The Routledge Introduction to the Canadian Short Story

This volume aims to introduce undergraduates, graduates, and general readers to the diversity and richness of Canadian short story writing and to the narrative potential of short fiction in general. Addressing a wide spectrum of forms and themes, the book will familiarise readers with the development and cultural significance of Canadian short fiction from the early 19th century to the present. A strong focus will be on the rich reservoir of short fiction produced in the past four decades and the way in which it has responded to the anxieties and crises of our time. Drawing on current critical debates, each chapter will highlight the interrelations between Canadian short fiction and historical and socio-cultural developments. Case studies will zoom in on specific thematic or aesthetic issues in an exemplary manner. *The Routledge Introduction to the Canadian Short Story* will provide an accessible and comprehensive overview ideal for students and general readers interested in the multifaceted and thriving medium of the short story in Canada.

Maria Löschnigg received her Ph.D. at the University of Graz, where she is currently Associate Professor. Dr Löschnigg's previous publications include *The Epistolary Renaissance: A Critical Approach to Contemporary Letter Narratives in Anglophone Fiction*, *Green Matters: Ecocultural Functions of Literature*, and *The Anglo-Canadian Novel in the Twenty-First Century: Interpretations*.

Routledge Introductions to Canadian Literature
Series Editors:
Robert Lecker
McGill University
Lorraine York
McMaster University

Routledge Introductions to Canadian Literature is a series that provides critical introductions to important trends, issues, authors, historical, cultural and intellectual contexts in Canadian Literature. The series draws on the work of experts in the field to provide a detailed but accessible commentary on those works or conceptual issues which are taught with undergraduate students in mind but also graduate students and instructors.

The Routledge Introduction to Canadian Fantastic Literature
Allan Weiss

The Routledge Introduction to Auto/biography in Canada
Sonja Boon, Laurie McNeill, Julie Rak, and Candida Rifkind

The Routledge Introduction to Gender and Sexuality in Literature in Canada
Linda Morra

The Routledge Introduction to the Canadian Short Story
Maria Löschnigg

For more information about this series, please visit: www.routledge.com/Routledge-Introductions-to-Canadian-Literature/book-series/RICL

The Routledge Introduction to the Canadian Short Story

Maria Löschnigg

NEW YORK AND LONDON

Designed cover image: © Anna Bliokh / Getty Images

First published 2023
by Routledge
605 Third Avenue, New York, NY 10158

by Routledge
4 Park Square, Milton Park, Abingdon, Oxon, OX14 4RN

Routledge is an imprint of the Taylor & Francis Group, an informa business

© 2023 Maria Löschnigg

The right of Maria Löschnigg to be identified as author of this work has been asserted in accordance with sections 77 and 78 of the Copyright, Designs and Patents Act 1988.

All rights reserved. No part of this book may be reprinted or reproduced or utilised in any form or by any electronic, mechanical, or other means, now known or hereafter invented, including photocopying and recording, or in any information storage or retrieval system, without permission in writing from the publishers.

Trademark notice: Product or corporate names may be trademarks or registered trademarks, and are used only for identification and explanation without intent to infringe.

ISBN: 978-0-367-69649-8 (hbk)
ISBN: 978-0-367-69647-4 (pbk)
ISBN: 978-1-003-14268-3 (ebk)

DOI: 10.4324/9781003142683

Typeset in Bembo
by Apex CoVantage, LLC

Contents

Acknowledgements   vii

Introduction to the Volume   1

PART 1
The Genre of the Short Story and Its Emergence and Development in Canada   5

1 The Genre of Short Fiction and Its Position in the Canadian Literary Landscape   7

2 Sketchy Beginnings and "Becoming Canadian": From the Early 19th Century to Confederation Literature   26

3 From the Dawn of Modernism to the "Bursting Dam of the Sixties"   47

4 From the 1960s to the Mid-1980s: A Genre Establishes Itself   70

PART 2
The Canadian Short Story from the Mid-1980s to the Present   99

5 Metafiction and "Unnatural" Narrative Voices   101

6 Fragmentation in the "Era of the Vulnerable"   119

7 Gender Scripts and Queer Identities   139

8 Indigenous Short Fiction in English   164

9 Migration and Diaspora	189
10 Narratives of Loss – Domestic and Environmental Contexts	216
Afterword	243
Index	246

Acknowledgements

Although I have never had the privilege of meeting her personally, I feel I must first give my thanks to Alice Munro. It was through her stories, about 25 years ago, that my interest in and passion for Canadian literature in general and the short story in particular were sparked. At about the same time, in 1999, the Centre for Canadian Studies at the University of Graz was founded, which has fostered a vibrant exchange with authors and scholars from Canada. One of them, David Staines, has been an inexhaustible source of inspiration over the years and a dear friend. Thank you, David, for your encouragement and belief in the value of allowing internal *and* external perspectives on Canadian literature! Thank you also, Michelle Gadpaille from the University of Maribor, Slovenia, for always being ready to support the activities of the Graz Centre, enriching our students and staff through unforgettable guest lectures and providing invaluable guidelines for my research on Canadian short fiction.

In general, I want to thank all scholars and critics in the field of Canadian literature and the short story who have crossed my path and have added to my understanding of Canadian literature, among them Janice Fiamengo, Gerald Lynch, Sherrill Grace, and Coral Ann Howells. I feel honoured to have met authors like Daphne Marlatt and John Metcalf and will always treasure the friendship of Di Brandt. And whenever I teach Bill Valgardson's "A Matter of Balance", I make sure to let my students know about following that story's Goldstream Park trail with him and his dog Chico Bandito.

I am strongly indebted to my students, Austrian and international, who, over a period of 20 years of reading and discussing Canadian short stories, have greatly contributed to my own appreciation of their variety and richness. This book, therefore, also resonates with their voices. I want to extend special thanks to my Ph.D. students, above all Rebekka Schuh, Nikola Tutek, and Melanie Braunecker, whose work on epistolary modes, multimodal elements, and environmental concerns in the Canadian short story has led to much productive exchange.

Regarding the completion of this volume, I would like to express my gratitude to Marlene Arnold, who took care of the index, and to Jutta Klobasek-Ladler, who helped me with ever so many of the technicalities involved in producing the manuscript. Most of all, however, I would like to thank Martin, my husband and fellow Canadianist. Without his expertise, advice, and support, the present volume would never have seen the light of day.

In conclusion, I wish to dedicate this volume to everyone ready to embark on a journey into the vast and exciting landscape of Canadian short fiction, hoping that this book may be able to provide useful guidelines for that journey.

Introduction to the Volume

The Canadian short story fascinates. Slowly taking shape in the 19th and the early 20th century and gaining momentum in the 1980s, it has since evolved into Canada's most vibrant and diverse literary genre. Canada's first Nobel laureate in literature, Alice Munro, has entirely dedicated herself to short fiction – a fact which reflects the prominent position of the short story in Canadian writing today and which has proved a catalyst for the ongoing flourishing of the genre. There is today a proliferation of Canadian short story writing of great thematic and formal diversity. Impressive as this is, however, it makes it very difficult to do justice to the very wide range of authors and works. This is also one of the reasons, besides my personal expertise, that this book focuses on the Anglophone short story; however, it is to be hoped that a comprehensive account of Francophone short fiction from Canada will soon be available, too.

The Routledge Introduction to the Canadian Short Story has been designed as a companion to undergraduate and graduate courses on Canadian short fiction (in English) and as a guidebook for courses on Canadian literature and on the short story in general. In addition, this book will provide valuable source material for scholars working in the field of (Canadian) short fiction and may also appeal to general readers.

Aiming at a balanced representation of thematic and aesthetic issues, this volume is the first to provide an account of the development of Canadian short story writing from the 19th century to the very present of the early 2020s. Giving due consideration to canonical writers, it also introduces emerging authors that have not (yet) been dealt with in critical studies. The present volume thus differs from recently published works which exclude historical periods and/or concentrate on a rather small selection of authors, like Reingard M. Nischik's *The English Short Story in Canada: From the Dawn of Modernism to the 2013 Nobel Prize* (2017) or Laurie Kruk's *Double Voicing the Canadian Short Story* (2016). *The Contemporary Canadian Short Story in English: Continuity and Change* (2014), which I authored, deals exclusively with Canadian short fiction from the mid-1980s to the first decade of the 21st century and addresses scholars in the field rather than providing a systematic introduction to its subject matter. The latter also applies to John

DOI: 10.4324/9781003142683-1

Metcalf's voluminous *The Canadian Short Story* (2018), besides the problematic fact that the book largely excludes writers whose background is other than European Canadian.

The present volume offers an accessible and comprehensive account of Canadian short fiction in English, made primarily for undergraduate students but also for the general reader. Accordingly, the book also allows for selective reading along historical, aesthetic, or thematic lines. The two parts comprise ten chapters, reflecting different approaches called for by, on the one hand, the earlier history of the short story and, on the other hand, the genre's boom regarding subject matter, style, and form from the mid-1980s to the present. Except for the introductory survey and discussion of generic characteristics, all chapters include a reader-friendly case study. These case studies illustrate how Canadian short fiction has addressed historical, political, social, cultural, and ecological sensibilities and moments of crisis and how writers have used an array of narrative techniques in order to provide novel and alternative perspectives on these issues.

The four chapters in Part 1 deal with the position of the short story within Canadian literature and with the stages in the history of the genre up to the 1980s. The overarching objective of the first chapter is to embed short fiction in the Canadian literary context and to make readers aware of the specifics of short fiction as a literary genre as a basis for a full appreciation and recognition of what short fiction can do. Chapters 2 to 4 are organised chronologically. "Sketchy Beginnings and 'Becoming Canadian'" (Chapter 2) traces early short prose forms like the sketch and the emergence of the Canadian linked-story cycle and explores the Canadian animal story prevalent in the late 19th and early 20th centuries. Chapter 3 focuses on the formative phase of Canadian short fiction from the 1920s to the "bursting dam of the sixties", elucidating how this development is inextricably linked to shifts in the cultural infrastructure of the 1940s and '50s. The final chapter of Part 1 sheds light on the multiple factors that contributed to the establishment of the short story as the most vital literary genre in Canada in the 1960s, '70s, and '80s. This phase is associated with some of Canada's most influential practitioners of the short story: Alice Munro, Mavis Gallant, Jack Hodgins, and Alistair MacLeod. However, their careers have continued into the new millennium, illustrating the fact that chronological divisions in Canadian short story writing since the early 1970s are sometimes problematic and can be made only for practical purposes.

Part 2 is concerned with the Canadian short story from the mid-1980s to the present, a period in which the genre has received strong impulses from a growing number of Indigenous writers and from authors with recent immigrant backgrounds. Countering views that the Canadian short story has been lacking in innovation, the first two chapters of this section critically engage with an intriguing range of aesthetic forms in contemporary short fiction. While Chapter 5 is dedicated to metafictional stories and unusual narrative voices, Chapter 6 focuses on the aesthetics of fragmentation. Since form and content are always interrelated, these two chapters will also provide insight into how narrative experiments have been made functional for thematising the mechanisms of literature itself, but also for effectively (and affectively) shedding light on crises and liminal experiences (like for instance the challenges of migration or the unsettling impact of climate change) and for thought-provoking approaches to issues of gender.

The remaining four chapters are organised according to thematic and culture-specific concerns. Thus, gender scripts and queer identities are at the centre of Chapter 7, which explores feminist aspects and pays tribute to stories which address the increasing relevance of LGBTQ issues. Chapter 8 deals with the invaluable contribution of Indigenous writers to Canadian short fiction. As the chapter will show, the "translation" of oral storytelling elements into the printed medium allows for momentous aesthetic and affective effects. Similarly, the "explosion" of voices from different cultures in the wake of Canada's implementation of multiculturalism has greatly invigorated Canadian short fiction. Chapter 9 looks at how writers have addressed questions of living with or between cultures and have creatively used paradigms of short fiction in doing so. The final chapter (Chapter 10) explores how the contemporary short story approaches experiences of loss, a prominent motif in Canadian literature in general. The chapter first discusses loss in the context of the personal, the domestic, and the everyday before turning to one of the most urgent concerns of our time – the environmental crisis. Contrary to eminent voices (like that of Margaret Atwood) lamenting its absence, the Canadian eco-story *does* exist. A particularly prominent topic in Indigenous short fiction, environmental loss and the urgency to respond to it are now also prominent in non-Native short fiction.

Case studies offer in-depth readings of exemplary stories and provide readers with anchor points for approaching short fiction, followed by concise tables that sum up the most important structural and thematic aspects of these narratives:

- Ernest Thompson Seton, "Silverspot, The Story of a Crow" (1898); Charles G.D. Roberts, "Do Seek Their Meat from God" (1892) – a comparative view on the Canadian animal story (Chapter 2)
- Sinclair Ross, "The Lamp at Noon" (1938); Sharon Butala, "Gabriel" (1990) – prairie "realism" and deep-mapping the prairies (Chapter 3)
- Alice Munro, *Lives of Girls and Women* (1971) – storified autobiographical fiction (Chapter 4)
- George Bowering, "Discoloured Metal" (1994) – visualising ambiguity (Chapter 5)
- Carol Shields, "Dying for Love" (2000) – the rhetoric of fragmentation and aggregation (Chapter 6)
- Margaret Atwood, "My Last Duchess" (2006) – in search of empowering role models (Chapter 7)

Introduction to the Volume

- Thomas King, "One Good Story, That One" (1993) – the interfusional story (Chapter 8)
- Madeleine Thien, "Simple Recipes" (2001) – migration and generational conflict (Chapter 9)
- Lee Maracle, "Cedar Sings" (2010) – the Canadian eco-story (Chapter 10)

It goes without saying that within its limited space, this *Introduction to the Canadian Short Story* is by necessity selective, and choices regarding authors and works have often been difficult. Emphases regarding themes, as well as writers, collections, and stories, might have been placed differently. Concerning emerging writers in particular, it is always challenging to decide who and what to include. As it is, decisions have been based on extensive reading and have been made with a view to providing the reader with a lucid and balanced introduction to Canadian short fiction. It is the overriding goal of this volume to illustrate how the short story, through its wide thematic spectrum and an array of narrative forms and techniques, contributes to a deeper understanding of Canada's multifaceted culture and the complexities of human lives in general. It is to be hoped that the volume not only provides readers with viable access to Canadian short fiction but will also incite them to delve more deeply into this captivating field.

Part 1

The Genre of the Short Story and Its Emergence and Development in Canada

1 The Genre of Short Fiction and Its Position in the Canadian Literary Landscape

1.1. The Position of the Short Story in Canada

The prominence of the short story within the Canadian literary landscape has by now become a generally acknowledged phenomenon and has been additionally boosted in 2013, when the Nobel Prize in Literature was awarded to Alice Munro. It has been especially since the 1960s that the short fiction form developed into a "particularly productive and vital genre" (Nischik 2017: 1). Within short story criticism, it has been since the 1980s in particular that critics started to recognise the significance and vitality of the form. In 1980, Helmut Bonheim (1980–81: 659) referred to the short story as "the most active ambassador of Canadian literature abroad", and Wayne Grady (1980: vi), in the preface to *The Penguin Book of Canadian Short Stories*, called it "Canada's healthiest and most versatile genre". This is also confirmed by W.J. Keith in the mid-1980s (1985: 170), who claims in his *Canadian Literature in English* that some of the "most notable fiction in Canada is now written in the short story form", as well as by Michelle Gadpaille in her 1988 book on the Canadian short story, where she describes the short fiction form as an "exceptionally strong genre in Canadian literature" (vii). A particularly emphatic statement on the significance of short fiction in Canada has come from Aritha van Herk (1990: 925), who attests to short stories the role of being the "heartbeat of Canadian literature, in so far as they collapse the erratic, the elemental and the reluctant into a version of multiplicitous and wildly contaminatory fiction". Van Herk's diagnosis, in particular, touches on short fiction's inherent potential to reflect an almost infinite spectrum of thematic concerns, presenting them from ever new angles and in ever new aesthetic shapes.

Thus, it comes as no surprise that in the new millennium, too, the short story in Canada has continued to be a vibrant and potent form that seems ideally suited to respond to and critically reflect cultural, social, political, environmental, emotional, and psychological moments of crisis and encounters. Against the prediction voiced in the 1960s that the genre was dying (New 2009: 381), it was actually in the process of being fully born. The genre's eventual "success story" is not least reflected in the flood of

8 The Genre of the Short Story and Its Emergence and Development

Canadian short story anthologies and of single-author collections that have emerged over the past decades. In *The Cambridge History of Canadian Literature*, William H. New (2009: 381) summarises this unabated upsurge as follows:

> By the first decade of the twenty-first century approximately fifty collections were appearing every year, the increase in numbers coinciding with social growth, changes in the means of production, and extended critical attention. While markets for the genre remained fragile, short fiction nevertheless became more visible and more varied, with publishers seeking further ways to attract commercial attention and new writers keen to address readers in a different manner and voice.

Alexander MacLeod (2016: 439f) draws attention to yet another proof of Canada's "unique passion for the short story". Triggered, in particular, by John Metcalf's polarising commitment to the development and circulation of the genre, there erupted "a series of 'anthology wars'" (see also Lecker 2013) that culminated in the publication of the voluminous *Penguin Book of Canadian Short Stories* (2007), edited by Jane Urquhart. The ensuing heated debate about who should have been included or omitted even made it into the national news – a phenomenon, as MacLeod observes, that would rarely happen outside Canada (2016: 440). As to the reasons for the unabated flourishing of the Canadian short story, the country's cultural infrastructure that – from the mid-20th century onwards – proved to be particularly conducive to the promotion of the form, must be adduced. This not only includes a vibrant network of literary magazines and small presses with a focus on the short story but also initiatives such as the annual *Best Canadian Short Stories* or *The Journey Prize Anthology* that appears every year, as well as literary awards specifically geared to the genre (see Macleod 2016: 441f. for a more detailed account of these factors).

In Canada, the emergence of the "short story proper" coincides with the advent of the modernist short story. Starting rather tentatively in the late 19th century with Duncan Campbell Scott's short story cycle *In the Village of Viger* (1896), it was with authors like Raymond Knister and Morley Callaghan that the Canadian short story began to take shape in the 1920s (see Chapter 3). Though strongly influenced by the American short story, both authors, at the same time but in different ways, advocated an independent development of the genre in Canada. While Callaghan rather saw himself as an internationalist, it was, above all, Knister who contributed to the visibility of Canadian short fiction, not only through his short story oeuvre (of about 100 stories) but also through his editorship of the first anthology of Canadian short stories in 1928. Both Knister's and Callaghan's stories display distinctly modernist techniques. This includes a limited external plot in favour of internal focalisation, as well as an elliptic and allusive style, indirect mediation of information, and a tendency towards epiphanic closure that, to a large extent, have come to be considered typical markers of the genre of the short story as such (see Section 1.2.).

Regarding thematic issues, too, the Canadian short story of the early 20th century adheres not only to modernism but also reflects elements that, in recent short story criticism, have been identified as intrinsically connected to short fiction. One such element is the frequent focus on isolated outsiders, on characters that exist on the margins of society, which can be found in Knister's and Callaghan's stories but also frequently appears in Sinclair Ross's short fiction, written in the 1930s and '40s. With Ross in particular, another feature related to modernist writing needs to be mentioned – namely, a strong semanticisation of space in order to capture the inner crisis of his characters. Lonely and alienated characters also inhabit the short stories of Ethel Wilson, "English Canada's most important female modernist writer" (Nischik 2017: 23). As with Knister and Callaghan, suggestive ambiguity and the probing of mental spheres are hallmarks of her art, as is her depiction of space (mostly the West Coast) as liminal. In fact, the modernist paradigm, with its shift from external action to internal explorations of the characters' psyche, has become a feature that is now more generally associated with the genre of the short story and its "marked de-emphasis of plot" (Hunter 2007: 7).

Despite the prominence in Canadian short fiction of modernist manifestations of the genre, the short story from the early 20th century onwards has also continued to be informed by realist paradigms; this is evident, for example, in Frederick Philip Grove's and Hugh Garner's short stories. In fact, the combination of realist and modernist modes has remained a hallmark of Canadian short fiction, defining much of the writing of authors such as Mavis Gallant, Alice Munro, or Guy Vanderhaeghe. However, often the impression of verisimilitude is used by these authors to create deceptive surfaces under which there unfolds a counter-realistic deep-mapping evoked by a rich semantic web of implication and allusion. The ongoing presence of modernist and (neo)realist narrative paradigms in Canadian short fiction may, at first glance, render an impression of the Canadian short story as a relatively conventional genre. However, the innovative manner in which Canadian authors have exploited the aesthetic potential of this form and adapted it to shifting thematic concerns proves the contrary, as will be demonstrated in this book.

English-Canadian short stories may not have followed postmodernist trends as radically as their American or French-Canadian counterparts, and their strength rather lies in subtle experiments with modernist modes of expression, often combined with realist or postmodernist/antirealist elements. Still, the postmodernist trends that saw their heyday in the 1960s and '70s were not ignored by all Canadian authors. Early traces of postmodernism can already be seen in Joyce Marshall's short stories and, above all, in Sheila Watson's work, which – in addition to her experiments with collage techniques – displays a strong use of intertextuality and meta-referentiality. Further names that can clearly be associated with postmodernist short fiction are Ray Smith, George Bowering, Diane Schoemperlen, and Margaret Atwood. Innovative incentives regarding both unusual and provocative subject matter, as well as stylistic experiment, have also come from Barbara Gowdy, Annabel Lyon, André Alexis, Mark Anthony Jarman, Zsuzsi Gartner, and Lynn Coady, among many others.

Beyond aesthetic and periodic categories like *realist*, *modernist*, or *postmodernist*, the Canadian short story has brought forth a number of distinct forms that deserve attention. There have been *multimodal* forms of short fiction (e.g. Schoemperlen), *flash fiction* (e.g. Atwood), and *iconic* and strongly *metafictional* modes of writing (e.g. Bowering). Orality, as rendered most memorably in Thomas King's *trickster stories*, has engendered unique forms of narrative expression, as will be shown in Chapter 8. Another format which has come to be seen as quintessentially Canadian is the *short story cycle* (Lynch 2001). Due to its appearance in all periods of Canadian short fiction and its manifold thematic orientation, it will receive attention in many chapters and will be addressed in a number of contexts. In addition to these forms, three modes of narrative discourse have made a strong imprint on Canadian short fiction: the *epistolary mode*, *you-* and *we-narration*, and the *composite or fragmented story*. The distinct aesthetic potentials of these rather unconventional variants will be given space in Chapters 5 and 6, where the focus is more strongly on experimental aspects of contemporary Canadian short fiction.

As this book will demonstrate, the Anglophone Canadian short story is characterised by an astounding plurality. Nonetheless, it will be necessary, before turning to developments, individual authors, specific thematic concerns, and aesthetic forms in the following nine chapters of this book, to first attempt a definition of the generic parameters of the short story as such.

1.2. What Is a Short Story?

The short story is neither a miniature novel nor is it comparable to a novel's chapter; still, it is shortness which serves as the basis for a definition and understanding of the specific aesthetic qualities of the genre. In other words, it is essential to investigate the nature and effect of the short story's shortness – what Barbara Korte (2003: 5) has aptly termed its "calculated brevity" and what A.L. Kennedy (2008: 3) has pointedly described as "small in a way that a bullet is small". Thus, the question at stake here is what techniques authors employ in order to make maximum use of the short story's restricted textual space and to create the impression that "we read not a 'partial object' but a 'total object, complete with missing parts'" (Hunter 2007: 140). A Canadian writer who has repeatedly reflected on the short story and the different mechanisms that govern a short story and a novel is Douglas Glover (see, for example, *Attack of the Copula Spiders and Other Essays on*

Writing, 2012). In "Anatomy of the Short Story" (2019), he again returns to this issue and describes the suggestive aesthetics of the short story as follows:

> Story form is an object, a translucent shimmering thing with words tacked to the surface of its swirling involutions. The words glitter with their own reflective colouring; in them you see the momentary reflections of other words.
>
> (23)

While contemporary critics mostly agree on the short story's distinct and elaborated quality of composition as well as on its literary value, this has not always been the case. One of the first impulses toward a genre-conscious theorising of the short story came from Edgar Allan Poe in the 1840s, who already named "unity of effect or impression" (1976: 46) as a quintessential feature of the genre and noted that in the "whole composition there should be no word written, of which the tendency, direct or indirect, is not to the one pre-established design" (1976: 48). However, while Poe still used the term "tale" for his short fiction, it was Brander Matthews who in his 1885 essay *Philosophy of the Short-Story* coined the term "short-story" (then still spelt with a hyphen) (Korte 2003: 6). Interestingly, Margaret Atwood, in her latest collection of short fiction to date, has gone back to the term "tale", attributing to it a stronger emphasis on fictionality. Thus, in the "Acknowledgements" following the nine tales collected in *Stone Mattress* (2014) she notes: "Calling a piece of short fiction a 'tale' removes it at least slightly from the realm of the mundane works and days, as it evokes the world of the folk tale, the wonder tale, and the long-ago teller of tales" (2014). However, whether we refer to a piece of short fiction as a "tale" or a "short story", what is at stake in the context of this chapter is the establishment of short fiction as a distinct form of literary expression.

In fact, we owe a decisive step in recognition of the short story as an autonomous genre to Elizabeth Bowen, whose seminal introduction to the *Faber Book of Short Stories* (1936) for the first time defined the short story's brevity as a positive quality rather than a flaw (1976 [1936]: 153, 157). This shift in the appreciation of the short story is not least linked to "a creative transaction between brevity and complexity – the art of saying less but meaning more" (Hunter 2007: 2), which became a central aesthetic concept for modernist practitioners of short fiction like James Joyce, Virginia Woolf, and Katherine Mansfield. The "distilled essence" (Head 1992: 6) of modernist narrative with the epiphany as its key feature is still a characteristic of contemporary short story writing and also figures strongly in contemporary short story criticism (Delaney and Hunter 2019: 2f). At the same time, the short story which, according to Clare Hanson (1985: 9) "exhibits a protean variety", is one of the most hybrid and innovative forms and thus calls for ever new critical approaches and models of definition. A workable concept of the short story must pay tribute to the wide spectrum of different forms possible within this genre, disentangling short narratives from their long "relatives" while at the same time acknowledging genre blurs and overlaps. In this context, Delaney and Hunter (2019: 2) state the following with regard to the short story's unstable position:

> The sense of the short story's identity as equivocal or unfixed – bracketed somewhere between the prose poem and the novella – is compounded by other factors: by a literary culture overwhelmingly geared to recognizing and rewarding the longer form; by the relegation of the short story to low-capital venues such as the magazine and anthologies, whose multi-author, thematized modes of publication can conspire to diffuse and degrade the text's singularity; and particularly in recent decades, by institutionalised reproduction and programmatisation through the Creative Writing industry.

As critics, students and readers of short fiction, we can contribute to its re-evaluation as long as we are willing to engage with this challengingly artful and compact form and take pleasure in "the free play of interpretive possibility" (Hunter 2007: 48), and as long as we dismiss any rigid expectations of "what a short story should be". In fact, Delaney and Hunter (2019: 3) regard the "disorderly history" of short story criticism as a part of its innovative power since it confirms the form's elusiveness and liveliness.

I shall now come back to the question posed at the beginning of this section and explore the distinct quality of the short story's brevity with the aim of establishing a generic framework that defines the "essence" of short fiction. This attempt at providing a concise definition of the short story is informed by an awareness that not all texts will fit into this framework and that the short stories produced now and in the future will, again and again, inspire us to rethink and revise our generic concepts.

A. Length

Having talked about the short story's brevity, it is now time to address this – albeit problematic – criterion in more detail. First, it is important to emphasise that it is not so much its textual shortness as such that makes for the generic specificity of the short story but rather the question of *how* it is short. Still, we cannot completely eschew the question of textual length. Following Beevers's assertion (based on Bonheim 1982: 166) that a "short story can be any length between a few hundred words and fifty thousand" (2008: 20), it already becomes clear that the spectrum of length overlaps on one end of the scale with flash fiction and on the other with the novella or short novel. In this context, it also needs to be noted that length was more often than not dictated by the medium in which a story was published. Thus, for example, Valerie Shaw (1983: 8) mentions V.S. Pritchett, who deemed the short story "an inextinguishable lost cause, pointing out that it is difficult to publish stories longer than 7,000 words, and after 10,000 impossible". While most short stories range between 2,000 and 10,000 words, the only way to recognise ultra-long texts as short stories is again through their concentrated structural makeup (as will be shown later). Regarding the condensed and artful composition of the short story, it also makes sense to use Poe's famous demand that it should be possible to read a short story "at one sitting" (1976 [1842]). It is also its condensed form that has led Michael Basseler (2019: 26) to see the short story as "a privileged literary form of life knowledge" or an "*organon of life knowledge*" (17), which demands a concentrated and undisturbed perusal for its full receptive effect to unfold.

While publication in magazines coerces authors into the straitjacket of brevity, book publications in the form of short story anthologies and single-author collections pose the problem of publishers' preference for the long monolithic form of the novel. With regard to interlinked stories, this problem has repeatedly been circumvented by selling short story cycles as novels, as has been the case with Alice Munro's famous *Lives of Girls and Women*, to name but one example. While the short story has also been defined as a text type that is too short to be published autonomously, this again is only partly true, since especially established authors have also managed to publish single stories in book form – an example would again be Alice Munro, whose "Queenie" appeared as a slim book in 1999, after having been published in 1998 in the *London Review of Books* and before being included in her 2001 collection *Hateship, Friendship, Courtship, Loveship, Marriage*. However, these can only be tentative approaches; as far as Canadian short fiction is concerned, there are, on one end of the scale, ultra-brief flash fictions or micro-stories such as Margaret Atwood's "She" and "Eating the Birds", which cover not even a page, and "like aphorisms distil form and inflect it with irony and implication" (Glover 2019: 80); on the other, there are more spatially extended forms such as many of Alice Munro's later stories. Among these, "Too Much Happiness" or "The Love of a Good Woman" range between 60 and 75 pages in different editions. However, what all these texts have in common is a dense configuration of meaning and a brevity that is "calculated" (Korte 2003: 5), which makes it necessary to examine this quality in more depth.

B. *Style*

In the short story, density and concentration result to a large extent from a "vertical" configuration of meaning. In contrast to the tendency in novels to present events and/or story elements in a more linear and "horizontal" way, coherence in the short story is often established more indirectly through thematic and/or semantic equivalences, thus replacing "the syntagmatic dimension of discourse with a set of paradigmatic possibilities" (Heble 1994: 5). Even though this technique has often been linked to the modernist type of the short story in particular, it can be identified as a stylistic feature that applies to short fiction in general. This paradigmatic density is created through multivalent symbolic signification, through recurring elements in different semantic guises and strongly metaphoric language – in short, through techniques which also define poetry. It, therefore, comes as no surprise that British author A.L. Kennedy (2008: 5) says about writing short fiction: "It's the most concentration that you will ever do as a writer; you're certainly in the kind of territory that poets have appropriated, where every word counts on the page". The rhetorical density of short fiction is also confirmed by Beevers (2008: 21), who claims that the "successful short story will demonstrate a more harmonious relationship of all its aspects than will any other art form, excepting perhaps lyric poetry", adding that it "provides a 'single and unique effect' towards which every word contributes".

British-Canadian author Kathy Page's story "Red Dog" (*The Two of Us*, 2016) may serve as an example to briefly demonstrate what I have explained in the previous paragraph. The story captures a significant moment in the life of Katie, an eight-year-old girl with special needs who normally lives in a home but is taken to stay with her father, his new wife and "three ordinary children" (142) over Christmas. Her longing to be included and her craving for emotional warmth when she is left outside in the cold while the rest of the family do their Christmas shopping is powerfully mediated through recurring words related to brightness and mesmerising smells: "Bottles . . . stacked in pyramids, glittering", "The windows glow and shine; the air bristles with women's fragrances", "People in bright coats" (140); even the eyes of the woman with the dog who approaches her "glitter with promise, like the lights in Christmas windows" (141). These are semantic isotopies and metaphors rich in allusive meaning that emphasise, through stark contrasts, the desperate situation of the girl.

In addition, Page introduces a strongly suggestive symbolism through the image of the "dog". When Katie strokes the woman's dog and buries her hands in its warm fur, she is reminded of her Christmas wish: a dog. The dog, however, not only stands for the warmth and protection she longs for but also for the girl herself. Not only is Katie receptive to smells (like a dog), but she also seems to be treated like a dog by her family. When the girl's family finally emerge from the shopping centre and pick her up, the woman with the dog observes them: "She is following them, the woman thinks, shocked, the way a dog does" (142). On Christmas Eve, Katie gets a toy dog, but "it isn't warm and it has no smell" (143); Katie falls into a fit and, as a punishment, is made to wait in the "small room" used for "knick-knacks that don't fit in anywhere else" (143), another allusion to Katie's own status in the family. The girl's desperate preoccupation with the dog is rendered in multiple variations, as, for example, when her racing heart is metaphorically described as having paws (144). When suddenly, through the window, she sees a "red dog" in the garden that seems to look at her, she calms down and tells her family, in her one-word sentences, that she wants to go outside. While her family drink wine and discuss Katie, she is out in the cold in pursuit of the fox. The girl's body is warm and she can smell the "red dog", yet the last words of the story, "not knowing yet about the hedge" (146), imply another disappointment, opening up the possibility that her emotional freezing might materialise into her actually freezing to death. Thus, though the story is only eight pages long, its rich poetic texture offers multiple entry points for interpretation. It sheds light not only on the events of that particular day but on the dire life of the girl in general and her relationship with her "family", which is characterised by emotional neglect.

C. Plot

The plot of a short story is characterised by "tactical omissions" (Hunter 2007: 2). These may consist, for example, in the (extreme) reduction of expository material that in a novel may be necessary for narrative coherence; in the short story, in turn, coherence is often created through suggesting and implying meaning rather than explicating it. "Tactical omission" in short fiction is also evident in the focus on a significant incident, "an elemental human experience or a situation of crisis rather than developments over a long span of time" (Korte 2003: 6). Thus, it is often an experience of recognition rather than development that is featured in the short story.

The story "A Matter of Balance" (*What Can't Be Changed Shouldn't Be Mourned*, 1990) by William Dempsey Valgardson, for example, starts *in medias res* with the sentence: "He was sitting on a cedar log, resting, absent-mindedly plucking pieces from its thick layer of moss, when he first saw them" (130). Only later do we find out that the main character's name is Harold, that "them" refers to two bikers who seem to follow him and, as it turns out, actually want to harm him, and that the setting is a hiking trail in Goldstream Park on Victoria Island. Even though the whole plot is limited to this hike, Harold's growing panic and the eventual climax when he and the bikers are trapped in "an area where the rock fell from the side of the trail like a frozen set of rapids" (140), the story at the same time provides an insight into Harold's whole life *via* fragmented flashbacks and implicature. Harold, in the end, has the upper hand and leaves the two criminals to die on the rough rock, where nobody will hear their cries for help as the moss that already figures in the first sentence of the story will muffle every sound. Even though this is, at first sight, a suspenseful story about the characters' efforts to keep their balance on the rock, the title "A Matter of Balance" by no means refers to the physical level only. Through the story's intricate configuration of suggestive elements, it is shown to also refer to the reversal of power between victim and perpetrators, the mental balance Harold has tried to regain after his wife was killed by men just like those who followed him, the balance between reason and fear during his struggle for survival on the rocks, and the very "dubious moral balance that Harold establishes by avenging himself on his pursuers for the death of his wife" (Löschnigg and Löschnigg 2007: 329). This moral dilemma also results in "a 'balance' between openness and closure" (Löschnigg and Löschnigg 2007: 329), so that it is up to the reader to weigh the protagonist's motifs against their own notions of right or wrong.

While Valgardson's story is a memorable example demonstrating how minimal plot and the focus on a single incident can be surrounded by a dense web of meaning, thus making "maximum use of [the short story's] restricted scope" (Korte 2003: 5), this does not necessarily mean that short stories cannot also feature multiple plots. A prime example of an author who has frequently experimented with the multiple-plot format is Carol Shields. In "Keys" and "Dying for Love" (both in *Dressing Up for the Carnival*, 2000), for example, Shields arranges the different plot strands that make up these stories synchronically rather than chronologically (Löschnigg 2014: 60f) and links these parallel micro-stories through powerful analogies (see also Chapter 6). In other words, even though we do have multiple and seemingly separated plots, they are again arranged paradigmatically rather than in a linear way, thus making visible a plethora of mutually implicative cross-references.

D. Setting

Regarding temporal and spatial settings, too, the short story tends to be defined by "an economy of means" (Korte 2003: 6). It is thus not surprising that the core plot of a great number of short stories tends to cover a rather brief time span (which may nonetheless reverberate with implications of the character's entire life) and frequently focuses on one semantically charged locale.

As to the temporal frame of short fiction, both Kathy Page's "Red Dog" and W.D. Valgardson's "A Matter of Balance" may serve as illustrative examples of the semantically significant handling of time in this genre. In "A Matter of Balance", the core story only covers a few hours. However, through a number of analepses (flashbacks) triggered by Harold's crisis as he is pursued and threatened by the two bikers, the story offers suggestive glimpses of his whole life, resonating with earlier crises that can be recognised as anticipations of the situation he now finds himself in. In "Red Dog", too, the story only covers one afternoon and evening in the life of Katie. However, through cleverly contrived implications, the events of that day shed light on her entire miserable life. Thus, when Maria, the new partner of Katie's father, mysteriously asks herself: "How much does Katie remember?" (139), this could refer to some horrible incident in the past that may have caused Katie's disability.

In short fiction in particular, space is a vital dimension for the creation of meaning, one that can be exploited in various ways to enhance semantic concentration and productive ambiguity. As Valerie Shaw (1983: 150) puts it, "whatever the relationship between place and people, the scene in which a story is set often contributes in decisive ways to the total effect". The short story writer must, therefore, carefully establish the setting in order to make it functional rather than merely ornate, in the sense that it ties up semantically with plot, characterisation and other narrative constituents.

In "A Matter of Balance", Valgardson strongly semanticises space through, for example, creating analogies between the setting and the focaliser Harold. Thus, when he comes upon an arbutus tree, "[i]ts bark deep earth-red, [hanging] in shreds" (134), he links it to his own precarious post-traumatic state: "That is the way he felt, like a snake or an arbutus, shedding his old skin for a new, better one" (134). In this story, space also adopts symbolic meaning when Harold reflects on the silence of the forest that seems to be void of any signs of life; he is aware that the "moss that covered the rock and soil, the moss that clung thickly to the tree trunks, the moss that hung in long strands from the branches, deadened everything, muted it, until there were no sharp lines, no certainties" (148). The way the focaliser perceives his surroundings (the focalised space) foreshadows the ending, that is the very likely death of his pursuers. The significance of the moss that mutes everything (and that figuratively also blurs the lines between right and wrong), is highlighted not only through repetition but also through its appearance in the very first sentence of the story. While in "A Matter of Balance" space is used in analogy to the main character's emotional state, the representation of space in Page's story rather works towards the establishing of contrasts. Thus, Katie's despair when she waits in the cold outside the shopping mall is dramatically emphasised through the contrast of the glittery brightness by which the girl is surrounded.

E. Characters

The short story's concentration and limited scope necessarily also affect character constellations and techniques of characterisation. As with all genre-defining categories discussed in this chapter, however, those that refer to the presentation of characters, too, must be seen as tendencies rather than rules and will apply most accurately to prototypical forms of short fiction.

In many short stories, brevity is achieved not least by the economical use of characters. Mostly, the number of characters in a short story does not exceed half a dozen, with a clear concentration on their overall semantic function. Again, Valgardson's story serves as a good example since in the core story we have one protagonist confronted by two antagonists, with other characters making only brief, schematic appearances in analepses. Even in a relatively long story like Alice Munro's "Child's Play" (*Too Much Happiness*, 2009), the cast of major characters consists of only three, the narrator Marlene, her childhood friend Charlene, and their "antagonist" Verna, a child with special needs, whom the two girls eventually kill. Other characters, such as Marlene's mother, Charlene's husband, the counsellors at the camp, and a priest, have only very marginal roles. Nonetheless, and keeping the short story's "organic" structure in mind, even these secondary characters become important in the web of meanings woven by the text. Thus, the way Marlene remembers her mother's reaction to what "happened" to Verna and how she describes, in retrospect, the neglect on the part of the counsellors on that fateful day contribute in multiple ways to an indirect characterisation of Marlene rather than delineating either the mother or the counsellors as story characters themselves.

There is a tendency in short fiction for characterisation to be implicit and conveyed indirectly rather than through (extended) explication. In Munro's "Child's Play", Marlene's personality and how it has been affected by the crime she committed as a ten-year-old girl must be inferred from her way of telling the story. Indications are provided, for example, by the way she circumvents the actual murder: it is only after recounting a number of childhood incidents and summing up her later life that she is finally able to describe how she and Charlene drowned Verna on the last day in the camp. This story is also an excellent example of how, in short fiction, explicit and implicit elements of characterisation are frequently made to clash: while Marlene explicitly states that she has gone on with her life and come to terms with the past in her own way, the narrative still indicates that her life has been haunted by what she did and that her crime may well have been the reason that she never married and never had children.

F. Beginnings and Endings

The "opening of a short story", as Helmut Bonheim claims, "is more important than that of a novel". This is due not only to the fact that mostly the opening of a short story "occupies a greater percentage of the text" (1982: 91) but also, and more importantly, to the short story's condensed structure. Each element of the short story's opening, from the tone to thematic allusions, is shaped in a way that makes it reverberate throughout the text. Without much introductory information and with only indefinite references to characters, places and incidents, openings in short fiction tend to place the reader right in the middle of things. Frequently, therefore, short stories have emic (viewed from an internal perspective) rather than etic (viewed from an external perspective) entry points into the text, i.e. they begin with so-called referentless pronouns instead of first defining the subjects. Once again, Munro's "Child's Play" is a case in point:

> I suppose there was talk in our house afterwards.
> How sad, how *awful*. (My mother.)
> There should have been supervision. Where were the counsellors? (My father.) (188)

Not only is there no information about the first-person narrator, but the reader is also confronted, by way of foreshadowing, with what Marlene's parents deplore as an avoidable accident, yet which will turn out to have been a horrid crime. Never does any of the characters besides Marlene and her accomplice, Charlene, come to know about the murder. The "awful" incident, as it will be seen by the others, and, most importantly, the way the murderess herself will try to come to terms with it later in life are already implied in this opening; this will surface repeatedly throughout the story. As to the tone of the opening, the reader is already given, at this early stage, a taste of Marlene's endeavours to play down what she and her friend did. This is achieved through her intimating, in her very first words, that she does not even remember exactly what happened after the "accident"/murder at the camp ("I suppose").

What goes for openings is also relevant for short story titles, which often indicate a key motif that informs the story. Thus, the ironic and/or apologetic title of Munro's "Child's Play" signals that the murder committed by the narrator in the past will be dealt with in a complex and multiply refracted manner. Another illustrative example is Alistair MacLeod's "Clearances" (*Island*, 2002 [2001]), whose title functions on three different historical levels. First, the story refers to the Highland Clearances in Scotland between 1750 and 1860, which are then linked with the clearing of the land by Scottish settlers on the Canadian Atlantic Coast. On a third level, the title also points to present-day land clearances on Cape Breton – now with the help of powerful machinery – for the sake of modern tourism.

Hugh Hood (1987 [1962]: 17), in his introduction to *Flying a Red Kite*, emphasised the importance of titles: "I paid special attention to my closing paragraphs and above all to my titles". In the much-anthologised title story, in particular, the title's significance as a polyvalent leitmotif becomes strikingly evident: it refers to the protagonist Fred's epiphanic experience at the end of the story and functions as an objective correlative for both spiritual and emotional processes in the story, as well as on the side of the reader. Moreover, the red kite can be seen as an emblem of the human soul, while its metaphorical link with the crushed raspberries on Fred's daughter's face seems to suspend the division between the spiritual and the physical.

It is not only titles and beginnings, however, that assume specific importance in short fiction; closure, too, as Hugh Hood already indicated in the statement quoted earlier, plays a disproportionally large role in a short story's overall effect. In general, the endings of modern stories tend to foreground ambiguity and unsettle/undermine fixed notions of meaning. "After 1914", as Susan Lohafer (1989: 109) notes, "to write a story that tied up experience, summed things up, or gave clear answers was to reveal a simplicity, a banality – not to mention an innocence – that just wasn't 'modern'". In contrast, in the American short story of the early 19th century (and especially with Poe), the totality of effect also included the providing of the "'final' piece in a puzzle" (Lohafer 1989: 109). In Canada at that time, it was the sketch that dominated short prose writing. When towards the end of the

19th century, the Canadian short story as such was born, a modern(ist) aesthetic already prevailed, according to which forms of closure that suggested semantic completion were somehow regarded as obsolete.

A general classification of endings in short fiction proves to be extremely difficult. What can be said for certain is that endings decisively contribute to the effect of a story, an observation supported, for example, by Bonheim (1982: 118): "We expect endings, much more than beginnings, to show what the story was about, what special effect was to be achieved". But how is the special effect of an ending achieved? There is, in fact, a wide spectrum of techniques employed by authors to make their stories "click" at the end. One, for example, is linking the end with the beginning. In "Child's Play", the final scene in which Marlene discloses the murder links up with the "awful" incident referred to at the beginning. Another technique is the epiphanic mode, when the story closes with a sudden realisation or insight, as is the case, for example, in Hood's "Flying a Red Kite". Often, endings involve a punchline or twist (frequently ironic), as, for example, in Margaret Atwood's short short story "Gertrude Talks Back" (*Bones & Murder*, 1994). The surprise effect is here produced by Gertrude's proudly delivered confession that it was she herself who killed her husband, old Hamlet. Twists can also arise from meta-narrative elements, as found, for example, in the title story of Thomas King's *One Good Story, That One* (1993). Here, the narrator's concluding remark, which refers to the trickster figure of Native mythology ("I clean up all the coyote tracks on the floor", 10), provides the reader with an implicit instruction on how to read the story.

It also needs to be considered that a clear differentiation between closed and open endings is often impossible since a story may suggest closure on one level and openness on another. Thus, Valgardson's "A Matter of Balance" at first sight seems to offer a closed ending: Harold has won the battle on the rocks against the two bikers and leaves them to die in the river gorge. We cannot know for certain, though, if the two men will, in fact, die since all the details indicating this are rendered from Harold's point of view and may, therefore, represent wishful thinking rather than factual information. What much more strongly prevents a sense of closure, however, is the moral dilemma that is anything but resolved at the end of the story. Similarly, closure is only implied in Kathy Page's "Red Dog", where the ending leaves enough space for the reader to fill the gaps in the text with different interpretations.

No matter which strategy an author employs to end a short story, though, and no matter whether the ending is more obviously open or renders the impression of closure, there is a tendency in short fiction to leave significant *Leerstellen* to be indeterminate and open-ended (Hunter 2007: 45). Ideally, this leads to a unique and genre-specific impact on the reader, or as Lohafer puts it, "The end of the story may not end our involvement with it; we may be forced to reread and rethink. Any good story is going to leave the reader cogitating . . . , and some stories require a great deal of thought even to yield tentative meaning" (1989: 112f).

G. Readers

The challenge a short story may pose for the reader not only lies in its ending. The reception of short fiction in general – and in particular, this means the short story since the early 20th century – is "at the difficult end of the reading spectrum" (Beevers 2008: 22). This is also confirmed by Hunter (2007: 8), who refers to the short story as "a medium . . . adapted peculiarly to that alert intelligence, on the part of the reader, which rebels sometimes at the *longueurs* of the conventional novel". The observation that the short story speaks to the "alert, not the fatigued reader" (Hunter 2007: 8), a statement that similarly applies to poetry, may go a long way to explain why short stories, in Charles May's words, are "essential but seldom read" (2004: 24). As Ailsa Cox (2008: ix) explains, short stories "typically engage with the inexplicable, reminding us of those aspects of reality which escape our standard modes of cognition and classification". The reader's interpretive act is further challenged by the paradox inherent in the receptive process, which Glover describes as follows: "You read a story forward but understand it backward, only fully comprehending the journey when you have reached the end and rehearse it in memory. Even then it is difficult to capture a story in its entirety, as a simultaneous entity, without dedicated re-reading" (2019: 23f). In general, due to its thematic and aesthetic resistance to mainstream discourses, which to a large extent results from its tightly knit, allusive, and indeterminate configuration of meaning, the short story form demands intensive concentration on the part of both writer and reader and is, therefore, a particularly potent literary genre.

Ian Reid (1989: 299) addresses yet another aspect which distinguishes the reception of short stories from that of novels – namely, their framing. The novel, as opposed to the single short story, is "closely aligned with the form of the book" (Reid 1989: 310). With novels, therefore (and, for this purpose, also with bound short story collections), paratextual frames offer first entry points into the main text. A single short story, in contrast, is framed either by the stories surrounding it in a collection or by other texts in the case of magazine publication. These frames influence the reading (usually inadvertently so), as do the titles of single-author collections or anthologies of stories by different authors. Titles such as *West by Northwest: British Columbia Stories* (eds. David Stouck and Myler Wilkinson 1998) or *Strike the Wok: An Anthology of Contemporary Chinese Canadian Fiction* (eds. Lien Chao and Jim Wong-Chu 2003) incite us to read these stories along regional or ethnic lines. While such framings are not in themselves positive or negative, it is important to be aware of their effect when reading and/or analysing short fiction.

H. The Short Story as a "Minor" Genre

Inspiring impulses for short story criticism have come from Adrian Hunter's investigation of the short story as a "minor genre" – "minor" not in the sense of being less important than, say, novels, but in the sense that due to its "elliptic, fragmentary, fleeting, suggestive and ambiguous nature", the short story "is ideally calibrated to the experience of modern life" (Hunter 2007: 2, 46). It has thus been used as a powerful instrument for rendering social alienation and personal crisis and has been preoccupied, to a considerable extent, with marginalised groups and the experience of loneliness. Seen from this point of view, its shortness may clearly be an asset in the sense that the short story can "embody an experiential condition of modernity – a sense of chronic uncertainty, historical sequestration and social isolation" (Hunter 2007: 3). In the same vein as Hunter, Cox (2008: ix) points out that short stories "typically engage with the inexplicable, reminding us of those aspects of reality which escape our standard modes of cognition and classification". It, therefore, comes as no surprise that the short story has "played such a prominent role – disproportionately so – in cultures that have experienced colonial disruption" (Hunter 2007: 4).

Since the late 19th century, as Hunter (2007: 4) observes, the short story "has been found to be peculiarly amenable to the expression of 'minority', eccentric and counter-normative identities and ideological positions". This may offer one explanation for why in Canada, a country which, since its official confederation in 1867, has been struggling to assert itself vis-à-vis its overpowering neighbour, the short story occupies such a prominent position. Second, looking at the short fiction output in Canada over the past decades, it becomes obvious that the short story has been used particularly often by authors who belong to cultural and/or ethnic minorities and who tackle, in their works, experiences of migration, displacement, and racism. Examples are, among many others, Austin Clarke, Rohinton Mistry, Neil Bissoondath, Evelyn Lau, Madeleine Thien, Shyam Selvadurai, André Alexis, and David Bezmozgis. In Native Canadian literature, too, short fiction occupies a prominent position, thinking, for example, of Thomas King, Lee Maracle, Drew Hayden Taylor, Eden Robinson and many others.

Moreover, many Canadian short stories engage with marginalisation resulting from disability, invalidity, illness, and/or ageing, with crises due to substance abuse, alcoholism, and criminal histories and with loss and grieving (see also Chapter 10). They often also deal with the distorted identities produced by the clash between heteronormative binaries and anything that goes against them. Canadian short fiction thus confirms Hunter's argument that the short story is "particularly suited to the representation of liminal or problematized identities" and speaks "directly to and about those whose sense of self, region, state or nation is insecure" (2007: 138).

The discussion of the short story's generic markers in this section should by no means be understood as prescriptive. However, I agree with Bonheim that there should be "first classification, then differentiation" (1982: 265). In order to underscore the claim that the short story is a literary genre with a distinct aesthetic potential, it is necessary to produce a set of generic markers, however tentative and flexible these may be. I have approached the short story with the help of eight different categories, which, I should add, apply most fittingly to somewhat "prototypical" short stories. Many of the features described earlier may also be found in novels, and many short stories will only fulfil some of these criteria. In short, definitions of the short story must be based on the awareness that they will continuously have to be adapted to new developments within short fiction and that they will have to remain as open as possible. This is in line with what Ann-Marie Einhaus (2016: 5) has referred to as the genre's capacity to "contain within it the greatest possible degree of variety and idiosyncrasy".

Regarding the cultural significance of the short story in Canada, it may be worth considering Alexander MacLeod's argument that "the supposedly marginalized form of the short story has been consistently central to the major aesthetic and cultural shiftings of Canadian literature" (2016: 430). As MacLeod convincingly shows in his chapter for the *Oxford Handbook of Canadian Literature* (2016), the short story in Canada has been a catalyst of aesthetic and cultural change rather than just a mere reflection of the literary and social status quo. Thus, Hunter's concept of the short story as a literary form specifically suited to explore margins (on socio-cultural and aesthetic levels) and to express states of instability, disruption, and transition assumes a particularly strong relevance for Canadian short fiction.

Works Cited

Primary Works

Atwood, Margaret (1995 [1994]). *Bones & Murder*. London: Virago.
Atwood, Margaret (2014). *Stone Mattress: Nine Tales*. New York and London: Doubleday.
Chao, Lien and Jim Wong-Chu, eds. (2003). *Strike the Wok: An Anthology of Contemporary Chinese Canadian Fiction*. Toronto: TSAR.
Hood, Hugh (1987 [1962]). *Flying a Red Kite*. Erin: The Porcupine's Quill Press.
King, Thomas (1993). *One Good Story, That One*. Toronto: Harper Collins.
MacLeod, Alistair (2002 [2001]). *Island: Stories*. London: Vintage.
Munro, Alice (2009). *Too Much Happiness*. London: Chatto & Windus.
Page, Kathy (2016). *The Two of Us*. Windsor, ON: Biblioasis.
Stouck, David and Myler Wilkinson, eds. (1998). *West by North West. British Columbia Short Stories*. Vancouver: Polestar.
Valgardson, William Dempsey (1990 [1982]). "A Matter of Balance". In: Klaus Peter Müller, ed. *Contemporary Canadian Short Stories*. Fremdsprachentexte. Stuttgart: Reclam. 130–149; also in: Valgardson, William Dempsey (1990). *What Can't Be Changed Shouldn't Be Mourned: Short Stories*. Vancouver: Douglas & McIntyre. 8–18.

Secondary Works

Basseler, Michael (2019). *An Organon of Life Knowledge: Genres and Functions of the Short Story in North America*. Bielefeld: Transcript.
Beevers, John (2008). "The Short Story: What Is It Exactly, What Do We Want to Do with It, and How Do We Intend to Do It?". In: Cox. 11–26.
Bonheim, Helmut (1980–81). "Topoi of the Canadian Short Story". *Dalhousie Review* 60.4: 659–669.
Bonheim, Helmut (1982). *The Narrative Modes: Techniques of the Short Story*. Cambridge, MA: Brewer.
Bowen, Elizabeth (1976 [1936]). "The Faber Book of Modern Short Stories". In: May. 152–158.
Cox, Ailsa, ed. (2008). *The Short Story*. Newcastle upon Tyne: Cambridge Scholars Publishing.
Delaney, Paul and Adrian Hunter, eds. (2019). *The Edinburgh Companion to the Short Story in English*. Edinburgh: Edinburgh University Press.
Einhaus, Ann-Marie, ed. (2016). *The Cambridge Companion to the English Short Story*. Cambridge: Cambridge University Press.
Gadpaille, Michelle (1988). *The Canadian Short Story in English*. Oxford: Oxford University Press.
Glover, Douglas (2019). "Anatomy of the Short Story". In: Douglas Glover, ed. *The Erotics of Restraint: Essays on Literary Form*. Windsor, ON: Biblioasis. 23–82.
Grady, Wayne (1980). "Preface". In: Wayne Grady, ed. *The Penguin Book of Canadian Short Stories*. Harmondsworth: Penguin. v–vi.
Hanson, Clare (1985). *Short Stories and Short Fictions, 1880–1980*. Basingstoke: Macmillan.
Head, Dominic (1992). *The Modernist Short Story: A Study in Theory and Practice*. Cambridge: Cambridge University Press.
Heble, Ajay (1994). *The Tumble of Reason: Alice Munro's Discourse of Absence*. Toronto: University of Toronto Press.
Hunter, Adrian (2007). *The Cambridge Introduction to the Short Story in English*. Cambridge: Cambridge University Press.
Keith, William J. (1985). *Canadian Literature in English*. London: Longman.
Kennedy, Alison L. (2008). "Small in a Way That a Bullet Is Small". In: Cox. 1–9.
Korte, Barbara (2003). *The Short Story in Britain: A Historical Sketch and Anthology*. Tübingen: Francke.
Lecker, Robert (2013). *Keepers of the Code: English-Canadian Literary Anthologies and the Representation of the Nation*. Toronto: University of Toronto Press.
Lohafer, Susan (1989). "How Does a Story End?". In: Lohafer and Clarey. 109–114.
Lohafer, Susan and Jo Ellyn Clarey, eds. (1989). *Short Story Theory at a Crossroads*. Baton Rouge and London: Louisiana State University Press.
Löschnigg, Maria (2014). *The Contemporary Canadian Short Story in English: Continuity and Change*. Trier: WVT.
Löschnigg, Maria and Martin Löschnigg (2007). "Figures in a Landscape: William Dempsey Valgardson, 'A Matter of Balance'". In: Reingard M. Nischik, ed. *The Canadian Short Story: Interpretations*. Rochester and New York: Camden House. 321–330.
Lynch, Gerald (2001). *The One and the Many: English-Canadian Short Story Cycles*. Toronto: University of Toronto Press.
MacLeod, Alexander (2016). "The Canadian Short Story in English: Aesthetic Agency, Social Change, and the Shifting Canon". In: Cynthia Sugars, ed. *The Oxford Handbook of Canadian Literature*. New York: Oxford University Press. 426–447.

May, Charles E., ed. (1976). *Short Story Theories*. Athens: Ohio University Press.
May, Charles E. (2004). "Why Short Stories Are Essential and Why They Are so Seldom Read". In: Per Winther, Jakob Lothe and Hans H. Skei, eds. *The Art of Brevity: Excursions in Short Fiction Theory and Analysis*. Columbia: University of South Carolina Press. 14–25.
New, William H. (2009). "The Short Story". In: Coral Ann Howells and Eva-Maria Kröller, eds. *The Cambridge History of Canadian Literature*. Cambridge: Cambridge University Press. 381–401.
Nischik, Reingard M. (2017). *The English Short Story in Canada: From the Dawn of Modernism to the 2013 Nobel Prize*. Jefferson, NC: McFarland & Company.
Poe, Edgar Allan (1976 [1842]). "Review of Twice-Told Tales". In: May. 45–51.
Reid, Ian (1989). "Destabilizing Frames for Story". In: Lohafer and Clarey. 299–310.
Shaw, Valerie (1983). *The Short Story: A Critical Introduction*. London: Longman.
Van Herk, Aritha (1990). "Scant Articulations of Time". *University of Toronto Quarterly* 68.4: 925–938.

Suggestions for Further Reading

Glover, Douglas (2012). "How to Write a Short Story: Notes on Structure and an Exercise". In: Douglas Glover, ed. *Attack of the Copula Spiders and Other Essays on Writing*. Windsor: Biblioasis. 23–42.
Lohafer, Susan (2003). *Reading for Storyness: Preclosure, Theory, Empirical Poetics and Culture in the Short Story*. Baltimore: Johns Hopkins University Press.
May, Charles E., ed. (1994). *The New Short Story Theories*. Athens: Ohio University Press.
Patea, Viorica (2012). *Short Story Theories: A Twenty-First Century Perspective*. Leiden and Boston: Brill, Rodopi.
Thacker, Robert (2004). "Short Fiction". In: Eva-Marie Kröller, ed. *The Cambridge Companion to Canadian Literature*. Cambridge: Cambridge University Press. 177–193.
Winther, Per (1995). "The Canadian Short Story in English: An Alternative Paradigm". In: Jørn Carlsen, ed. *O Canada: Essays on Canadian Literature and Culture*. Aarhus: Aarhus University Press. 65–78.

2 Sketchy Beginnings and "Becoming Canadian"

From the Early 19th Century to Confederation Literature

"At the time of Confederation in 1867", Michelle Gadpaille (2001: 2898) notes, "short fiction already filled the magazines of the new country". However, these short prose pieces were mostly sketches and anecdotes with a strong local colour element rather than what would later be regarded as the short story proper. Nor were these "earliest antecedents of the Canadian short story" (Gadpaille 1988: 1) comparable to the closely knit tales of Edgar Allan Poe, Nathaniel Hawthorne, or Herman Melville, which, already in the early 19th century, led to a climax in American short fiction that was recognised internationally. The most important names regarding the early 19th-century sketch are Thomas McCulloch and Thomas Chandler Haliburton.

The sketchy and anecdotal form was also used in writings by Anna Brownell Jameson (*Winter Studies and Summer Rambles*, 1838), Catherine Parr Traill (*The Backwoods of Canada*, 1836), and Susanna Moodie (*Roughing It in the Bush*, 1852; *Life in the Clearings versus the Bush*, 1853). Of these works, it is, above all, *Roughing It in the Bush* which has had a lasting impact on the Canadian imaginary. Moodie's fictionalised account of her Upper Canadian pioneering experiences in the 1830s, whose chapters all represent closed and rounded-off prose sketches, has made the author a cultural icon of early "Canada", resonant in the country's literary landscape. Her impact is reflected, for example, in the "survival myth" that Margaret Atwood propagates in *Survival* (1972), and that still informs critical works on Canadian literature. Atwood has also engaged with Moodie in her literary works, most memorably in her poetry collection *The Journals of Susanna Moodie* (1970), but also in her only historical novel so far, *Alias Grace* (1996). Other authors who have been inspired by Susanna Moodie's sketches of pioneering life are, for example, Carol Shields (*Small Ceremonies*, 1976), Margaret Laurence (*The Diviners*, 1974), and Timothy Findley (*Headhunter*, 1993).

Other female voices that contributed to short fiction in the 19th century – in particular to the romantic story that flourished at this time – are Rosanna Leprohon, Isabella Valancy Crawford, Susan Francis Harrison, Eliza Lanesford Cushing, and May Agnes Fleming. Leprohon's "mannered romances" (New 1989: 76), for example, were published between the 1840s and 1880s

DOI: 10.4324/9781003142683-4

in magazines such as the *Literary Garland*, the Boston *Pilot* and the Montreal *Family Herald*. Harrison produced a collection of short prose, *Crowded Out and Other Sketches*, that came out in 1886. Her sketches are strongly satirical, attacking, for example, "the colonial-mindedness of British publishers, who are willing to accept only wilderness versions of Canada" (New 1989: 104), or social manners in general. Although, as Nischik (2007: 4) argues, these authors are known today mainly "for a few of their less formulaic stories reprinted in anthologies of Canadian short fiction", and even though "sentimental romances, plot-driven adventure tales, and formula writing were the order of the day", the contributions of these authors should not be completely dismissed. After all, as Gerald Lynch (2002b: 1042) notes, these women were writing from "the fringes of patriarchal society" and their stories "often address aesthetic matters absent in the works of the engaged male writers".

Towards the end of the 19th century, the first signs of the advent of modernism in Canadian short fiction can be discerned, with Duncan Campbell Scott's *In the Village of Viger* (1896; see Section 2.2.) representing a decisive "break with the popular genres of romance, the frontier tale, and the local colour story" (Gadpaille 1988: 13). The time when Scott's *In the Village of Viger* appeared also saw the emergence of another – distinctly Canadian – genre, the realistic animal story. Charles G.D. Roberts's and Ernest Thompson Seton's animal stories were not only popular during their day but still enjoy a steady readership. Since the controversy as to who of the two authors invented the genre has not been solved yet, I agree with Lynch that "it may be most accurate to consider them jointly as the creators of this distinctly Canadian form" (2002a: 30). The different approaches of the two authors will be discussed in more detail in Section 2.3. Seton's and Roberts's wild animal stories cater to the trope of the Canadian wilderness, which still resonates strongly in the Canadian cultural imaginary.

2.1. The Sketch and the Local Colour Tradition

"The Canadian short story has a history with sketchy beginnings at least as far back as the early nineteenth century" (Lynch 2001: 3). While Thomas McCulloch and Thomas Chandler Haliburton are the most important names regarding the early 19th-century sketch, Stephen Leacock's *Sunshine Sketches* mark both the climax of this anecdotal form in the early 20th century as well as its end, since in the 1920s more modernist forms of short fiction took over. In contrast to the tale or the short story, the sketch is static rather than dynamic. While in the short story proper, the character develops or is profoundly impacted by the events rendered in the narrative, the sketch "is a static description of a character or place where the character remains constant" (Beevers 2008: 19). Due to its heavily dialogic structure and its humour, the sketch is also akin to the anecdote; both adopt a chatty and familiar tone, and even though their main purpose may be entertainment, their often ironic tenor also fulfils didactic or socio-critical functions.

Thomas McCulloch (1776–1843), a Nova Scotian Presbyterian minister, is now mostly known for his *Letters of Mephibosheth Stepsure*, which appeared in the *Acadian Recorder* (from December 1821 to May 1822 and from January 1822 to March 1823) and came out as a book in 1862. In his "Introduction" to the New Canadian Library Edition of the *Stepsure Letters*, Northrop Frye calls McCulloch "the founder of genuine Canadian humour" (1960: ix). This form of humour, as well as elements of local colour, would be taken up later by Haliburton and Leacock. Moreover, all three authors use the form of connected stories for their short prose collections, thus heralding a tradition that was to crystallise into a particularly prominent form in Canada.

As mentioned, the sketch and anecdote frequently have a didactic dimension. In McCulloch's *Letters*, this arises, to a large extent, from his ironical rendering of "lame Meph's" (101) self-righteousness, which Jennifer Andrews (2002: 515) aptly captures as follows: "By juxtaposing verbal cleverness with Stepsure's dismissive treatment of his neighbours, McCulloch creates a cautionary tale for readers who are inclined to see themselves as superior". A device through which the narrator makes his neighbours the butt of his satirical portraits is the mock-heroic: thus, for example, Captain Hector Shootem's (Hec's) bravery is ridiculed through a comparison of "the battle of Scorem's Corner" (*Letters* 103), in fact an encounter of Hec and his men with a herd of pigs, with the Battle of Waterloo. From today's point of view, a number of Mephibosheth's humorous remarks will appear sexist and racist; allowing for the distinction between author and narrator, however, they may invite discussions on prevailing attitudes in early 19th-century settler societies and changing sensibilities.

In his *Stepsure Letters*, McCulloch combines the sketch with the epistolary mode. Staging his anecdotes as letters, the author manages to create a more personal atmosphere between his narrator and his readership, who appear to be directly addressed and included. With the letter-form, McCulloch, in fact, uses a narrative mode that was to become – in different ways – a recurring element in modern Canadian short fiction.

Thomas Chandler Haliburton (1796–1865), a Nova Scotian lawyer, first published his satirical and highly colloquial *Sam Slick* stories in *The Novascotian (1835)* before they appeared in book form as *The Clockmaker; or the Sayings and Doings of Samuel Slick, of Slickville* in 1836. *The Clockmaker* was followed by a number of other *Sam Slick* books, but it is the first series that has survived and become part of the Canadian literary canon. Haliburton's sketches enjoyed immense popularity during their time and are said to have influenced no less a writer than Mark Twain (Thacker 2004: 179). In particular, the main character, Sam Slick of Slickville, Connecticut, "became a legend in his own time" and has granted the author the title "father of American humour" (McDougall 1958: x).

Haliburton's wit, as New (1989: 62) explains, "is broader than McCulloch's, his handling of dialect more firmly in control, his use of the letter form less recurrent than his reliance on anecdote". However, a letter it is which introduces and frames the actual stories, narrated by an English-born travelling circuit judge, who, in the later *Sam Slick* stories, "turns into a Nova Scotia-born gentleman named Thomas Poker, Esq." (New 1989: 63). The introductory fictional letter, "written" by Sam Slick and addressed to Mr. Howe (editor of the *Novascotian*), adds a meta-narrative element to the assembled sketches and gives the main character an opportunity to comment on the appropriation of his "*Sayins and Doins*" (*Clockmaker* 1). While first he claims that "[a]ccording to my idee you have no more right to take them, than you have to take my clocks without payin' for them" (1), he must soon admit that it is the "prettiest" and "wittiest" (2) book he has ever seen and also warms to the idea (consistent with his character, after all) that it brings profit. Moreover, he comes to see that it not only satirises the "Yankees" but also "wipes up the Bluenoses [i.e. the Nova Scotians] considerable hard" (2).

This letter is then followed by 33 short sketches and anecdotes. Here, Sam Slick, who travels around Nova Scotia with the Squire, is shown to explicitly criticise the Bluenoses for their backwardness, laziness, or, in Sam's words, being "much behind the intelligence of the age" (13). Even though, according to Sam, the province has more natural privileges than America, the Nova Scotians are "either asleep, or stone blind to them" (13). As Sam reveals to the Squire, "I tell you, if we had this country, you couldn't see the harbour for the shipping" (13). While the Bluenoses are explicitly attacked, Sam's profit-oriented pragmatic "Yankee" attitude is implicitly criticised through the exposure of his aggressively capitalist mindset, when he, for example, proudly declares: "We reckon hours and minutes to be dollars and cents" (8). In addition, the English also do not get away lightly, so that we can agree with Thacker (2004: 179) that "Haliburton uses Slick to lampoon the Nova Scotian, Englishman, and American alike". While, on the one hand, Haliburton's *Clockmaker* "testifies to a keen, not to say anxious, awareness of his position on the margins of two great cultures" (Lynch 2001: 9), it also reveals the author's colonial mindset. Even though the numerous racist remarks in the *Clockmaker* are mostly framed as Sam Slick's prejudices, they nonetheless perpetuate "obnoxious stereotypes of Blacks, women, other nationalities and various ethnic groups" (Davies 2002: 471). It thus does not come as a surprise that the title of George Elliott Clarke's keynote address at a symposium on the 200th anniversary of Haliburton's death was "Should We Burn Haliburton?" (Davies 2002: 471). However, eliminating racist texts does not eliminate racism. Rather, works like Haliburton's *Clockmaker* (and also McCulloch's *Stepsure Letters*) must be seen as documents of colonial and imperial mentalities that illustrate the necessity of critically engaging with racism and its cultural and literary manifestations.

While it may be true that these two early literary figures are the first representatives of Canadian humour and irony (Gadpaille 1988: 2) rather than the first representatives of the short story, their influence on short fiction should not be underestimated: first, they initiated a narrative tradition that three-quarters of a century later saw its most illustrious practitioner, Stephen

Leacock; and second, with their favouring of interlinked stories, they already used a form that "came increasingly to dominate the genre of the short story in Canada as distinct from England and America" (Lynch 2001: 9).

With a total of more than 60 books (including studies in political science, sketches and humorous stories, essays, and literary criticism), Stephen Leacock (1869–1944) was an exceptionally productive writer. After having worked as a schoolmaster for eight years, Leacock turned to economics and political science and eventually became a professor of political economy and long-time chair of the Department of Economics and Political Science at McGill University in Montreal. His career as a prolific creative writer only started relatively late, in 1910, with *Literary Lapses*, followed by more than two dozen further collections of humorous sketches. Of all his works, it is *Sunshine Sketches of a Little Town* (1912) on which his fame mostly rests today and which is seen as "one of the foremost examples of Canadian literary humor in short fiction" (Antor 2007: 53). Leacock's "masterwork" (Staines 2002: 641) appeared about three-quarters of a century after Haliburton's *Sam Slick* stories, and it seemed to continue the tradition of anecdotal, humorous short prose introduced by McCulloch and Haliburton (which is also why *Sunshine Sketches* will be included in this section). At the same time, however, and through their more consciously literary structure, Leacock's pieces already show a much stronger inclination towards the short story than earlier sketches. Moreover, the elaborate way in which the stories are interrelated and structured makes the book (just like Scott's *In the Village of Viger*) an early manifestation of the Canadian short story cycle, not only structurally but also in the sense of a generic form that supports and creates meaning. Regarding the sketch, Leacock's work marks a climax but also the end of this anecdotal form since around the turn of the century – and in particular from the 1920s onwards – modernist sensibilities strongly affected the short story in Canada. As far as Leacock's use of humour is concerned, however, continuities can be seen, for example, in the work of Jack Hodgins and Mordecai Richler and – even though often in darker shades – in Thomas King's short fiction and Margaret Atwood's flash fiction pieces and some of the tales collected in *Stone Mattress*.

The humour that defines *Sunshine Sketches of a Little Town* is benevolent rather than sarcastic; it is conveyed through irony rather than satire. Mariposa, the fictitious town that is also the major unifying element in this story cycle, stands for a still fairly intact world, a community that – despite the exposed weaknesses of its citizens – "is bound together by camaraderie, bound together by the essentially fraternal nature of its residents" (Staines 2021: 46). In this, it contrasts with the follow-up collection *Arcadian Adventures of the Idle Rich (1914)*, which satirises, "in a harsher, sharper tone the destructive and hypocritical activities of the plutocracy of a big capitalist American city" (Antor 2007: 54). The loss of small-town values and communal responsibility, however, is already anticipated in the concluding story of *Sunshine Sketches*, "L'Envoi. The Train to Mariposa". Here, the narrator brings home to his interlocutor that his obsessive pursuit of money in the city has alienated him from those who have held on to their roots in Mariposa and also from his true self.

The initial story, "The Hostelry of Mr Smith", provides the reader with the first introduction to Mariposa, which stands metonymically for any Canadian small-town setting but, in some way, also for Canada as such. It also sets the colloquial tone that defines the whole collection. From the beginning, the reader feels directly addressed and included in the story as one who is partly (or possibly) familiar with the town. Being evident already in the first sentence of *Sunshine Sketches* ("I don't know whether you know Mariposa", 1), this ambivalent role of the addressee is repeatedly referred to in the cycle. This is the case, for example, in the following passages from "The Marine Excursions of the Knights of Pythias":

> But if you've ever been on a Mariposa excursion you know all about these details anyway. . . .
>
> I suppose you have often noticed the contrast there is between an excursion on its way out in the morning and what it looks like on the way home.
>
> (*Sunshine Sketches* 47)

It is only in the final story, "L'Envoi", that the undecided status of the "you" is clarified when the narrator refers to his auditor's boyhood in Mariposa (148) and his alienation from it due to his adoption of the negative effects of city life, as has already been mentioned before.

The main techniques used by Leacock for his comical exposure of small-town foibles and parochial attitudes are bathos and hyperbole, as well as the subtle negotiation of incongruities between appearance and reality. Their clash is evident, for example, in Mariposa's grossly exaggerating the town's population (4) or in the description of Mariposa as a thriving town through which even the transcontinental railway runs, followed by the deflating remark: "It is true that the trains mostly go through at night and don't stop" (4). A striking example of Leacock's use of bathos and hyperbole can be found in "The Marine Excursions of the Knights of Pythias". Here, the aura of grandness that surrounds the description of the Mariposa Belle, Lake Wissanotti, and in fact, the whole atmosphere on the morning of the July excursion of Mariposa's "famous" steamer ship clashes with a later scene in which the steamer runs aground "on a reed bank" (50). Since Lake Wissanotti is only six feet deep and, contrary to what the enthusiastic narrator wants us to believe at the beginning of the story, is certainly none of the world's great attractions, the Mariposa Belle's accident is really not granted the tragic air of a "real" marine disaster but is flat-out ludicrous.

The narrator's passion for this town, no doubt, causes him to be carried away by his enthusiasm. Comparing, for example, the uniforms of the Knights of Pythias with those of the guards at Buckingham Palace and excessively using repetition and exclamation marks to underline the sublime greatness of this "marine excursion" suggest that the narrator – as opposed to the reader – is not fully aware of the inappropriateness of his grand pathos. It is, in fact, this amiably naïve conception of the narrator, who "invites both sympathetic understanding and critical distance", which "provides the basis for Leacock's kindly humour in *Sunshine Sketches*" (Antor 2007: 57). However, it must be noted here that there are instances in the book where the narrator *does* reveal an awareness of his biased depiction of Mariposa – for example, when he acknowledges that you will not be able to appreciate Mariposa's charm when "you come to the place fresh from New York" (3); also, he admits that his overly enthusiastic portrayal results, after all, from his familiarity with and love for this town.

Even though the sketch as a genre may have gone out of fashion, the notion of Canadian self-consciousness has not: in the *Sunshine Sketches*, it is displayed by the benevolently critical exposure of the townspeople's self-important demeanour, most memorably depicted in the mock celebration of Canadian greatness in "The Marine Excursions of the Knights of Pythias". It will appear again, for example, in a number of Mavis Gallant's stories, most prominently in "The Ice Wagon Going Down the Street". In "The Marine Excursions", this characteristically Canadian deflation of one's own supposed greatness is most strongly evident at the point when the people on the steamer wholeheartedly sing, "O – Can – a – da" (48), exactly at the moment when the steamer starts sinking.

With *Sunshine Sketches*, the short story cycle, which had been introduced in its full form by Duncan Campbell Scott's *In the Village of Viger*, had now come to stay. In fact, Scott's and Leacock's cycles can be seen as the first major instances of Canadian writers using the form to emphasise their themes. Having said this, it is now time to finally deal with Scott in more detail.

2.2. Duncan Campbell Scott: *In the Village of Viger* (1896)

Duncan Campbell Scott (1862–1947) was not only a renowned poet and short story writer but was also involved in Canadian politics, as his 53 years as a civil servant in the federal Department of Indian Affairs testify. While his role in Canada's assimilationist policies, the aftermath of which is still painfully felt within Aboriginal communities, is highly ambivalent, his central role regarding the establishment of a distinct Canadian literature and culture can hardly be ignored. As a writer, Scott was, above all, a poet, and it is this poetic and lyrical approach that also defines much of his short fiction.

Among Scott's short fiction, it is the story "Labrie's Wife" (in *The Witching of Elspie*, 1923) and, above all, the ten stories making up *In the Village of Viger* that have received the most critical attention. The *Viger* stories in particular have come to hold a "place at the head of the rich tradition of the Canadian short story cycle" (Lynch 2001: 33). First of all, *In the Village of Viger* is a cycle of place, like Leacock's *Sunshine Sketches*, the American Sherwood Anderson's *Winesburg Ohio* and James Joyce's *Dubliners*. The regional identity of Viger is conveyed through the volume's "detailed realization of its human and physical geography" (Dragland 1973: 11). However, like Leacock's, Anderson's, and Joyce's linked-story collections, *Viger*, too, acquires universal significance through its careful analysis of human nature, longing, and failure. Still, Scott's cycle – like Leacock's – shows itself as very Canadian by the emphasis that is given to the last story, which, in the Canadian short story cycle, more often than not implies a notion of return (Lynch 2001: 28, 32).

While Scott's cycle has repeatedly been linked to (psychological) realism with regard to its style (Dragland 1973: 13; Wicken 1997: 1044), it also shows elements of the sketch on the one hand and of modernist writing on the other. Thus, several characters are defined by a touch of eccentricity in the manner of Dickens and Leacock. In turn, Scott's impressionism, to be observed especially in the expository sections of his stories, and his foregrounding of fragmentation and disruption convey modern sentiments.

The fragmentation thematised in *Viger* is reflected in the choice of genre. "The discontinuous narrative of the short story cycle", as Lynch (2001: 37) observes, "with its implied formalistic challenge to the illusive unity of the master narrative of the novel . . . , provided Scott with a form ideally suited to the fictional dissolution and tentative reconstitution of what may be called Vigerian familial and communal life". In fact, *In the Village of Viger* confirms the premise underlying the present book: that genre is not just an instrument for the transmission of meaning but "that genre *is* meaning" (Lynch 2001: 28). In Scott's story cycle, that genre's distinct interplay between unity and disunity is manifest on many levels – most obviously in the function of the setting (a French-Canadian village in Quebec), which is the prime unifying element yet which is paradoxically also the space within which fragmentation is demonstrated.

Fissures evident in the "pleasant Viger by the Blanche" (*Viger* 18) are conveyed, for example, through the juxtaposition of idyllic descriptions with the first signs of the nearby city's rapid growth and eventual "embrace [of] the little village" (19), an embrace whose nature remains at first unknown. Thus, the pastoral depiction of the village in the poem that precedes the cycle clashes with the expository description of the village in the first story, "The Little Milliner". Here, "the mill . . . on the Blanche had shut down" and even "on still nights, above the noise of the frogs in the pools, you could hear the rumble of the street-cars and the faint tinkle of their bells, and when the air was moist the whole southern sky was luminous with the reflection of thousand gas-lamps" (19).

"Sedan", the fourth story, too, first creates an impression of exceeding pleasantness when the street where Paul Arbique keeps his inn is described. In the first paragraph alone, the word "pleasant" (with derivations such as "pleasantest", "pleasanter", and "pleasure") appears eight times, besides other positively connoted words, such as "happy", "idyllic", "contented", "dreamy", and "Arcadia". However, already at this point, the attentive reader will suspect that this overly pleasant street may be a mock-idyll – either due to the hyperbolic style or due to the conditional mode in the second sentence of the story: "It was a little street with little houses, but it looked *as if* only happy people lived there" (37, my emphasis). In the course of the story, the darkness looming underneath the idyllic surface comes to the fore more and more when the Franco-Prussian War breaks out in Europe and results in eruptions of hatred against the innocent German immigrant Hans Blumenthal, the clockmaker of the village. The story reaches a climax when Paul Arbique (who is from Sedan, where, in 1870, the French suffered a decisive defeat) organises a mob to "break into [Blumenthal's] house and give him a sound beating" (40). It is only due to the intervention of another outsider, Latulipe, the Arbiques's adopted and utterly neglected daughter, that Blumenthal escapes the attack and is rewarded with her love. The name of the river Blanche, too, which "meanders" through the stories and evokes notions of an unspoilt idyll, clashes with the general mood of a community which is about to lose its innocence.

Another motif that recurs throughout the cycle, giving it unity while in itself displaying disruption, is that of fractured families, which may be seen to stand symbolically for the disintegration of traditions in the wake of metropolitan intrusion. In fact, none of the stories features traditional family constellations of parents and children (Lynch 2001: 39). In "The Dejardins", for example, we encounter two brothers and a sister facing hereditary madness. It is eventually up to Philippe to take care of his brother, who has inherited his father's insanity and believes himself to be Napoleon. In "No. 68 Rue Alfred de Musset", too, we find siblings – in this case, an ambitious sister sacrificing an ill brother in a fraudulent attempt to marry rich and live an exciting life.

Structurally, "*Viger* is a story cycle full of parallels, inversions, doublings, and mirrorings, of recurrent motif and leitmotif, and, most appropriately, of echoes and resonances" (Lynch 2001: 37). In the stories, disruptive elements abound: in addition to the leitmotif of the fractured family and of the motifs of madness, disease, alcoholism, crime, and racism, the cycle resonates with images that illustrate the impact of technological progress, industrialisation and consumer capitalism. Their juxtaposition with images of an Arcadian idyll creates an elegiac tone. At the same time, however, the cycle also features "happy" stories such as "The Wooing of Monsieur Cuerrier" and "Josephine Labrosse", and a glimmer of hope is also evident in the concluding story, "Paul Farlotte".

"Paul Farlotte" is typical of the "return story" that concludes so many Canadian short story cycles. In addition, it reiterates thematic elements and motifs that define the whole cycle, such as destabilised family structures, madness, supernatural elements and the opposition of idyllic and destructive forces. The Arcadian is introduced through Paul's beautiful garden and little cottage and then contrasted with the "large gaunt-looking house" (*Viger* 70) of his neighbours, the St. Denis family. However, this time, the idyll is not a mock one but rather a replica of the place in France where Paul was born and to where he longs to return. The reason that he has not yet been able to fulfil his dream is his neighbours. Thus, the two contrasting houses are not only connected by the shadow which falls upon the little cottage in the morning and the large house in the evening (70) but also through Paul's altruistic commitment to the family. Guy St. Denis, just like his late father, has become obsessed with the futile invention of a matchbook-making machine, a fixation which threatens to destroy his family (i.e. his sister Mary and their younger siblings), for whom Mary cares like a mother. The story thus features another dysfunctional family, another variation of insanity and another image of the advent of modernisation and mechanisation. However, through Paul's decision to abandon his plans of returning to France in order to support the St. Denis family further, a new adaptive and constructive model of family and community is suggested. The story ends with Paul's trance-like vision of his mother's death back in France and his spiritual and mental return to Viger. The concluding story thus suggests the possibility of a revised conception of what family means among the disruptions caused by the modern world. The story, including the protagonist's return, does not really give a happy ending to the cycle. What it does, however, is to introduce a notion of hope and constructive transformation into an otherwise elegiac narrative of loss and disintegration.

The short story cycle, as made functional by Scott and Leacock for their depictions of place, community, and impending fragmentation, was to become one of the most successful narrative genres in Canadian literature. It started to boom in the 1970s and has remained a vibrant element of Canadian fiction ever since. Like the sequences by Leacock and Scott, later Canadian examples, too, have built on the meaning-creating capacity of the genre. Authors like Alice Munro, Margaret Laurence, and Isabel Huggan have used the linked-story paradigm as a medium of life-writing (see Chapter 4), while others, including Rohinton Mistry, David Bezmozgis and Rachna Mara, have employed its aesthetic specificity for narratives of migration (see Chapter 9).

2.3. The Realistic Animal Story

From the beginning, nature and the wilderness have figured prominently in the literature of what is now Canada. While nature and close observations of the fauna and flora of the backwoods of Ontario played a significant role already in Susanna Moodie's and Catherine Parr Traill's prose pieces, it is in particular with the realistic animal story, which emerged at the end of the 19th century, that a distinctly Canadian genre was born. In fact, as Wolfgang Klooß (2005: 88) proposes, the animal story came to stand as a synonym for Canadian short fiction as such. Through their focus on nature and wilderness, the two "founders" of this form, Charles G.D. Roberts (1860–1943) and Ernest Thompson Seton (1860–1946), contributed to Canada's literary emancipation from its epigonic orientation on Britain.

Both Roberts and Seton rejected animal fables and allegories where animals function as surrogate humans, and both pursued the aim of evoking a feeling of kinship with animals. However, despite this similarity in their intent, and even though both Seton's and Roberts's animal stories are based on close observation and scientific interest and are informed by Darwinian principles, their narrative approaches are nonetheless radically different. Seton did not see himself primarily as a writer but rather as an artist and a naturalist. Thus, the narrators in his animal stories are, above all, observers who minutely record the life and behaviour of strongly anthropomorphised animals. While the humans in his stories are thus passive observers rather than active participants in the events, the animals, in turn, clearly adopt human characteristics. This strong and unquestioned transfer of human attributes and human institutions onto the animal world is also one of the most severe points of criticism Seton's animal stories have repeatedly been confronted with. At the same time, these stories were immensely popular not only in Canada but also internationally. As opposed to Seton, Roberts regarded himself first and foremost as a writer. Comparing their animal stories, it cannot be overlooked that Roberts's work is more "literary" with regard to plot structure, focalisation, and psychological depth. In his stories, humans are not mere observers but active participants in the plot. While, again, animals assume characteristics that will be recognised as humanlike, this transfer is not unilateral in Roberts's stories, where often "humans discover the extent to which they, too, can become like animals" (Irmscher 2004: 108). Moreover, both Roberts's and Seton's animal stories, which feature animals as victims *and* victimisers, are striking examples of the survival pattern that Margaret Atwood has identified in Canadian literature and culture.

Ernest Thompson Seton, as mentioned before, regarded himself as a naturalist, "a term that for him had a visionary as well as scientific meaning" (Redekop 1997: 1055). This understanding of himself acquired a public dimension when he received the honorary position of "official naturalist for the Government of Manitoba". Seton was a self-educated scientist whose meticulous observations and studies of animals found expression in his numerous writings (e.g. *The Birds of Manitoba*, 1891), paintings, and illustrations. His first story, "Lobo – the King of Currumpaw", was included in his first collection, *Wild Animals I Have Known* (1898); this volume also contains the story "Silverspot, The Story of a Crow", which will be the subject of the following case study. Giving names to his wild animals and providing them with human attributes has counteracted Seton's pronounced scientific claim and earned him (as well as Roberts and others) the epithet of "nature-fakers" (Taylor 2002: 1035). However, anthropomorphising and individualising wild animals is a potent technique to help readers identify and empathise with them. It is, therefore, appropriate to read these stories, which, in the last resort, rely on the imagination and on metaphoric language, as works of fiction rather than scientific accounts of animal life, and to judge their merit according to how they affect our attitudes towards animals and foster cross-species thinking.

Of the two main representatives of the realistic animal story, Charles G.D. Roberts is usually seen as the more sophisticated writer, who had already made his name as a man of letters and a poet when he started to write animal stories. In fact, Roberts is regarded as the most eminent Canadian poet of the late 19th century and is also known for his novels, travel guides, histories, translations, and essays. His short fiction constitutes a substantial part of his work, however, and here the majority are animal stories, with "Do Seek Their Meat from God" (1892), published in *Harper's Magazine*, being his first attempt at this genre. Together with three others, "Do Seek Their Meat from God" was included in Roberts's first book of animal stories, *Earth's Enigmas: A Book of Animal and Nature Life* (1896); there followed several other collections such as *Kindred of the Wild* (1902) or *Wisdom of the Wilderness* (1922). The fact that Roberts is now mostly known for his animal stories may have to do with a new, ecologically based interest in nature that highlights the interconnectedness between different environmental agents and questions the supremacy of the human.

The following case study analyses Seton's "Silverspot, The Story of a Crow" and Roberts's "Do Seek Their Meat from God". Its aim is, first, to identify general defining features of the realistic wild animal story and, second, to make visible significant differences between Roberts's and Seton's approaches to this new and characteristically Canadian form of short fiction.

Case Study: A Comparative View on the Canadian Animal Story

Like Lobo the wolf, Raggylug the rabbit, Redruff the partridge, Scarface the fox, or Johnny the bear, Silverspot the crow is one of Seton's many individualised wild animals. Focusing on one particular specimen rather than on the species in general is of great importance for Seton, as he makes clear in the introduction to *Wild Animals I Have Known*: "The real personality of the individual, and his view of life are my theme, rather than the ways of the race in general, as viewed by a casual and hostile human eye" (online). The author – thinly disguised as the first-person narrator of the story – styles himself as a close observer of nature and is only rarely involved in the story's plot. The appeal to the reader is established by the frequent use of we/

us and occasional direct addresses. By employing the first-person plural, in particular, the narrator creates the impression of being on the same level as his readers. At the same time, however, he makes it clear that, through his superior knowledge of wildlife and his close observation, he is in a position to teach us about the life of an animal, a life that "may be more interesting and exciting than that of many human beings" (*Wild Animals* 48). This exceptionality is already asserted through the rhetorical question that begins the story: "How many of us have ever got to know a wild animal?" (47) Considering Seton's emphasis, in his introduction, that "[t]hese stories are true" and that "every incident in their [i.e. the animals'] biographies is from life" (online), the stories occupy an interesting position between short story and documentary. In "Silverspot", this documentary claim is also reinforced through precise indications of time and place. Thus, the narrative, which is divided into three parts, precisely documents when the observations in each part of the story were made. In the first part, the narrator follows his "hero" from late February 1885 until mid-April of the same year, that is, during the period when Silverspot "came with his troop, and for six weeks took up his abode on the hill" (50), the precise location of which is also meticulously documented. After the crows' mating and dispersal, the narrator comes upon Silverspot again in May, when he discovers him and his "wife" taking care of their nest high up in a pine tree. While these observations make up the second part of the story, the third and shortest section recounts his discovery of Silverspot's carcass about eight years later.

This impression of a scientific and factual claim is, however, curiously challenged by consistent anthropomorphising. From the beginning, Silverspot is introduced as "a great leader", "a genius" (47), who is in complete control of his band of about 200 crows. He is not only a perfect leader of his "troops", stationed at "Castle Frank" near Toronto but also an "excellent teacher" (61). In addition, he is endowed with a "quickness of wit" (59), can nearly count up to 30 (62) and has a hobby, as the narrator finds out when he comes upon the crow playing with his hidden treasure (58). Throughout the story, human institutions (e.g. schools, colleges), rituals (e.g. honeymoon, marriage), and social functions (e.g. soldier, sentry, teacher, wife) are used to describe the life and behaviour of the birds. These analogies between the lives of humans and crows form the basis of the narrator's claim that, in most instances, the achievements of the crows, led by the wise Silverspot, exceed those of humans. This is the case, for example, with regard to the discipline of soldiers: "Crows know the value of organizations, and are as well drilled as soldiers – very much better than some soldiers, in fact, for crows are always on duty, always at war, and always dependent on each other for life and safety" (49). This passage clearly reveals that in Seton's "Darwinian, non-judgemental, value-free, survival-of-the-fittest world, there remain parallels with the human world which are not-value-free" (New 1989: 115). Also, Seton's idealisation of the crow community and his elevation of Silverspot to the position of tragic hero at the end of the story suggest a division of wild animals into good and bad: "Alas! It was the head of old Silverspot. His long life of usefulness to his tribe was over – slain at last by the owl that he had taught so many hundreds of young crows to be aware of" (67). The division becomes strikingly evident in the narrator's reference to the owl as a "murderer" who "still hung about the scene of his crime" (66). At the same time, the "cruel tricks" Silverspot uses when robbing the small birds' nests are defended by reference to similar cruelties committed by humans: "But we must not judge him for that, as it is just what we ourselves do to the hens in the barnyard" (59). Seton's insistent anthropomorphising of animals and the suggestion that the most "humane" behaviour is that of the animals (Irmscher 2004: 108) are problematic from the perspective of the natural sciences, as are the descriptions of animal behaviour in terms of "wit", "knowledge", and "intention".

However, it is exactly this drawing of analogies between the world of the crows and that of the human species that makes it possible for readers to identify with the birds and to see them not as pests to be dealt with but as creatures with a complex social organisation and communication system. By singling out an individual animal, giving it a name, observing it closely over a longer period, and describing its behaviour in terms humans can relate to, Seton challenges the notion of a radical division between species that has long defined the coexistence of humans and animals and has, not least, served to justify the *in*human treatment of the latter. The most striking device to make the "other" familiar is Seton's use of musical scores for rendering the crows' complex communication. Paying close attention to different cadences and rhythmic patterns in the cawing of the crows, the narrator tries to translate "Crow" into English. He thus notices that Silverspot sends a different message to his band when the narrator passes without carrying anything than when he carries a gun, sometimes combining various "melodies" when the situation becomes more complex. The score below imitates the sounds the narrator hears the crows gurgling out when "making love" – it is, in other words, "I love you" in Crow:

Of course, the notion remains in the story that crows are interesting and valuable because they are like humans and not due to their own distinct nature. However, it is precisely through endowing his animal characters with human-like personalities and allowing them a "tragic" death that the author is able to achieve his aim – to make readers recognise parallels between species and thereby make them susceptive to the suffering of their fellow creatures, or as the author explains it, "Since, then, the animals are creatures with wants and feelings differing in degree only from our own, they surely have their rights" (online).

Roberts's story "Do Seek Their Meat from God" parallels two panthers caring for their cubs with a prosperous pioneer's defence of his son. While the human sphere in Seton's story is mostly excluded from the plot, Roberts's narrative intertwines and juxtaposes the lives of the panthers with those of the human characters. Due to its aesthetic and rhetorical concentration, "Do Seek Their Meat from God" – like most of Roberts's animal stories – clearly follows the generic parameters of a short story proper. It is characterised by a "totality of effect", a strong semanticising of space, and suggestive imagery. However, there is also a tightly knit plot structure that follows the pattern of exposition, rising action, climax, and denouement of classical drama, which structurally supports the transfer of concepts of the "tragic" to the animal world in Roberts's fiction, as discussed by Konrad Groß (2020: 363–367), and the notion of the animals as tragic heroes (Seifert 2007: 49f).

The highly poetic and evocative exposition, which introduces the panthers and their habitat, already discloses the dualism which informs the whole narrative. It is evident, for example, in the description of the two sides of the ravine where the panthers live – one habitable and enveloped in protective darkness, the other illuminated by moonlight and "barren, unlike its fellow, bossed with great rocky projections, and harsh with stunted junipers" ("Do Seek Their Meat" 175). The male panther's summoning cry when he moves out of the dark into the moonlit steep, too, is characterised by ambivalence since it is "at once plaintive and menacing" (175). The crows, which are disturbed by the panther's cry and are mentioned again a little later, when the female panther answers her mate, already anticipate death. At the same time, however, the coexistence of panthers and crows points to natural cycles, which the story also reflects structurally when the final scenario repeats, almost verbatim, a passage from the initial description of the ravine, "from whose bottom came the *brawl of a swollen* and *obstructed stream*" (180, my emphasis). The dualism that defines the description of the setting and of the male panther, which "is both vulnerable and harmful, gentle and rough, endangered and dangerous" (Seifert 2007: 46), is also evident in the juxtaposition of the male panther and the male human, and is continued in the opposition between the prosperous settler and his impoverished neighbour, disparaged as a drunkard by the former and living in a small cabin with his child.

The heterodiegetic narrator first focuses on the two panthers and their search for food. Sometimes, the animals become focalisers – for example, when they suddenly hear the "voice of a child crying" and we read, "Soon would they break their bitter fast" (176). This point in the story comes as a cliff-hanger since the narrative then digresses in order to summarise the story of the "shiftless fellow" (177), whose seven-year-old son used to visit the home of the rich settler to play with the latter's five-year-old boy. The focus then shifts to the settler's boy and relates why he ended up crying in the poor man's cabin: since the proud settler did not approve of the two boys' friendship, his son secretly sneaked into the cabin, not knowing that its owners had left. The narrative now switches to the settler, who hears the screams and mistakes them for the wailings of his despised neighbour's son, of whose departure he, too, was unaware. At this point, the two strands merge at first only through both parties listening to the child's screams:

> He stopped, lowered his burden to the road, and stood straining his ears and eyes in the direction of the sound. It was just at this time that the two panthers also stopped, and lifted their heads

> to listen. Their ears were keener than those of the man, and the sound had reached them at a greater distance. (178)

Roberts takes great care to foreground the parallels between animals and humans: not only do their actions concur in time, but they are also described as *being* very similar. In an instant of dramatic irony, the settler pities the neglected boy, as he thinks, and continues on his way home. It is only when the wailing becomes fiercer that the man eventually turns to take a look at the cabin and find his own son threatened by the panthers. Now the two plotlines finally seem to connect, yet the narrator interposes again, engaging in a lengthy comment before rendering the fatal encounter. In this comment, he exculpates the panthers, emphasising that we should not regard them as cruel or hideous but acknowledge instead that they "were but seeking with the strength, the cunning, the deadly swiftness given to them to that end, the food convenient for them" (179). The climax is reached when both the "two great beasts" (179) and the man reach the open door of the cabin. When the female animal is shot, the stage is set for the confrontation between the two males, strong representatives of their respective species. Overpowering and killing the animal, the settler seems to assert man's superiority, yet there is no triumph in his victory. In fact, there is a coda to the story that recounts the settler's discovery of the decaying bodies of panther cubs a few weeks later. This will make the reader feel sympathy for the animals. The story focuses on the "grim irony of the food cycle" (Seifert 2007: 44) without offering the reader easy solutions. The moral integrity of the settler, too, remains ambivalent. Due to his prejudice and initial reluctance to help the child he took to be that of his neighbour, he almost loses his own child. In addition, it is, after all, due to civilisation's (including the settler's) encroachment upon the habitats of wild animals that the panthers are forced to "seek their meat" in the vicinity of human dwellings. This is made clear in another didactic passage in the story:

> The settlements of late had been making great inroads on the world of the ancient forest, driving before them the deer and smaller game. Hence the sharp hunger of the panther parents, and hence it came that on this night they hunted together. They purposed to steal upon the settlements in their sleep, and take tribute of the enemies' flocks. (176)

Parallels between animals and humans are suggested on many levels of the story. Both the panthers' as well as the settler's actions are driven by instinct and their urge to protect and care for their young. Also, Roberts takes great care to foreground similarities between the child and the cubs by "using similar diction and imagery" (Seifert 2007: 47), evoking sympathy for both parties. In general, the rich metaphoric language of the story creates an intricate connection between nature and the human sphere. Thus, for example, the panther's cry is compared to "the fierce protestation of a saw" (175), the forest is described as "cloth[ing] the high plateau" (176), and the animals are featured as sentient and cognizant creatures who "*knew* of a solitary cabin" (176, my emphasis), in addition to the male panther *telling* his mate "that the hour had come when they should seek their prey" (175). This passage also echoes the title and reflects the story's combination of biblical myth and a Darwinian struggle for life. Shortly before the panthers' and the settler's storylines merge, there is another such reference ("those great beasts which had set forth to seek their meat from God", 178), which refers to Psalm 104:21 in the Old Testament: "The young lions roar after their prey and seek their food from God". In Roberts's story, the uneasy coalescence of God-given "laws" and natural laws of survival adds yet another element of ambiguity to an already complex narrative.

There are a number of elements which Seton's "Silverspot" and Roberts's "Do Seek Their Meat from God" share. The following list highlights commonalities in the two authors' conceptions of the realistic animal story:

- Kinship between animal and human is suggested, mediated through analogies, metaphors, and anthropomorphism.
- Awareness of cross-species thinking is created.
- Empathy with animals is evoked.
- Both stories are based on close observation and scientific interest.
- Both stories are informed by Darwinian principles.
- Categories of the "tragic" are transferred onto the realm of wild animals.
- There are didactic elements.

> At the same time, as has been shown, Seton's and Roberts's narrative and aesthetic approaches to their subject matter are very different. The following juxtaposition identifies these differences:
>
> | Seton, "Silverspot" | Roberts, "Do Seek Their Meat from God" |
> | --- | --- |
> | • Episodic, loose structure | • Tightly knit structure, totality of effect |
> | • Documentary claim prevails; reinforced by precise indications of time and place | • Aesthetic and artistic claim prevails; strong semanticising of space |
> | • First-person narrator = observer (I-as-witness); only rarely involved in the plot | • Third-person omniscient narrator; heterodiegetic, outside the world of the story; occasional instances of focalisation |
> | • Frequent communication with the implied reader | • A rather covert narrator; only very rarely does the reader feel directly addressed |
> | • Human characters not playing an active part in the plot | • Plot centres on the juxtaposition of animal and human characters; both are major agents in the story |
> | • Animals named and individualised | • Animals as representatives of their species |
> | • Strong anthropomorphising of animals | • Anthropomorphism much more subtle; cross-species elements not only mediated in a unilateral way but reciprocally allocated |

The realistic animal story that boomed in the late 19th and early 20th centuries "spoke to the Zeitgeist of cultural criticism, nature worship, and the rediscovery of the archaic and the instinctual" (Seifert 2007: 43). While the hype about animal stories declined in the 1930s, the preoccupation of Canadian literature with nature and the wilderness has not. In novels and semi-fictional writing especially, animals have continued to play a considerable role. Examples are Farley Mowat's *Never Cry Wolf* (1963) and *A Whale for the Killing* (1972), Marian Engel's *Bear* (1976), and more strongly ecologically oriented works in the past few decades, such as Barbara Gowdy's *The White Bone* (1998), Katie Welch's *The Bears* (2012), or Jennifer Dance's young adult novel *Hawk* (2016). However, with growing concerns about the environmental effects of the Anthropocene, nature and ecological issues have also found their way into Canadian short fiction again (see Chapter 10). Examples can be found in Margaret Atwood's short stories (in particular in her flash fiction), in Kathy Page's mythopoeic stories, and in a number of stories by Indigenous Canadian writers like, for instance, Lee Maracle or Warren Cariou.

It is not only thematically, however, that the realistic animal story has impacted the development of short fiction in Canada. Roberts's rhetorically refined stories, in particular, which make ample use of the distinct meaning-making possibilities of the genre, can also be regarded as early specimens of the Canadian short story proper.

Works Cited

Primary Works

McCulloch, Thomas (1960 [1862]). *The Stepsure Letters*. Toronto: McClelland and Stewart.
Haliburton, Thomas C. (1958 [1836]). *The Clockmaker*. Toronto: McClelland and Stewart.
Leacock, Stephen (1960 [1912]). *Sunshine Sketches of a Little Town*. Toronto: McClelland and Stewart.
Roberts, Charles G.D. (1976 [1892]). "Do Seek Their Meat from God". In: David Arnason, ed. *Nineteenth Century Canadian Stories*. Toronto: Macmillan. 175–180.
Scott, Duncan Campbell (1973 [1896]). *In the Village of Viger and Other Stories*. Toronto: McClelland and Stewart.
Seton, Ernest Thompson (1977 [1898]). *Wild Animals I Have Known*. Toronto: McClelland and Stewart.

Secondary Works

Andrews, Jennifer (2002). "Humour and Satire". In: New. 514–521.
Antor, Heinz (2007). "Tory Humanism, Ironic Humor, and Satire: Stephen Leacock, 'The Marine Excursion of the Knights of Pythias' (1912)". In: Nischik. 53–65.
Beevers, John (2008). "The Short Story: What Is It Exactly, What Do We Want to Do with It, and How Do We Intend to Do It?". In: Ailsa Cox, ed. *The Short Story*. Newcastle: Cambridge Scholars Publishing. 11–25.
Benson, Eugene and William Toye, eds. (1997). *The Oxford Companion to Canadian Literature*, 2nd ed. Oxford: Oxford University Press.
Davies, Richard A. (2002). "Haliburton, Thomas Chandler". In: New, William H., ed. *Encyclopedia of Literature in Canada*. Toronto: University of Toronto Press. 469–472.
Dragland, S.L. (1973). "Introduction". In: Duncan Campbell Scott. *In the Village of Viger and Other Stories*. Toronto: McClelland and Stewart. 9–16.
Frye, Northrop H. (1960). "Introduction". In: Thomas McCulloch. *The Stepsure Letters*. Toronto: McClelland and Stewart. iii–ix.
Gadpaille, Michelle (1988). *The Canadian Short Story in English*. Oxford: Oxford University Press.
Gadpaille, Michelle (2001). "Canadian Short Fiction". In: Charles E. May and Frank N. Magill, eds. *Critical Survey of Short Fiction*, 2nd rev. ed., vol. 7. Hackensack, NJ: Salem Press. 2898–2907.
Groß, Konrad (2020). "Two Tragic Tales of *ursus canadensis*: Animal Perspectives in Charles G.D. Roberts's *The Heart of the Ancient Wood* and Antonine Maillet's *L'Oursiade*". In: Maria Löschnigg and Melanie Braunecker, eds. *Green Matters: Ecocultural Functions of Literature*. Leiden and Boston: Brill, Rodopi. 358–373.
Irmscher, Christoph (2004). "Nature-Writing". In: Kröller. 94–114.

Klooß, Wolfgang (2005). "Die anglokanadische Literatur und die Suche nacheiner kulturellen Identität". In: Konrad Groß, Wolfgang Klooß and Reingard M. Nischik, eds. *Kanadische Literaturgeschichte*. Stuttgart and Weimar: Metzler. 71–94.

Kröller, Eva-Maria, ed. (2004). *The Cambridge Companion to Canadian Literature*. Cambridge: Cambridge University Press.

Lynch, Gerald (2001). *The One and the Many: English-Canadian Short Story Cycles*. Toronto: University of Toronto Press.

Lynch, Gerald (2002a). "Animal Stories". In: New. 29–30.

Lynch, Gerald (2002b). "Short Story and Sketch". In: New. 1039–1046.

McDougall, Robert L. (1958). "Introduction". In: Thomas C. Haliburton, ed. *The Clockmaker*. Toronto: McClelland and Stewart. xi–xvi.

New, William H. (1989). *A History of Canadian Literature*. New York: New Amsterdam Press.

New, William H., ed. (2002). *Encyclopedia of Literature in Canada*. Toronto: University of Toronto Press.

Nischik, Reingard M., ed. (2007). *The Canadian Short Story: Interpretations*. Rochester and New York: Camden House.

Redekop, Magdalene (1997). "Seton, Ernest Thompson". In: Benson and Toye. 1054–1055.

Seifert, Martina (2007). "Canadian Animal Stories: Charles G.D. Roberts, 'Do Seek Their Meat from God'". In: Nischik. 41–52.

Seton, Ernest Thompson. "Introduction". In: Ernest Thompson Seton. *Wild Animals I Have Known*. Online: www.gutenberg.org/cache/epub/3031/pg3031.txt [accessed 8 January 2021].

Staines, David (2002). "Leacock, Stephen". In: New. 640–642.

Staines, David (2021). *A History of Canadian Fiction*. Cambridge: Cambridge University Press.

Taylor, Peter A. (2002). "Seton, Ernest Thompson". In: New. 1034–1036.

Thacker, Robert (2004). "Short Fiction". In: Kröller. 177–193.

Wicken, George (1997). "Duncan Campbell Scott". In: Benson and Toye. 1042–1045.

Suggestions for Further Reading

Bentley, D.M.R. (1999). "'The Thing Is Found to Be Symbolic': Symbolist Elements in the Early Short Stories of Gilbert Parker, Charles G.D. Roberts and Duncan Campbell Scott". In: Gerald Lynch and Angela Arnold Robbeson, eds. *Dominant Impressions: Essays on the Canadian Short Story*. Ottawa: University of Ottawa Press. 27–52.

Campbell, Wanda (1999). "Of Kings and Cabbages: Short Stories by Early Canadian Women". In: Lynch and Robbeson. 17–26.

Fiamengo, Janice, ed. (2007). *Other Selves: Animals in the Canadian Imagination*. Ottawa: University of Ottawa Press.

Lecker, Robert (2010). "Nineteenth-Century English Canadian Anthologies and the Making of a National Literature". *Journal of Canadian Studies* 44.1 (Winter): 91–117.

Lynch, Gerald (2009). "Short Fiction". In: Coral Ann Howells and Eva-Marie Kröller, eds. *The Cambridge History of Canadian Literature*. Cambridge: Cambridge University Press. 166–184.

MacLeod, Alexander (2016). "The Canadian Short Story in English". In: Cynthia Sugars, ed. *The Oxford Handbook of Canadian Literature*. New York: Oxford University Press. 426–447.

3 From the Dawn of Modernism to the "Bursting Dam of the Sixties"

The advent of the modern(ist) short story in Canada can be ascribed to the 1920s, with Raymond Knister and Morley Callaghan being the central figures of this first phase, followed by Sinclair Ross and Ethel Wilson in the 1930s and '40s. With its focus on significant revelatory moments, its rejection of schematically structured plots, its economical and succinct narrative style, and its suggestive and allusive character, the modernist short story can be seen as the prototype of short fiction as described in Chapter 1 of this volume. Featuring but fragments of life, it nonetheless suggests the whole and derives its aesthetic effect from "that which is concealed" (Knister 1975: 392). Displaying both an imitation of American forms and traditions and an attempt to forge a distinct Canadian form, Knister's and Callaghan's endeavours must be evaluated against the backdrop of short fiction developments south of the border. Their importance for the Canadian short story will be elaborated on in Section 3.1. of this chapter.

With the beginnings of modernist tendencies in Canada, urban settings became more prominent. Thus, the metropolis forms the backdrop of most of Morley Callaghan's stories, many of which are set in his hometown Toronto, while in some New York or Montreal feature as the urban space against which the narratives unfold. Ethel Wilson, too, evocatively charted urban space in her short stories. In her rather untypical cityscapes, Wilson, in Nischik's words, "portrays Vancouver as a liminal space, a space of transition and even escape, but also as the awaited sanctuary from disappointing if not dangerous human relationships" (2017: 22). Another female author who, like Wilson, published her first story in the late 1930s and frequently employed urban settings (Toronto, Montreal) is Joyce Marshall.

The city, mostly Toronto, also plays a major role in Hugh Garner's stories. However, while Callaghan's, Wilson's and Marshall's city stories clearly reflect modernist sentiments, Garner's stories are defined by social realism; this as well as his explicit declaration that his major aim was to entertain (Nischik 2017: 24) has led to his being somewhat neglected by critics. Examples of his most successful stories are "The Yellow Sweater", "The Legs of the Lame", and "One-Two-Three Little Indians". The latter in particular has repeatedly been referred to as his best story. In this story

DOI: 10.4324/9781003142683-5

(published in *The Yellow Sweater*, 1952), Garner – like in so many of his works – depicts the plight of the underprivileged in a critical and genuinely moving manner. Through its Indigenous protagonist, Big Tom, who cannot save his sick baby from dying in his arms, this story also addresses issues of racism. Working in a trailer park that, among other "attractions", promises "INDIAN GUIDES" (51), Big Tom is reduced to the status of an exhibit. His act of pulling off the feather he has been wearing in order to come across as more "authentic", and throwing it in a ditch, has been interpreted as an "explicit refusal to conform to stereotypes imposed upon him by society" (Ferguson 2007: 134). However, from a 21st-century perspective, the depiction of Tom and his wife is also, to some extent, problematic as it contributes to the narrative of victimisation that has been stereotypically associated with Native Canada. A glimpse at more contemporary stories by Indigenous Canadian writers shows how the elegiac mode of Garner's story has made way for stories of empowerment that aim at processes of decolonisation. In particular, Thomas King has critically addressed and subverted the commodification of Indigenous culture and the marketing of clichés by the tourist industry in stories such as "One Good Story, That One", "Totem", "A Seat in the Garden" and "Tidings of Comfort and Joy" (see Chapter 8).

Another author – besides Garner – who employed a realist style is Frederick Philip Grove, who published his first story in 1926. In Grove's prairie stories, the setting is depicted as hostile, often rendering the characters devoid of agency and driven to fatalism. While these sentiments are still present in Sinclair Ross's stories of the 1930s, '40s, and '50s, Ross's fictional accounts of the Saskatchewan prairies during the time of the Depression are clearly indebted to modernist narrative parameters, as will be shown in Section 3.2.

The Canadian short story of the first decades of the 20th century is defined not only by forms of social realism and the advent of modernism but also already prefigures postmodernist tendencies. The key figure in this context is Sheila Watson. Even though her short fiction oeuvre is rather slim, her significance for the development of Canadian short fiction should not be underestimated. With a focus on Wilson, Marshall, and Watson, Section 3.3. will trace the specific impact these female authors had during these formative decades for the short story in Canada, followed by a delineation of the changes in Canada's cultural infrastructure which eventually led to the flourishing of the genre from the 1960s onwards.

3.1. The Emergence of the Modernist Canadian Short Story: Raymond Knister and Morley Callaghan

When, in 1928, Raymond Knister (1899–1932) brought out the first anthology of Canadian short fiction and, in his introduction, anticipated a thriving period for this genre in Canada, an actual market for short fiction did not yet exist in the country. There were but a handful of magazines that published short stories and "very little interest in story collections among publishers" (Thacker 2004: 186). The cultural climate of the first decades of the 20th century may also explain why Knister's promotional efforts and achievements on behalf of a modern Canadian canon in general and of the modern Canadian short story in particular only started to be recognised in the wake of the upsurge of Canadian literature in the 1960s and '70s. As an author of short fiction, Knister, like so many others, had to turn to American magazines for publication. In his conception of a poetics of short fiction, Knister tried to combine American and British modernist sentiments with Canadian subject matter. The latter was strongly defined by his experiences in rural Ontario, where he grew up on a farm. In fact, as Peter Stevens (xvii) notes in his introduction to the 1976 edition of selected work by Raymond Knister, his short stories were characterised by "local colour and surface minutiae".

Memorable examples of Knister's southwestern Ontario farm stories are, among many others, "Mist Green Oats" and "Peaches, Peaches". Apart from their focus on rural communities and the harsh realities of farm life, they feature another recurring element in Knister's oeuvre – namely, a sensitive adolescent protagonist. Thus, Len in "Mist Green Oats", who functions as a focaliser in this third-person narrative, experiences the never-ending chores that make up his life as entrapment and increasingly fantasises about a world beyond the narrow confines of the farm.

Whereas "Mist Green Oats" and "Peaches, Peaches" are illustrative examples of Knister's combination of local colour and the relatively plotless modernist story, "The Fate of Mrs. Lucier" is an example of Knister's more daring experimentation with modernist forms of writing. In an almost Joycean manner, oscillating between an impersonal objectified authorial voice and figural narration, the story charts the psychological crisis the elderly female protagonist, Mrs. Lucier, experiences on her journey back from a visit to her daughter's farm. Waiting for the connecting inter-urban car to the city at a small train station, she gradually works herself into a state of terror. While at first she imagines all sorts of possible accidents that may happen, the focus then shifts to the three men with whom she shares the waiting room. In her growing panic, she interprets each motion of the three as evidence of their evil intentions:

> The tall man lounged to a seat near the door. Why *must* he sit near the door? . . . Anyway, imagine three men travelling together! A long man and a short looked sinister enough, too chummy ("thick as thieves"). But when there were three, and they looked as travel-worn as these, tired and as familiar. . . . With an effort of the neck she stared all about. There was no place. In the ceiling was a trapdoor the colour of plaster. Could she be sure the shadow did not swerve? If it opened suddenly and a rope descended. All kinds of places for putting victims' bodies. The

stove yawned before her hot eyes! . . . They made a suspicious move. The wicket was closed, the door closed – Perhaps all

(183f)

Using free indirect discourse, elliptic sentences, and a strongly impressionistic semanticising of space, Knister manages to offer compelling glimpses into Mrs. Lucier's panic-stricken mind.

Another hallmark of Knister's narrative art, in addition to this new – modernist – interest in finding apt ways to depict processes of the psyche, is his extensive use of dialogue. This technique – amply used, for example, in "Horace the Haymow", among many others – is part of Knister's aspiration to create an objectivist tone, a stylistic device that is in some ways reminiscent of Hemingway. As Hill (2012: 63) puts it, "Knister's narrators are almost always reporters, not the interpreters, judges, and evaluators who often narrate more traditional realist fiction". Combining rural Canadian settings, elements of referential realism, and modernist aesthetics, Knister seems to anticipate characteristic developments in the Canadian short story, with Alice Munro's stories being among the most memorable examples of this still prevalent mode. Thus, what Knister said about Canadian short fiction in the 1920s still captures the genre's essence in the 21st century: "I think that while there must be experiment, the main line of tradition will be continued, and changes will be represented by a curve rather than a corner" (Knister 1923: n.p.).

In the "Introduction" to his 1928 anthology, Knister lamented the fact that talented writers were "obliged to adjust their contributions to foreign markets", while Canadian magazines "were encouraging, in the main, third-rate imitators of third-rate foreign models" (1976: 397). Having drowned in 1932, at the age of 33, Knister was denied the satisfaction of witnessing the coming real of his prophecy about the dawn of an era in which the Canadian short story would flourish. This era began in the 1950s and '60s, and the genre has been alive and kicking ever since. As a writer who was not only exceptionally well-read but also full of great artistic potential when he died so young, Knister has rather unsurprisingly been compared to John Keats, and indeed the English Romantic poet features in his novel *My Star Predominant* (1934) (Stevens 1976: xi).

To sum up, Knister deserves attention not only for his role as an important catalyst for the development of the Canadian short story but also because his critical and artistic approach points out the way in which the short story in Canada has evolved. Moreover, Knister's inclusive attitude towards the "Canadianness" of Canadian literature (Hill 2012: 58) must be seen as an important incentive for overcoming provincial and nationalistic sentiments. This attitude is also shared by Frederick Philip Grove, who remarks in a letter to Knister, "So long as the work turned out by any Canadian writer is worth its salt, it will be Canadian, no matter whether it deals with Canada or China" (Grove 1929). This debate gained new relevance with the emergence of authors that represent the multicultural world, which started to pick up momentum in the 1980s. Thus, from the point of view of the 21st century, we can now say, with David Staines (2014: 27), that "*here*, that famous designation we have been looking at, is now an indefinable area, encompassing Canada and the world, an area with no centre and therefore no periphery, with neither the possibility nor even the need of definition".

Even more than the undogmatic Canadianness of Knister's work, the stories of Morley Callaghan (1903–1990) challenge narrow concepts of national affiliation. Callaghan, who knew Ernest Hemingway, had met Francis Scott Fitzgerald and James Joyce in Paris and saw Sherwood Anderson as his "literary father" (Staines 2021: 61), "catered mainly to an American audience" (Goetsch 2007: 96) and saw himself as a North American or an internationalist rather than a Canadian. Callaghan's fiction appeared in the *New Yorker* and other American magazines, and several of his stories were included in Edna O'Brian and Martha Foley's annual edition of *The Best American Short Stories*. However, as Robert Thacker notes, Callaghan is "now little known outside of Canada. He was, after all, a Canadian – and in ways vexed and difficult to define, that meant he was a North American of another sort, one something like, yet different from, Americans from the United States" (2004: 184). At the same time, for the taste of Canadian audiences, his stories were not sufficiently Canadian. As Paul Goetsch (2007: 96) explains, "[a]lthough many of his stories are set in Canada . . . , Callaghan usually does not emphasize the Canadian setting. Nor does he regularly 'Canadianize' his works by addressing specifically Canadian issues in the manner of several of his contemporaries".

Like Knister, Callaghan combines techniques that "objectify and document while engaging the reader" (Nischik 2017: 20), a style which may have been influenced by these authors' occasional work as journalists, in addition to influences that came from modernist movements in the U.S. and Europe. The issue of writing and style, in fact, figures as a leitmotif in Callaghan's immigrant story "Last Spring They Came Over" (1927), which juxtaposes objective journalistic writing and imaginative writing (emblematised, here, as letter writing). Callaghan's sparse and laconic language has repeatedly been compared to that of Ernest Hemingway. However, as Goetsch (2007: 96), among others, has argued, "some critics have exaggerated Hemingway's importance for Callaghan's development". A major difference between these two authors is that between Hemingway's preference for the showing mode – or what has repeatedly been referred to as his "camera-eye technique", through which events are rendered more scenically – on the one hand, and Callaghan's less suggestive style in which the telling mode and subjective filtering still prevail on the other.

A hallmark of Callaghan's stories is the use of items as "objective correlatives", according to T.S. Eliot (1934: 145), the use of "a set of objects, a situation, a chain of events which shall be the formula of that particular emotion; such that when external facts, which must terminate in sensory experience, are given, the emotion is immediately evoked". Thus, in both "The Shining Red Apple" (1935) and "A Cap for Steve" (1952), the objects mentioned in the titles adopt a strong symbolic function with regard to the child characters in these stories. The shining red apple, temptingly displayed by the greengrocer, is an object of longing that evokes all the boy's neediness. At the same time, it is a correlative for "getting on in the world" (to use another of Callaghan's story titles) for the storekeeper himself, from whose perspective the story is told. In "A Cap for Steve", too, the cap functions as an objective correlative – in this case, for the shy boy Steve's longing to be acknowledged by his peers. In the course of the story, Steve manages miraculously to get hold of the outfielder Eddie Condon's cap, when the Phillies, a famous baseball team, come to town. A little later, when the cap is stolen and cannot be retrieved, a void opens up in the boy. However, it is eventually filled by something more precious: Steve's bonding with his estranged father. Like "The Shining Red Apple", this story, too, denies the reader an internal focus on the boy and is filtered instead by the perspective of his father, Dave.

While "A Cap for Steve" centres on a conflicted father-son relationship, "All the Years of Her Life" focuses on a son, Alfred Higgins, and his mother, this time rendering the point of view of the former. Alfred, who "had been getting into trouble wherever he worked" (10) since he left school, is caught shoplifting at the drugstore where he has been employed for the past six months. The owner, Sam Carr, summons Alfred's mother, who manages to impress him through her dignity, "her lack of terror and simplicity" (11); as a result, he just "bow[s] low to her in deep respect" (11) and lets Alfred go. Back home, Alfred is so imbued with a feeling of "admiration of [his mother's] strength and repose" (12) that he decides to go downstairs to the kitchen in order to tell her that "she sounded swell" (12). However, watching her through the open door, he sees how she shakes and trembles and seems to have aged. The story ends with an epiphanic moment when he suddenly sees, for the first time, what he has done to her and her life over the years:

> He watched his mother, and he never spoke, but at that moment his youth seemed to be over; he knew all the years of her life by the way her hand trembled as she raised the cup to her lips. It seemed to him that this was the first time he had ever looked upon his mother.
>
> (13)

Through his rejection of the plot-centred story, his "stripped-down language with the words as transparent as glass" (Staines 2021: 60), his charting of his characters' inner worlds, his foregrounding of the everyday, and his experimentation with epiphanic endings and objective correlatives,

Callaghan, like Knister, plays a central role for the further development of the distinct realist-modernist pattern of short fiction in Canada. As opposed to Knister, however, Callaghan is also noteworthy as "Canada's first internationalist" (Boire 1992: 208) and as one of the first significant urban writers in Canadian short fiction.

3.2. From Prairie Realism to Deep-Mapping the Prairies

In the 1920s, romantic images of the Canadian West, as shaped by writers such as Joseph Edmund Collins or Ralph Connor, began to make way for bleaker imaginaries of rural life in the prairies. These now concentrated on the experience of the agricultural frontier as characterised by dust storms, blizzards, and – in the 1930s – the Depression. It is this image of survival in a hostile environment which has dominated notions of the prairie as a "region of the mind" for decades. More than such writers of short fiction like Frederick Philip Grove or W.O. Mitchell, it was Sinclair Ross whose stories have shaped stereotypical notions of the Canadian prairies and have led critics like Alison Calder (1997: 51) to conclude, "Prairie writing is a cliché, gophers and grain elevators erect themselves against an oppressive sky. Dwarfed by natural forces, a man battles his way through a blizzard and someone lights a lamp at noon". In fact, Ross's "lamp at noon" denotes not only the dire scenario of the eponymous short story but seems to have become a symbol of the prairies as such, a region where things are threateningly at odds.

Apart from earlier exceptions like the stories of Henry Kreisel, it was only from the 1970s onwards that more multifaceted representations of the prairie regions emerged: Margaret Laurence's *A Bird in the House* (1970), Sandra Birdsell's *Agassiz Stories* (1987), Guy Vanderhaeghe's *Man Descending* (1982), and stories by Rudy Wiebe may serve as examples here. In particular, the androcentric tendency of conventional prairie writing, as identified by Cheryl Lousely (2001: 72), was increasingly challenged by authors who offered alternatives to the stereotypical images of the prairie as a hostile wilderness to be conquered, broken, and cultivated, or serving as a setting for male adventures. Two writers whose works are informed by such a new perception are Gloria Sawai (*A Song for Nettie Johnson*, 2001) and Sharon Butala (see, for example, *Fever*, 1990). While Sawai works with polyvocality and presents a multitude of different ethnic identities, Butala reinvents the prairies through her inclusion of intertextual and supernatural elements. In addition, she endows stories such as "The Prize" or "Gabriel" with a historical deep structure that goes beyond the region's here and now, reaching back not only to pre-European Indigenous culture but also to prehistoric times. Thus, both Sawai and Butala reinvent the prairies through "deep-mappings" (Maher 2001) that are characterised by multiple border-crossings:

between past and present, rural and urban spaces, nature and culture, and the natural and supernatural. Also, the stories are characterised by unusual narrative perspectives and the inclusion of previously neglected and marginalised aspects.

Sinclair Ross's (1908–1996) collection *The Lamp at Noon and Other Stories* (1968), as well as his novel *As For Me and My House* (1941), assumed an almost emblematic status with regard to literary depictions of the prairies in the first half of the 20th century. Ross, a banker by profession, grew up on prairie farms in northern Saskatchewan, which is the backdrop of the nine stories collected in *The Lamp at Noon*. In these stories, the land is featured as bleak and hostile and is strongly semanticised in order to mirror the – mostly afflicted – emotional states of his characters. The inner torment of the characters is always externalised through the caprices of the land and the weather and mirrored by blizzards ("The Painted Door"), dust storms ("The Lamp at Noon"), or thunderstorms ("A Field of Wheat").

The setting – Saskatchewan during the 1930s Depression – is a recurring element in the stories, defined by extremes of drought in the summer and ravaging blizzards in the winter, victimising families physically, mentally, and economically. Another recurring element is that of couples at odds – usually a hardworking but uneducated husband and a more cultured and sensitive wife. While one may agree with Aritha van Herk's (1997: 961) comment that Ross's stories are "a significant if overrated contribution" to prairie literature, the psychological impact of his depictions of fated relationships cannot be overrated. Thus, Ross presents us with male characters who are hopelessly caught up in stereotypical gender scripts that prevent them from showing tenderness, communicating their grief to their wives, or showing any "weakness" that may go against traditional notions of masculinity. In fact, the only companionship these men seem to have is with their horses, as is evident in "The Lamp at Noon", "Not by Rain Alone", and "A Field of Wheat". Thus, not only the women in these stories are terrifyingly lonely but also the men. After the disclosure of Ross's homosexuality in his friend Keath Fraser's memoirs (1997), speculations came up that this might explain the author's preoccupation with problematic marriages. Considering, however, how both male and female characters are depicted in the stories, allowing both to become focalisers at times and granting the reader access to their innermost feelings, it seems that it is rigid and constricting gender norms rather than the institution of marriage that are being criticised.

I shall now more closely describe typical thematic and structural elements of Ross's writing with a focus on "The Lamp at Noon", followed by a comparative look at Sharon Butala's contemporary "rewriting" of this story, where the clichés of prairie realism are revised, and new angles of perception materialise.

Case Study: Prairie Realism and Deep-Mapping the Prairies

"The Lamp at Noon" (1938) is a tightly knit short story which, like most of Ross's, is informed by the tradition of prairie realism while at the same time reflecting the aesthetic mode of modernism. The story's time covers but a few hours, and its focus is not on external action but on the characters' mental and emotional crises. In the centre is a young couple, Paul and Ellen, who struggle to make a living on a prairie farm. It is the third day of a dust storm that has again destroyed their wheat and the third day of quarrelling about their future – with Paul stubbornly holding on to the farm and the desperate vision that in the following year everything will be better, and Ellen begging for alternatives, for a way out of the trap of debt and poverty.

The beginning of the story features Ellen around noon, waiting for her husband while trying to soothe her baby boy and protect him from the omnipresent dust. Her precarious state is indicated by references to her "fixed and wide" eyes (13), her "wide immobile stare" (14) and the wind that is described as "demented" (13) and which Ellen perceives as two winds – one in flight and one in pursuit (14). The one that "sought refuge in the eaves, whimpering, in fear" (14) may stand for Ellen, while the other, which "assailed it there, and shook the eaves apart to make it flee again" (14) may stand for her husband, whose obstinacy in the end drives her out into the storm and finally into madness. In addition, the story

> synchronizes the couple's quarrel with the dust storm that supplies the text's temporal structure. Storm and quarrel reach their climax and subside on the third day between the lighting of the lamp at noon and its extinction towards the evening, that is, the time span that contains the story's action. (Meindl 2007: 107)

The most prominent image, however, is the lamp at noon, which Ellen lights at the beginning and which is repeatedly referred to throughout the story. While a lamp is usually associated with the hearth and home, the fact that it is lit at noon gives it a sinister quality, making it a symbol of things being at odds. The lamp also directly stands for Ellen, "the soft, diffusing light, dim and yellow" (13), indicating her last but futile flames of hope that she might change Paul's mind. When Paul comes back to the house to look for her, he notices that the lamp was blown out (22) – the extinct light, thus foreshadowing Ellen's insanity and the baby's death.

"Ross never takes sides", as Margaret Laurence (1968: 11) claims, "men and women suffer equally. The tragedy is not that they suffer, but that they suffer alone". While agreeing in general with Laurence, one still wants to add that in "The Lamp at Noon", it is Ellen who eventually breaks, whereas Paul, with his strength and grimness (15) and his "harsh and clenched virility" (15), may even recover from the blow of his infant boy's death and his wife's mental breakdown. However, the reader is clearly led to feel for both, which is due to the narrative structure of the text. In the first part of the story, where Ellen functions as a focaliser, her mental crisis is foregrounded. The dilemma of their relationship becomes evident when Paul enters the scene. In his presence, Ellen's imminent fears subside, and the longing for his "arms supporting her" (15), which dominated while she had been anxiously waiting for him, is again eclipsed by the antagonism that has been haunting them for some time. Thus, against her previous intentions, she resumes the quarrel they had the day before. In the midst of their altercation, "with the lamp between them" (15), the point of view switches to Paul, and we follow him on his way to the stables, where he seeks comfort from the horses. Comparing their conflicted dialogue with the thoughts Ellen and Paul have once they are on their own, it becomes clear that they are unable to share what they really feel. This is true especially for Paul, who fiercely fights his urge to check on his wife even though her "eyes frightened him" (18) when he left her after lunch because he is afraid it would be registered as a weakness. His stubborn clinging to twisted notions of masculinity and strength turns out to be his fatal weakness: when he finally *does* come back to the house, Ellen is already out in the storm in a state of madness, trying to shield her baby and possibly smothering him in the act. Luce Irigaray's reconception of hysteria as "the unheard voice of the woman who can only speak through somatic functions" (1991: 26) may apply here. When Ellen comprehends that she cannot escape her unbearable isolation, entrapment, and despair through protest and arguments, she protests with her body (Meindl 2007: 114). Only in her mentally damaged state, it seems, can she respond to her husband in a way he expected her to: "'You were right, Paul. . . . You said tonight we'd see the storm go down. So still now, and a red sky – it means tomorrow will be fine'" (23). The story ends on an almost unbearably bleak irony suggesting that only by becoming "mad" is it possible to see anything positive in their situation and to establish this uncannily false harmony. While in "The Lamp at Noon", madness is but a deceptive form of female empowerment, it adopts a much more life-affirming dimension in Alice Munro's epistolary pioneer story "A Wilderness Station" (1992) or Margaret Atwood's historical novel *Alias Grace*.

"The Lamp at Noon" also subtly destabilises conventional associations of the male with the reasonable and rational on the one hand and the female with the irrational and emotional on the other. While Paul, through his exhibiting of "masculine" strength and his conviction "that it was his self-respect and manhood against the fretful weakness of a woman" (18), seems to be the rational one, the story also indicates that his way of farming and his misjudgement of his wife's state are anything but sensible. It is, in fact, Ellen who knows about farming and has repeatedly advised her husband to quit monoculture. Also, her covering her baby's crib to fend off the dust is more life-affirming than most of Paul's actions seem to be.

Through the farmer couples that feature in his stories, and most notably through Ellen and Paul in "The Lamp at Noon", Ross "sketches a gendered microcosm of tragic humankind" (Meindl 2007: 107). A major factor in most of Ross's stories, however, is the land itself, crushingly hostile, that Margaret Laurence (1968: 7f) has described so aptly:

> In spite of its deceptive moments of calm promise, it is an essentially violent and unpredictable land, quixotic, seeming to bestow grace and favour, then suddenly attacking with arrows of snow, shrieking armies of wind, bludgeons of hail, or the quiet lethal assault of the sun. (Laurence 1968: 7f)

These two aspects in particular – the toxic effect of gender scripts on relationships and the notion of the land as hostile – are taken up and revised in Sharon Butala's "Gabriel", a story that may serve as an example of more holistic, contemporary approaches to the Canadian prairies.

Sharon Butala (1940–) is a prolific Saskatchewan author, having published 20 books of fiction and non-fiction, in addition to a number of plays. As Geoff Hancock (1997: 160) notes, "her best work is found in her short stories", collected in *Queen of the Headaches* (1985), *Fever* (1990), *Real Life* (2002), and *Season of Fury and Wonder* (2019). Butala's interest in the geological, historical, and Aboriginal past of the prairies and her commitment to the importance of biodiversity and ecological aspects of agriculture in general are most memorably evident in her non-fiction works *The Perfection of the Morning* (1994) and *Coyote's Morning Cry* (1995). However, they have also informed a number of her short stories. Examples are the two metafictional stories "Saskatchewan" (in *Real Life*) and "The Prize" (in *Fever*), which both feature writer-protagonists struggling with an adequate depiction of the prairies. In "Gabriel", in turn, Butala refers to and plays with existing prairie myths and traditions. Implicitly but nonetheless recognisably referring to Sinclair Ross's "The Lamp at Noon", Butala's story is an intertextual response to the cliché of prairie realism or even a parody of the familiar Depression-story pattern.

Thus, we find in "Gabriel" the ruined crops, the extremes of weather and problems of communication between husband and wife, the latter — just like Ellen in "The Lamp at Noon" — representing the educated but timid wife from the city, while Gabriel is again a farmer who "had no education" and "couldn't imagine life without the farm" (133). The description of Frannie, who has not been well since she had a miscarriage, echoes that of Ellen in Ross's story: "She stared at him, her eyes big and dark" (127) or "she called, a note of panic in her voice, 'Don't stay out after dark!'" (128). Also, the looming threat of having to give up the farm due to debts haunts both Ross's Paul and Butala's Gabriel, the latter dreading the day "when the final foreclosure notice came" (138).

However, while the basic situation in the two stories seems to be very similar, Butala's story ends on a much more optimistic note. Her revision of the Depression-story pattern is closely linked to the inner development of Gabriel, who functions as the sole focaliser in this story. Gabriel's transformation, in turn, is triggered by supernatural elements. The prairie is haunted by strange lights and mysterious sounds and incidents, culminating in a tremendous boom that tears up the sidewalk on which Gabriel and Frannie were standing a few moments earlier (138). These supernatural elements reflect the couple's precarious psychological state but also create an eerie and threatening atmosphere. Increasingly, a causal connection between the apocalyptic prairie scenario and the extinction of Native culture and pre-European wilderness emerges so that towards the end of the story, Gabriel seems to be able to see these strange apparitions as messages from the prairies' spiritual past, revealed to him in order to make him give up, to make him stop trying to conquer and cultivate this land. Already earlier in the story, Gabriel seemed to be susceptible to the regenerating power of the uncultivated prairie:

> It was a relief finally to be walking in the prairie grass in the steep, rocky hills, too rocky, too steep to cultivate, and he was secretly glad, though he'd never say so out loud, that he had an excuse to leave this last little bit of real prairie. (129)

That "Gabriel" can be read as an eco-story (see also Chapter 10) is evident from numerous references to detrimental anthropogenic impacts on the environment. Thus, Gabriel notices, among others, "that there were hardly any insects left" (129), that "as the grass died, the hills had begun to erode", and that the trees "were dead and dying" (130), apart from references to "a regular epidemic of miscarriages that people were blaming on the grasshopper spray" (133). In a moment of epiphany, Gabriel suddenly sees that the strange occurrences for which he secretly blamed Frannie were actually "ghosts" that had been trying to alert him to the history of the land, to the time when it was inhabited by buffalos and Indigenous peoples, and to the beauty of the wilderness. In the vision that closes the story, Gabriel sees himself and Frannie starting a new life in the city, with Frannie recovering and finding a job, having children and himself working as a maintenance man – they would be content while "his dreams would be of the farm" (142). Giving up the trope of "man fighting against a hostile land", Gabriel also gives up the destructive concepts of masculinity that haunt Ross's stories.

What makes "Gabriel" such an interesting story is not least the fact that it draws on a great number of literary traditions: the Depression story à la Sinclair Ross, Jack Hodgins's magical realism, the ghost story in the manner of Henry James's "The Turn of the Screw", dystopian literature, and the parable. Most of all, however, it deep-maps the prairie through imagining its unconquered, unbroken, and unsubdued past, a past in which people endeavoured to live in harmony with its shifts and rhythms, a past before the agricultural practices of the Europeans came to threaten its ecological balance.

> **Parallels between "The Lamp at Noon" and "Gabriel"**
>
> - Ruined crops and extremes of weather
> - Character constellation of an educated, timid wife and an uneducated farmer husband
> - Lack of communication between husband and wife
> - Similarities in the description of the terrified wife
> - Looming threat of having to give up the farm
>
> **Revisionist Aspects**
>
> | *"The Lamp at Noon"* | *"Gabriel"* |
> | --- | --- |
> | • Realist depiction of the prairies | • Use of supernatural elements/magical realism |
> | • Land seen as hostile and in need of being conquered/cultivated | • Increasing recognition of the land's intrinsic beauty and value |
> | • Focus on the agricultural value of the land | • Appreciation of the ecological value of wilderness |
> | • One-dimensional temporal structure | • Envisioning the prairie before European – or even human – settlement |
> | • Exclusive focus on settler perspective | • Inclusion of Indigenous sentiments |
> | • Ironic epiphany (Paul) – eclipsed by the tragic ending: his wife's insanity and the baby's death | • Epiphanic ending suggests Gabriel's adaptability and hope for the couple's future |

3.3. Innovation and the Female Voice

Focusing on Ethel Wilson, Joyce Marshall, and Sheila Watson, this section aims to acknowledge the importance of female writers for the consolidation of short fiction in Canada, a form which should become even more significant from the 1960s onwards, and to show on the example of their work how diversely these authors play with realist, modernist, and postmodernist modes of writing.

Vancouver-based Ethel Wilson (1988–1980) published her first story, "I Just Love Dogs", in 1937 in *The New Statesman*. Most of her stories appeared in magazines in the 1940s and '50s and came out in a collected edition titled *Mrs. Golightly and Other Stories* in 1961. This volume, as David Stouck (1990: 210) notes in his introduction, "holds a special place in the Wilson canon because here is the author in the abbreviated forms that she believed suited her best". Characterised by elusiveness and fragmentation and by impressionistic depictions of – especially natural – settings, Wilson's stories are clearly modernist. In the true modernist manner, their focus is on psychological insight rather than outward action, yet these closely knit stories are nonetheless full of suspense. Another hallmark of Wilson's stories is unconventional punctuation (or the lack thereof), through which she compellingly simulates the rhythm of natural speech and the fragmentation of thought. Regarding settings, many of her stories are located in and around Vancouver, such as "The Window", or in the rural interior of British Columbia, such as "On Nimpish Lake". However, a number of stories also feature settings outside of Canada, such as California in "Mrs Golightly", Austria and Germany in "We Have to Sit Opposite", and Egypt in "Haply the Soul of My Grandmother".

In many of her stories, the atmosphere of the ordinary established at the beginning proves to be deceptive, anticipating the narrative technique of Alice Munro's murder mysteries. An example is "Hurry, Hurry", which starts with a pleasant hike and ends with a female corpse beside a "salt water ditch" (115). Typical of Wilson's marked symbolism, the wounded hawk upon which the hiker Miriam came earlier on prefigures the murdered woman. When Miriam encounters the murderer, however, she is ignorant of the corpse in the ditch and of the danger she is in herself. Similarly, an alcoholic mother's abuse of her daughter looms under the quiet surface of a wool shop in "Till Death Us Do Part", a story that mostly employs the form of a journal and also includes meta-narrative elements.

While in "Till Death Us Do Part" and "Hurry, Hurry", the lurking violence is eventually made explicit, "Haply the Soul of My Grandmother" remains allusive to the very end, thus making the events even more uncanny. The story features a Canadian couple, the Forresters, who are on a guided tour to an ancient tomb in Egypt. In the beginning, Mrs. Forrester, from whose perspective the story is mostly presented, seems to be the main character as we witness her growing panic and difficulty breathing in one of the tombs they visit. However, as the narrative progresses, it more and more surfaces that it may really be her husband Marcus's past that is the focus of interest. After all, the little hand "wrapped in grave-clothes" (31), which an old man tries to sell to them as a souvenir ("Nice hand. Buy a little hand, lady. Very good very old very cheap. Nice mummy hand", 31), causes a very strong emotional reaction in Marcus, followed by a fever, thus making the reader wonder about possible connections; suspicion is further aroused by the words he utters in his delirious sleep: "A LITTLE HAND" (35). During the visit to the tomb already, his wife noticed that her husband seemed to be looking for something, followed by a reference that he "had been in Egypt in the last war" (32). With the story oscillating between the point of view of a covert narrator and that of Mrs Forrester, it remains open as to what extent his wife suspects a connection between the small hand and her husband's doings during the war and whether the reference to the hand as a "little raped hand" (32) is already a sign of her suspicions. However, the ending of the story clearly renders Mrs Forrester's thoughts: "Marcus, whose was that little hand, she thought and would think . . . whose was it? . . .

Did it ever know you . . . did you ever know that hand? . . . Whose hand was it, Marcus? . . . Oh let us get away from here!" (35) Like Mrs Forrester, the reader is not granted knowledge about what Marcus did or did not do during his service in Egypt, a gap that is agonisingly unsettling, with the potential to make the reader think of unimaginable atrocities. And the war *does* have a presence in Wilson's oeuvre: the last two sentences of "We Have to Sit Opposite", published in 1945, for example, evoke Hitler's unimpeded rise to power: "Many people slept until they reached Munich. Then they all began to wake up" (66). Literally, these concluding lines refer to the passengers on a train from Salzburg to Munich. However, the sudden switch from the main characters, two Canadian women and a German family sharing a train carriage, is an oddity that can hardly be dismissed. "Bearing in mind that Munich was the capital of the Nazi movement and a symbol of the failure of British appeasement policy" (Kück 2007: 124), this laconic ending may not only metaphorically be related to the rise of the Nazis but also sheds a different light on the patriarchal German father on the train, who now comes to stand emblematically for those receptive to the Nazi ideology.

Wilson proves to be most convincing when she combines the motifs of fear and violence with the psychological dimension of her characters. This is the case, for example, in "Mr. Sleepwalker", where a young woman is stalked by a man with a frightening animal smell. The fact, however, that nobody else notices the smell and that, in the end, it turns out that the man only followed her because he was drawn to her own "delicious smell" (150) allows for reading the story as a psychological study of the young woman, from whose unreliable perspective the story is told in the first place.

The most convincing story, in this respect, is "The Window". The main character, Mr. Willy, has withdrawn from society and built a large window in his Vancouver house from which he can overlook the sea between "Spanish Banks and English Bay" (196). The window, a barrier between himself and society, allows him to enjoy the world without having to meet people, while at night it transforms into a mirror that reflects Mr. Willy in his own room "like a stranger" (203). Much like Mr. Duffy in James Joyce's "A Painful Case", Mr. Willy, too, experiences a "strong shock of recognition" (204), an epiphanic realisation of his life as sterile and meaningless. However, while "A Painful Case" *ends* with Mr. Duffy's insight into his own isolation and loneliness, Mr. Willy's epiphany occurs in mid-story. In other words, he is allowed to develop. When in the final climax of the story, he barely manages to escape with his life from the attack of a robber, the near-death experience of a man who has already been dying emotionally leads him to realise "that a crack had been coming in the great wall that shut him off from the light" (49). Thus, the ending, though highly mysterious, does render the note of hope that is denied Joyce's Mr. Duffy.

Although Joyce Marshall (1913–2005) published her first story in 1936, it was only in 1975 that *A Private Place*, the first of her three collected volumes, appeared (the other two being *Any Time at All*, 1993, and *Blood and*

Bone, 1995). Considering the psychological depth of Marshall's well-crafted stories, it is surprising that her work has received comparatively little critical attention. Through their focus on psychological portraits of the mostly female protagonists, their beginnings *in medias res*, and their frequent use of free indirect discourse, Marshall's stories are quintessentially modernist in style. In fact, of the seven stories assembled in *A Private Place*, only "The Little White Girl" features a first-person narrator, while in the others, figural narration prevails, allowing the author to explore her female focalisers' consciousness.

In "The Enemy" and "Salvage", storytelling itself acquires a therapeutic function. The enemy in the eponymous story turns out to be a vandal who keeps wrecking the apartment of Miranda, who – as the name suggests – has until then been miraculously lucky and lived a happy, though somewhat superficial, life. These attacks of vandalism shatter her confidence in the way she has led her life and make her want to see the culprit when he has been caught. That Miranda craves to see "the face of what is the real enemy, whether within or without" (34) indicates that the vandal may also embody a part of her own personality that has turned against her. It is only by telling the story over and over again (and not necessarily as it happened) (23) that she is able to live to the next day – as if talking about it could fend off other threats (34). In "Salvage", too, storytelling becomes a tool for survival. Rhoda, a middle-aged woman, saves the life of a young homeless girl who tries to kill herself with a mixture of drugs. Even though Sylvie verbally abuses Rhoda once she is able to speak, she knocks on Rhoda's door two days later, having run away from the hospital. Feeling somehow responsible, Rhoda ends up taking her in. As it turns out, the confrontation with this human wreck gradually unravels Rhoda's own crisis. Since Sylvie would not speak about her shattered life, Rhoda finds herself telling her own story – above all, her inability to come to terms with her divorce from Rex. Even though the girl hardly responds and Rhoda keeps asking herself why she even tells this stranger the story of her broken life, she begins to feel that "she'd begun to live in this girl's eyes" (55). In fact, as she tells the girl, "[w]ith you as my private largely silent shrink, I seem to have straightened a few things in my own head" (57). Even though the relationship between Sylvie and Rhoda is at no point featured as an easy one, it seems the two very different women have engaged in a symbiosis that enables them both to live.

While "Salvage" ends with a note of hope, Marshall's most frequently anthologised story, "The Old Woman" (1952), draws a radically bleak portrait of human isolation. Joining her husband in a secluded location in Northern Quebec after three years of separation, Molly has to accept that Toddy has become "bushed" and is now incapable of engaging in human interaction. Toddy's increasing madness is rendered concrete in "the old woman", the electrical power station he is not only in charge of but literally in love with. Moreover, Molly, "her mind bruised with horror and fear" (83), is forced to realise that her husband watches her as if she were a machine: "Perhaps that's what he wants me to be – a generator, quiet and docile, waiting for him here, moving only when he tells me to move" (83). In the end, the now entirely insane Toddy cannot be reached anymore – neither by his wife nor by his coworker, who explains to Molly at the end of the story: "For years I watch him fall in love with her [the machine]. Now she has him for herself" (91).

The stories mentioned so far all appeared in Marshall's first collection, *A Private Place*, and are all defined by narrative devices typical of modernism. In her later work, however, in particular some stories from *Blood and Bone*, Marshall also started to experiment with postmodernist techniques. However, before the 1960s, it was only Sheila Watson who really moved beyond the boundaries of modernist writing.

With only six stories, Sheila Watson's (1909–1998) short fiction oeuvre is relatively small. And yet, due to her interest in the aesthetics of narratives and her endeavour to move away from the prevalent realist and modernist paradigms, she does provide an important incentive for the development of short fiction forms in Canada during this period. Watson's technically challenging stories display a high degree of meta-referentiality and abound with intertextual allusions, thus clearly following postmodernist trends. In this respect, mainly those stories are of interest which the author herself referred to as her "mythic cycle" (Irvine 1999: 115). These are "Brother Oedipus", "The Black Farm" (1956), "Antigone", and "The Rumble Seat", in which Watson transposes the characters of Sophocles's Theban plays (Oedipus and his descendants) into a modern Canadian setting. That the "kingdom" in Watson's stories is a mental hospital has an autobiographical background, as Kuester (2007: 164) notes: Watsons's father was the superintendent of a British Columbia Mental Hospital. More importantly, however, the psychiatric setting is highly functional within the stories: through the figure of Oedipus, "the keystone of Freudian psychoanalysis, Watson re-enters the psychiatric institution . . . and deconstructs its structures from the inside" (Irvine 1999: 115). In other words, Watson exploits this setting for her playful rewriting of classical myths and for tracing the thin – or even blurring – line between sanity and madness.

The frequently anthologised "Antigone" (1959) is probably her best-known story. In the original myth, as rendered by Sophocles, Antigone is the daughter of Oedipus and his wife (and mother), Jocasta. She is buried alive by the Theban king Creon, her mother's brother, for having herself buried her rebel brother Polynices against the king's commands. Haemon, the son of Creon, who is engaged to Antigone, then kills himself. In Watson's version, it is the son of the doctor-king reigning over the asylum who tells the story and who prefers Antigone to her more compliant sister Ismene. Father and son remain unnamed but will be identified as Creon and Haemon by those familiar with Sophocles's plot. Like Antigone, the narrator resents the heartlessly pragmatic rule of his father's "kingdom" and, with her, crosses the river that separates the orderly and controlled realm of Creon from the wilderness on the other side. It is, in fact, from their position on the bridge that Haemon tells his/their story in the mode of simultaneous first-person narration interspersed with memories and general reflections on his father's tyranny:

> I turn away from her and flatten my elbows on the high wall of the bridge. I look back at my father's kingdom. I see the terraces rolling down from the red-brick buildings with their barred windows. . . .
>
> The inmates are beginning to come out on the screened verandas. They pace up and down in straight lines or stand silent like figures which appear at the same time each day from some depth inside a clock.
> (245)

The meticulous organisation of the mental institution, a cypher for restriction and confinement, is juxtaposed with Antigone's defiant nature. This nature is expressed, in the 20th-century version, just like the original myth, by her conducting a forbidden burial. While in Sophocles's *Antigone*, however, the burial is that of Polynices, it is but a dead sparrow that is interred in Watson's version. Watson thus revives and, at the same time, deflates the old myth. Her ludic rearrangement of mythemes also modifies the ending: even though "Creon", on whose thigh is written "King of Kings" (248), does confront Antigone with her "crime", he not only fails to make any impression on her but is outwitted by her reply:

> This ground is public property, he says. No single person has any right to an inch of it.
>
> I've taken six inches, Antigone says. Will you dig the bird up again?
> (148)

In contrast to the gruesome fates of the ancient lovers, Watson's "Haemon" lives to tell the tale of Antigone, and the last sentence ("From Antigone he simply turned away", 249) denotes the king's defeat – at least regarding the disciplining of the unruly girl.

Sheila Watson's stories clearly deviate from the majority of Canadian short fiction in the 1940s and '50s. Nonetheless, and even though postmodernist narrative forms have never been prominent in Canadian short fiction, the experimental dimension which they represent must not be dismissed from a critical appreciation of the genre in Canada. Thus, two other early representatives of Canadian postmodernism are Ray Smith and Raymond Fraser, who were both affiliated with the Montreal Story Tellers (see Chapter 4). In the 1970s and '80s, two of the most interesting postmodernist short story writers were George Bowering and David Arnason, whereas in the contemporary context, the most striking narrative experiments have come from Diane Schoemperlen and Margaret Atwood, as will be shown in Chapter 5.

66   *The Genre of the Short Story and Its Emergence and Development*

Through her parodic engagement with mythological pretexts in several of her works (including short fiction), Atwood in particular reaches back to Sheila Watson's intertextual experiments.

3.4. Towards the "Bursting Dam of the Sixties": Infrastructures and Mentors

From the 1940s until the 1960s, the output of Canadian short stories became more and more promising. Thus, the 1940s saw the emergence of two magazines, *Preview* and *First Statesman* (both based in Montreal), which fused to form the *Northern Review* in 1945 (Weaver 1997: 1059) and were committed to contemporary literature. One of the most important Canadian short story writers, Mavis Gallant, published her first stories in *Preview* before her works appeared in the *New Yorker*. The disappearance of the *Northern Review* in the mid-'50s was compensated by the emergence of *The Tamarack Review*, which became an influential medium for the publication of short fiction between 1956 and 1982 and brought out stories by writers such as Alice Munro, Hugh Hood, and Mordecai Richler. Other outlets for short fiction in the 1940s and '50s were the *Queen's Quarterly*, *The Canadian Forum*, and *The Fiddlehead*, to which *The Malahat Review*, *Exile*, *Descant*, and the *Canadian Fiction Magazine* can be added in the 1960s.

A key publication of the post-war period is Desmond Pacey's anthology *A Book of Canadian Stories* (1947), which appeared in a revised edition in 1950 and then again in 1962. Despite the steady upsurge of short fiction in the 1940s and '50s, it was still difficult for authors to publish their collected works in volume form. Among the handful of collections that still appeared are the debut volumes of Hugh Garner (*The Yellow Sweater and Other Stories*, 1952) and Mavis Gallant (*The Other Paris*, 1956). The course of the short story in Canada changed radically in the 1960s. Three factors in particular led to what Michelle Gadpaille (1988: 99) has pointedly referred to as "the bursting dam of the sixties". One was the launch of several programmes by the Canadian Broadcasting Corporation (C.B.C.) dedicated to the arts and literature; the other was an expansion of opportunities for publication. This was due to, first, a new interest in short fiction on the part of major commercial publishing houses like McClelland & Stewart and Macmillan of Canada and, second (and possibly even more significantly), the emergence of small presses that dedicated much of their efforts to short fiction, as will be discussed in Chapter 4. The third factor is related to the Massey Commission (the Royal Commission on National Development in the Arts, Letters, and Sciences), which was appointed in 1949, with the aim of investigating the situation of the arts and culture in Canada, and culminated in the so-called Massey Report of 1951.

The role of the C.B.C. in the development of the Canadian short story cannot be overestimated and is closely linked to Robert Weaver, who was hired in 1948 as a programme organiser in the Talks and Public Affairs Department (Woodcock 1997: 1172). As such, he was responsible for a number of cultural programmes on Canadian radio. Through his function as a radio producer, Weaver literally made the Canadian short story audible and, in the process, discovered authors like Alice Munro, Mordecai Richler, and others. It is thus no exaggeration when W.H. New claims that Weaver "rapidly became identified with the Canadian short story" (1989: 181). It is a striking coincidence that the first story Weaver bought from the then 19-year-old Alice Laidlaw (later Munro), "The Strangers", was meant to be broadcast on the 1st of June, 1951, the day on which the Massey Report was published. Due to the C.B.C.'s obligations to broadcast the details of the Report, "The Strangers" had to be postponed to a later date. However, the fact that the Massey Report, which led to the funding of the National Library of Canada (now Library and Archives Canada), the creation of the Canada Council for the Arts, and several other initiatives that fostered the development of Canadian literature, should in this way be connected to Alice Munro is fitting. After all, Munro really came to embody the Canadian short story in the following decades (Thacker 2004: 178) and, since her 2013 Nobel Prize, maybe even the status and quality of Canadian literature as such.

Robert Weaver was influential in the development of the short story not only through his activities at the C.B.C. Together with William Toye and others, he also produced the aforementioned *Tamarack Review* and further boosted the short story through a number of anthologies, among them five series of *Canadian Short Stories* (between 1960 and 1991, Oxford University Press) and the *Oxford Book of Canadian Short Stories* (1986; 2nd ed. 1995), coedited with Margaret Atwood. Largely ignoring the earlier output of short fiction in Canada, Weaver's *Canadian Short Stories: First Series* (1960) lays its focus on post–Second World War stories. Among the youngest writers included in this volume are Mavis Gallant with "The Legacy" (later included in *The Other Paris*) and Alice Munro with "The Time of Death" (later included in her debut collection *Dance of the Happy Shades*, 1968).

Through the significantly improved conditions of the 1950s and '60s, the way was paved for a more prominent status and an enhanced presence of the short story in Canada. In fact, the favourable climate encouraged authors to engage with the genre as a major form of literary expression, as was the case with Mavis Gallant, Norman Levine, William D. Valgardson, and above all, Alice Munro. As Thacker aptly notes, "as the 1960s closed, the audience for the short story . . . was being born" (2004: 188), a shift that also affected the publishing industry and made them look more favourably on this narrative "stepchild". Also, the stronger readiness of publishing houses to bring out short story books may have fostered the considerable emergence of linked story collections from the 1970s onwards, with Margaret Laurence's *A Bird in the House* (1970) and Alice Munro's *Lives of Girls and Women* (1971) having become classics of Canadian literature.

Works Cited

Primary Works

Butala, Sharon (1990 [1980]). *Fever: Stories*. Toronto: HarperCollins.
Callaghan, Morley (1997 [1936]). "All the Years of Her Life". In: Margaret Atwood and Robert Weaver, eds. *The New Oxford Book of Canadian Short Stories in English*. Toronto, Oxford and New York: Oxford University Press. 9–13.
Knister, Raymond (1976 [1925]). "The Fate of Mrs. Lucier". In: Peter Steven, ed. *Raymond Knister. The First Day of Spring: Stories and Prose*. Toronto and Buffalo: University of Toronto Press.
Marshall, Joyce (1975). *A Private Place*. Ottawa: Oberon Press.
Ross, Sinclair (1968). *The Lamp at Noon and Other Stories*. Toronto: McClelland & Stewart.
Watson, Sheila (1990 [1959]). "Antigone". In: Michael Ondaatje, ed. *The Faber Book of Contemporary Canadian Short Stories*. London and Boston: Faber and Faber. 241–249.
Wilson, Ethel (1990 [1961]). *Mrs. Golightly and Other Stories*. Toronto: McClelland & Stewart.

Secondary Works

Benson, Eugene and William Toye, eds. (1997). *The Oxford Companion to Canadian Literature*, 2nd ed. Oxford: Oxford University Press.
Boire, Gary (1992). "Morley Callaghan 1903–1990". *Canadian Literature* 133: 208–209.
Calder, Alison (1997). "Reassessing Prairie Realism". In: Christian Riegel and Herb Wyile, eds. *A Sense of Place: Re-Evaluating Regionalism in Canadian and American Writing*. Edmonton: The University of Alberta Press. 51–60.
Eliot, T.S. (1934). "Hamlet". In: T.S. Eliot, ed. *Selected Essays*, 2nd ed. London: Faber and Faber. 141–146.
Ferguson, Stefan (2007). "Social Realism and Compassion for the Underdog: Hugh Garner, 'One-Two-Three Little Indians' (1950)". In: Nischik. 129–139.
Fraser, Keath (1997). *As for Me and My Body*. Toronto: ECW Press.
Gadpaille, Michelle (1988). *The Canadian Short Story*. Oxford: Oxford University Press.
Goetsch, Paul (2007). "Psychological Realism, Immigration, and City Fiction: Morley Callaghan, 'Last Spring They Came Over' (1927)". In: Nischik. 95–103.
Grove, Frederick Philip (1976 [1929]). "Frederick Philip Grove to Raymond Knister, 15 November 1929". In: Desmond Pacey, ed. *The Letters of Frederick Philip Grove*. Toronto: University of Toronto Press.
Hancock, Geoff (1997). "Butala, Sharon". In: Benson and Toye. 160–161.
Hill, Colin (2012). *Modern Realism in English-Canadian Fiction*. Toronto, Buffalo and London: University of Toronto Press.
Irigaray, Luce (1991). *The Irigaray Reader*, ed. Margaret Whitford. Oxford: Basil Blackwell.
Irvine, Dean (1999). "Oedipus and Anti-Oedipus, Myth and Counter-Myth: Sheila Watson's Short Fiction". In: Gerald Lynch and Angela Arnold Robbeson, eds. *Dominant Impressions: Essays on the Canadian Short Story*. Ottawa: University of Ottawa Press. 115–125.
Knister, Raymond (1975). *Raymond Knister: Poems, Stories and Essays*, ed. David Arnason. Montreal: Bellrock.
Knister, Raymond (1976). "Introduction to Canadian Short Stories". In: Peter Stevens, ed. *Raymond Knister. The First Day of Spring: Stories and Prose*. Toronto and Buffalo: University of Toronto Press. 392–398.
Knister, Raymond to Merrill Denison, 3 May 1923, box 1, The Raymond Knister Collection, McMaster University.

Kück, Nina (2007). "'An Artful Artlessness': Ethel Wilson, 'We Have to Sit Opposite'". In: Nischik. 117–127.
Kuester, Martin (2007). "Myth and the Postmodernist Turn in Canadian Short Fiction: Sheila Watson's 'Antigone'". In: Nischik. 163–173.
Laurence, Margaret (1968). "Introduction". In: Sinclair Ross, ed. *The Lamp at Noon and Other Stories*. Toronto: McClelland and Stewart. 7–12.
Lousley, Cheryl (2001). "Home on the Prairie? A Feminist and Postcolonial Reading of Sharon Butala, Di Brandt and Joy Kogawa". *ISLE: Interdisciplinary Studies in Literature and Environment* 8.2: 71–95.
Maher, Susan (2001). "Deep-Mapping the Great Plains: Surveying Literary Cartography of Place". *Western American Literature* 36.1: 5–24.
Meindl, Dieter (2007). "Modernism, Prairie Fiction, and Gender: Sinclair Ross, 'The Lamp at Noon'". In: Nischik. 105–116.
New, W.H. (1989). *A History of Canadian Literature*. New York: Macmillan.
Nischik, Reingard M., ed. (2007). *The Canadian Short Story: Interpretations*. Rochester and New York: Camden House.
Nischik, Reingard M. (2007). "The Canadian Short Story: Status, Criticism, Historical Survey". In: Nischik. 1–39.
Nischik, Reingard M. (2017). *The English Short Story in Canada: From the Dawn of Modernism to the 2013 Nobel Prize*. Jefferson, NC: McFarland & Company.
Staines, David (2014). "Canada in the World: Literatures at the Crossroads". In: Waldemar Zacharasiewicz and Fritz Peter Kirsch, eds. *Immigration and Integration in North America: Canadian and Austrian Perspectives*. Göttingen: V & R unipress. 15–29.
Staines, David (2021). *A History of Canadian Fiction*. Cambridge: Cambridge University Press.
Stevens, Peter (1976). "Introduction". In: Peter Stevens, ed. *Raymond Knister. The First Day of Spring: Stories and Prose*. Toronto and Buffalo: University of Toronto Press. xi–xxvi.
Stouck, David (1990). "Afterword". In: Ethel Wilson, ed. *Mrs. Golightly and Other Stories*. Toronto: McClelland & Stewart. 212–216.
Thacker, Robert (2004). "Short Fiction". In: Eva-Maria Kröller, ed. *The Cambridge Companion to Canadian Literature*. Cambridge: Cambridge University Press. 177–193.
Van Herk, Aritha (1997). "Prairie Writing". In: Benson and Toye. 960–965.
Weaver, Robert. (1997). "Short Stories in English: To 1982". In: Benson and Toye. 1058–1061.
Whalen, Terry (2002). "Montreal Story Tellers Fiction Performance Group". In: William H. New, ed. *Encyclopedia of Literature in Canada*. Toronto: University of Toronto Press. 751–752.
Woodcock, George (1997). "Weaver, Robert". In: Benson and Toye. 1172.

Suggestions for Further Reading

Boire, Gary (1999). "'The Language of the Law': The Case of Morley Callaghan". In: Lynch and Robbeson. 75–86.
Breitbach, Julia (2007). "The Beginnings of Canadian Modernism: Raymond Knister, 'The First Day of Spring' (Written 1924/25)". In: Nischik. 67–82.
Calder, Alison (2016). "Retracing Prairie Literature". In: Cynthia Sugars, ed. *The Oxford Handbook of Canadian Literature*. New York: Oxford University Press. 691–708.
Doyle, James (1999). "'Just Above the Breadline': Social(ist) Realism in Canadian Short Stories of the 1930s". In: Lynch and Robbeson. 65–74.
Lynch, Gerald and Angela Arnold Robbeson, eds. (1999). *Dominant Impressions: Essays on the Canadian Short Story*. Ottawa: University of Ottawa Press.

4 From the 1960s to the Mid-1980s

A Genre Establishes Itself

A number of factors are responsible for the "explosion" of short fiction in Canada in the 1960s, one of them being Robert Weaver's ongoing activities at the C.B.C. His programme *Anthology* (1953–1985), which can be seen as the Canadian equivalent to *The New Yorker* as the nation's most prestigious venue for short story publication, boosted the recognition of this genre in Canada and encouraged authors to dedicate themselves to the form. In fact, as Nischik (2017: 49) notes, "[e]very year, approximately 40 stories by well-known and lesser-known Canadian writers were broadcast to an average audience of 55,000 listeners per week". Through this programme, the suitability of the genre for audio performance was underlined, too, a feature that would be recognised and further developed by the Montreal Story Tellers in the 1970s.

Also in the 1960s, the effects of government policies to support the arts and culture in Canada, implemented in the wake of the Massey Report of 1951 (see also Section 3.4.), came to full fruition. Thus, the newly created Canada Council for the Arts (1957) offered aid-to-publish programmes (Thacker 2004: 188) and subsidised a number of new periodicals like the *University of Windsor Review*, the *Wascana Review*, the *Malahat Review*, and the *Lakehead Review*. These periodicals, as Norman Levine memorably recorded in his story "We All Begin in a Little Magazine" (1972), were essential venues for emerging writers. Another factor that contributed to the promotion of the short story was the foundation of a number of publishing houses that specialised in Canadian literature and which also profited from government funding: the House of Anansi Press, Talonbooks, Oberon Press, Coach House Press, and others (see also MacLeod 2016: 441f). Not all the mentors of the Canadian short story embraced the massive subsidising campaigns uncritically. Thus, John Metcalf, one of the most influential and uncompromising advocates of the genre, feared that "government gold" (2018: 111) would inevitably lead to literary mediocrity by favouring Canadian content as against aesthetic quality, with the Council thus "skew[ing] and distort[ing] the nature of our literature and the workings of our literary world" (2018: 111). As Thacker (2004: 188) notes,

> the 1960s saw the rise of what might be called a more conscious Canadianism – a patriotism or nationalism born variously of that decade's social unrest, Canada's 1967 Centennial celebrations, the Vietnam War, the Quiet Revolution in Quebec, and the appearance as prime minister of Pierre Elliott Trudeau.

Looking back at this crucial decade, it is evident that by its end, the short story had developed and matured, and a number of authors are now recognised internationally.

In his article on the short story in English in *Canadian Literature* (1969: 128), Donald Stephens marks 1961 as the year in which the "dam burst". Even though such definite demarcations may be problematic, one piece of evidence that confirms Stephens's observation is the emergence of an impressive number of debut collections in that decade, starting in 1961 with Norman Levine's *One Way Ticket* and Ethel Wilson's *Mrs. Golightly and Other Stories*. There followed Hugh Hood's *Flying a Red Kite* (1962), Margaret Laurence's *The Tomorrow Tamer* (1963), Audrey Thomas's *Ten Green Bottles* and Dave Godfrey's *Death Goes Better with Coca-Cola* (both in 1967), Alice Munro's *Dance of the Happy Shades* (1968), and Ray Smith's experimental *Cape Breton Is the Thought Control Center of Canada* (1969). That decade also saw the publication of Mavis Gallant's second collection of short fiction, *My Heart Is Broken*, in 1964, and of Hugh Hood's *Around the Mountain*, a volume of stories linked by place (Montreal), in 1967. Also, in 1968, Sinclair Ross's collected stories appeared in a New Canadian Library edition.

Since the 1970s, it has become more and more difficult to keep track of new publications and emerging writers. New incentives came from the Montreal Story Tellers (see Section 4.1.), including John Metcalf, Hugh Hood, Raymond Fraser, Clark Blaise, and Ray Smith, the latter an exponent of the postmodernist short story in Canada. Even though postmodernist experiments are not as prominent in English-Canadian short fiction as in French-Canadian or U.S. writing, there are some authors who challenged the dominant modernist-realist paradigm – at least in some of their stories. Apart from Smith, these are Dave Godfrey, Audrey Thomas, Leon Rooke, Matt Cohen, and Keath Fraser. Two further authors who started to publish experimental short fiction in the early 1970s and early 1980s, respectively, are George Bowering and Margaret Atwood. Metafictional elements can be found, for example, in Bowering's "How Delsing Met Frances & Started to Write a Novel" (*Flycatcher*, 1974) and, above all, in the programmatic "A Short Story" (*A Place to Die*, 1983). Here, fictionality is highlighted through chapter headings which refer to those elements of a narrative text that would be addressed in a course on literature and/or creative writing. Atwood's early experiments in short fiction are most memorably represented by the genre-bending pieces collected in *Murder in the Dark* (1983). Experimental Canadian short fiction, including stories by the authors mentioned here, will receive more attention in Chapters 5 and 6 of this volume. However, a name that should be mentioned here is that of Geoff Hancock, who was an early advocate of more pointedly experimental forms. His rejection of the modernist-realist mode in favour of the postmodernist is evident from the focus of the *Canadian Fiction Magazine*, whose editor he was from 1975 to 1998, as well as from his numerous author interviews and edited anthologies.

Metafictional and surreal elements can also be found in some stories by Rudy Wiebe (e.g. "Where is the Voice Coming From" and "The Angel of the Tar Sands"). In Marian Engel's stories (collected in *Inside the Easter Egg*, 1975, and *The Tattooed Woman*, 1985), too, shifts from the realistic to the surreal and fantastic can be identified. Myths and the Gothic, in turn, make an appearance in the work of Jack Hodgins (see Section 4.3.) and in William D. Valgardson's stories, as is evident especially in "Bloodflowers", the title story of his 1973 debut collection. Many of Valgardson's stories chart the life of Icelandic communities in Manitoba's Interlake area between Lakes Winnipeg and Manitoba (see also *God Is Not a Fish Inspector*, 1975, and *Red Dust*, 1978) and have gained him the epithet "Icelandic mystic" (Gunnars 1989: 16). Valgardson moved to Vancouver Island in 1974, which is also the backdrop of most of the stories in *What Can't Be Changed Shouldn't Be Mourned* (1990); he seems to be most comfortable concentrating on the short story, like the two foremost Canadian practitioners of the genre, Mavis Gallant and Alice Munro. Gallant's short fiction, which ranges from the 1950s to the 1990s, will be discussed in Section 4.2, and Munro's in the context of the short story cycle (Section 4.4.).

Characteristic of the first instances of short prose in Canada (see Chapter 2), linked stories have never lost their attraction for Canadian writers. Hugh Hood's *Around the Mountain* (1968) and Ray Smith's *Cape Breton Is the Thought Control Centre of Canada* (1969) may serve as examples. Another noteworthy story cycle based on place and community is Mordecai Richler's *The Street* (1969). The ten stories, which pay homage to the author's hometown of Montreal and especially to Saint Urbain Street and its Jewish community, are set against the backdrop of the Second World War. Like his novels, *The Street* testifies to Richler's skill in combining the comic and the tragic to great effect. While in the examples mentioned here the stories are mainly linked by place, a new type of short story cycle emerges in the early 1970s, with Alice Munro's *Lives of Girls and Women* (1971) and Margaret Laurence's *A Bird in the House* (1970). These mark the birth of the Canadian "life cycle" (Löschnigg 2014: 298), providing models for later works of fragmented autobiographical fiction (see Section 4.2.).

The high standing of the Canadian short story since the 1960s and '70s is also reflected in the distribution of literary prizes. For instance, short story collections account for a third of the Governor General's Awards since 1978 (Nischik 2017: 55), among the winners being Alice Munro's *Dance of the Happy Shades* (1968), *Who Do You Think You Are?* (1978) and *The Progress of Love* (1986), Mavis Gallant's *Home Truths* (2001 [1981]), and Guy Vanderhaeghe's *Man Descending* (1982). In 2015, Vanderhaeghe again sealed the prize for short fiction with *Daddy Lenin and Other Stories*.

4.1. John Metcalf and the Montreal Story Tellers

The *Montreal Story Teller Fiction Performance Group*, thus its full name, was formed in the winter of 1970–1971 (Whalen 2002: 752) in order to take creative writing – in particular, short fiction – to schools, universities, and community groups. Between 1971 and 1976, the Story Tellers presented and discussed short fiction in many institutions, mostly in the Montreal area, and these performances also affected their writing style. Even though the Group's audiences were, at times, quite small, the Story Tellers' efforts to forge and disseminate a Canadian canon distinct from the "crude thematic tradition of Canadian writing" (Garebian 1985: 188) decisively contributed to the maturing of the Canadian short story and to what has been referred to as the Canadian Renaissance in the 1960s and early 1970s (Nischik 2007a: 16). Ironically, none of the five members of the Montreal Story Tellers was actually born in Montreal, and only one of them, Toronto-born Hugh Hood, made Montreal his home. Both Ray Smith and Raymond Fraser were Maritimers, while Clark Blaise and John Metcalf were born outside Canada.

Originating from Carlisle, England, John Metcalf (1938–) came to Canada in 1962, became a Canadian citizen in 1970 and embarked on a mission to promote short fiction. Besides his activities with the Performance Group, he edited about 40 anthologies and became the most avid (and acrid) critic of short fiction in Canada. While Metcalf's impressive achievements as a mentor of Canadian short fiction cannot be overestimated, his controversies with those who did not meet his expectations must be seen in a critical light. Adverse to both the plot-oriented story and the anti-mimetic, postmodernist mode, Metcalf is known as an unflinching advocate of the modernist paradigm, which is also reflected in his own short stories. Metcalf's work includes seven collections of short fiction, of which three reprint earlier publications, like his latest collection *Standing Stones: The Best Stories of John Metcalf* (2004). His meticulously constructed stories, freighted with intertextual references and characterised by concentration and fragmentation, may not appeal to a wider reading public. As Metcalf polemically claims, "the mass can't read" (Metcalf 1982a: 1). Rather than drawing readers into the text, Metcalf's stories tend to place obstacles before them in order to prevent too quick an understanding.

Committed readers, however, will find many of the stories aesthetically rewarding. Metcalf's concern with rhythm, which to him conveys emotion, endows his stories with unique cadences. This is achieved by conscientious punctuation and layout, the use of italics for unuttered thoughts or to "indicate faintness and distance" (Metcalf 1982b: 179), and the use of capital letters for emphasis. Dialogue is also prominent, testifying to Metcalf's conviction that "speech creates character much faster than description" (1982b: 176), and so are parody and caricature.

All these elements are prominently represented, for example, in "Gentle as Flowers Make the Stones". Featuring a writer-protagonist like so many of Metcalf's stories, the narrative charts the creative efforts of Jim Haine, who struggles with a poetic adaptation of the Roman poet Martial. Providing lines from Martial in Latin – as they run through Jim's mind when he ponders on the most fitting words – and synchronising these intellectual musings with trivial, albeit existential, concerns about money and food, the story echoes the style of the first chapters of Joyce's *Ulysses*. Synchronisation, omission, and fragmentation occur in the following passage, which has Jim thinking about his unconventional friend Carol while being preoccupied with his poetry project:

> He wondered if she still brushed her teeth with twigs, still washed her hair with honey.
> He strained and grunted.
> *Veteres patronos*
> He was being too literal. Again. He needed to get further from the text. To preserve. Intact. The main line of. Intent. But let. The.
> The outer door banged shut; the bolt of the next cubicle slotted home. Checkered trousers rumpled over a pair of brown shoes.
> *Inter tam veteres ludat lascivia patronos*
> *Et nomen blaeso garriat ore meum.*
> "Care!" said Jim.
> The brown shoes cleared his throat.
> Yes.
> Expand it.
>
> ("Gentle as Flowers", 145f)

The story ends on a similar synchronising of artistic creation and, in this case, a superficial sexual encounter. As Jim completes a poem in his mind, he ejaculates on the back seat of the car where his acquaintance has just gratified him orally. This is both highly self-referential and ludicrous, and the comic effect mostly results from the woman's complete ignorance of Jim's aesthetic preoccupations. Thus, when Jim cries – most probably out of joy about having finally managed to finish his poem – the woman takes it as an emotional response to her "services", just as she mistook his earlier poetic scribblings on a piece of paper as his wish to note down her phone number.

The creative process in the story reflects Metcalf's own. When the protagonist has completed his perfect poem, the "perfect" story, too, has come to an end. Like Jim in the story, Metcalf, too, carefully ponders on the most fitting and resonating expressions. Metcalf, in general, uses much autobiographical material for his stories. Apart from his experiences as a writer in Canada and his encounters with the Canadian art industry, Metcalf also draws on his childhood and youth in England, which features in many stories as a place of memory for the "exiled" writer character (as in "The Years in Exile"). Formally, many of Metcalf's eight *Best Stories* from the 2004 collection are, in fact, novellas ("Private Parts", "Girl in Gingham", and "Polly Ongle"), thus confirming Keith Garebian's statement that Metcalf's "truest form is, perhaps, the novella" (1985: 200).

Like Metcalf, Hugh Hood (1928–2000), too, was indebted to modernism and preoccupied with form and style. However, his stories are strongly informed by his Catholic background and often suggest an allegorical meaning. They address transcendental issues and incorporate supernatural elements. At the same time, these elements are framed by and combined with realistic setups. Hood "starts with the commonest of things – streets, buildings, geography, ordinary people – and significant emblems emerge" (Garebian 1985: 204). Having regarded himself as "*both* a realist and a *transcendental allegorist*", the term Hood coined for his aesthetic style is "super-realism" (Mathews 1978–79: 211). Notwithstanding his ambitious 12-volume novel project, *The New Age/Le nouveau siècle*, Hood is today mostly known for his short stories. In fact, his ten collections (starting with *Flying a Red Kite* in 1962 and concluding with the posthumously published *After All!* in 2003) make him one of the most prolific representatives of short fiction in Canada. The cyclical form that defines his novel project is also evident in his story collections *Around the Mountain* (1967), *None Genuine Without Its Signature* (1980), and *August Nights* (1985).

Above all, however, Hood's work is defined by the fusion of the physical and concrete with notions of the divine, an aspect best illustrated in the title story of *Flying a Red Kite* (1962), Hood's probably best-known story. "Flying a Red Kite" can be divided into three parts. Starting with "The ride home began badly" (302), it immediately introduces the atmosphere of failure that accompanies the protagonist Fred Calvert's journey home from a shopping tour in downtown Montreal. His thoughts of failure and guilt and his physical and mental exhaustion are emphasised when, on the bus, he witnesses a drunk Catholic priest ogling the legs of some female passengers. As they pass the cemetery, Fred also overhears him saying, "It's all a sham . . . , they're in there for good" (306) – apparently, the priest has lost his faith. The second part shows Fred at home with his wife and daughter, half up the hill, while the third part and climax of the story takes Fred and his daughter to the top ridge of the mountain, making Fred realise that "He'd never been up this far before" (311).

This upward spatial movement reflects Fed's spiritual growth, reaching its zenith – literally and emotionally – with the red kite "that began to soar up and up" (312). The titular red kite which Fred buys for his daughter Deedee figures prominently in all three parts. On his way home, it is but a nuisance and reminder of past failures: "two flimsy wooden sticks rolled up in red plastic film, and a ball of cheap thin string – not enough, by the look of it, if he should ever get the thing into the air" (303). At home, it is Fred's wife, Naomi, who puts the kite together, almost damaging it in the process. Nonetheless, this act, as well as Naomi's countering of Fred's identification with the "spoiled priest" on the bus, prepares the ground for the epiphany in the third part.

The fact that it is a Sunday when Fred and Deedee make their way up the hill underlines the spiritual dimension of this enterprise, as does the cemetery that lies beside the field where Fred finally makes the kite fly. It appears again at the end of the story, when Fred watches the kite "two hundred feet and more above him up over the cemetery where it steadied and hung, bright red in the sunshine" (312). The kite's symbolic meaning as an emblem of the human soul and its immortality is made explicit in the story when Fred takes it as proof that the priest on the bus was wrong. What is only implied, however, is that the kite also reflects Fred's emotional and spiritual "ascent", as suggested in particular by the metaphoric merging of the red kite and the red of the crushed wild raspberries that Fred sees on his daughter's face in the concluding paragraph. The spiritual meaning of the red kite is reflected in the physical here and now, embodied in Deedee's raspberry-stained face. Both images viewed together become an "objective correlative" (see Section 3.1.) for a divine pattern manifest in the physical and secular.

Clark Blaise's (1940–) eight collections of short stories to date span a period from 1973 (*A North American Education*) to 1992 (*Man and His World*). Informed by his divided American, Canadian, and French-Canadian heritage and his affiliation with Indian culture through his marriage to Bharati Mukherjee, Blaise's work is characterised by a wide spectrum of different settings, a strong focus on identity – or, rather, the loss thereof – and a general notion of alienation. This is already evident in his debut collection, whose subtitle, *A Book of Short Fiction*, also indicates Blaise's preoccupation with reflection rather than plot. The stories in *A North American Education* are organised in three groups: "The Montreal Stories", "The Keeler Stories", and "The Thibidault Stories". Named only in the title story, "A Class of New Canadians", Norman Dyer also seems to be the protagonist in "Eyes" and "Words for the Winter". While Dyer, a frustrated English instructor in Montreal, is the focaliser in the first story, rendered in the third person, the second story, "Eyes", relates the events from a you-perspective, thus occupying a liminal position between the third-person mode in the first story and the concluding "Words for Winter", which features a first-person narrator.

The effect of the you-form and use of the present tense in "Eyes" is of particular interest. While the present tense creates the illusion of immediacy, the second-person mode not only suggests universality (when understood in the generic sense of "one") but also draws the reader into the text, making them participate in the protagonist's struggles to fit in. The "eyes" of the title denote the motif of voyeurism that haunts the whole story, the protagonist being both voyeur and an object of voyeurism; they materialise in the eyes of a pig at a Greek butcher's shop at the end of the story:

> You remove your gloves and touch the skin, you brush against the grainy ear. How the eye attracts you! How you would like to lift one out, press its smoothness against your tongue, then crush it in your mouth. And you cannot.
> (*A North American Education* 23)

Using second-person narration for this story of alienation, Blaise is one of the first Canadian short story writers to exploit the aesthetic potential of this destabilising voice for rendering characters undergoing a crisis or being at a distance from themselves. Decades later, authors like Margaret Atwood, Elyse Gasco, Lynn Coady, or Steven Heighton would amply use this form for their narratives of crisis (see Chapter 5). A story where fluid movements between different settings and cultural contexts are particularly evident is "Meditations on Starch" (1992), which shifts between Canada, India, and Europe – especially (Kafka's) Prague and (Freud's) Vienna. In the story, the narrator's "meditations on starch" are, in fact, meditations on how the rise of Nazism was possible and how it affected his family. Standing in front of the Sigmund-Freud-Haus in Vienna's Berggasse 19, he is overcome by the agonising political impotence of the arts and sciences: "And it chokes me, suddenly, the realization that science and music can be so advanced, and do nothing to influence a political culture in its infancy. Austrian democracy was younger than Ghana when Nazis crushed it" ("Meditations" 75).

The fact that the short fiction output of the Montreal Story Tellers is by no means stylistically and/or thematically homogenous is shown most strikingly, although in radically different ways, by the stories of Ray Smith (1941–2019) and Raymond Fraser (1941–2018).

Fraser's stories, collected in *The Black Horse Tavern* (1972), are defined by colloquial language, an acute ear for the verbal register of the "common folk" and a focus on social "losers". Fraser's impact on the Canadian short story has been relatively short-lived, and his work has hardly received critical attention. In contrast, Ray Smith established himself as the most experimental member of the Montreal Story Tellers Fiction Performance Group and as one of Canada's early postmodernist writers of short fiction.

Smith's first published story, "Cape Breton Is the Thought-Control Centre of Canada" (*Tamarack Review*, 1967), is the title story of his first collection, published in 1969. A new edition of that collection published in 2006 contains an extensive introduction by the author as well as the drawings by Ken Tolmie that had been rejected by Anansi in 1969. The title story – in fact a compilation of mini-stories, dialogues, reflections, and aphorisms – deals with Canadian nationalism vis-à-vis the economic and cultural dominance of the United States. What the story is meant to imply, in Smith's words, is that "the Canadian nationalist, with few home grown dreams, dreams in American terms" (2006: 6). Smith's innovative style, which is alternately informed by the aesthetics of music and the visual arts, results from the idea that what he writes about "should be embodied, not talked through" (2006: 5), thus conveying a certain mood through the mode of the textual surface structure. In the story "Smoke", for example, the author tries "to produce a story as pungent, as elusive, as evocative as smoke through an autumn wood" (2006: 21). In his second linked-stories collection, *Lord Nelson's Tavern* (1974), too, Smith experiments with narrative voice and tries to capture "the fluidity of boundaries in human experience and to unite form with content" (Gadpaille 1988: 103).

4.2. In Transit – of Exiles and Outsiders: Norman Levine and Mavis Gallant

Norman Levine and Mavis Gallant not only share their dedication to the genre of short fiction but are also comparable with regard to their self-imposed exile. Born in Ottawa to orthodox Jewish parents who had emigrated to Canada from Poland, Levine left Canada in 1949 to settle in England (Cornwall). In the mid-1960s, he returned to Canada but moved again to Europe in his later years, living in France and in the north of England. Gallant moved to Europe in 1950, settling in Paris after having travelled and lived in the south of France, Austria, Italy, and Spain.

Norman Levine (1923–2005), who started out as a poet, is now mostly known for his short fiction (comprising eight collections between 1961 and 2005). Levine's stories are characterised by a minimalist style and a preference for first-person narration. Thematically, they often revolve around artists, as in "In Lower Town" (*I Don't Want to Know Anyone Too Well*, 1971), where the protagonist is a successful author. Also, the theme of the Canadian author in exile is a recurring element (e.g. "A Canadian Upbringing" and "I Like Chekhov", both in *I Don't Want to Know*), testifying to a strong autobiographical impulse behind his works. This can also be observed in his best-known story "We All Begin in a Little Magazine" (1972; collected in *Thin Ice*, 1979), which is set in England and features the typical writer-protagonist who can be regarded "as a persona for the thinly disguised Levine" (Bölling 2007: 276). However, as with many Canadian short story authors, this does not detract from the artistic quality of the work. Levine's stories were widely recognised internationally and especially in Europe, his German translators being none less than Nobel Prize winner Heinrich Böll and his wife, Annemarie. In 2017, Biblioasis brought out a collected stories edition that again bears the title *I Don't Want to Know Anyone Too Well* and is complemented with a foreword and afterword by John Metcalf.

Mavis Gallant (1922–2014) is not only the most important Canadian expatriate author but also one of the most seminal and most frequently anthologised representatives of Canadian short fiction in general. She began her career in the early 1950s, when "Madeline's Birthday" was published by *The New Yorker*, where altogether 116 of her stories would appear. Her first book of stories, *The Other Paris*, was published in 1956, with nine further collections to follow, in addition to compilations such as *The Collected Stories of Mavis Gallant* (1996) – the most comprehensive collection of Gallant's prolific output – or *The Cost of Living* (2009), which assembles early and previously uncollected stories. For a long time, Gallant – the expatriate whose stories were often regarded as not being "Canadian enough" – was denied full acknowledgement in Canada. This changed with the publication of *From the Fifteenth District* (1979) and, above all, *Home Truths: Selected Canadian Stories* (1981), the latter including Gallant's strongly autobiographical "Linnet Muir" stories.

Even though she was brought up bilingually herself, Gallant doubted the possibility of true bilingualism; in her "Introduction" to *Home Truths*, she wonders "if such a phenomenon can exist this side of schizophrenia" (xvii). For Gallant, language forms the basis of cultural identity. Thus, for the child characters in her stories who are forced to abandon their mother tongue, "[l]anguage was black" (*Home Truths* 69), as is the case for the Collier girls in "Orphan's Progress" or for Gérard in "Saturday". In the latter story, it is the French-Canadian mother of Gérard (and his six siblings), who tries to remodel the linguistic and cultural identities of her children as part of an attempt to escape from her own Catholic past. Consequently, Gérard, who longs to think and dream in French, speaks it only "as if through a muslin curtain" (39). "Deprived from the all-important first language", Gallant explains, "he is intellectually maimed. The most he can do is to hobble along" (xviii).

Many of Gallant's stories render the sad fates of abandoned, uprooted, and displaced children. The author described her own childhood as traumatic, having attended no less than 17 schools of different religious and cultural orientations (Besner 1988: 3). Like the fictional Linnet Muir of her stories, Gallant's strong personality may have turned these disruptive experiences to the positive, yet the cultural homelessness of her juvenile characters is often depicted as damaging their self. "Up North" (*Home Truths*) may serve as an example here. The story describes the train ride of a young British war bride and her small son up to Abitibi, a construction camp north of Montreal. A notion of darkness permeates the whole story, colouring all other impressions, which are rendered mostly from the child's point of view. Dennis and his mother are in the dark – not just because everything on the train and what they see from the window is sooty, black, and dirty but also because they are completely disoriented in their new existence. The boy's increasing fear takes shape in a dreamlike observation he makes during a short stop. The little bent men he sees, carrying bundles and speaking in a foreign language, become a cypher for the strangeness of Dennis's new surroundings. By ignoring or even denying the child's observation, his mother and their fellow traveller McLaughlin transform his fear into a state of panic, which, in the end, leads to the gradual disintegration of the boy's self. Being scolded for repeating his strange story ("'You didn't see anyone. Now shut up'"), the boy can do nothing but insist that he "Sor 'em", eventually "in a voice as low as he could descend without falling into a whisper" (63). His state of terror reaches a climax when stories about Indians mix with his observations and feelings of abandonment: "'The Indians!', the boy cried, clinging to the train, to air; to anything. His face was momentarily muffled by McLaughlin's shirt. . . . He screamed, 'Where's mum? I never saw anything!'" (64) In this moment of panic, Dennis realises that he has to say whatever is expected of him in order not to be a burden to his mother. His crisis is underlined when he abandons his British vernacular "sor" in favour of the standard "saw", which will not indicate his origin. In addition, the muffling of his face suggests the stifling of his voice and of his own self.

The focus on cultural displacement and disorientation is also visible in numerous stories that feature adult characters – those "At Home" and those "Canadians Abroad", as the first two sections of *Home Truths* are titled. Gallant was a transcultural person *par excellence* and a truly cosmopolitan writer. Nonetheless, she refused to be seen as anything other than Canadian, being convinced that a strong sense of one's own background is a prerequisite for understanding and living in other cultural contexts. Lacking this strong sense of cultural and linguistic identity, Gallant's characters often fail to come to terms with cultural transition, feeling alienated, lonely, depressed, or even physically affected. In general, the characters in Gallant's stories tend to find themselves suspended between two or more cultures, suffering from the "transcultural slippage" that Coral Ann Howells (1992: 23) has defined as "no smooth transition but a traumatic defection". Such feelings of displacement characterise, for example, Peter Frazier and Agnes Brusen in "The Ice Wagon Going Down the Street" or Lottie and Vera in "Virus X". Lottie, a student of sociology from Winnipeg who is in Paris to do research, feels more and more "dislocated, perhaps forever" (*Home Truths* 234), a psychological crisis that also turns physical when she becomes seriously ill.

In "The Ice Wagon Going down the Street", Gallant's most frequently anthologised story, the uneasiness with cultural identity surfaces when Peter Frazier and Agnes Brusen, two Canadians, are made to share an office in Geneva. In Peter's case, his conflicted attitude is evident in his derogatory and almost cynical references to his and Agnes Brusen's shared Canadian origins. Peter, an urban Canadian, from whose perspective the story is mostly told, supposes that "they had been put together because they were Canadians; but they were as strange to each other as if 'Canadian' meant any number of things, or had no real meaning" (133). In expectation of a more glamorous career, he is unhappy not only about Agnes's Norwegian-Saskatchewan background but also about the fact that this unprepossessing young woman, this "mole" (134) – so different from the colourful peacocks with which Peter and his wife, Sheila, are associated – is supposed to be his boss. His reflection that "their being Canadian, and suddenly left together was a sexual damper" (134) is reiterated towards the end when he reminisces that "[t]hey were both

Canadians, so they had this much together . . . Anyway, nothing happened" (153). Something, however, *does* happen and is linked to the title image of "the ice wagon going down the street", which appears three times in the story. The episode of Peter and Agnes's encounter in an office in Geneva is, in fact, a memory that keeps crossing Peter's mind when the Fraziers are back in Canada again, staying with Peter's sister in Toronto until their future will settle. He remembers the evening when Agnes sneaked out of a fashionable party in Geneva, displaced, miserable, and utterly drunk, and Peter picked her up and took her home. It was at this point that Agnes recalled the ice wagon, whose early morning rounds through her prairie hometown she associated with the solitude of those cherished moments when she seemed to have the world to herself, yet which had since become a memory emblematic of her loneliness. At the same time, this memory also stands for her Canadian background. By sharing it with Peter and thus drawing on their common Canadianness, the memory of the ice wagon compensates – if only for a moment – for the experience of displacement. It is this very moment that Peter remembers when he and Sheila talk "about those times" (153), but which he keeps secret from his English-born wife as if it were something too precious to share with someone who would probably not understand:

> He thinks of the ice wagon going down the street. He sees something he has never seen in his life – a Western town that belongs to Agnes. Here is Agnes – small, mole-faced, round-shouldered . . . She watches the ice wagon and the trail of ice water in a morning invented for her: hers. He sees the weak prairie trees and the shadows on the sidewalk. Nothing moves except the shadows and the ice-wagon and the changing amber of the child's eyes. The child is Peter.
>
> (154)

In this moment of epiphany, Peter is not only united with Agnes but also with his Canadian heritage. He may be lost, as the last words of the story suggest, but at least he is granted recognition of what he has lost.

Stylistically, Gallant's stories are characterised by a detached narrative voice and laconic language. Gallant's matter-of-fact style creates a "puzzling distance between narrator, character and readers" (Kulyk Keefer 1989: 45). It appears almost as an iconic device, mirroring the cold and disconcerting nature of the worlds she portrays in her stories. Through their use of subtle implications, however, the stories have a strong emotional impact and do not preclude compassion. Sometimes, it is merely the incongruity between the detached narrative voice and the emotional significance of what is represented which reveals the distress felt by many of her characters due to a lack of empathy that characterises their social environments. One of the most effective of Gallant's emotive devices is her encoding of the psychological dimension of loss and displacement into physical correlatives. The reader's decoding process, which often takes place unconsciously, is triggered by the accumulation of suggestive references to such correlatives. The motif of the bed in "Orphan's Progress" is a memorable example of how Gallant combines the abstract with the concrete to great effect. The story traces the alienation of the two Collier sisters from their hybrid English and French background but also from each other. The large bed that the girls share with their French-Canadian mother at the beginning of the story symbolises an emotionally intact bicultural identity. Later, when the girls are torn from their mother by social workers, the growing gap between the sisters, who are now forced to use English exclusively, is rendered concrete through the image of a pull-out divan on which the siblings "wrangled about bedclothes" (*Home Truths* 69). Still later, in a convent where English words are forbidden, Cathie and Mildred, for the first time, sleep in separate beds, even in different dormitories. Like the ice wagon, physical images which are employed to designate psychological conditions usually have no symbolic meaning as such. Rather, they achieve it through Gallant's "rhetoric of accumulation", as Martha Dvorak calls it – that is, a recurrence of similar references which results in a "textual web of ramifications [taking on] the shape of a whole cloth, through the winding web of concatenation" (2002: 68). Gallant's exploiting the full potential of the short prose form, her terse style, her suggestive gaps, and the almost agonisingly detached narrative voice have drawn readers to her work and puzzled them; they have influenced younger writers like, for example, Janice Kulyk Keefer and have attracted considerable critical attention, in particular from the 1980s onwards. It speaks for itself that for the 2001 EMBLEM edition (McClelland & Stewart) of *Home Truths*, the subtitle *Selected Canadian Stories* was not deemed necessary anymore.

4.3. From Coast to Coast: Jack Hodgins and Alistair MacLeod

Regarding the importance of regional contexts, two authors have made a particularly strong impact on the Canadian short story: Jack Hodgins and Alistair MacLeod. Both started to publish stories in the late 1960s, remained productive well into the new millennium, and have decisively contributed to shaping the literary landscapes of the West Coast (Hodgins) and the East Coast (MacLeod), respectively. MacLeod's last collection, *Island* (2000), comprises the stories from his two earlier collections, *The Lost Salt Gift of Blood* (1976) and *As Birds Bring Forth the Sun* (1986), as well as two new stories, "Island" and "Clearances". His last story, "Remembrance", appeared in 2012, one year before his death. With *Spit Delaney's Island*, Hodgins, too, launched his first collection of stories in 1976, followed by *The Barclay Family Theatre* in 1981. His most recent book of stories is *Damage Done by the Storm* (2004).

Jack Hodgins (1938–), one of the foremost writers from the Canadian West Coast, successfully transforms "his local backyard into an image of the whole creative universe" (Keith 1981: 31). Firmly rooted on Vancouver Island, Hodgins has explored the Canadian West Coast in novels and short stories, especially those collected in *Spit Delaney's Island*. As Waldemar Zacharasiewicz (1986: 97f) has pointed out, Hodgins's "use of [his] specifically regional material in order to convey stories of general human significance" shows the influences of writers from the American South such as William Faulkner, Eudora Welty, and Flannery O'Connor.

Through his first novel, *The Invention of the World* (1977), Hodgins has been associated with magical realism, yet the author himself has been rather reluctant about this label (see, for example, Hancock 1987: 61). However, the magical and mythical (including Indigenous myths) *do* figure prominently in several of his stories, testifying to a metaphysical conception of the "real", which the author explores in his writing. His narratives tend to be peopled by eccentric and, at times, even grotesque and freakish characters. These are not flat, however, like the characters typical of, for example, the satirical prose sketch. Also, Hodgins's almost hyperbolic handling of character and plot does not preclude compassion. Rather, his short fiction allows space for both the comedy and tragedy of human existence.

In *Spit Delaney's Island*, the ten stories are linked by place but also by a focus on characters who are isolated and estranged from each other and on their attempts to overcome this alienation. A further unifying element is the two stories that frame the collection, with the concluding title story continuing the story of Spit Delaney, who is first introduced in the initial story, "Separating". It is in this story that Hodgins's "interest in margins and borders of all kinds" (Kruk 2016: 13) is particularly evident. Spit, who "only admits to being a figure on the edge" (3), is more and more preoccupied with the question of "*Where is the dividing line?*" (7), which moves centre stage after the loss of his beloved steam locomotive in the paper mill to a museum. His obsession with the locomotive ("'Spit and Old Number One, a marriage made in heaven', people joked", 6) shows strong parallels to Joyce Marshall's "The Old Woman" (1952) (see Section 3.3.); in both stories, an obsessive attachment to a machine incapacitates the protagonists for human relationships and eventually destroys their marriage. What is most interesting, however, is how Spit's personal crisis and separation from his wife, Stella, are set in analogy to Indigenous tales of sea monsters and their traffic across the "dividing line" between sea and land and to the allegedly scientific account of "a crack that runs all around the ocean floor" (18). These juxtapositions lend a cosmic dimension to Spit's personal experiences, linking them to mythical marital separations, "to the separation of island from mainland, of land from sea, and ultimately, of mind from self" (Gadpaille 1988: 112).

"Spit Delaney's Island", the final story (and the only one told in first-person form), is set some time after Spit's separation from Stella and his expulsion from their home. He undergoes a severe crisis, expressed in nightmares in which he finds himself transformed into a marine animal helplessly stranded on the beach and is helped by the mysterious and eccentric poet Phemie Porter. Her correct diagnosis of his crisis gives Spit the feeling that, for the first time, he is being recognised: "She's in there [the poem she sent him] somewhere looking at me clearer than anyone's ever seen me before" (199). Moreover, her disclosure of her own ability to "store everything important in her own mind" (193) liberates Spit from his dependence on physical objects and signals a departure out of his paralysing dilemma onto new shores.

Of the other stories in this collection, some are quite surreal or even Kafkaesque (Zacharasiewicz 1986: 99), like "At the Foot of the Hill, Birdie's School", while others strike a lighter note, like "Every Day of His Life", Hodgins's first published story. In a hilariously comical manner, this story illustrates how a husband and father for her son is caught by Big Glad Littlestone, an obese 36-year-old woman about whom people make vitriolic remarks that "there won't be a church aisle on the island wide enough for her to walk down", while the more sensitive would say, "Poor girl . . . The size of a logging truck and almost as loud" (86). The reader is taken by her sparkling vitality, though, and sympathies are with her rather than with her prospective bridegroom, whose name, Mr. Swingler, sounds all too much like "swindler". In general, Mr. Swingler is just as eccentric as Big Glad and macabre when he relates how he ate the ashes of his late wife. Instead of being taken aback by this admission, however, Big Glad wishes that he would do the same for her, which he denies since "after the first time there's nothing to it" (97). Unsurprisingly, the story concludes upon a note of unease, even though the bride and groom set out to be married.

Probably the most haunting story in the collection is "Three Women of the Country", which is tellingly set in the village of "Cut Off". Consecutively, the three parts of the story shed light on the private dilemmas of three women, whose role as focalisers alternates with the occasional use of an ironical authorial voice. At first, these women are introduced as harmless eccentrics, yet the narrative increasingly reveals how "cut off" from each other they are and which abyss lurks underneath a seemingly harmless surface. The first chapter renders the perspective of Mrs. Milly Wright, a self-righteous woman, as the name already implies, who is prone to racism and gossip. The second chapter focuses on Charlene Porter, a teenage girl, whose views on truth and reality are shattered when she discovers a retarded boy hidden in her neighbour Mrs. Starbuck's attic. In the third chapter, Mrs. Starbuck's dark secret is revealed: she complied with her husband's locking away their disabled child. The story ends dramatically when Mrs. Starbuck is crushed by her own car in a rushed attempt to leave the village with her son to make a new start. However, the boy "was leaping free of the car, squealing" (67), and the description of the painfully grotesque figure of the boy running is followed by the climactic scene in which the frantic mother leaps out of the car herself, stumbling to her death while trying to catch her son. It seems that Edna Starbuck's vain struggles against the darkness within her are rendered concrete as she collides with the car "as if she were fighting a monster she couldn't see" (68). The story ends upon an ambivalent note:

even though this chapter renders Edna Starbuck's point of view, the final paragraphs return to Charlene and Mrs Wright, and the story concludes with the latter contemplating the reflections of their startled faces in the window of the car. However, the additional information that the window was "only an inferior sort of mirror" (69) suggests that there is no moment of recognition or self-awareness after this cataclysmic event; rather, the two remaining women may just carry on as before.

In contrast to Hodgins's first collection, *The Barclay Family Theatre* includes stories that are set outside of Vancouver Island. In addition to familial links between characters, the arts as such function as a unifying element in this short story cycle, being explored in various ways. In contrast, *Damage Done by the Storm* lacks any features characteristic of the linked-stories pattern. Still, through their focus on "an odd assortment of outsiders, escapees, and loners coping with various kinds of 'damage'" (Kruk 2016: 13), there are themes that connect the ten stories in this collection, even if they are more varied as to narrative voice than the earlier books. Thus, in the title story, we encounter a senator in Ottawa trying to keep a promise he made to his grandson (and failing to do so again), while in "Astonishing the Blind", the first-person narrator, Meg, is a concert pianist settled in Germany. "Galleries", in turn, features a Faulkner scholar on a tour through Mississippi with her son, a conflicted photographer from whose perspective the story is presented.

Among the stories set on the Canadian West Coast, "Over Here" is of particular interest. A young boy befriends an "Indian" girl, Nettie, who has been adopted into a white family and is not supposed to know about her heritage. In order to "protect" the new pupil, the school stops teaching the kids about Indigenous Canadian cultures: "There were no more lessons about life in an Indian village. No more stories about ravens. We learned about Incas and Mayans instead" (*Damage* 45). In the course of the story, the boy projects all his stereotypical notions of "Indians" onto Nettie, even though, as he somewhat disappointedly observes, she "didn't have the beauty of a Mohawk girl in a book" (41). Told from the naïve perspective of an eight-year-old, the story subtly dismantles and revises essentialist misconceptions about "Indians".

Revisionary features also define the humorous "The Drover's Wife". The story about South Australian Hazel, "The Terror of the Woods" (*Damage* 74), who crossed the Pacific and established a logging imperium on the Canadian West Coast, is interesting both as an intermedial and an intertextual narrative. Thus, in the fictional world of the story, Hazel is the woman who stood as a model for Russell Drysdale's famous painting *The Drover's Wife* (1945); the painting, in turn, was supposedly inspired by Australian author Henry Lawson's well-known story "The Drover's Wife" (1892). Hazel had "always wanted to be the biggest thing in the picture" – not only literally (after all, her sturdy figure dominates the painting) but also figuratively as "she wanted to boss the whole coast" (78). The story, thus, inverts the notion of female victimhood that imbues the painting and even more so Lawson's tale – so much so that the peripheral first-person narrator concludes,

> I understand there is a good deal of sympathy in Australia for the figure Hazel cuts in the famous painting – an unhappy woman, dependent upon the wishes of a man while at the mercy of a harsh environment. Those who see in that young Hazel the symbol of a female victim would, I imagine, be heartened to learn that she succeeded in altering her destiny once she arrived on these shores. Look at the legs. She was never meant to be toppled.
>
> (86)

The ongoing relevance of Hodgins's short stories has, in fact been confirmed by a new and expanded edition of *Damage Done to the Storm* that came out in 2019.

Alistair MacLeod (1936–2014), whose ancestors came to Nova Scotia from the Scottish island of Eigg in 1790, assumed the role of a bard for the Atlantic region of Canada in general and Nova Scotia's Cape Breton in particular. This was in spite of the fact that MacLeod's childhood was spent in Saskatchewan, where his father worked as a miner, and that he lived most of his life in Ontario, where he taught English and creative writing at the University of Windsor. For their summers, however, MacLeod and his large family would "all return like pilgrims to their spiritual home in Cape Breton" (Gibson 2014: 284). In MacLeod's strongly poetic stories, Cape Breton is most of all a "mnemonic region" (Sandrock 2009: 176), a region of the mind strongly informed by myths of an Edenic past. In several stories, elegiac depictions of intact communities based on strong familial bonds and governed by a strong sense of tradition and continuity are linked to an even remoter past in Gaelic Scotland. Regarding the universal significance of MacLeod's regionally based stories, one may say with Irene Guilford (2001: 10) that their author's "birthplace is Canadian, his emotional heartland Cape Breton, his heritage Scottish, but his writing is of the world". The fact that the cultural relevance of his stories transcends the regional is also confirmed by their having been translated into several languages, among them French, Norwegian, Italian, German, and – fittingly and yet surprisingly – Gaelic.

With only one novel and fewer than 20 short stories, MacLeod's oeuvre is relatively slim; however, this lack in quantity is amply compensated by the refined and rhythmically elaborate style of MacLeod's narratives. Producing stories at the rate of roughly one per year earned MacLeod the nickname the Stone Carver, "chipping out each perfect word with loving care" (Gibson 2014: 285, 288). The theme of loss (see also Chapter 10) runs through MacLeod's fiction, including his novel *No Great Mischief* (1999). The loss of traditions and of communal and familial structures passed on from one generation to the next is causally connected to the onslaught of urbanisation and modernisation. As the traditional industries of the Maritimes (mining, fishing, farming, and lumbering) have gone down, they have made way for tourism and new economies, such as those related to cybercommunication. In MacLeod's stories, the old ways, while depicted as doomed, are at the same time idealised in memories of a shared community. However, MacLeod also shows himself as conscious of how this kind of nostalgia can be exploited by the tourist industry. In "The Tuning of Perfection" (1984; later included in *As Birds Bring Forth the Sun*), the commodification of folk music and culture is criticised when Archibald, the protagonist, refuses to comply with ignorant producers of a "Scots Around the World" show in Halifax, where he was supposed to sing Gaelic songs with his granddaughter. Others from their community *do* present Gaelic art that has been tailored for mainstream tastes. However, they do so in a subversive manner, feeding the audience a "song" called "Brochan Lom", which, as Archibald immediately recognises, "isn't even a song. It's just a bunch of nonsense syllables strung together" (*Island* 303). The fake performance can be regarded as an act of cultural resistance comparable to that of the Elder in Thomas King's "One Good Story, That One". In King's story, ignorant "whitemen" who have come to record authentic "Indian" stories are treated to a version of their own creation myth (the biblical Genesis) in thin Indigenous disguise (see also Section 8.1.).

Five of the seven stories in *The Lost Salt Gift of Blood* conform to the pattern of the initiation story, featuring boys or adolescents as their protagonists and (in four cases) first-person narrators. In "The Boat", MacLeod's first published story (1968), the teenage narrator is torn between his mother's wish that he continue his father's trade as a fisherman and his father's endeavours to enable him to pursue a different life. In "The Return", too, the tensions between a father and a mother are filtered through the first-person perspective of their son, the ten-year-old Alex. The story recounts a fortnight's visit at home (a Cape Breton mining town), after ten years of absence, by the lawyer Angus, his Montreal wife and their son. The boy, who has never met his numerous paternal relations, including his grandparents, is embraced by the family and realises, for the first time, that "I have been lonely all of my short life" (*Island* 85). The bond between him and his "clan" is strengthened by the initiation he undergoes when, after their shift in the mine, his grandfather embraces him so vigorously that the blackened boy has to join him and his uncles in the shower. While Alex, to the great chagrin of his mother, becomes more and more integrated into the life of the mining family, he also becomes increasingly aware of his father's alienation. This is rendered in three closely linked episodes. Coming back from a long and adventurous day with his cousins, Alex sees his father approaching: "He is not disturbed that I have been away so long and seems almost to envy us our unity and our dirt as he stands so straight and lonely in the prison of his suit and inquires of our day" (87). The father's isolation is also conspicuous when Alex comes out of the washhouse, seeing his father "still sitting at the bench by himself" (91). It is now that an earlier scene may be recognised as a symbolic reference to Angus. While waiting for the ferry, Alex and his parents have watched a mottled brown gull ousted by a flock of white gulls which "peck at *him* and drive *him* away" (75, my emphasis). It seems that, for Angus, there is no real return – neither to his clan nor to his life as a partner in his father-in-law's firm. Physically, he returns to Montreal, yet his emotional outbursts when they arrived on Cape Breton and his confessing to his son how hard it had been to give up chewing tobacco (the habit standing, of course, for all he had to give up in order to fit into genteel urban life) suggest that he will remain suspended in between the two worlds.

The theme of loss is also prominent in MacLeod's last stories, "Clearances" (1999) and "Remembrance" (2013). However, in the former story pining over loss and rigidly holding on to traditional values and social structures in a changing world tend to be regarded critically. The elderly protagonist of this "heritage preservation narrative" (Hodd 2008: 194f) reflects on his past on Cape Breton, where he still lives "in the house his grandfather had built" (*Island* 416). He also reminisces over his visit to the place of his Highland ancestors in Scotland when he was on leave during his service in the Second World War. He remembers that he was immediately identified as being "from the Clearances" (419) and now – many decades later – becomes painfully aware that he is "the descendant of victims of history and changing economic times" (420). More than this, he even shares their fate as he feels coerced into selling his property to a tourist enterprise. The title "Clearances" thus adopts several meanings: it refers to the 18th-century Highland Clearances and, by analogy, to the vanishing of the old ways of life on Cape Breton but also to the clearing of land by the Scottish settlers and their descendants themselves when they claimed the Atlantic Coast of Canada. This also includes the protagonist and his sons, as well as the modern clearcutters he views so negatively. The story as such, however, implies the inevitability of change and the necessity of adapting to new circumstances. Even though close family ties and the passing of traditions down the generations are essential to the protagonist's vision of an intact world, it is, ironically, his stubborn refusal to compromise which drives his own son away. Because the fish have disappeared from the Atlantic Coast, John has no choice but to go to Ontario, "fishing Lake Erie" (423) and living apart from his family most of the time – a situation that could be prevented if part of their property were sold and transformed into tourist facilities.

In general, MacLeod's fictional worlds are male-dominated, requiring physical strength and endurance. Men and women live in separate spheres, and husbands are mostly unable to share their experiences and grievances with their wives – an exception being the short marriage of Archibald in "The Tuning of Perfection". In conclusion, one may say with Laurie Kruk (2016: 11f) that "MacLeod has documented the silences of masculinity, especially within a working-class context where orality and textuality, the clan and modernity, are frequently in conflict". Through their imaginative mapping of Celtic Nova Scotia, his stories can be seen as "poignant reminders of our embeddedness in landscape as well as language" (Kruk 2016: 11).

4.4. The Birth of the Canadian "Life Cycle"

Even though the form of linked stories/sketches has had a long tradition in Canada, starting with McCulloch's and Haliburton's contributions in the 19th century, the use of the short story cycle as a medium for life writing was introduced and popularised only in the early 1970s, with Margaret Laurence's *A Bird in the House* (1970) and Alice Munro's *Lives of Girls and Women* (1971). Both cycles feature a first-person narrator and protagonist who relates her life in the fragmented mode of autonomous but linked stories, and in both works the cumulative effect of their episodic structure creates great narrative depth. Even though Munro first referred to her *Lives* as a novel (which she later revised) and the book was hailed by critics as "the best Canadian novel" (Nischik 2017: 91), it clearly conforms to the genre of the short story cycle. The same holds for Margaret Laurence, who initially – and upon the pressure from her publisher – struggled to turn her stories into a novel (Nischik 2017: 90). However, *A Bird in the House* remains a memorable collection of linked stories, which – like *Lives* – is now a Canadian classic. Both collections contain eight stories each that add up to "portraits of the artist as a young woman". Place functions as a unifying element in both books. In *A Bird in the House*, Vanessa MacLeod grows up in the 1930s in the fictive prairie town of Manawaka. Based on Neepawa, Margaret Laurence's Manitoban birthplace, Manawaka is also the setting of several of Laurence's novels. In the same way, the setting of *Lives*, Jubilee, was modelled after Munro's birthplace Wingham, Ontario.

The prominence of the linked-stories format in Canada may be attributed to the country's then still vulnerable book market – after all, short story sequences, as opposed to novels, also allow for publications of single stories in magazines (Nischik 2017: 88) – but also to a general preference on the part of publishers (and possibly also readers) for longer and more strongly unified volumes of short fiction. At the same time, it can be observed that, in the period from the 1960s to the mid-'80s, the status of the short story in Canada had risen significantly. All the same, it cannot be ignored that the novel still enjoys a higher prestige – with the effect that a number of short story cycles have been marketed as novels. The short story cycle, as Gerald Lynch (2001: 18) argues, has, in general, had a specific appeal for Canadian authors and is "a quintessentially Canadian form"; as it seems, Canadian writers suspicious of the more totalising aesthetics of the novel "have found in the story cycle a form that allows for a new unity in disunity, reflecting a fragmented temporal sense, and incorporating a more authentic representation of modern sensibilities". Before discussing in more detail Munro's *Lives* and before providing an overview of other noteworthy works that have followed and modified the life-cycle model, I shall, therefore, briefly look at the aesthetic specificities of this distinct subgenre.

Critics have made little distinction between story sequences only linked by place or recurring motifs and those additionally connected by narrative voice and/or focalisation. However, this differentiation is important when it comes to approaching the episodic makeup of the short story cycle as a vehicle of life writing, in contrast to the more linear and totalising impression created by the traditional novel. The main difference between autobiographical novels and autobiographical story cycles is that of coherence versus fragmentation. Story sequences will highlight significant moments in the lives of the protagonists. Thereby, they establish an "iconic relationship" between "the episodic quality of life" they render and the "selective nature of memory" (Löschnigg 2011: 111). As Martin Löschnigg further explains, "[t]he open and discontinuous quality of lives as rendered by this particular genre tends towards the contingency that characterizes a life *as lived* rather than towards the structural coherence of life as narrativized in conventional forms" (2011: 110). Gerald Lynch (2001: 22), too, acknowledges the distinctive aesthetic of the short story cycle, describing it metaphorically as the

> world and life seen by stroboscope, held still momentarily, strangely fragmented into new arrangements, moving unfamiliarly in the minds of readers accustomed to the spatial and temporal panorama of novels. That steady beam, itself an illusion of novelistic codes, is broken up in storified autobiographical fiction.

Case Study: Storified Autobiographical Fiction

Alice Munro (1931–) has exploited the aesthetic potential of "storified" lives in three of her publications: in *Lives of Girls and Women*, in *Who Do You Think You Are?* (1978) (published as *The Beggar Maid* in the U.S.), where Rose's perspective is refracted using third-person narration, and in *The View from Castle Rock* (2006). In the latter volume, the author uses the short story cycle for an innovative mix of family chronicle and autobiographical writing, creating a "heritage narrative" that crosses "the borders between history, personal memoir and fiction" (Howells 2007: 166).

The eight chronologically arranged stories in *Lives of Girls and Women* relate the development of Del Jordan from childhood to young adulthood, concluding with her being on the threshold of becoming a writer. While the book can be described as a *Bildungsroman* with regard to its content, its structure runs counter to the linear chronology of conventional autobiographical writing. Instead, the narrative focuses on significant experiences and transitional moments in Del's early life in rural Ontario, these being further accentuated by significant gaps in time between the individual stories. Thus, "Age of Faith" focuses on Del's troubled search for religion, while "Baptizing" renders her first experiences with boys; the "brainy" but inhibited Jerry Storey is followed by Garnet French, whose sex appeal ignites her physical passion – an infatuation that almost leads her to surrender to conventional expectations regarding women. When Garnet tries to forcefully baptise her in the Wawanash River, Del is amazed "that anybody could have made such a mistake, to think he had real power over me" (264) and abruptly breaks up their relationship – feeling "free" and "not free", "relieved" and "desolate" (267) at the same time. The Wawanash River, in fact, is a central unifying element, full of suggestive meaning, appearing already in the first sentence of the initial story "Flats Road" and in almost all the other stories. It is also in this river that Miss Farris, Del's former teacher, and Marion Sherriff, her former schoolmate, drown themselves.

Gender roles and Del's increasingly critical awareness of them define the whole narrative. In "Princess Ida", for example, Del's mother Ada is shown to stand for reason, pragmatism and a cognitive approach to the world – features in a woman that make her an outsider in small-town Jubilee but, at the same time, an important role model for her daughter, albeit approached with caution by Del. In the title story, Ada lectures her daughter to use her brains:

> "There is change coming I think in the lives of girls and women. Yes. But it is up to us to make it come. All women have had up till now has been their connection with men. All we have had. No more lives of our own, really, than domestic animals". (195)

At this point, Del cannot yet fully fathom the essence of her mother's advice and sees it as just another instance of the conviction that "being female made you damageable" (195). However, in the course of "Baptizing" and, in particular, when she realises what her friend Naomi and the other girls at the creamery office where Naomi works regard as a "normal" and desirable life for a woman, she knows that this is not for her. Like Rose in *Who Do You Think You Are?* and, in fact, like a number of Munro's female characters, she rejects an either-or. She neither sees herself as able to put up with the feminine masquerade that is expected of girls and women nor wants to be excluded from love, passion, and romance; she wants to be a woman *and* to be recognised as an intellectual and artist. This vision in favour of a "this *and* the other" appears in a great number of configurations in Munro's work; it is central to her undogmatic feminism (Löschnigg 2016: 60).

The recognition of reality as double or multiple is also at the core of Del's development into an artist, another recurring element in this cycle. Del's emergence as a writer who has a novel worked out in her mind in the concluding story, "Epilogue: The Photographer", is already anticipated in the preceding stories. Thus, it appears, for example, in "Heirs of the Living Body" where, after her Uncle Craig's death, she is bequeathed his manuscript of an exhaustive history of Wawanash County. As the girl feels uncomfortable putting it "back with the things [she] had written", it becomes evident that she has already authored a "few poems and bits of a novel" (69). References to Del's belief in the power of the imagination can also be found in "Changes and Ceremonies", where the narrator muses in retrospect, "I was happy in the library. Walls of printed pages, evidence of so many created worlds" (131). In fact, with each story, material which will eventually be transformed into art accumulates – be it actual encounters, experiences, observations, or confrontations with texts and stories of all kinds, which the burgeoning writer absorbs like a sponge.

Strongly metafictional, the final story provides glimpses into Del's artistic "laboratory", reflecting on how the author transforms her experiences into fiction. Regarding the Sherriff family, whose "share of Tragedy" (269) has attracted her attention as a writer, the narrator meticulously recounts how she has moulded facts to make them fit her story: "In my novel I had got rid of the elder brother, the alcoholic; three tragic destinies were too much even for a book, and certainly more than I could handle" (271f). For the novel Del has devised in her head, she "had changed Jubilee, too" (274), populating it with eccentrics and using hyperbolic language to transform it into the derelict setting, incessantly plagued by "brutal heat" (274), which would fit her version of Ontario Gothic. Revisiting Jubilee, the ordinariness of Bobby Sherriff and the Sherriff's house to which Bobby invites her for cake and lemonade make her realise that "some damage had been done" to her novel. "From now on", as Margaret Atwood (2016: 113) comments on this decisive point in Del's life, "her work will be to find out how to combine the creation of fiction with the solidity of 'reality' that does justice to both". Del must revise her approach to "reality" (278) as she recognises the danger also implied in the artist's absolute command of her "material" – a danger that is also expressed through the sinister Photographer in her novel. At the end of the book, we thus find the narrator at a threshold concerning her artistic awareness, while it is suggested, at the same time, that the book we have just finished is her revised version of imaginatively revisiting Jubilee.

In contradiction to Atwood, who keeps referring to *Lives* as a novel and to the eight stories as chapters, I shall stick to my view that this work reveals the characteristics of a short story cycle. All the pieces can be appreciated as autonomous, aesthetically satisfying stories in their own right, a fact that is confirmed by their individual appearance in many anthologies. When the book is understood as self-referential, as is strongly suggested by the concluding story, it makes sense to read the stories as Del's successful revision of her aborted first mental draft of a novel. As it were, the book thus stages the rejection of the linear, unified novel structure in favour of fragmentation and the mirroring of memory that the linked-stories format suggests. At the same time, this makes *Lives* a self-begetting narrative, that is, a story, usually in the first-person, that follows the protagonist to the point where she is about to compose the text we have just read, thus "project[ing] the illusion of art creating itself" (Kellman 1976: 1245).

The concluding "Epilogue" is self-referential also with regard to Munro's own way of transforming "reality", evident in particular from Del's proleptic statement about her hometown: "It did not occur to me then that one day I would be so greedy for Jubilee" (280). Like Del, Munro has again and again imaginatively revisited Huron County in rural Southwestern Ontario, which is not only her personal but also her artistic world (Staines 2016b: 7). Del's recognition of the ambiguity and/or multiplicity of reality, of all things that were "dull, simple, amazing, and unfathomable" at the same time, like "deep caves paved with kitchen linoleum" (280), leads her to a new concept of art: "for what I wanted was every last thing, every layer of speech and thought, stroke of light on bark or walls, every smell, pothole, pain, crack, delusion, held still and held together – radiant everlasting" (280). This is exactly what Alice Munro herself has achieved so admirably and in a unique manner in her stories ranging from the 1950s to her 2012 farewell as a writer, *Dear Life*.

Unifying Elements

- Narrative voice: in all eight stories, Del Jordan functions as a first-person narrator.
- Place: Huron County, Jubilee, the Wawanash River.

***Lives* as a Portrait of the Artist as a Young Woman**

- Each of the stories foregrounds Del's development towards being a writer – through references to texts she encounters and consumes, as well as through explicit comments on her creative activities.

***Lives* as a Self-Begetting Short Story Cycle**

- As Del has discarded the flawed Gothic novel stored in her mind and achieved a more complex understanding of the relationship between fact and fiction, the book *Lives of Girls and Women* can be read as her successfully revised attempt at capturing the essence of her hometown and its people.

Self-referential Aspects

- The concluding story, in particular, can be understood as a comment on Munro's own art of writing and unique mode of using her "material".

The life cycle in Canada is very much alive. Since Munro's and Laurence's publications, the short story cycle has proliferated in Canadian writing and has remained a prominent genre until today. Also focusing on women, Edna Alford's *A Sleep Full of Dreams* (1981) and Sandra Birdsell's *Night Travellers* (1982) and *Ladies of the House* (1984) have repeatedly been compared to Laurence's and Munro's cycles; however, their stories are connected mainly through place and community, not the consistent narrative voice and/or focalisation that characterises life cycles. Even though in Alford's book, the nurse Arla appears in most of the stories, the strongest composite effect is created by place – a dreary nursing home for elderly and terminally ill women in Calgary. The same applies to the two collections by Birdsell, later combined under the title *Agassiz Stories* (1987), in which the individual pieces are linked by the setting (the fictive Manitoban town of Agassiz) and the cast of characters (the Lafrenière family). One collection from the 1980s that *does* continue the life cycle pattern is Isabel Huggan's *The Elizabeth Stories* (1984). Once again, there is a sequence of eight stories. These portray the early years of Elizabeth Kessler in Garten, a fictive small town in Ontario like Munro's Jubilee or Hanratty (in *Who Do You Think You Are?*). Another feature that Huggan's cycle shares with Munro's *Lives* is the way in which both combine the impression of experiential immediacy with the insight of the mature narrating self.

Numerous life cycles have followed since the 1990s, expanding the boundaries of this genre. Examples are Connnie Barnes Rose's *Getting Out of Town* (1997), Frances Itani's *Leaning Leaning Over Water* (1998), and Margaret Atwood's *Moral Disorder* (2006), her most strongly autobiographical book to date. Urban settings are taken up in Linda Svendsen's *Marine Life* (1992) and Debbie Howlett's *We Could Stay Here All Night* (1999). Exploring the aesthetic potential of linked stories for fictional life-writing is also frequent in works by recent immigrants to Canada, as Makeda Silvera's *Remembering G* (1991) and David Bezmozgis's *Natasha and Other Stories* (2004) testify (see also Chapter 9). In Shyam Selvadurai's *Funny Boy* (1994) and Téa Mutonji's *Shut Up You're Pretty* (2019), storified life-writing is used expressively for rendering the respective first-person narrators' sexual and cultural liminality (see also Chapter 7). Regarding migration narratives, it is, above all, the generic variant of the polyvocal short story cycle that authors have used to great effect – with Rohinton Mistry's *Tales from Firozsha Baag* (1987), M.G. Vassanji's *Uhuru Street* (1990), and Rachna Mara's *Of Customs and Excise* (1991) serving as memorable examples (see also Chapter 9).

Works Cited

Primary Works

Blaise, Clark (1974 [1973]). *A North American Education: A Book of Short Fiction*. Don Mills, ON: PaperJacks.
Blaise, Clark (2001 [1992]). "Meditations on Starch". In: George Bowering, ed. *And Other Stories*. Vancouver: Talonbooks. 61–75.
Gallant, Mavis (2001 [1981]. *Home Truths*. Toronto: McClelland & Stewart.
Hodgins, Jack (1977 [1976]). *Spit Delaney's Island*. Toronto: Macmillan.
Hodgins, Jack (2004). *Damage Done by the Storm*. Toronto: McClelland & Stewart.
Hood, Hugh (1966 [1962]). "Flying a Red Kite". In: Giose Rimanelli and Roberto Ruberto, eds. *Modern Canadian Stories*. Toronto: Ryerson Press. 302–313.
MacLeod, Alistair (2002 [2000]). *Island. Collected Stories*. London: Vintage.
Metcalf, John (1982 [1975]). "Gentle as Flowers Make the Stones". In: John Metcalf, ed. *Making It New: Contemporary Canadian Stories*. Toronto: Methuen. 139–158.
Munro, Alice (1994 [1971]). *Lives of Girls and Women*. London: Bloomsbury.
Smith, Ray (2006 [1969]). *Cape Breton is the Thought-Control Centre of Canada*. Windsor: Biblioasis.

Secondary Works

Atwood, Margaret (2016). "Lives of Girls and Women: A Portrait of the Artist as a Young Woman". In: David Staines, ed. *The Cambridge Companion to Alice Munro*. Cambridge: Cambridge University Press. 96–115.

Besner, Neil K. (1988). *The Light of Imagination: Mavis Gallant's Fiction*. Vancouver: University of British Columbia Press.

Bölling, Gordon (2007). "The Canadian Writer as Expatriate: Norman Levine, 'We All Begin in a Little Magazine' (1972)". In: Nischik 2007a. 271–281.

Dvorak, Marta (2002). "Mavis Gallant's Fiction: Taking the Rhetorical Measure of the Turning Point". In: Nicole Cote and Peter Sabor, eds. *Varieties of Exile: New Essays on Gallant*. New York: Peter Lang. 63–74.

Gadpaille, Michelle (1988). *The Canadian Short Story*. Oxford: Oxford University Press.

Gallant, Mavis (1982 [1981]). "Introduction". In: Mavis Gallant, ed. *Home Truths: Selected Canadian Stories*. Toronto Macmillan. xi–xxii.

Garebian, Keith (1985). "In the End, a Beginning: The Montreal Story Tellers". In: J.R. (Tim) Struthers, ed. *The Montreal Story Tellers. Memoirs, Photographs, Critical, Essays*. Montreal: Véhicule Press. 188–213.

Gibson, Douglas (2014 [2011]). *Stories About Storytellers*. Toronto: ECW Press.

Guilford, Irene (2001). "Introduction". In: Irene Guilford, ed. *Alistair MacLeod: Essays on His Works*. Toronto: Guernica. 7–10.

Gunnars, Kristjana (1989). "'Voyage on a Dark Ocean': Interview with W.D. Valgardson". *The Icelandic Canadian Magazine* (Spring): 14–19.

Hancock, Geoff (1987). "Jack Hodgins". In: *Canadian Writers at Work: Interviews with Geoff Hancock*. Toronto: Oxford University Press. 51–78.

Hodd, Thomas (2008). "'Shoring Against Our Ruin': Sheldon Currie, Alistair MacLeod, and the Heritage Preservation Narrative". *Studies in Canadian Literature/Études en littérature Canadienne* 33.2: 191–209.

Howells, Coral Ann (1992). "'Parables of Our Time': Canadian Women's Transcultural Fictions". *Australian Canadian Studies* 23: 17–30.

Howells, Carol Ann (2007). "Writing Family History: Review of *The View from Castle Rock* by Alice Munro". *Canadian Literature* 195 (Winter): 166–168.

Keefer, Janice Kulyk (1989). *Reading Mavis Gallant*. Toronto, New York and Oxford: Oxford University Press.

Keith, William (1981). "'Jack Hodgins' Island World': Review of *The Barclay Family Theatre*". *The Canadian Forum* (September–October): 30–31.

Kellman, Steven G. (1976). "The Fiction of Self-Begetting". *Comparative Literature* 91.6: 1243–1256.

Kruk, Laurie (2016). *Double-Voicing the Canadian Short Story*. Ottawa: University of Ottawa Press.

Löschnigg, Maria (2014). *The Contemporary Canadian Short Story in English: Continuity and Change*. Trier: WVT.

Löschnigg, Maria (2016). "'Oranges and Apples': Alice Munro's Undogmatic Feminism". In: Staines 2016a. 60–78.

Löschnigg, Martin (2011). "Short Story Cycles as Media of Life Writing in Contemporary Canadian Literature". In: Sabine Coelsch-Foisner, ed. *From the Cradle to the Grave: Life-Course Models in Literary Genres*. Heidelberg: Winter. 107–117.

Lynch, Gerald (2001). *The One and the Many: English-Canadian Short Story Cycles*. Toronto: University of Toronto Press.

MacLeod, Alexander (2016). "The Canadian Short Story in English: Aesthetic Agency, Social Change, and the Shifting Canon". In: Cynthia Sugars, ed. *The Oxford Handbook of Canadian Literature*. New York: Oxford University Press. 426–447.

Mathews, Lawrence (1978–1979). "The Secular and the Sacral: Notes on a New Athens and Three Stories by Hugh Hood". *Essays on Canadian Writing* 13–14: 211–229.

Metcalf, John (1982a). *Kicking Against the Pricks*. Downsview, ON: ECW Press.

Metcalf, John (1982b). "Building Castles". In: John Metcalf, ed. *Making It New: Contemporary Canadian Short Stories*. Toronto: Methuen. 175–180.

Metcalf, John (2018). *The Canadian Short Story*. Windsor: Biblioasis.

Nischik, Reingard M., ed. (2007a). *The Canadian Short Story: Interpretations*. Rochester and New York: Camden House.

Nischik, Reingard M. (2007b). "Canadian Artist Stories: John Metcalf's 'The Strange Aberration of Mr Ken Smythe' (1973)". In: Nischik 2007a. 283–297.

Nischik, Reingard M. (2017). *The English Short Story in Canada: From the Dawn of Modernism to the 2013 Nobel Prize*. Jefferson: McFarland & Company.

Sandrock, Kirsten (2009). "Scottish Territories and Canadian Identity – Regional Aspects in the Literature of Alistair MacLeod". In: Petra Rüdiger and Konrad Gross, eds. *Translations of Cultures*. Amsterdam and New York: Rodopi. 169–182.

Smith, Ray (2006). "The Age of Innocence". In: Ray Smith, ed. *Cape Breton Is the Thought-Control Centre of Canada*. Windsor: Biblioasis. 1–34.

Staines, David, ed. (2016a). *The Cambridge Companion to Alice Munro*. Cambridge: Cambridge University Press.

Staines, David (2016b). "From Wingham to Clinton: Alice Munro in Her Canadian Context". In: Staines 2016a. 7–25.

Stephens, Donald (1969). "The Writing of the Decade: The Short Story in English". *Canadian Literature* 41: 126–130.

Thacker, Robert (2004). "Short Fiction". In: Eva-Marie Kröller, ed. *The Cambridge Companion to Canadian Literature*. Cambridge: Cambridge University Press. 177–193.

Whalen, Terry (2002). "Montreal Story Tellers Fiction Performance Group". In: William H. New, ed. *Encyclopedia of Literature in Canada*. Toronto, Buffalo and London: University of Toronto Press. 751–752.

Zacharasiewicz, Waldemar (1986). "The Development of Jack Hodgins: Narrative Art in His Short Fiction". In: Franz K. Stanzel and Waldemar Zacharasiewicz, eds. *Encounters and Explorations: Canadian Writers and European Critics*. Würzburg: Königshausen and Neumann. 94–109.

Suggestions for Further Reading

Clement, Lesley D. (2000). *Learning to Look: A Visual Response to Mavis Gallant's Fiction*. Montreal and Kingston: McGill-Queen's University Press.

Creelman, David (2003). *Setting in the East: Maritime Realist Fiction*. Montreal: McGill-Queen's University Press.

Lecker, Robert (1988). *The Fictions of Clark Blaise*. Toronto: ECW Press.

New, William H. (2009). "The Short Story". In: Coral Ann Howells and Eva-Maria Kröller, eds. *The Cambridge History of Canadian Literature*. 381–401.

Struthers, J.R. (Tim), ed. (1985). *The Montreal Story Tellers: Memoirs, Photographs, Critical, Essays*. Montreal: Véhicule Press.

Wyile, Herb (2011). *Anne of Tim Hortons: Globalization and the Reshaping of Atlantic-Canadian Literature*. Waterloo, ON: Wilfrid Laurier University Press.

Part 2

The Canadian Short Story from the Mid-1980s to the Present

5 Metafiction and "Unnatural" Narrative Voices

Although much criticism has emphasised the relative conventionality of Canadian short fiction and although it cannot be denied that many contemporary stories are still indebted to realist and modernist traditions, this chapter (as well as the following one) will demonstrate that the Canadian short story from the mid-1980s onwards *does* display a wide spectrum of experimental modes and styles. For instance, several authors have toyed with metafiction and the disruption of aesthetic illusion. Their experiments, which are often ludic in nature, may sometimes be seen as continuing postmodernist practices; however, they also reveal efforts by contemporary writers to unsettle conventional expectations on the part of their readers.

For this purpose, intriguing effects have been produced, for instance, by visual experiments that complement, complexify, challenge, or contrast the verbal text. Another tendency that can be observed is that of flash fiction. Margaret Atwood, in particular, has repeatedly toyed with this concentrated form and leveraged it to produce metafictional effects. The recent penchant for micro-stories that straddle the boundaries between short fiction and poetry "may well reflect", as Russell Smith (2018: 13) has observed, "habits of communication that come from writing for social media and websites". Besides Atwood, examples are Douglas Glover's ten micro-stories included in *Savage Love* (2013), Patrick Roscoe's "The Cage" (*The Truth About Love*, 2001), Kathy Page's "Lak-ha" (*Paradise & Elsewhere*, 2014), or Reg Johanson's epistolary "A Titan Bearing Many a Legitimate Grievance" (*Best Canadian Stories 2018*). With three collections of flash fiction, including *The Kingdom of Heaven: 88 Palm-of-the-Hand Stories* (1996), *Kilter: 55 Fictions* (2003, shortlisted for the Giller Prize), and *the end of me* (2020), John Gould seems to have adopted this variant as his favourite form of short fiction. Using the example of *Kilter*, Neta Gordon (2010) convincingly demonstrates that the choice of form cannot be separated from the content. "The shortness of Gould's stories", as Gordon explains, "gives shape to Kilter's exploration of how the present age produces various kinds of doubt and fear: doubt about the possibility of metaphysical and/or epistemological resolution; fear associated with problems of misinterpretation or miscommunication; and a sense of loss regarding the failure of explanatory models, such as systems of

DOI: 10.4324/9781003142683-8

justice or faith" (2010 online: 2f). Examples of metafiction, visual experiments and flash fiction will be dealt with in Section 5.1.

Fascinating aesthetic effects have also been achieved using you-narration, a form which tends to destabilise ontological boundaries and to create the impression of directly inviting the reader into the text. Blurring the narrator/protagonist/addressee's identity and distancing the "you" from their own self, the very "essence" of second-person narration "is to eschew a fixed essence" (Richardson 2006: 19). We-narration, too, has been taken up by a considerable number of writers experimenting with the mediation of collective consciousness and agency. The use of these two intriguing "unnatural" narrative forms will be further elaborated in Section 5.2.

While the following examples of experimental Canadian short fiction are by no means exhaustive, they *do* shed light on representative authors and forms. Regarding "unnatural" perspectives one could, of course, further mention stories which feature "impossible" narrators, such as a dead man in Lee Maracle's "Sojourner's Truth" (*Sojourner's Truth*, 1990). Other examples, in this context, are Zsuzsi Gartner's "The Second Coming of the Plants", which gives voice to the flora, or Tom Thor Buchanan's "A Dozen Stomachs" (*Best Canadian Stories* 2018), which is told from the point of view of a stomach. Another interesting, innovative form that should at least be mentioned here but will receive ample attention in Chapter 8 is the "voice piece". Having been introduced by Indigenous writers, these voice pieces – or interfusional stories (King 1990: 13) – are characterised by a blending of oral traditions and print culture.

5.1. Metafictional Experiments

Metafiction is fiction that refers to itself by engaging in reflections on its own creative process or fictionality. Metafictional elements thus draw attention to a literary work's constructedness and its status as an artefact. The functions of metafictional devices are manifold; frequently breaking the aesthetic illusion, they may undermine the reader's immersion in the story, eliciting instead an awareness of the nature of literary composition and of the conventionality of literary techniques. Such devices, which lead to a distancing of the reader from the story, may also have parodistic effects and/or function as an intellectual stimulus for critical engagements with fiction, literature, and/or art in general (meta-reference). Metafictional effects may also be engendered by instances of metalepsis, that is, the transgression of ontological boundaries. Metatextual strategies like (deconstructive) references to language, literary form, and the mechanisms of storytelling are not an invention of postmodernism; however, they made a particularly strong appearance during the heyday of literary postmodernism in the 1960s and '70s.

Regarding the Canadian short story in English, metafictional forms have existed from the mid-20th century onwards and have continued to exist alongside their less self-conscious "siblings" right into the 21st century.

Authors who have repeatedly worked with metafictional techniques are, for example, Audrey Thomas, Carol Shields, Leon Rooke, Dave Godfrey, Matt Cohen, Keath Fraser, Lisa Moore, Cynthia Flood, David Arnason, Anosh Irani, Thomas King, André Alexis, Douglas Glover, and above all, George Bowering, Margaret Atwood, Diane Schoemperlen, and Lynn Coady. In the following, selected authors and stories will be discussed that provide memorable illustrations of the array of metafictional techniques.

The cosmopolitan Audrey Thomas (1935–) has experimented with metafictional strategies in several of her stories. Thus, "Initram" (*Two in the Bush*, 1981) begins with "Writers are terrible liars" (185). The story, whose title is an anagram of "martini", thematises the necessity of addressees. While, on one level, it features two women-writers who need each other as an audience for the narratives of their breakups with their partners, it is also a self-referential story in the sense of a self-begetting one: at the end, the first-person narrator discloses to her friend that she "was thinking of writing a story about her" (203) and makes her pick a name for her fictional persona. The writer-friend – perhaps a fictionalised Alice Munro? – chooses "Lydia" as the name of her storified self, and this is what the friend's name is in the story we have read.

Leon Rooke (1934–), too, has repeatedly toyed with metafictional devices, as in "Want to Play House" (1992) or "The Heart Must from Its Breaking" (1991), both included in *Painting the Dog* (2001). "Art" (1992; *Painting the Dog*) is particularly fascinating with regard to the relationship between fiction and reality. In this surrealist story, the characters, a married couple, are painted as part of an artwork and "die" when the wife spills her drink, thus wetting the paint. The story ends upon a metalepsis that has the narrator bleeding to death, reflecting on the people who would come in and decide to throw out the painting in which "the house, the cow etc. have all bled together. You can't recognize the woman any more, or see that this once was a bed and . . . well it's all a big puddle except these flowers" (120). Fictive characters are usually understood as being contained within the ontological boundaries of a work of art. Stepping out of the frame and onto a different diegetic level, the characters in "Art" are given agency, and their status as painted figures is relativised. In turn, this makes the reader empathise with the couple as if they were real, branding the way in which the art dealers commodify the paintings as a violation. At the same time, the story can be read as a comment on impressionistic writing styles, drawing attention to the form and texture of experimental writing in general.

Interesting metafictional experiments can also be found in John Gould's (1959–) collection of flash fiction *the end of me* (2020). Thus, in "Pulse", the focaliser reflects on his intention of writing a story about a man who wants to record the moment of his death, "not a poem" (89); rather, he "wants to do this with Twitter" (91). In "Squirrel", a boy is preoccupied with a 250-word essay on "What do you believe in?", which he is supposed to write for school and in which he is "supposed to use details" (257). In the end, the story "Squirrel", including the narrator's metatextual reflections, is at the same time his accomplished assignment.

In several of Lynn Coady's (1970–) short stories, the relationship between fact and fiction plays a significant role. Thus, in "Clear Skies" (*Hellgoing*, 2013), Sara, an author whose fame rests mostly on her teenage memoir *Escaping Eden*, insists on reconsidering the distinction between fiction and memoir: "My point is, they're all still going to be *stories*, no matter what category we choose to pit them in – fiction or non" (119). Finding herself to be one of four creative writing instructors at a workshop in the prairies, Sara's reflections disclose how her dramatic "life story" does not feel like her own anymore when she reads from it after many years:

> She read the words like they were someone else's – stumbling, missing key inflections, having to go back and start entire sentences again. The book started at the end of the story – a fairly conventional structure, suggested by the editor – with the night of Sara's escape.
> (134)

On the one hand, the story problematises any clear distinctions between memoir and fiction, indicating how autobiographical writing, too, is shaped by narrative style and structure. On the other hand, it also thematises the desire, on the part of readers, for "real life" stories. Thus, Sara, who has, in the meantime, written and published two novels and a collection of short fiction, is forced to realise that she is still mostly known for her teenage memoir. The organiser of the creative writing "retreat" displays the book and has ordered 20 copies to sell, while there are only "five copies of her second novel, and no copies of her first or her collection of stories" (121f).

The way in which serial characters, especially those in popular TV series, may sometimes become "real" is memorably illustrated in Coady's "The Drain", included in *Best Canadian Stories 2020*. The nameless first-person narrator is a screenwriter who, with her team, is faced with the problem of having to "kill" one of the characters in their show: "Marietta did not fit and the audience needed her to die" ("Drain" 209). What haunts the story, however, is a continuous blurring of the boundaries between Marietta, the character in the show, and Annie, the actress impersonating her:

> I hated her, however. Why did I hate her? Why did *anyone* hate her, was the question? She was good. She wasn't TV-generic. You could call her bland – Annie had a lopsided and bashful smile that recalled a young Renée Zellweger.
>
> I mentally addressed the viewing audience – *Why do you hate her?*
>
> *Because you want me to love her,* the viewing audience replied. *You want it so badly.*
> (213)

The merging of the real woman (Annie) with the character (Marietta) is also what seems to make it more and more difficult for Sara's boss, Liz, to handle the situation and come up with a decision. In the end, being discarded is Liz's fate, too. As she loses her job, her "fading away" is rendered physical through the flushes (the "melting away") which she suffers in the course of her climacteric. However, Liz continues to work on Marietta, keeping her suspended between life and death. When she tells the narrator at the end of the story that "Marietta is still dying" (226), she seems to refer to her own transitional situation.

Three authors who have repeatedly been associated with innovative modes of writing and who have radically challenged aesthetic illusion and reader expectations are Margaret Atwood (1939–), Diane Schoemperlen (1954–), and George Bowering (1935–). Another feature these authors share is their occasional experimentation with visual elements.

Margaret Atwood's meta-critical engagements with writing can be found, above all, in her collections of short short fiction: *Murder in the Dark* (1983), *Good Bones* (1992), *Bones & Murder* (1994; mostly a compilation of the two earlier collections), and *The Tent* (2006). All the short prose pieces in these collections are defined by a genre-transgressing hybridity, oscillating between the short story proper and the prose poem, the essay-fiction and the short short story. A term that best fits all these texts is "flash fiction", which Sharon Rose Wilson (2003: 20f) defines as a "750-word story . . . that can be apprehended in a flash" and, what is more, conveys the implication of surprise.

Because of its suggestion of sudden twists, the term "flash fiction" is particularly appropriate for Atwood's parodic experiments and her "poetics of inversion" – that is, her "technique of undermining conventional thought patterns, attitudes, values, or textual norms by turning them on their heads" (Nischik 2003: 6). Many of Atwood's flash fiction pieces are overtly metanarrative and metafictional, forcing readers to probe their accepted ideas about the distinction between art and life, and how these two may indeed interact. Examples are "Happy Endings", "Murder in the Dark", "There Was Once", "Women's Novels", "The Page" (see *Bones & Murder*), "Life Stories", "Orphan Stories", "Three Novels I Won't Write Soon", and "The Tent" (see *The Tent*).

A particularly interesting text is the dialogic "There Was Once", where a writer's attempt at writing a story is devastated by a merciless critic:

- There was once a poor girl, as beautiful as she was good, who lived with her wicked stepmother in a house in the forest.
- Forest? *Forest* is passé, I mean, I've had it with all this wilderness stuff. It's not a right image of our society, today. Let's have some *urban* for a change.
- There was once a poor girl, as beautiful as she was good, who lived with her wicked stepmother in a house in the suburbs.

- That's better. But I have to seriously query this word *poor*.
- But she was poor!
- Poor is relative. She lived in a house, didn't she?
- Yes. Then socioeconomically speaking, she was not poor.
- . . .
- There was once a middle-class girl, as beautiful as she was good –
- Stop right here. I think we can cut the beautiful, don't you? Women these days have to deal with too many intimidating role models as it is, what with those bimbos in the ads. Can't you make her, well, more average?
- There was once a girl who was a little overweight and whose teeth stuck out, who –
- I don't think it's nice to make fun of people's appearances. Plus, you're encouraging anorexia. (22ff)

First, the impression is created that the story questions and parodies conventional narrative patterns (the fairy tale metonymically standing for such conventions). However, this impression is dismantled until it is no longer the writer but the critical voice itself that becomes the target of the criticism. In the end, not a single word of the fictive writer's first sentence stands the test of verbal and stylistic accuracy, and this leads to the eradication of the text or (implicitly) of literature in general. Thus, while the story, on the one hand, displays how freighted the genre of the fairy tale is with stereotypical images, it can, on the other hand, also be read as a parody of the consequences of obsessive political correctness and its detrimental effects on creative writing.

In many of her flash fiction pieces, Atwood toys with different forms of you-narration, investing the text with a strong appellative quality. In "Happy Endings", for example, the use of the second-person pronoun introduces an interactive element into the story, inviting the reader to participate in the creative act, as it were:

> John and Mary meet.
> What happens next?
> If you want a happy ending, try A.
> (55)

In the story, the reader addressed is offered six different versions of how the story of John and Mary may proceed; however, the outcome is always the same, no matter which choice is made:

> The only authentic ending is the one provided here:
> *John and Mary die. John and Mary die. John and Mary die.*
> (61)

The text foregrounds the difference between the story and discourse levels of narratives, highlighting the importance of how a story is written. Since plots "anyway are just one thing after another, a what and a what and a what" (62), the text ends upon encouraging the addressee to "Now try How and Why" (62). It may also be read as a rejection of the plot- or action-dominated story in favour of narratives that explore motives, modalities, and what lies hidden underneath the succession of events.

As mentioned earlier, Atwood's flash fiction sometimes combines metafictional techniques with visual elements. This is the case, for example, in "The Little Red Hen Tells All" and "Let Us Now Praise Stupid Women" (both in *Bones & Murder*), where the author's own – somewhat cryptic – illustrations both complement and question the highly ironical narratives.

Visual elements play an even more striking role in the works of Diane Schoemperlen, who, in her own words, has "always been fascinated by form and structure, that postmodern thing" (Whetter 1996: 135). In many of her stories, collected in six volumes which stretch from 1986 into the new millennium, she has experimented with literary conventions and techniques and has thus contributed to an ongoing reconsideration of rigid categorisations. After her experiments with "phototextual narratives" (Lucas 1992: 76ff) in *Double Exposures* (1984), Schoemperlen turned to multimodal and genre-bending forms of storytelling in her Booker Prize–winning *Forms of Devotion* (1998), in which all stories are accompanied by prefabricated illustrations – some in their original form and some in the form of collages created by the author.

Of the 11 pieces collected in *Forms of Devotion*, "How to Write a Serious Novel About Love" is the most interesting concerning metafictionality. Like Atwood's "Happy Endings", the story offers several versions of the boy-meets-girl pattern and suggests "John" and "Mary" as names for the protagonists. Another feature that the story shares with Atwood's text is the use of the hypothetical you-form, with its imitation of the user manual and the staging of an interactive engagement between narrator and (implied) reader. Step by step, the story instructs the reader on how to tackle the different components of a narrative text, starting with the naming of the characters:

> Begin with a man and a woman.
> . . .
> First of all, your man and woman will need names. Consider their selection very carefully. *Vinny* and *Ethel* cannot possibly live out the same story as *Alphonse* and *Olivia*. The reader may well have trouble taking seriously the fates of *Mitzi* and *Skip*. Sometimes neutral names are best. After much deliberation, decide to name your characters *John* and *Mary*. Avoid thinking about John the Baptist, Mary Magdalene, Mary Poppins, or the Virgin Mary. . . .
> Describe John.
>
> (93)

Often comically absurd, the instructions and suggestions for naming, character description, setting, and so on all come with illustrations that visualise what the manual describes in words. However, the illustrations (like the one showing what John and Mary might look like) subvert the openness which the "manual" seems to suggest through the very fact that they render concrete the characters' appearance. In addition, the text, too, is characterised by a deceptive double structure: while the narrator keeps suggesting that it is the addressee who decides, the latter is, in fact, denied this creative liberty. Sentences that offer no real choices (like "decide to name your characters *John* and *Mary*", 93) or just absurdities and clichés (e.g. "John has brown hair and brown eyes. John has blond hair and blue eyes. John has black hair and green eyes. John has no hair and no eyes. Pick one", 94) interfere with the act of writing as projected in the story. Schoemperlen's story can thus be read as a parody of the self-help manual it feigns to imitate.

However, this is not the only possible reading. At the end of the story, the narrator predicts the addressee's failure and encourages them to start all over again: "Realize that you will have to write another novel. What else can you do? Begin with a man and a woman" (114). The circularity of the pseudo-manual (instructions for the second attempt will be completely identical to those for the first) could either indicate that being creative cannot really be *learned* or that the way to success is trying again and again. Each attempt will differ from the previous one, as the story suggests: "Realize that you know more about love now than you did when you started to tell the story of John and Mary" (114). However, there is yet another aspect that needs to be considered. Since the second-person mode is quintessentially protean (Richardson 2006: 19), the "you" that is addressed may very well also refer to the narrator (or author) herself, who, somehow addressing herself, reflects playfully on her own writing.

Many of George Bowering's stories are characterised by postmodernist playfulness. Thus, he breaks the aesthetic illusion in his by now almost canonical "A Short Story" (*A Place to Die*, 1983). Other examples are "Staircase Descended" and "Being Audited" (both in *The Rain Barrel*, 1994). In the former, the first-person narrator allows the reader a close-up glimpse into how he transforms the material of his everyday life into a story, repeatedly establishing the illusion of directly involving the reader, whose possible dropping out of the story is a recurring issue: "In fact it is unlikely that you have made it this far. If you have, please sign your initials right here: " (212); or "But you are here, aren't you, you did sign in, didn't you?" (212); or "It is a story, don't you agree?" (214). All the different elements that make up a story are "discussed" with the reader, thus undermining, on the one hand, any emotional immersion while, on the other, enhancing cognitive involvement and sensitising readers to the significance of *how* stories are told, the effects of images, and the choice of words. "Staircase Descended" is a particularly illustrative example of Bowering's aim to create, through his writing, "a shared space that privileges communication and collaboration between writer and reader" (Garrett-Petts 1992: 558).

"Being Audited" again features a writer; it relates the story of how his wife tries to get him to see a tax accountant in order to get a tax rebate. To enjoy the maximum benefit, this involves not only getting officially registered as an "author" but also moving into bigger and bigger houses to create rooms (study, personal library, etc.) that could be written off for tax refunds. The use of the house, however, as we are reminded by the narrator, "is symbolic, either of the house of fiction in Jamesian terms, or as the psyche's image of self in the Freudian sense" (200). Problems arise when the new accountant finds that "George Bowering is not a 'serious writer'" (205). Destabilising the fictional status of his story through the use of his own author-persona, Bowering then offers the reader, in true postmodernist style, two different endings to choose from.

Ludic engagements with the author's own persona have also been adopted by other writers and assume an uncanny effect, for example, in André Alexis's "My Anabasis" (*Despair and Other Stories*, 1994). Here, not only the narrator, living in Ottawa, Ontario, is called André Alexis but also a character he suspects of having had an affair with his wife and whom he visits in Ottawa, New York. On the train, however, he meets another person of this name, which leads to intricate configurations involving all the writer's alter egos.

Case Study: George Bowering, "Discoloured Metal" – Visualising Ambiguity

Regarding visual effects, one of Bowering's most intriguing stories is "Discoloured Metal" (*Rain Barrel and Other Stories*, 1994). In this story, the first-person narrator finds himself on a transatlantic flight, the "empty" space between Canada and Europe being visually rendered through a circular blank in the middle of the page. While in the beginning this blank only blots out a small segment of text, it becomes increasingly larger in the course of the story so that readers are eventually forced to give up trying to reconstruct the missing words and sentences. Rather, they have to put up with the fragments on the margins of the page and, eventually, with two completely empty pages. At this point, however, the reduction of text and meaning is reversed as, page by page, the text comes back, first in small circles and eventually as a full page.

While the visual elements in this story are not explicitly metafictional, they can nonetheless be seen as an iconic representation of Wolfgang Iser's *Leerstellen* – that is, the gaps of meaning in a literary text meant to be filled by the reader. Rendering concrete the ambiguity of literature, the expanding empty circles and their subsequent filling up invite several interpretations indeed. Thus, they may, first, stand for the "loss" and "gain" of time which affect the traveller between different time zones. On the eastward trip, time is blotted out and restored on the return trip. This interpretation is further encouraged by the circular shape of the erased text, which evokes the shape of the globe.

Second, the gradual vanishing and coming back of text may visualise the narrator's memory gap – his inability to make sense of "the very bad thing in the middle, which we had eventually to stop discussing" (92), which may refer to a plane accident or another moment of crisis during the flight. Following this reading, one will find a number of references to safety measures: "As a result, any commercial plane which conforms to the official criterion of strength and has been certified by the airworthiness authorities of the government can, *if operated sensibly*, carry passengers with complete safety" (92, my emphasis). The conditional "if operated sensibly", followed by the (ironic?) remark "[a]nd everybody remembers to do everything. Remembers for life" (92), is of particular significance here. If one interprets the holes in the text and the blank pages as visual manifestations of gaps in the narrator's memory, the previous statement (about everybody remembering everything) is made invalid, and with it, the assertions about the complete safety of modern aeroplanes. In this context, also the narrator's reflections on the (in)appropriateness of the word "air terminal" ("What a word", 92) are of significance and further support the version of an accident.

Third, the gradual dis- and reappearance of language could also be read as a reflection of the precarious hyphenated status of the German-Canadian passengers on board. The way the narrator describes these passengers highlights the notion of their being at odds with time and place. Thus, an old man across the aisle "wore round Kafka eyeglasses, but he was unaware of the Kafka-book in the blue and white flight bag in front of his neighbour's feet", and the field glasses "hanging from his neck" were "from World War One" (93). Not understanding any English, he is not aware that he is not supposed to use his tape recorder, so he "merrily" records "the roar and voices of his first ascent in this winged silver. Up and away, away" (93). On yet another level, the vanishing words and their gradual reemergence could also be seen to visualise the protagonist's feelings of alienation as the plane tears him away from his home and his wife. Such a reading could be supported by the fact that the full restoration of the printed page coincides with their reunion. On a more concrete level, the round shape of missing text could also represent the impaired vision due to the jet engine blotting out the protagonist's view – literally and, maybe, also metaphorically.

Last but not least, the lines from W.H. Auden and Louis MacNeice's *Letters from Island* (1937) ("So we have come/As trippers North", 96) will induce the "educated" reader to restore the lost text with the subsequent lines from their poetic travelogue. In addition, this intertextual reference may also open up new venues for speculations about "the very bad thing in the middle". However, the point here is not to decipher the "real" meaning and thus to demystify the story. Rather, the story is a celebration of ambiguity which the author foregrounds, in an idiosyncratic manner, through the conspicuous absence of text. "The ambiguity stands", John Moss (1989: online) says about Bowering's concept of storytelling, and continues that "[t]his is what his fiction says: the barriers between life and art must fall; let's meet in the text for a while, free among words to become ourselves". Thus, the text's iconic representation of *Leerstellen* foregrounds the importance of ambiguity as an essential feature of literature.

Semantic implications of the textual gaps:

- Iconic representation of ambiguity and of *Leerstellen* – gaps of meaning which invite and necessitate the collaboration of the reader
- Visualisation of the narrator's possible memory gap and/or a traumatic event that happened on the transatlantic flight
- Visual reference to the loss and gain between time zones – evoked through the circular shape of the textual gap and its restoration (shape of the globe)
- Visual image denoting the liminal, hyphenated situation of German-Canadian passengers on board
- Visual reference to the protagonist's feeling of alienation.
- Graphic representation of the narrator's impaired view – vista blotted out by the jet engine (literally and metaphorically)
- Intertextual reference as an additional semantic option for filling the gap.
- Creation of a semantic space shared between writer and reader, which invites the reader into the text and highlights the importance of textual openness and ambiguity.

5.2. Unusual Narrative Voices

One of the most fascinating narrative voices is the you-form. As demonstrated in the previous section, the use of the second-person pronoun has been employed by a number of authors to create metafictional effects and to foreground the underlying mechanisms of storytelling. In these cases, the second-person pronoun usually designates an addressee who is not, at the same time, also the narrator. Rather, the illusion is created that extratextual readers themselves are addressed and drawn into the story. While these variants of you-narration result in metalepses, authors have also used the second-person form to consistently address a character who is placed on the same diegetic level as the narrator.

Thus, in Mark Anthony Jarman's (1955–) dystopian story "In Terminal Three (More Fun in the New World with the Symbionese Liberation Army)" (*My White Planet*, 2008), the "you" refers to a collective of passengers commanded by an authoritarian voice to board an aircraft and told: "You travel all the time, yet you go nowhere. Move over the madder globe, fly up, up and away, but you can't escape the red interior of the skull that houses you" (202). The uncanny atmosphere that increasingly builds up in the story is, to a considerable extent, due to the consistent addressing of the unspecified group of passengers, implying the inclusion of the readers themselves. Jarman, in general, has introduced new facets of style to the Canadian short story. Referring to the author's earlier collections, *New Orleans Is Sinking* (1998) and *19 Knives* (2000), W.H. New describes this style as follows: "language bursts in play, voice taking over from print as sentences rush forward as obsessively as characters do" (2009: 399).

Another author who has experimented with this mode is Patrick Roscoe (1967–). Both "The Truth About Love" and "Touching Darkness" (*The Truth About Love*, 2001) address gay sexuality and love *in extremis*, and in both cases, the story is addressed to the narrator's lover. The former can be read as a manifesto of unconditional love and an investigation of the destructive intersection of Eros and Thanatos. At the same time, the interior monologue directed to the lover also adopts the function of a requiem – a goodbye note for someone who lives on the edge, who is, in fact, a serial killer and who might be caught any minute. If "The Truth About Love" allows glimpses into the abyss of human desire, this is even more unsettling in "Touching Darkness". In this extremely disturbing story, both men – narrator and addressee – are haunted by the trauma of child abuse, an experience which has seeped into body and mind and which surfaces again after many years. Having enjoyed 12 years of emotional and sexual happiness and satisfaction, the narrator's lover suddenly withdraws into the spare room, avoiding light and rejecting clothes and eventually also food. At the same time, he desires the narrator to torture and abuse him until, after a period of three years, he is reduced to a bundle of blood, bones, and excrement and literally disintegrates. In the course of the story, this destructive masochistic drive is more and more related to the lover's past when, as a boy, he was locked in a dark room, neglected and abused. At the same time, the employed narrative voice radically complexifies the explicitly narrated and implicitly suggested horror. It thus raises the question, is the addressed lover possibly an alter ego of the narrator himself? Or is Billy, the orphaned boy who lives nearby and mysteriously dies, an incarnation of the lover? Or has Billy been sexually abused by the narrator and/or the lover? Due to his masterly command of the you-address and the shockingly graphic voice of his narrators, Roscoe provides unsparing and thought-provoking portraits of the depths of human nature.

That you-narration is a congenial form for the representation of states of crisis is evident, in particular, in stories that feature what Brian Richardson (2006: 19ff) has termed the "standard type of second-person narration" or, in Monika Fludernik's (1994: 289) terminology, "second-person fiction proper". Here, the "you" not only designates the narratee and/or character but also the narrator. As Richardson (2006: 36) has pointed out, this variant of second-person narration is "admirably suited to express the unstable nature and intersubjective constitution of the self". It is this function in particular which Canadian authors of short fiction have successfully employed for narratives of crisis. The you-narrators in their second-person stories create the impression of being at a distance from their own self. At the same time, the "you" implants the personal and subjective into the universal since the second-person pronoun also tends to carry the meaning of the generic "one". In addition, the second-person pronoun always suggests a certain inclusive appeal to the reader.

Examples of such uses of the second-person form for narratives of crisis are manifold. Margaret Atwood has employed it for a number of her pieces of eco-fiction (see also Chapter 10), such as "The Tent" or "Tree Baby" (*The Tent*, 2006). Other noteworthy authors who have experimented with the standard type of the you-form in dazzling ways are Lynn Coady, Elyse Gasco (1967–), and Steven Heighton (1961–2022).

Lynn Coady has used standard you-narration to capture her narrator-protagonists' identity crisis in two coming-of-age stories, "Ice Cream Man" and "Batter My Heart" (*Play the Monster Blind*, 2000). In the former, the young protagonist struggles to come to terms with an inefficient father and a mother who was ostracised because she did not conform to their town's norms and who is now dead. The story poignantly foregrounds the townsfolk's hypocrisy and their equation of cleanliness and outward piety with a decent life. The narrator's mother, cynically referred to as "Herself" behind her back, may have been an eccentric, but she nonetheless constituted a stabilising presence for the girl. Now that she is dead, things start to fall apart, and the teenage girl realises more and more the sham of religiously tinged surfaces. Thus, being sent to religion classes by her father, she reflects: "You come in late, and all the worst kids are there. The kids whose parents are the most strict about prayer and chastity – they automatically become the ones who smoke and drink and curse. You'd think people would see this connection" (46). The narrator mourns her mother quietly, untangling the mother's "outrageously" long hair from the button of her sweater or using her hairbrush. Standing in the bathroom, she muses: "You could hypnotize yourself if you think too long about the drain of the bathtub, of how much of Herself remains clogged down there" (44). It is never explicitly said, yet strongly suggested that Herself died in the bathtub – during one of the many long baths she "scandalously" used to take. Thus, the daughter's decision, at the end of the story, to take a bath *herself* strikes an alarming note, confirmed by the story's final line: "And for God's sake, it's great, once you get in there" (47). In the context of the story, this expression of pleasure must be approached with caution. Having been agonisingly confused by contradicting impressions and demands, the narrator appears alienated from her own self – a state so convincingly mediated through the second-person voice that mutes, diffuses, and finally collapses subjectivity (Richardson 2006: 26). Now, indulging in a bath herself, she finally solves the problem through merging with Herself. Considering her mother's fate, however, it is difficult to regard this as a happy ending. In "Batter My Heart", this split between seemingly irreconcilable selves is again memorably rendered through you-narration. The story provides an internal view of how the narrator tries to balance her self-image of being a "walking sin" (55) with her endeavours to at least *appear* pious.

Another writer who has experimented with you-narration is Elyse Gasco, whose *Can You Wave Bye Bye, Baby* (1999) features four stories (out of seven) in this form. The author uses this "slippery" technique for her profound explorations of motherhood and her mediation of the psychological processes which accompany the experience of maternity from the perspective of the mother (or prospective mother) as well as from that of the (abandoned) daughter. In "You Have the Body", for example, the protagonist experiments with different selves:

> You imagine that you are the body of the one [her biological mother] who could not keep you. . . . At other times, you are your mother [referring to her adoptive mother], and when no one is looking, you ease your fingers into yourself, looking for terrible blood.
>
> (*Can You Wave* 29)

At other times, the "you" also refers to the narrator's unborn baby: "Who knows what you are making in there, what strange materials you are actually made of" (37). Through this blurring of the boundaries between self and other, the you-form is a congenial vehicle for rendering the young mother's ambivalent feelings concerning her identity, which she senses as being connected in a complex way to her two mothers as well as to her unborn child. At the same time, referring to herself in the second person also conveys a certain distance, on the part of the narrator, from her own self – a distance which, in this case, facilitates self-reflection.

One of the most intriguing stories that use you-narration to depict a character's split personality is Steven Heighton's "OutTrip". Together with "Swallow", it is one of two second-person stories in *The Dead Are More Visible* (2012), and both deal with the effects of substance abuse. In "OutTrip", the you-narrator Ben is going through the third day of five on a therapeutic survival trip which is the climax of a detox-program. Struggling with the heat, "parched and hungry" (78), Ben notices that the man who had been following him for some time and whom he refers to as "the Fisher" is catching up. The way the story is told, the Fisher could be a real person – namely, Ben's former dealer who wants to lure him back into drug consumption, or Ben's own addictive and destructive self, that part of his self he tries to vanquish during this trip. The Fisher seems to represent the narrator's worst fears: "Delirium, psychosis, either is preferable to being trapped out here with the real Fisher, hours from help, in the remote Northern spur of a desert that goes on forever" (86). More and more, it dawns on the increasingly delirious narrator, however, that the possibility of the Fisher being a figment of his imagination is an even more frightening threat because "if the Fisher is a chimera – and he must be: he can't be real – then really it's just *you* goading yourself toward death" (90). Throughout the story, the reader, like the main character, is left in the dark whether the figure of the Fisher actually appears in person or is a delusion produced by Ben's mind. Is Ben, when he addresses him, actually addressing the damaged part of his own self? This is indicated by passages like the following: "You're just me! This isn't for real – I'm dreaming you" (80); "You're in my mind" (84).

The story reaches a climax when Ben, utterly dehydrated and exhausted, thinks he hears water trickling. Following the sound into a cave, he encounters the Fisher again, who blocks the way to the water and uses this tantalising situation to tempt Ben back into the vicious circle he had tried so hard to get out of. However, Ben withstands, and when the Fisher grabs his hand, Ben overpowers him and flees from the cave and from the "precious water" (97), which seems to have been another trick of his mind. Or maybe not? The final part of the story renders the impression that Ben has now overcome his moment of crisis, emerging "into the night", and "the deep valley seems brilliant as morning" (97). The Fisher, in turn, who now seems more real than ever, is brought down by three wild animals, and his cries for help seem to Ben better than water. Using you-narration in this narrative of substance abuse and addiction, and further complicating the representation of the protagonist's mental struggles by introducing a physical incarnation of his afflicted and addicted self (which, too, is addressed as "you"), makes his struggles tangible and relatable to a degree that is rarely achieved in the literature on this subject matter.

Second-person fiction proper, as these stories demonstrate, has a particularly strong emotional impact. Told in the present tense, as they typically are, second-person narratives create the illusion that we follow the characters while they look at themselves during moments of crisis. The reader is denied the comfort of knowing that, whatever may have happened, the character is now out of danger, unlike in retrospective first-person narration, where narrators relate their story from a safe point in the future. What is more, the consistent use of the second-person pronoun induces readers to share the struggles of the narrator-protagonist – much more so than is the case with any other narrative voice.

We-narration, too, creates interesting aesthetic effects as it "straddles the line between first-and third-person fiction, as a homodiegetic narrator discloses that which can only be known by an external heterodiegetic intelligence" (Richardson 2006: 60). In addition, in we-narration, the identity of the group which the first-person plural pronoun designates tends to fluctuate. This is the case, for example, in David Arnason's "A Prelude to America" (*The Demon Lover*, 2002). In "Succession" (*The Demon Lover*), too, Arnason employs we-narration – in this case, to render ironically the attitudes of the citizens of Winnipeg towards the Queen and the monarchy in general. Grouping individual thoughts in the form of opinion blocks, the author humorously points to the conservatism and stagnation which, according to the story, dominate the city, while at the same time indirectly questioning the arrogant and simplifying assumption that "we" always know what others think.

Regarding we-narration, Richardson (2006: 43) notes, "One is particularly struck by the intensely political use the technique is recently put to". Looking, for example, at Margaret Atwood's, Kathy Page's, or Zsuzsi Gartner's experiments with the collective first-person pronoun, this observation can definitely be confirmed. Margaret Atwood, in particular, has made ample use of the collective first-person voice in *The Tent* (2006). All the stories told in this mode, including "Post-Colonial", "Heritage House", "Resources of the Ikarians", "Eating the Birds", and "Something Has Happened", display a strong political or ecological agenda (see also Chapter 10), as does "We Want It All" from *Bones & Murder* (1994). What Natalya Bekhta (2020: 97f) says about the "we" in "We Want It All" can also be applied to the other flash fiction pieces listed earlier – namely, that it "does not establish any narratological agency and does not acquire the performative force of a collectivity. The text becomes, rather, a musing on the state of ecology, on threats to our existence as humans for which we have only ourselves to blame". Through this, however, Atwood's we-texts create the illusion of metalepsis since the designation of the "we" tends to spill over to the reader, who may feel included in this collective, which is exposed as having brought about their own demise through insatiable greed. In "Post-Colonial", we find the "us versus them" dynamics (Bekhta 2020 165ff). The "we" here designates the collective of Canadian settler cultures, while "they" refers to Indigenous inhabitants of Canada. This seemingly clear division, however, is more and more destabilised in the course of the text. Thus, referring to the genocide of Native peoples, the narrator muses, "*We did that*, we think, *to them*. We say the word *them*, believing we know what we mean by it; we say the word *we*, even though we were not born at the time" (*The Tent* 98f). At the end, the narrative switches to the here and now, inviting the reader to reflect on problematic dichotomies which are still part of our cultural discourse, even though they have become (or should have become) obsolete: "It's a constant worry, this *we*, this *them*. And there you have it, in one word, or possibly two: post-colonial" (100).

Against the repeatedly diagnosed conventionality of the Canadian short story in criticism, this chapter's aim was to draw attention to the fascinating breadth of different narrative forms it employs. In particular, Atwood's, Schoemperlen's, and Bowering's ludic engagements with metafictional aspects have enriched the genre, as have the latter two authors' experiments with visual elements or Atwood's and many other writers' creative explorations of the aesthetic potential of flash fiction. Another feature that defines a considerable body of stories is the use of second-person narration. Lynn Coady, Elyse Gasco, and Steven Heighton, in particular, have demonstrated that the you-mode allows for effective depictions of characters in crisis. Even though not as prominent as the second-person form, we-narration, too, has been employed in a number of stories to highlight political and ecological issues.

Epistolary forms (including the staging of digital modes) could have been included in this chapter, too. However, since I am interested, especially in showing how authors employ the epistolary mode to break up linear storylines and to create polyvocality, I decided to include epistolarity in the context of techniques of fragmentation discussed in the following chapter.

Works Cited

Primary Works

Atwood, Margaret (1995 [1994]). *Bones & Murder*. London: Virago.
Atwood, Margaret (2006). *The Tent*. London: Bloomsbury.
Bowering, George (1994). *The Rain Barrel and Other Stories*. Vancouver: Talonbooks.
Coady, Lynn (2000). *Play the Monster Blind*. Toronto: Vintage Canada.
Coady, Lynn (2013). *Hellgoing. Stories*. Toronto: House of Anansi Press.
Coady, Lynn (2020). "The Drain". In: Paige Cooper, ed. *Best Canadian Stories 2020*. Windsor: Biblioasis. 203–226.
Gasco, Elyse (1999). *Can You Wave Bye Bye, Baby? Stories*. Toronto: McClelland & Stewart.
Gould, John (2020). *the end of me*. Calgary: Freehand Books.
Heighton, Steven (2012). *The Dead Are More Visible: Stories*. Toronto: Alfred A. Knopf.
Rooke, Leon (2001). *Painting the Dog: The Best Stories of Leon Rooke*. Toronto: Thomas Allen.
Roscoe, Patrick (2001). *The Truth About Love*. Toronto: Key Porter Books.
Schoemperlen, Diane (1998). *Forms of Devotion*. Toronto: HarperCollins.
Thomas, Audrey (1981). *Two in the Bush and Other Stories*. Toronto: McClelland and Stewart.

Secondary Works

Bekhta, Natalya (2020). *We-Narratives. Collective Storytelling in Contemporary Fiction.* Columbus: Ohio State University Press.

Fludernik, Monika (1994). "Introduction: Second Person Narrative and Related Issues". *Style* 28: 281–311.

Garrett-Petts, W.F. (1992). "Novelist as Radical Pedagogue: George Bowering and Postmodern Reading Strategies". *College English* 54.5 (September): 554–572.

Gordon, Neta (2010). "Shortness as Shape in John Gould's *Kilter: 55 Fictions*". *Journal of the Short Story in English* 54 (Spring): 1–10 (online).

King, Thomas (1990). "Godzilla vs. Post-Colonial". *World Literature Written in English* 30.2 (Autumn): 10–16.

Lucas, Belen Martin (1992). "Photo-Textual Narratives: Double Exposures *and* Still Sane". *Tessera* 13 (Winter): 76–90.

Moss, John (1989). "Life/Story: The Fiction of George Bowering". *Essays on Canadian Writing* 38 (Summer): 1–15 (online).

New, William H. (2009). "The Short Story". In: Coral Ann Howells and Eva-Marie Kröller, eds. *The Cambridge History of Canadian Literature.* Cambridge: Cambridge University Press. 381–401.

Nischik, Reingard M. (2003). "Murder in the Dark: Margaret Atwood's Inverse Poetics of Intertextual Minuteness". In: Sharon Rose Wilson, ed. *Margaret Atwood's Textual Assassinations: Recent Poetry and Fiction.* Columbus: Ohio State University Press. 1–17.

Richardson, Brian (2006). *Unnatural Voices: Extreme Narration in Modern and Contemporary Fiction.* Columbus: Ohio State University Press.

Smith, Russell (2018). "Introduction". In: Russell Smith, ed. *Best Canadian Stories 2018.* Windsor: Biblioasis. 7–16.

Whetter, Darryl (1996). "'In the Language of Schoemperlen': Interview by Derryl Whetter". *Studies in Canadian Literature/Études en littérature Canadienne* 21.1: 131–140.

Wilson, Sharon Rose (2003). "Fiction Flashes: Genres and Intertext in Good Bones". In: Sharon Rose Wilson, ed. *Margaret Atwood's Textual Assassinations: Recent Poetry and Fiction.* Columbus: Ohio State University Press. 18–41.

Suggestions for Further Reading

Deville, Michel (1995). "Murdering the Text: Genre and Gender Issues in Margaret Atwood's Short Short Fiction". In: Michel Deville, ed. *The Context and the Culmination.* Liège: University of Liège. 57–67.

Hönnighausen, Lothar (2007). "Realism and Parodic Postmodernism: Audrey Thomas, 'Aquarius' (1971)". In: Reingard M. Nischik, ed. *The Canadian Short Story: Interpretations.* Rochester and New York: Camden House. 247–259.

Lane, Richard J. (2011). *The Routledge Concise History of Canadian Literature.* Abington and New York: Routledge.

Nischik, Reingard M. (2017). *The English Short Story in Canada: From the Dawn of Modernism to the Nobel Prize.* Jefferson, NC: McFarland & Company.

Nischik, Reingard M. (2021). "Margaret Atwood's Later Short Fiction". In: Coral Ann Howells, ed. *The Cambridge Companion to Margaret Atwood*, 2nd ed. Cambridge: Cambridge University Press. 157–170.

Stacey, Robert David, ed. (2010). *RE: Reading the Postmodern: Canadian Literature and Criticism After Modernism.* Ottawa: University of Ottawa Press.

6 Fragmentation in the "Era of the Vulnerable"

The "last few decades have seen a renewed popularity of fragmentation in works of fiction that deny completeness, linearity and coherence in favour of incompleteness, disruption and gaps" (Guignery and Drąg 2019: xi). This trend can also be observed in contemporary Canadian short fiction, and it finds its expression in a wide spectrum of forms and techniques employed to break up the text and challenge the aesthetic experience of unity. David Malcolm (2019: 35) and other critics have emphasised that "fragmentariness is integral to short fiction" in general, yet in contemporary short fiction, this genre-specific fragmentariness has often been intensified through radically breaking unity and linearity. Rather than constituting a jumble of bits and pieces, however, such fragmented narratives, as shall be shown, are subtle systems of meaning-making, which derive their semantic potential from the relationships between the parts and the whole. At the same time, the fissures that are evident through breaks in the textual structure and that often mirror fragmented experiences and selves keep resonating, no matter how the reader may strive to integrate them in the act of interpretation.

The short story cycle, which may be referred to as a fragmented novel, has had a long tradition in Canadian writing and has been frequently employed, in the past decades, for stories of migration, cultural displacement, and acute situations of crisis. This variant of the short story collection, "in which individual texts enter into complex, modifying, and amplifying semantic relations with each other" (Malcolm 2019: 38), plays a significant role in several chapters in this volume, where it is discussed in the context of various periods and thematic concerns. It, therefore, suffices at this point to mention it briefly as a major genre signalling fragmentation. Through its "unique balancing of the one and the many" (Lynch 2001: 18), that is, its foregrounding of both unity *and* disunity, the linked-stories composition is ideally suited to mediate and reflect the tension between individuals and the larger framework of cultural, communal, or national identities and expectations. While many of the earlier Canadian examples of linked stories are unified by place and community, a new variant emerged in the 1970s – namely, the life cycle. The specific aesthetics of storified autobiographical fiction are addressed in Chapter 4, regarding Alice Munro's *Lives of Girls and*

Women. From the mid-1980s onwards, many authors have used the story cycle in order to avoid smoothly linear and unified storylines in narratives that render migration, the intricacies of cultural and/or sexual identity, and the complexity of modern life in general (see also Chapters 7 and 9).

"Fragmentariness", as Guignery and Drąg (2019: xii) argue, "is . . . commonly associated with loss, lack and vulnerability". Following Jean-Michel Ganteau, who defines our age as an "era of the vulnerable" (2015: 5), it is, therefore, not surprising that techniques of disruption define modern fiction and are manifested not only in the "storified" novel but also in an astounding number of individual short stories. In Canadian short fiction, the most frequent form of fragmentation is the division of the text into clearly separated sections, often additionally marked by means of chapter headings or typographically foregrounded topic sentences. In many stories, however, this propensity for composite structures is not evident at first glance. Here, the accumulation and synchronising of seemingly disparate fragments within one individual story can be recognised only in the process of reading. Examples of the composite short story, its variants and aesthetic effects will be discussed in Section 6.1., which also includes a case study of Carol Shields's "Dying for Love".

The second section (Section 6.2.) is dedicated specifically to epistolary forms as a distinct technique of multimodal fragmentation. The inclusion of letters, notes, e-mails, and other forms of e-communication again leads to a fragmentation of the storyline. The integration of staged forms of electronic communication into printed novels and short stories testifies to the role of digital media as an "important catalyst for generic change" (Nünning and Rupp 2013: 202). Multimodality is also produced through the inclusion of lists, footnotes, or visual elements, including passages that are typographically set off from the main text (see Section 6.3). In general, multimodality is often used for producing polyphony and ambiguity, calling for reconstructive strategies of reading. In addition, we may say with Guignery and Drąg (2019: xi) that multimodal fragmentation "might be a way for contemporary writers to reflect today's accelerated culture and social media and overcommunication within which long-form fiction seems increasingly anachronistic".

6.1. The Composite Short Story

As mentioned earlier, the division of stories into clearly separated units is the hallmark of a considerable body of contemporary Canadian short fiction. One would think that this might bring the short story closer to the novel. However, rather the opposite is the case. Unlike the chapter of a (conventional) novel, the clearly separated sections of the composite story eschew linear progression and indicate semantic connections rather in a vertical, paradigmatic manner, thus revealing suggestive connections between different time levels, settings or seemingly disparate plot elements. In some cases, in fact, such composite stories seem to be miniature replicas of the larger form of the short story cycle. In this, they follow a representational mode which Paul Ricœur describes as follows: "while the episodic dimension of a narration draws narrative time in the direction of the linear representation of time . . . the configurational dimension, in its turn, presents temporal features directly opposed to those of the episodic dimension" (1984: 67).

The composite format has been used in so many stories published over the past decades that only a rough overview of selected authors and stories can be provided here. Thus, Douglas Glover has experimented with fragmentation in several stories collected in *A Guide to Animal Behaviour* (1991) and *Savage Love* (2013). Mark Anthony Jarman uses fragmentation to great effect in "Bear on a Chain" (*My White Planet*, 2008), as does Paige Cooper in "Slave Craton" and "Vazova on Love" (*Zolitude*, 2018). The composite format also defines Michael Crummey's "Roots" (*Flesh and Blood*, 1998), which traces a young journalist's quest for his own and his hometown's history when he returns to Black Rock, a Newfoundland mining town, and in which Crummey skilfully juxtaposes pieces of public and personal history. Some writers use the names of the respective focalisers as titles of the story segments in order to foreground the stories' polyphonic makeup. This is the case, for example, in Shauna Singh Baldwin's "Simran" and "Toronto 1984" (*English Lessons and Other Stories*, 1996) or in Caroline Adderson's "The Maternity Suite" (*Pleased to Meet You*, 2006), a disturbing story about fake pregnancies.

A particularly appealing example of fragmentation is Deborah Willis's (1982–) "Last One to Leave" (*The Dark and Other Love Stories*, 2017), where each spatially separated section is introduced by (partly fragmented) topic sentences highlighted in bold print. Alternatingly, the individual units tell the stories of Sidney and Havryl, which eventually merge. Sidney escaped "the provincial city of her birth" (115) as a young woman to live in a small and remote logging town, hours north of Victoria, B.C., where she worked as a copy editor and later as the sole editor of the local paper. Havryl is a young Jewish orphan from Ukraine, who was sent to Canada in 1950. Having "a name no one could pronounce" and being "from a place no one could pronounce" (117), he lives outside the town limits in a shack he built himself after his boss at the mill where he worked for some time had died in an accident. While the townspeople think he is mad and mute and possibly dangerous, Sidney resolves to visit him for an interview for her column but finds him rather reluctant to talk. At the moment when Sidney wants to give up and leave, he suddenly says "Stay" and "it felt like yanking a tooth when he dragged the word up from where it had been buried" (127). The strongly moving story is a striking example of how fragmented narrative structures are employed to mimic fissures of the self and how, through putting together fragment after fragment, some notion of healing and wholeness is created – a wholeness, however, which still shows the adumbrations of the cracks.

An author who has repeatedly employed the form of the composite short story in striking ways is Steven Heighton (1961–2022). Thus, in several stories collected in *Flight Paths of the Emperor*, Heighton uses multilayering in order to emphasise how the hostilities between Japan and America during the Second World War resonate in the present. In "A Man Away from Home Has No Neighbours", the historical scope even extends to the Russo-Japanese War of 1904–1905 and shows, through an intricate configuration of commonalities between seven seemingly unrelated time levels, that people act more recklessly and atrociously when they can remain anonymous, lacking neighbours to check their actions.

Fragmentation also plays a major role in many of Annabel Lyon's (1971–) stories. This is how "Song" (*Oxygen*, 2000) begins:

> Two boys went into a house. A girl waited in the car.
>
> ★★★
>
> It happened like this. The boys went into the house while the girl waited in the car. When they came out the girl drove them away. For some time it wasn't clear to her what had happened.
>
> (77)

The story focuses on the (possible) murder of an elderly lady by the two boys and features their and the girl's confusion about what actually happened in the house. The various "stanzas" of this "Song", written in a sparse and unaffected style, juxtapose contradicting versions of a crime which represent the different points of view of the teenagers involved and of official reports that were released afterwards. The sentences "Two boys went into a house" and "it happened like this" appear in almost every "stanza", resembling the refrain of a song. While the first statement can be considered a fact within the framework of the story, the second one is highly deceptive as, again and again, it promises what it fails to do. With each new gap in the text, which zigzags between different time levels and perspectives, accumulating repetitions with variation, the menace which lurks in "Song" (and, in fact, in many of Lyon's stories) becomes more and more threatening. The story is daring in many ways. It not only centres on the horror that most likely went on in the house and is only gradually and elliptically disclosed; at the same time, it also depicts the two young criminals and their (innocent?) driver as traumatised – shocked about what they had done and were capable of. This mostly results from Lyon's radical rhetoric of fragmentation and (frantic) repetition.

While, in most stories, fragmentation is apparent at first glance and thus shapes the recipient's expectations from the start, there are also several examples where narrative disruption can be recognised only gradually during the reading process. Such stories display no clearly marked semi-autonomous story units but nonetheless configure seemingly disparate elements to create semantic depth. An early example of such an accumulative style is Audrey Thomas's (1935–) "If One Green Bottle" (*Ten Green Bottles*, 1967), which renders elliptically the afflicted and associative thoughts of a woman giving birth. The woman's stream of consciousness zigzags between her own liminal experiences between birth-throes, the biblical Virgin Mary's "maculate delivery" (11), Picasso's *Guernica*, Auschwitz, nursery rhymes, Robert the Bruce, Orpheus, and Lot's wife, among many other fragments of thought. The baby being stillborn, the story ends upon a note of futility: "The battle over . . . the death within expelled . . . cast out . . . the long hike over . . . Ararat . . . It's over . . . eyes heavy . . . body broken but relaxed. All over . . . Yet one would be grateful . . . at the last . . . for a reason . . . an explanation . . . a sign. . . . Not this nothing" (18).

A more recent writer who experimented with the evocative synchronising of apparently dissimilar elements and episodes in several of her stories is Carol Shields (1953–2003). In her cumulative stories, too, fragmentation is usually not highlighted by spacing, chapter heading or other obvious markers of division. Shields, who has repeatedly named Alice Munro as her role model (Löschnigg 2014: 55) and who – like Munro – has given emphasis to the quotidian and the domestic, shares yet another feature with the Nobel Prize winner: her favouring of configurational rather than sequential connections. In her metafictional story "Ilk" (*Dressing Up for the Carnival*, 2000), the narrator comes up with striking metaphors for these two opposed approaches when she compares the theme-driven "ovarian" mode with the conventional plot-driven "ejaculatory" mode (*Collected Stories* 442). Writer figures and artists, in general, make a strong appearance in Shields's oeuvre, providing an occasion for numerous implicit and explicit metafictional reflections as, for example, in "Flitting Behaviour" (*Various Miracles*, 1985), "Block Out" (*The Orange Fish*, 1989), or "A Scarf" and "Edith-Esther" (*Dressing Up for the Carnival*). While there are without doubt several commonalities between Munro and Shields, the latter has nonetheless developed her own idiosyncratic style and has – more strongly than Munro – "restore[d] familial context and a sense of the domestic *to* the avantgarde" (Ramon 2008: 10).

Shields's innovative style is, most of all, defined by her "rhetoric of aggregation" (Löschnigg 2014: 58), that is, the sum of techniques the author employs to produce cumulative effects. This is most strikingly evident in her composite stories, which are characterised by the seriation and synchronicity of phenomena and incidents. Memorable examples of such stories, which are, in fact, cycles of micro-stories, are "Various Miracles" and "Home" (*Various Miracles*), as well as "Dressing Up for the Carnival", "Keys", and "Dying for Love" (*Dressing Up for the Carnival*). The following case study of "Dying for Love" will demonstrate how Shields, in her composite stories, puts synchronicity over chronology and commonality over singularity.

Case Study: Carol Shields, "Dying for Love" – The Rhetoric of Fragmentation and Aggregation

The story combines three narratives about women who are on the verge of committing suicide. In all three micro-stories, the protagonists are "at the end of love" (439) due to having been abandoned by their husbands or partners for another woman. The thematic link between these micro-stories is further underscored by the similarity not only of the protagonists' names but also of those of their rivals: Beth/Charlotte, Lizzie/Carlotta, Elizabeth/Coral. Despite these obvious correlations, the situations the three main characters find themselves in are quite different. The middle-aged Beth and Ted have been together for four or five years before he leaves her for the dancer Charlotte, whose skinny body is a special provocation for Beth, whose weight problems had been an issue between her and Ted. Lizzie, by contrast, is only 18 and has been impregnated by her boyfriend during the short time they shared their lodgings before Ned "became sodden with love, and for a music hall performer named Carlotta" (*Collected Stories* 434). Elizabeth, in turn, has been married for 25 years and struggles with the recognition that she "had lost forever the power to stir ardour" (438). Knowing that her husband no longer loves her, she imagines a lover for him, "Coral of the swervy body and rhythmic hands" (438). While Beth contemplates ending her life with the help of pills, and Lizzie intends to fling herself from the new bridge, Elizabeth tries to suffocate herself with a dry cleaner's plastic bag. The disparities in the women's ages, relational situations and methods of "dying for love" dissolve again at the end of each narrative through the image of the handrail. It is a cypher of hope and "ongoingness" which suddenly materialises for each of the women as an option, something to hang on to.

In order to make sense of this "triptych of abandoned women in different historical circumstances, each of whom is 'called back' from suicide by projecting her thoughts onto a more affirmative vision of the future" (Ramon 2008: 150), it is necessary to consider the story's overall narrative structure. All three micro-stories are narrated by an emotionally involved first-person narrator. The introductory passages to the first two pieces, in particular, suggest that the narrator knows the afflicted women personally:

> My first thought this morning is for Beth, how on earth she'll cope now that Ted's left her for the dancer Charlotte Brown. . . . Will she

> get through the first days and nights? The nights will be terrible for her, I'm sure of that, long and heavy. (431)
>
> But then there's Lizzie in Somerset; my fears for Lizzie grow day by day. Her predicament is clear, and so is her fate, although I can perhaps imagine a way to assist her in the avoidance of that fate. (434)

While these passages are quite consistent with the narrative conventions of (peripheral) first-person narration, the narrator more and more moves beyond the limitations of homodiegetic narration – within each story but also with each story. Thus, the concluding account of Beth's story clearly displays authorial omniscience:

> Then she wanders into her bathroom, her hot milk in hand, and permits herself an admiring look in the ripply mirror, but nonchalantly, coolly, out of the corner of her eye. What she sees is the profile of someone who had considered joining that tiny company of women who have died for love. She salutes the side of her face with her thick pottery mug, across which is written the word SMILE.
>
> Life is a thing to be cherished, she thinks, and this thought, slender as a handrail, gets her through one more night. (434)

In the third story, the narrator is clearly extradiegetic; in other words, in the account of Elizabeth's story the narrator and protagonist are situated on different ontological levels. Interestingly, however, this external perspective is, at the same time, destabilised through hints that suggest that Elizabeth is "much nearer home" (437) and, in general, more closely connected to the narrator. Thus, the micro-story (and the entire story) concludes with "Not that this is much of a handrail to hang on to – *she knows that, and so do I* – but it is at least continuous, solid, reliable as a narrative in its turnings and better than no handrail at all" (439, my emphasis).

Elizabeth can be understood as a "persona" of the narrator herself, which is also supported by the former's "power to create parallel stories that offer her a measure of comfort" (439). This is exactly what the narrator does – and Carol Shields, for that matter. The "handrail", it seems, is the resource of stories which makes visible the underlying pattern experienced by different people in different situations. While in Beth's and Lizzie's stories, this awareness remains still vague, it materialises as a clear insight in Elizabeth's case. In fact, her name – being a

> composite of "Liz" and "Beth" – may also suggest that the two younger women are earlier versions of herself.
>
> "Dying for Love" celebrates the "saving capacity" (439) of storytelling. Through telling, imagining, and listening to parallel stories of loss, of "the legions of other women who have almost died for love" (438), the narrator uncovers patterns of despair but also of recovery from it. What first seems like a dead end for these women becomes a possibility as soon as they see themselves linked to a larger narrative that transcends the particular and rather provides insight into larger underlying patterns. Like many of Shields's cumulative stories, "Dying for Love" radiates strength through highlighting commonalities.
>
> "Dying for Love" and Shields's "rhetoric of aggregation":
>
> - Fragmentation through featuring three seemingly separate stories
> - Framing by a first-person narrator whose ontological status is slippery
>   - Narrator is both inside *and* outside the stories she recounts.
> - Synchronisation of the stories through thematic correspondences, similarity of names, and recurring images
> - Visible underlying patterns in apparently different experiences by women of different ages and in different life situations
> - Recognising commonalities as a source of comfort, a "handrail", for abandoned women, which is evident on three levels:
>   - It dawns on the three women in the respective micro-stories who, in the end, all choose life over suicide.
>   - It defines the meta-narrative considerations of the frame narrator.
>   - It affects the extratextual reader, who is led to see the stories as a "handrail" to help them to get through their own grief.

6.2. Fragmentation Through Epistolary Elements

Fragmentation is also achieved through the inclusion of letters. In fact, in contemporary fiction, epistolary forms have seen a renaissance (Löschnigg and Schuh 2018: 1–12). Interestingly, the digitisation of modern culture has not only led to a proliferation of epistolary modes endemic to the Internet but has also prompted a new interest in the conventional letter. In Canadian short fiction, the letter and, increasingly, also its digital siblings occupy an exceptionally prominent position (Schuh 2021) and constitute a powerful tool to break up storylines and refract meaning. Of Alice Munro's stories, 22 include letters or are written entirely in the epistolary mode. Among other Canadian authors who have experimented with letters are Sandra Birdsell, André Alexis, Lynn Coady, Dede Crane, Caroline Adderson, Kathy Page, John Gould, and Emma Donoghue.

As the epistolary stories by Austin Clarke, Olive Senior, Rabindranath Maharaj, Rohinton Mistry, David Bezmozgis, and Caterina Edwards show, letters are particularly frequent in migration stories and stories which thematise cultural displacement (see also Chapter 9). Memorable examples – among numerous others – are Rabindranath Maharaj's "The Diary of a Down-Courage Domestic" (*The Book of Ifs and Buts*, 2002), Austin Clarke's "Waiting for the Postman to Knock" (*They Never Told Me and Other Stories*, 2013), and Caterina Edwards's "Home and Away" (*Island of the Nightingales*, 2000). As Rebekka Schuh (2021: 158ff) has demonstrated, letters are ideally suited to mediate the liminal experience – spatially and mentally – of migrant subjects, the exchanged letters designating the push and pull motivations of the migrant or immigrant, signifying both distance and the desire to bridge it.

Whether written entirely in letter form or only including letters, epistolary elements lead to a fragmentation of a story's plotline. Often not occupying much space, embedded letters within short fiction nonetheless constitute essential story elements. Thus, a short letter at the beginning of André Alexis's "My Anabasis" (*Despair and Other Stories*, 1994), for example, is the catalyst for all the following events. In Dede Crane's "What Sort of Mother" (*The Cult of Quick Repair*, 2008), in turn, the letter that concludes the story provides the narrative with the daughter's voice in a text that is otherwise exclusively narrated from the point of view of the mother.

In general, the multiplication of voices is one of the most striking effects of epistolary short fiction. This is evident, in particular, in Alice Munro's (1931–) "A Wilderness Station" (*Open Secrets*, 1994), a piece of historical fiction which consists of 11 letters and one article in the Carstairs magazine *Argus*. The story centres on Simon Herron's (mysterious) death in the backwoods of Canada in the mid-19th century. Whether Simon's death was an accident or whether he was killed either by his brother George or his wife, Annie, is never really clarified in the story. Rather, the story asks to be read as a narrative of female empowerment. In all official letters and in her brother-in-law's seemingly objective recollections in the Carstairs magazine about 50 years after the fatal incident in the backwoods, Annie is defined by others. Through a careful placing of Annie's own letters, Munro stages her gradual emergence from a muted person to a woman who speaks up with her own voice. Refusing to be defined by others and eluding clear definitions altogether, Annie, in the end, manages to live a fairly fulfilled life (Löschnigg 2014: 30ff).

While the effect of fragmentation is hardly an issue in one-letter stories, such as Lee Maracle's "Dear Daddy" (*Sojourner's Truth and Other Stories*,

1996), these stories nonetheless tend to challenge a unilateral reception. Since the essential genre-defining element of epistolary fiction is the presence of an internal reader, this envisioned addressee not only shapes the epistolary text's content, style, and purpose but also invites a double reading. Thus, the letter the 14-year-old girl addresses to her absent father in "Dear Daddy" not only renders her own story but also suggests insight into her father's life. The function of the epistolary mode as a tool to "write back" to someone who had failed the addresser, which is evident in "Dear Daddy", plays an even stronger role in Alice Munro's "Before the Change" (*The Love of a Good Woman*, 1998). The story consists of ten imagined letters addressed to the female narrator's ex-lover Robin, who wanted her to abort their child and whose hypocrisy and misogyny destroyed their relationship. In her letters, the deeply wounded writer excavates the past and confronts Robin with *her* version of *his* story through the ample use of you-narration. At the same time, the letters serve a therapeutic function so that, with the tenth and last letter, the narrator has managed to get Robin out of her system.

The displacement of letters, spatial and especially temporal, makes an excellent device for having a character build up illusions. Since communication through letters excludes the non-verbal signals effective in face-to-face dialogues, it encourages the addressee to indulge in imaginary constructions which are further intensified by the time lag between letters. This time lag leads the recipient of a letter to "take something which is already past as present and to fix fluid entities as something permanent" (Löschnigg and Schuh 2018: 24). Alice Munro, for example, exploits this element of temporal deferral and lack of non-verbal information in "Carried Away" and "Hateship, Friendship, Courtship, Loveship, Marriage". In "Carried Away", the main character, Luisa, develops larger-than-life images of Jack Agnew, who serves in the First World War and starts a correspondence with her. How strong the impact of Luisa's "epistolary illusion" (Schuh 2018: 80) is on her life becomes apparent only after the war is over and Luisa waits in vain for Jack's return, feeling increasingly haunted by his "shadow" or "ghost". The letters in "Hateship, Friendship, Courtship, Loveship, Marriage" are forged, yet they nonetheless have a similar illusory effect on the main character, Johanna, who, by acting upon them, ironically and unwittingly causes her fate to turn in her favour.

The epistolary form also lends itself ideally to meta-narrative experiments. In many epistolary stories, we find a narrativising of writing and reading processes. This is the case in Rohinton Mistry's "Swimming Lesson" (*Tales from Firozsha Baag*, 1987), where, in Bombay, the main character Kersi's parents discuss not only their son's stories but also his letters and send their comments back to their son in Canada. A particularly interesting story in this regard is Steven Heighton's e-mail story "Noughts & Crosses" (*The Dead Are More Visible*, 2012). It consists of Janet's sent e-mail, in which she tells her lesbian lover Arnella that she wants to end the relationship, and Arnella's successive responses, which, step by step, dissect and critically deconstruct Janet's message but are never sent. At the same time, the story also critically reflects on the difference between letter and e-mail as apt means of communication. Heighton's story is also indicative of the influence of the New Media on literature in general and the short story in particular.

While the impact of the digital turn on Canadian literature has now been widely recognised (Eichhorn 2016), the staged integration of electronic media on the printed page is often excluded from considerations of this impact on literature. In fact, the renaissance of epistolary fiction, especially from the 1990s onwards, seems to be "linked to the catalytic impact of the Internet on fiction" (Löschnigg and Schuh 2018: 27). At the same time, the combination of staged electronic modes with more conventional ones opens up novel possibilities of narrative expression while also channelling and questioning the communicative practices of the digital age. Interestingly, the transposition of digital modes onto the printed page also "reinstalls the physicality and materiality of semiotic practices" (Hallet 2009: 146).

An author who has experimented both with conventional letters and electronic forms is John Gould (1959–). While "Ex", "Via Negativa", "10 Things", and "Welcome" can all be regarded as letter stories, "Bones" and "Customer Review" (all in *the end of me*, 2020), which also display a strong metafictional element, stage digital modes of communication. "Bones" leads us into a chatroom where a user suggestively named *penumbra* asks for advice regarding a novel he wants to write. The book is to be about "the first man, how he lived but mostly how he died" (223). What the prospective author is struggling with in particular is "how to get inside this guy's head", considering he lived "million years ago" (223). The user *penumbra*'s reaching out into digital space elicits 25 responses in addition to comments among the chatters and foregrounds the dynamics of this form of communication, as well as sheds light on how stories are constructed. The ending, "◄◄ Previous Thread Next Thread ►►" (228), typographically imitating the screen, highlights the openness and also multiplication of possibilities of such communication tools. The theme of death, which is the common denominator in all 56 micro-stories assembled in *the end of me*, is approached in a particularly unsettling manner in "Customer Review". Shaped in the format of an online review of a book titled "The Sinking Lifeboat: How Death Could Save Us [Hardcover] R.L. Clark (Author)" (249), the story mostly consists of the "review" of the already provocative book and the customer's additional musings on the duty of rich Western people to die in order "to make life possible for all living creatures" (250). How we read this thought-provoking review is further framed and complicated by the final "Was this review helpful to you? Yes ☐ No ☐ **Report Abuse**" (251). Needless to say, this piece of flash fiction is also interesting from an ecocritical view.

Further Canadian stories which stage digital correspondences are Doretta Lau's "God Damn, How Real is This?" (*How Does a Single Blade of Grass Thank the Sun?*, 2014), Deirdre Simon Dore's "Your Own Lucky Stars" (*Best Canadian Stories 2018*), and Casey Plett's "Hazel & Christopher" (*Best

Canadian Stories, 2020). Lynn Coady, too, has implemented elements of the new media in "Dogs in Clothes" (*Hellgoing*, 2013) and "Someone's Recording" (*Best Canadian Stories 2018*).

Lynn Coady's (1970–) "Someone's Recording" testifies to the influence of new technologies not only on literature but also on lives. The story features university professor Gary's e-mailed responses to his ex-partner's social media campaign, accusing him of sexual misconduct 15 years earlier. While Gary tries to settle the issue by privately contacting Erica, she is adamant about making it known to her rapidly growing cache of followers. Thus, she posts his private e-mails on her Instagram platform, and increasingly, her fan base starts to harass Gary. He is forced to lock his Facebook account and is finally suspended from work because "[s]tudents have started boycotting [his] classes en masse" (*Best Canadian Stories*, 2018: 49). This ambiguous story, which relates to the #MeToo movement, raises more questions than it answers. As the story alludes to sexual harassment and abuse, the reader never really finds out what Gary is accused of. This is because the text only renders his reactions to Erica's accusations, while there is no first-hand insight into her point of view or her activities on various social media channels. Since Erica's attacks become more and more gleeful, however, it can be assumed that something must have happened back then that explains her destroying Gary's life. At the same time, there can be no doubt about the story's critique of the problematic and destructive function of the "(il)legal court" of social media. These issues will again be taken up with regard to Margaret Atwood's "alternative" feminisms (Section 7.1.).

Another author that should be mentioned in this context is Russell Smith (1963–). Known, in particular, for his at times provocatively frank depictions of sex (most strongly evident in his pornographic novel *Diana: A Diary in the Second Person*, 2003), Smith has also repeatedly worked with staged digital forms in his stories. This is the case, for example, in "TXTS" (*Confidence*, 2015), where someone receives text messages from a person he does not know, and a woman publicises her experiences during a date in her blog. In "Raccoon" (*Confidence*), in turn, a woman gives vent to her anger about her husband through Twitter hashtags.

In addition to epistolary modes (including conventional letters and e-epistolarity), which are all informed by their orientation towards private and/or public addressees, the diary form is another device used in the Canadian short story with a tendency to refract storylines. Thus, in "Maggie", Lee Maracle complements the first-person narrator Stacey's story about her older sister with passages from 11-year-old Maggie's diary. This doubling of the points of view of children, who are victims of a school system brutally enforced on Indigenous children (Maggie, in the end, freezes to death), strongly intensifies the affective impact of this story. John Gould's "From the Journal of Dr. Duncan MacDougall of Haverhill, Mass" (*the end of me*) is entirely composed of diary entries, which trace the titular character's daily reflections on (his own) death from 18 October 1906 to 27 October 1906.

A particularly interesting story in this context is Lucia Gagliese's topical "Through the Covid-Glass" (*Best Canadian Stories*, 2021), which meaningfully attunes subject matter and structure. In 20 journal entries spanning about half a year, the narrator, a psychotherapist, records the increasingly suffocating experiences of isolation due to the COVID-19 pandemic, of being forced to support her patients solely through telemedicine, and of the growing feeling of "Fatigue. Lethargy. A sloth but without the equanimity" (75). While the first entry (12 March 2020) and that on the narrator's birthday (26 June 2020) come with an exact date, other entries only count the number of days this state of emergency has dragged on until, finally, the loss of a sense of time is reflected in increasingly vague temporal signifiers such as "It seems years" (72), "Still Summer" (73), and "Third Sleepless Night" (75). The only information in the headings that is provided consistently, though, and provides the entries with a haunting frame is the exactly stated, steadily rising, and eventually exploding number of deaths and infected people in Canada, starting with "1 death/117 cases" (63) in the first entry and ending with "9184 deaths/130,918 cases" in the last one, titled "Today" (75). Yet, as the narrator realises, "statistics . . . don't tell the true story. Humanity is in the singular. In my colleagues waving silly goodbyes at the end of Zoom meetings. . . . In my niece hugging herself as proxy. In my mum, reading page after page of obituaries in the Italian newspaper" (65). Thus, Gagliese's diary story is a great example of the value of literature, of stories' power to translate data into something relatable and reflecting the impact pandemics like the recent COVID-19 crisis can have on individual lives. The narrative, broken up as it is into a series of entries of different lengths, is further fragmented by to-do lists, compilations of ingredients for a meal the narrator shares with her friend in a fake online dinner for two, and the titles of the films she watches on each day, which are all movies featuring Cary Grant. The last two entries suggest a climax. In the penultimate entry, the increasing blurring of everything is captured through the blurring and overlapping of words:

RisKisSinGamblinGGatherinGermSchooL
. . .
IsolateDespairinGrieFeaRemoEndurE
ZooMuteDistancEmployeDeliverieSavingSafEconomY
RecoverDeceaseD
PropagandAntivaxxeResistancE
PoliticS (75)

In the last entry, not even the Cary Grant movies provide consolation anymore, and it is in this slump of despair that the story ends with "This cannot be how it ends" (75), thus suggesting ongoingness after all.

6.3. Other Forms of Multimodality

Authors have not only experimented with letters, e-epistolarity and diary modes to disrupt the unity of the text through multimodal strategies. The juxtaposition of all kinds of non-epistolary textual and visual modes, too, is frequent in contemporary Canadian short fiction, contributing to an aesthetics of fragmentation. Thus, many stories that are divided into clearly separated (and often titled) units are additionally fractured through the use of different typologically accentuated passages or other visual elements. Examples are Leon Rooke's "Sing Me No Love Songs I'll Say You No Prayers" (*Painting the Dog*, 2001), André Alexis's experimental "Horse" (*Despair and Other Stories*, 1994), and George Bowering's "Little Me" (*The Rain Barrel*, 1994). In "Sing Me No Love Songs I'll Say You No Prayers", Leon Rooke (1934–) breaks up the storyline through numerous "chapter headings" which suggest interpretive guidelines for the reader; he also includes drawings, one of them, for example, visualising "*What the Dream Looked Like When He Tried Recalling It Later*" (*Painting the Dog* 220). George Bowering's (1935–) "Little Me" consists of nine diary entries which stage the gradual disintegration of the narrator's mind and self through their increasingly regressive language. Whereas the penultimate entry already displays clear signs of amnesia, the "narrator" is forced to resort to analogic codes in the last entry, which only consists of a drawing – suggesting the skills of a small child.

André Alexis's (1957–) composite Gothic narrative "Horse" (*Despair and Other Stories*, 1994) is a particularly forceful example of how structural fragmentation mirrors fissures of the self. Belonging to the second generation of Caribbean-Canadian writers (Chariandy 2004), many of Alexis's stories render, "in relatively transparent or matter-of-fact language, absurd, 'exotic', and macabre circumstances, and they suggest indebtedness to such short fiction writers as Poe, Bowles and Borges" (Chariandy 2004: 82). Since "Horse" is one of the stories that make up the third part of *Despair*, which is titled "ANDRÉ", we can assume that the otherwise unnamed first-person narrator of this story also bears the same name as the author. In "Horse", which is divided into six chapters, the narrator's recurring dreams – one of them featuring men whose detached heads sit on tables in front of them – become his reality. The enigmatic quality of his nightmares further materialises in ominous signs that appear within these dreams. These signs are represented visually on the page and are doubled by the dreams of the narrator's mother (now dead), of which André reads in a letter that is included in the second chapter of the story. It is only later, when the narrator's boarder, Dr. Enrico Pascal, comes to use his landlord for his sinister experiments to find out whether it is possible to separate the body from the mind/soul, that the dreams can be seen as foreshadowing André's own fate. Through the effect of the drugs Dr. Pascal feeds him, André is made to see his body from the outside and feels a loathing and disgust for his physical self (*Despair* 141): "Of course, I had realized some time before that I was a negro, but this 'niggerness' still

Fragmentation in the "Era of the Vulnerable" 133

surprised me" (137). What, on the one hand, reads like an absurdist horror story materialises, on another level, as a disturbingly powerful reflection on the psychological aftermath of colonialism, as described memorably by postcolonial thinkers such as Frantz Fanon (see *Black Skin White Masks*) and Homi Bhabha (see, for example, "Remembering Fanon: Self, Psyche and the Colonial Condition"). Thus, Dr. Pascal – representing Western society – forces the protagonist to see and feel his "otherness" as a deficiency, an "amputation" that results in a ruptured self. Even though, eventually, André reinserts himself into his body, this only leads to the transformation of his zombie-like state into that of an animal-like creature: "Not only had I lost my language(s), the one(s) I used to communicate, but I had also lost the language I used to speak with my body, the one my body used to speak to me" (145). It is with the help of a stick that Dr. Pascal now brutally inculcates language into the protagonist. This is how the story ends:

– Le mot anglaise "joual"?
– Horse.
(147)

The dehumanised André loathes his victimiser but cannot yet free himself since he is too dependent on the doctor to rehumanise him. This, of course, will be on Dr. Pascal's own terms since he is the one who has the power to remodel his "subject" in any way possible. Regarding its structure, which compellingly mirrors André's broken self, the text is not only disrupted through the division into chapters and the inclusion of a letter and enigmatic visual signs. The first chapter also features a list the narrator makes of the rooms in his house, which he classifies with letters from A to Z. This classification appears again in the fourth chapter, where the microcosm of the house is amplified to become the macrocosm of Ottawa. Dr. Pascal's list of districts in Ottawa to which he sends André's body is again codified with letters A to Z and included in its entirety in the story, as are the routes of the trips he is commanded to make – for example, "1. diewcoeu" and "2. eltiraso" (142). However, rather than yielding any clarity, these alienating codifications of tracks through the city are tools to further obfuscate meaning and exercise power. The story is a compelling example of how techniques of fragmentation can be effectively employed to reflect "schisms of selfhood" (Chariandy 2004: 85) against the backdrop of postcolonial contexts.

Guignery and Drąg (2019: xii) claim that "works of fiction which relate personal and collective traumas, with a focus on bodily frailty and a dramatisation of loss, should opt for the trope of vulnerability and for modes of fragmentation and dislocation". While Alexis employs this poetics for his stories of collective (postcolonial) trauma, Caroline Adderson (1963–) uses modes of fragmentation for narratives of personal trauma in "Shhh: 3 Stories About Silence" (*Pleased to Meet You*, 2006). Here, a cartoonist "outsources" his damaged self by inventing the character of "Self-Loathing", who appears in almost all panels of his cartoons. The three separate narratives that make up the story are linked by their thematic concern with the meaning of silence. For the protagonist in the first story, a stutterer who worked with the B.B.C. and whose job it was to edit out the pauses when they got too long in interviews, silences were "profoundly moving" (*Pleased* 138). In the second story, the focus is on Eric and Nat, both from *The Sun*, who are on an excursion to meet someone for an interview. Eric is an incessant talker and, ironically it turns out now, is the one who told Nat about the B.B.C. man who loved silences in the first story. Silences flow into the second story through a phone call Nat receives from her husband, Don. His pauses, which "Nat thinks, should be edited out" (141), lead over to the third story, in which Don is in the centre. Don is a cartoonist also for the *Sun* but has lost his sense of humour and has taken time off from work. In all his cartoons, there is "that nasty hedgehog", which, as Nat explains to Eric in the second story, is not a hedgehog, "That's his Self-Loathing" (140). In the third and longest story, the narrative – rendered from Don's point of view – alternates with descriptions of his cartoon panels, which are set off from the parts in figural narration through spacing, a different font, and the exclusive use of capital letters. These 30 ekphrastic pieces, or verbal representations of the visual cartoon panels, turn out to be Don's way of coming to terms with traumatic experiences during his schooldays. His former torturer, Blake Alderson, has now turned to religion and has rented part of Don and Nat's land to provide a space for his sect and their rituals. Don and Nat accepted because they needed the money, even though, as it turns out, Blake has not yet paid any rent at all. It is this unhealed old wound and the renewed humiliation that seem to have catapulted Don into his recent state of crisis. Through his cartoons which feature BLAKE, his daughter "GEMMA, THE TALKING BABY", SELF-LOATHING, and DON himself, the traumatised man can distance himself from his own person while still working through his problem. Simultaneously confronting Blake and reworking their encounter artistically, Don finally manages to drive off the shadows of the past. In the final panel, his fictionalised self can let go of SELF-LOATHING, "the spiky mound that appears in every one of his cartoons" (156) and which, as the reader will have realised by now, represents a pile of dog shit – that is, the offensive item used by Blake and his gang to torture and humiliate Don: "PANEL: DON CLASPS HIS HANDS; DON'S BALLOON: OKEY! ENOUGH! SCAT! HIS SELF-LOATHING SKEEDADDLES OVER ITS SPINY SHOULDER" (159). The silence that concludes "Shhh: 3 Stories About Silence", when Don has finally defeated his antagonist and "[n]either of them speaks for several minutes" (159), could not be charged with more meaning.

Notions of trauma also pervade Kaie Kellough's (1975–) "Ashes and Juju" (*Dominoes at the Crossroads*, 2020). In this unsettling story, the author approaches a historical incident of racism that happened at Concordia University (Montreal) in 1969. In the story, the narrator is still haunted by the incident in which he played an ambivalent role. To exorcise his guilt, it seems, he wants to make a documentary film that focuses on the computer room on the 9th floor of the university building, which was occupied by hundreds of protesting students. When a fire broke out, the students were forced to leave the room and were not only arrested but also exposed to police brutality and public racism. In the narrator's mind, (hallucinatory) memories and envisioned scenes of the film he wants to create merge with scenes of his life decades after the incident. In addition, the story also provides a reproduction of the building plan of the ninth floor and an extract from a Caribbean community paper, where a young scholar is interviewed on her research project on the Concordia incident. Both the map and the fully provided interview are powerful elements to enhance the impression of authenticity.

Another noteworthy multimodal technique in Canadian short fiction is refracting the text through the use of footnotes. This is the case, for example, in Diane Schoemperlen's (1954–) "Innocent Objects" (*Forms of Devotion*, 1998), and Stephen Marche's (1976–) "Twinkle, Twinkle" (*Best Canadian Stories*, 2018). The latter is a "collaboration" between the author, a story-generating algorithm and Russell Smith, the editor of *Best Canadian Stories 2018*, who decided to "include with the story the author's notes on its creation (and his resistance to the machinery), as I think its genesis is actually what the story is about. This is both story and meta story" (13). Thus, in the version of "Twinkle, Twinkle" in Smith's 2018 anthology, the text is divided into the AI-generated narrative, which occupies the upper part of the page, and the 20 footnotes on the lower. Juxtaposing these two textual modes creates an interesting meta-referential dialogue between the algorithm and the actual human "author". Thus, via the notes, the reader is informed, for example, that, for Marche, the algorithm functions like an editor (*Best Canadian Stories*, 2018: 207) or that the choice of the title was not made by the algorithm but by the author himself (208).

An entirely different use of footnotes can be found in Schoemperlen's "Innocent Objects". This uncanny narrative about a burglary that takes place in the main character Helen Wingham's house synchronises four different sources of information. The main narrative juxtaposes an authorial account of Helen's life and the story of the thief – the latter presented through camera-eye technique, mostly written in the present tense progressive and set off from Helen's story by italics. In addition, all the objects in Helen's house which the thief touches or steals during Helen's absence come with footnotes. Thus, the lower part of the page is reserved for descriptions of these objects. Starting with informative descriptions as you might find them attached to exhibits in a museum, the texts in the footnotes increasingly morph into accounts of what these objects mean for Helen and what function they have in her life. In addition to the text, the footnotes also provide illustrations of the respective "innocent" objects. Confronting readers with four different representational modes on each page, the story engages them in puzzling speculations as to what exactly may have happened in Helen's house. The reading pleasure is not so much in solving the puzzle but rather in having to revise interpretations time and again.

One of the most striking experiments regarding the doubling of discourses through page division is Brian Fawcett's (1944–2022) *Cambodia: A Book for People Who Find Television Too Slow* (1986). Throughout the book, the lower part of the page is reserved for an essay on Cambodia and the Khmer Rouge, on the Belgian Congo and its reflections in Joseph Conrad's *Heart of Darkness* and Francis Ford Coppola's film *Apocalypse Now* (1979), on the Global Village and on meta-narrative reflections. The essay fulfils the function of a long footnote that discloses the subtext hidden in the 13 stories that occupy the upper parts (about two-thirds) of the pages. In fact, some of the stories again resemble essays rather than narratives. Most of the stories have a strong appellative impact, trying to establish an explicit interaction with the reader – much like Atwood's flash fiction pieces. In "A Small Committee", for instance, the reader is invited to secretly observe a committee meeting from an adjoining room. While the (implied) reader and the narrator are watching, they engage in a critical dialogue about what they see.

Fawcett's primary concern in *Cambodia* is the effect of globalisation which, according to the author, destroys individualism and memory, a factor, in the author's view, which also characterises genocide. The major crime in the genocides which took place in the Belgian Congo and in Cambodia, Fawcett argues in his essay, was the extermination of cultural memory. Similarly, modern society dictated by global techno-culture makes people forget what they are and where they are, as is illustrated most drastically in the stories "Universal Chicken" and "The Huxley Satellite Dish". In *Cambodia*, Fawcett has developed a challenging new mode of literary expression. Doubling his stories by means of a documentary essay which is linked to the stories through daring analogies, Fawcett destabilises conventional reading practices and forces the addressee to contemplate parallels where one would never expect them.

In fragmentary literature, the "defiance of completeness, cohesion and continuity in the syntactic structure and the arrangement of text on the page appears suited to convey content that challenges the status quo" (Guignery and Drąg 2019: xxi). As shown in this chapter, the seams between the parts of which the stories are composed are more or less conspicuously exposed. In all cases, however, a notion of fragmentation remains, even after the reconstructive act of reading that such stories demand. Whether produced through clearly separated story sections in the composite story, through epistolary elements, typographically foregrounded text segments or techniques that involve page division, all strategies of fragmentation introduced in this chapter lend depth rather than breadth to the respective stories. They are thus techniques which further intensify the short story's general tendency towards the fragmentary as against the complete and the configurational as against the sequential. This penchant for fragmentation that characterises much of contemporary Canadian short fiction testifies to authors' attempts to search for ever new ways of exhausting the distinct aesthetic possibilities of the genre in order to create meaning and impact. The fact that the structure of these stories "mimic[s] fissures of the self" and "echo[es] the shattering effects of trauma" (Guignery and Drąg 2019: xii) suggests that authors are no longer satisfied with only *narrating* crisis but also aim at foregrounding mechanisms of alienation and disintegration through the form they use. It is apposite, therefore, that in the following chapters, fragmentation will also play a role – be it in connection with the overwhelming challenges of ecological issues or regarding destabilised identities and cultural trauma. However, while in this chapter and in Chapter 5, the focus was on different techniques of fragmentation, metafictional experiment, and "unnatural voices", the following four chapters will approach contemporary Canadian short fiction rather from a thematic angle, discussing it within contexts that have come to define the short story from the mid-1980s to the present.

Works Cited

Primary Works

Adderson, Caroline (2006). *Pleased to Meet You: Stories*. Toronto: Thomas Allen.
Alexis, André (1994). *Despair and Other Stories*. New York: Henry Holt.
Coady, Lynn (2018). "Someone's Recording". In: Russell Smith, ed. *Best Canadian Stories 2018*. Windsor: Biblioasis. 39–51.
Gagliese, Lucia (2021). "Through the COVID-Glass". In: Diane Schoemperlen, ed. *Best Canadian Stories 2021*. Windsor, ON: Biblioasis. 63–75.
Lyon, Annabel (2003 [2000]). *Oxygen: Stories*. Toronto: McClelland & Stewart.
Shields, Carol (2005). *The Collected Stories*. Toronto: Vintage.
Smith, Russell, ed. (2018). *Best Canadian Stories 2018*. Windsor: Biblioasis.
Thomas, Audrey (1977 [1967]). *Ten Green Bottles*. Ottawa: Oberon.
Willis, Deborah (2017). *In the Dark and Other Love Stories*. New York: Norton & Company.

Secondary Works

Bhabha, Homi K. (1994). "Remembering Fanon: Self, Psyche and the Colonial Condition". In: R. J. Patrick Williams and Laura Chrisman, eds. *Colonial Discourse and Post-Colonial Theory: A Reader*. New York: Columbia University Press.
Chariandy, David (2004). "Haunted Diasporas: The Second Generation Stories of André Alexis". *Journal of West Indian Literature* 12.1: 79–89.
Eichhorn, Kate (2016). "The Digital Turn in Canadian and Québécois Literature". In: Cynthia Sugars, ed. *The Oxford Handbook of Canadian Literature*. New York: Oxford University Press. 512–523.
Fanon, Frantz (1967). *Black Skin, White Masks*. New York: Grove Press.
Ganteau, Jean-Michel (2015). *The Ethics and Aesthetics of Vulnerability in Contemporary British Fiction*. London: Routledge.
Guignery, Vanessa and Wojciech Drąg, eds. (2019). *The Poetics of Fragmentation in Contemporary British and American Fiction*. Wilmington: Vernon Press.

Hallet, Wolfgang (2009). "The Multimodal Novel: The Integration of Modes and Media in Novelistic Narration". In: Sandra Heinen and Roy Sommer, eds. *Narratology in the Age of Cross-Disciplinary Narrative Research*. Berlin and New York: De Gruyter. 129–153.

Löschnigg, Maria (2014). *The Contemporary Canadian Short Story: Continuity and Change*. Trier: WVT.

Löschnigg, Maria and Rebekka Schuh, eds. (2018). *The Epistolary Renaissance: A Critical Approach to Contemporary Letter Narratives in Anglophone Fiction*. Berlin and Boston: De Gruyter.

Lynch, Gerald (2001). *The One and the Many: English-Canadian Short Story Cycles*. Toronto: University of Toronto Press.

Malcolm, David (2019). "The Short Story: Fragment and Augment". In: Guignery and Drąg. 33–43.

Nünning, Ansgar and Jan Rupp (2013). "Media and Medialization as Catalysts for Genre Development: Theoretical Frameworks, Analytical Concepts and a Selective Overview of Varieties of Intermedial Narration in British Fiction". In: Michael Basseler, Ansgar Nünning and Christine Schwanecke, eds. *The Cultural Dynamics of Generic Change in Contemporary Fiction: Theoretical Frameworks, Genres and Model Interpretations*. Trier: WVT. 201–234.

Ramon, Alex (2008). *Liminal Spaces: The Double Art of Carol Shields*. Newcastle upon Tyne: Cambridge Scholars Publishing.

Ricœur, Paul (1984 [1983]). *Time and Narrative*, trans. Kathleen McLaughlin and David Pellauer, vol. 1. Chicago: University of Chicago Press.

Schuh, Rebekka (2018). "Enveloped in Epistolary Illusion: The Aesthetics of Reading and Writing Letters in Selected Stories by Alice Munro". In: Löschnigg and Schuh. 73–89.

Schuh, Rebekka (2021). *Stories in Letters – Letters in Stories: Epistolary Liminalities in the Anglophone Canadian Short Story*. Berlin and Boston: De Gruyter.

Suggestions for Further Reading

Beran, Carol L., ed. (2014). *Contemporary Canadian Fiction*. Ipswich, MA: Grey House Publishing.

Dvorák, Marta and Manina Jones, eds. (2007). *Carol Shields and the Extraordinary*. Montreal and Kingston: McGill-Queen's University Press.

Hutcheon, Linda (1988). *A Poetics of Postmodernism: History, Theory, Fiction*. London: Routledge.

Lorre, Christine (2007). "'Dolls, Dolls, Dolls, Dolls': Into the (Extra)ordinary World of Girls and Women". In: Dvorák and Jones. 80–96.

Löschnigg, Maria (2017). "Carried Away by Letters: Alice Munro and the Epistolary Mode". In: Janice Fiamengo and Gerald Lynch, eds. *Alice Munro's Miraculous Art: Critical Essays*. Ottawa: University of Ottawa Press. 97–113.

McHale, Brian (1987). *Postmodernist Fiction*. London: Routledge.

Rose, Marilyn (2014). "Cool Empathy in the Short Fiction of Carol Shields". In: Staines. 197–221.

Staines, David, ed. (2014). *The Worlds of Carol Shields*. Ottawa: University of Ottawa Press.

York, Loraine (2007). "Large Ceremonies: The Literary Celebrity of Carol Shields". In: Dvorak and Jones. 238–255.

7 Gender Scripts and Queer Identities

In the wake of the second-wave feminism that defined the period from the 1960s to the 1980s, many female Canadian authors addressed issues of gender inequality and the restrictive impact of artificially imposed codes of feminine and masculine behaviour in their short fiction. The strong presence of women writers during this phase, especially in short fiction, may also explain the short story's "tendency to turn inward, towards the body, the emotions, and ultimately the mind – territories that have not received sustained or primary attention by male writers in Canada" (Gadpaille 1988: viif). Interestingly, authors whose writing careers started during or in the wake of the heyday of second-wave feminism have often dealt with gender issues and feminist concerns more explicitly than younger generation female writers, also in their later work. Examples are Carol Shields, Elisabeth Harvor, Sandra Birdsell, Isabel Huggan, Katherine Govier, Margaret Gibson, Frances Itani, Elizabeth Hay, Janice Kulyk Keefer, and Diane Schoemperlen – all born in the 1930s, '40s, or early '50s. In Itani's short story cycle *Leaning, Leaning Over Water* (1998), for example, the focus is on the narrator's mother, Maura, and her death by drowning – both literally and figuratively. Her inability to swim symbolises her inability to live her life with a man who loves her but who is nevertheless completely ignorant of her needs and the main source of her sorrow. Novel perspectives open up, in particular, in Margaret Gibson's stories (*Sweet Poison*, 1993; *The Fear Room*, 1996; *Desert Thirst*, 1998), many of which explore male-female power relations against the backdrop of mental issues. In Elisabeth Harvor's stories (*Let Me Be the One*, 1996), in turn, we often find female characters who are "trapped in mother and daughter roles" (Kruk 1992: 146).

The most noteworthy authors in the context of gender issues are, without a doubt, Alice Munro and Margaret Atwood. Launching their careers in the 1950s and '60s, they have indefatigably continued to tackle these issues and shed critical light on the constructedness of "gender scripts", as Laurie Kruk, following Judith Butler's elaborations in *Gender Trouble* (1990), terms the performativity of gender identity (2016: 43). Their recurring return to the exploration of male-female power relations not least reflects and critically responds to the vicissitudes of feminism. Thus, critics have identified

DOI: 10.4324/9781003142683-10

a third wave of feminism in the 1990s, one that rebelled especially against the foundationalist manifestations of second-wave feminism and responded to the impasse that, among others, resulted from "the collapse of the category of 'women'" (Snyder 2008: 175). Reflections of such inclusive, non-judgmental approaches to feminism can be found in Munro's reconciliation of the feminine and the feminist. Other critics prefer to term this phase post-feminism, referring to "an understanding of what it means to be a feminist in a society in which many vocal and influential people have said that feminism was no longer necessary" (Bailey 1997: 25). Since then, however, the gender debate has received another spin, with the #MeToo movement (2017) functioning as a decisive catalyst. It is indisputable that this movement created valuable global awareness of the ongoing problem of sexual harassment and assault and provided women with more efficient legal tools to persecute such abuses. At the same time, however, it is important to see that some of the messages conveyed by the movement may counter female empowerment through their tendency to project women, in a conservative manner, as the weaker sex who are in constant need of protection. Margaret Atwood's new-millennium stories apparently anticipated this danger, featuring female characters who refuse to be victims or, rather, find ways to assume a state of "creative non-victimhood", as Atwood calls the fourth position in the "victim theory" she developed in *Survival* (1972). Considering these shifts and turns of feminism as well as the different voices that define each "wave", it makes sense rather to talk about feminism*s* and thus foreground the productive diversity in criticism as well as literature (see also Devereux 2016: 850).

Arguing that explicitly feminist issues are not so prominent in stories by younger generation female authors does not mean that these writers refrain from addressing female experiences – quite on the contrary. However, these experiences tend to be no longer explicitly staged as a conflict between male and female interests or the result of hegemonic power relations. Also, what Cecily Devereux says about feminist theory – namely, that the fact that radical activism has "receded from the cultural foreground is a compelling sign of the changes effected through the work of the second wave" (2016: 857) – may also apply to creative writing. Examples of such younger-generation writers who feature female characters in novel ways are Lisa Moore, Caroline Adderson, Lynn Coady, Annabel Lyon, and Deborah Willis. Two further younger-generation writers who have enriched perspectives on gender in particularly inventive ways are Kathy Page and Elyse Gasco. The former has done so through her mythopoeic approaches as, for example, in "Of Paradise" and "Low Tide" (both in *Paradise & Elsewhere*, 2014). "Of Paradise" features a community of females living in a paradisiac state, while "Low Tide" is an inter-species story about a female sea creature (who is also the narrator of the story) and thematises the destructive effects of possessiveness. Elyse Gasco, in turn, dedicates her entire collection *Can*

You Wave Bye Bye, Baby (1999) to the experiences of pregnancy and maternity and does so in an aesthetically challenging way.

Another reason that may have prompted the shift from second- to third-wave feminism is a stronger focus – from the 1990s onwards – on intersections between gender, race, and class and on various manifestations of queerness. In "The Politics of Representation", Barbara Godard (1990: 202) highlights the intersection of gender and Indigeneity when she explains the precarious position of Native women:

> That an entire culture has been "raped", has made it impossible for them to love themselves, for Native men to cherish Native women. Admiring the dominant white culture, they adopt its values, seeing only "dark-skinned sensuality" in Native women as Other – the Squaw, not the Princess – raping them and beating them up. . . . Rage against the colonizer is deflected and turned inward on the colonized's own culture in a process of self-destruction.

Memorable examples of narratives which highlight the crippling mechanisms of colonialism on Indigenous women are Lee Maracle's "Too Much to Explain" and "Bertha", but also "Dear Daddy" and "Who's Political Here" (all in *Sojourner's Truth*, 1990). Authors who address questions of Caribbean identity in terms of gender and ethnicity are Dionne Brand, Olive Senior, and the emerging Zalika Reid-Benta, whose debut collection *Frying Plantain* (2019) has won numerous awards. Another young writer who has explored sex and gender against the backdrop of ethnic concerns is Téa Mutonji, whose debut collection *Shut Up, You're Pretty* (2019), too, has been accoladed with prestigious awards. Harrowing insights into cultural exclusion and the exploitation of the female body, in turn, are offered in Evelyn Lau's two collections, *Fresh Girls* (1993) and *Choose Me* (1999).

The stifling effects of constructed gender codes are not only addressed by female writers and do not only concern women. Three eminent Canadian authors who have repeatedly questioned cultural norms of masculinity in their short stories are Alistair MacLeod, Guy Vanderhaeghe and especially Timothy Findley. As Laurie Kruk (2016: 26) aptly remarks, Findley "uses his perspective as a gay man to reflect on the ways that gender roles entrap both sexes" (see also Section 7.2.). However, since gender scripts and gender inequalities have affected women more radically, it is not surprising that in short fiction, too, these issues have been taken up more strongly by female authors, especially Margaret Atwood and Alice Munro.

In the following, I shall, therefore, first, take a closer look at how these two eminent Canadian authors have approached the issue of gender and opened novel perspectives on womanhood and feminist sentiments in general. The second section is dedicated to the expanding body of short fiction which addresses LGBTQ issues, thus reflecting the growing sensitivity to gender fluidity and queerness. I shall round off this chapter with a look at intersections between sexual and ethnic identities on the example of Shyam Selvadurai's *Funny Boy* and Téa Mutonji's *Shut Up You're Pretty*.

7.1. Alternative and Undogmatic Feminisms: Margaret Atwood and Alice Munro

In her polemic reply to accusations in the wake of the #MeToo movement, Margaret Atwood (1939–) quite clearly articulates her understanding of feminism:

> My fundamental position is that women are human beings, with the full range of saintly and demonic behaviours this entails, including criminal ones. They're not angels, incapable of wrongdoing. . . . Nor do I believe that women are children, incapable of agency or of making moral decisions. If they were, we're back to the 19th century, and women should not own property, have credit cards, have access to higher education, control their own reproduction or vote.
> (*Globe and Mail* 2018)

Having been critical of a "guilty because accused" legal policy, as demanded for cases of sexual abuse after the #MeToo outcry, Atwood suddenly found herself denigrated as a traitor to the feminist cause. Over decades and especially in connection with novels like *The Handmaid's Tale* (1985), Atwood's work was classified as feminist, even though the author herself had repeatedly refused this label for her work (Parkin-Gounelas 2008: 935). Both attitudes, hailing the author as a feminist and accusing her of being anti-feminist, arise from an ideological and one-dimensional understanding of feminism, which in turn results in essentialist notions of women as exclusively good and in need of protection. Thus, what is at the core of Atwood's "alternative feminism", as I shall call her narrative empowering of women, is her characters' recognition and subsequent refusal of victim positions. Another central element of Atwood's approach to feminism is her rejection of ideology in favour of highlighting the complex ambiguities of gender relations – an attitude she shares with Alice Munro, despite their different ways of expressing these issues in their stories.

In the following, I shall demonstrate how Atwood's alternative feminism materialises in her short fiction, especially in several of her more recent stories. Female empowerment, for example, is a particularly prominent element in Atwood's rewritings. Thus, it is pointedly encoded, for example, in her inventive recycling of fairy tales, like the title story of *Bluebeard's Egg* (1983), and in her witty and subversive rewriting of *Hamlet*, "Gertrude Talks Back" (*Bones & Murder*, 1995); similarly, this applies to her reworking of the *femme fatale* in "Salome Was a Dancer" (*The Tent*, 2006) and to her unsettling revision of conventional interpretations in "My Last Duchess" (*Moral*

Disorder, 2006), a story which Eleonora Rao has fittingly called "an exercise in hermeneutics" (2009: 60) (see the following case study). However, refusing to be a victim defines not only a large body of Atwood's explicitly intertextual pieces but a considerable number of her stories from her latest collections in general. Noteworthy examples are "Hairball" (*Wilderness Tips*, 1991) and "Stone Mattress" (*Stone Mattress*, 2014).

Case Study: "My Last Duchess" – In Search of Empowering Role Models

"My Last Duchess" is the seventh story in Atwood's only short story cycle to date, *Moral Disorder*, also her most autobiographical work. The cycle follows the format of storified autobiographical fiction, a mode through which the transition between different phases in the protagonist's life is foregrounded. This effect is further enhanced, in *Moral Disorder*, by the sudden shift from first-person to third-person mode in stories six to nine. These stories feature as their main character a woman named Nell, who can be recognised as the unnamed narrator of stories one to five. It is especially in "The Art of Cooking and Serving" and "My Last Duchess" – set in the 1950s and '60s, respectively – that Atwood foregrounds gender as socially and culturally constructed.

In "My Last Duchess", the young first-person narrator's provocative reading against the grain of the eponymous Victorian poem arises from her fierce rejection of disempowering role models. The story captures Nell's last year at high school or, rather, the last weeks before the examinations which will decide about her future and – with her entrance into adulthood – will mark another stage in the protagonist's life. The text assigned in the literature class is Robert Browning's famous poem "My Last Duchess". Just like the "ancient, fermenting smell" (51) in the classroom mixes with the smell "given off by twenty-five adolescent bodies" (51), and with the newness of the modern desks and fluorescent lights, the Victorian poem functions as a ferment for Nell's evolving notions of womanhood and rejection of gender stereotypes.

While the adored and respected teacher, Miss Bessie, tries to sensitise her pupils to the ambiguities of the poem but, in the end, guides them to the most conventional and accepted interpretation, Nell secretly takes her own notes: "*Bumped off*, I wrote. The Duke had bumped off the Duchess. Cheap floozies often got bumped off" (54). From the beginning, the reader has access to Nell's subversive thoughts while the only character who is eventually confronted with her provocative reading is Nell's boyfriend, Bill. Bill hates literature for its ambiguity: "He wanted everything to be clear-cut, as in algebra" (62), as we learn from the narrator, who explains the poem to Bill, trying to make it as logical as possible so that he will be able to give the correct answers in the exam. To help him, she even puts together a list of opposites he could use for characterising the Duke and Duchess:

> Duke: ruthless, ~~stuck-up~~ proud, ~~oily~~ falsely polite, self-centred, shows off his money, ~~greedy~~ experienced, ~~psycho~~ art collector.
> Duchess: innocent, modest, ~~smarmy~~ sincere, earnest, ~~sickly sweet~~ kind to others, humble, ~~stupid~~ inexperienced, art object. (67)

Here, we have a juxtaposition of what Nell knows will be the expected answers on the one hand and the words that she chooses for herself but must discard because they are too slangy or inappropriate on the other. The more Nell ponders on the poem, the more annoyed she gets with the Duchess, comparing her with girls at her school "who smiled at everyone in the same earnest, humourless way":

> In the school yearbook, it usually said about them, "terrific personality" or "Our Miss Sunshine", but I'd never liked these girls very much. Their gaze slid over you, smile and all, usually coming to rest on some boy. Still, they were only doing what the women's magazines said they should do. *A smile costs nothing! A smile: the best makeup tip! Get smile appeal!* Such girls were too eager to please. They were too cheap. That was it – that was the Duke's objection: the Duchess was too cheap. (66)

When, finally, on a Saturday, Nell and Bill go over the poem again, it may not be a coincidence that she is wearing "a loose man's shirt" (69). Bill, who reads the poem like a news report rather than an aesthetically structured work of fiction, becomes so enraged about the Duke that he ends up attacking Nell for defending "the smug little pervert" (71). For Nell, this is the point when Bill must be replaced. As we read earlier in the story, "Bill had replaced my *last* boyfriend, who'd replaced the one before that" (60, my emphasis). Even though she sheds some tears over the breakup, this is not how the story ends. Rather, Nell concentrates on the next text assigned for Miss Bessie's literature class: *Tess of the d'Urbervilles*; and she comes to the conclusion that

> Tess was evidently another of those unlucky pushovers, like the Last Duchess, like Ophelia . . . These girls were all similar. They were too trusting, they found themselves in the hands of the wrong men, they weren't up to things, they let themselves drift. They smiled too much. They were too eager to please. Then they were bumped off, one way or another. (74)

The story concludes upon the narrator's reflections on why they were made to study these "hapless, annoying, dumb-bunny girls" (74), criticising those who choose the books for the curriculum and thereby perpetuate stereotypical notions of women as the "weaker sex". Considering Nell's precarious stage between girlhood and womanhood, it would miss the point, however, to take her rejection of these victimised women as a lack of female solidarity. Rather, Nell's frustration arises from her desperate need for and search for role models; as it is, these models only work in the negative.

It is also a noteworthy detail that Miss Bessie, who *does* function as a role model, is described by Nell as follows: "She trampled right over you if she thought you were fooling around – if you got in her way of teaching" (55). Does this not – if ever so slightly – remind us of the Duke? Nell longs for agency, and one is tempted to imagine that she would have enjoyed reading Atwood's version of Hamlet's mother in "Gertrude Talks Back", who finally admits to having herself killed her husband, whom she describes as an "awful prig" (*Bones & Murder* 20). Atwood's Gertrude also seems to share Nell's opinion of Ophelia when she advises Hamlet to look for another girlfriend, "not that pasty-faced, what's-her-name, all trussed up like a prize turkey in those touch-me-not corsets of hers. If you ask me, there's something off about that girl. Borderline. Any little shock could push her right over the edge" (*Bones & Murder* 20).

Nell's fierce rejection of the female victims that people canonical literature may also result from a vague awareness of her own fragility. Thus, walking across the football field after school is described by Nell as an ordeal for girls, exposing them to male gazing and catcalling

(*Moral Disorder* 59f). The issue of physical exposure is also implied in the image she uses to express her fear about the publication of their grades in the newspaper: "We dreaded this. It would be like having someone yank open the curtain when you were taking a shower" (57). At the same time, Nell feels that smartness was still seen as a deformity in girls (58), meaning that in order to step out of the gender script, they would have to work much harder than boys, whose professional future was already mapped out for them.

Adopting both Miss Bessie and the notorious Duke as role models is an essential handrail for the teenager during this precarious formative phase. Even though Nell's reading of the poem can be seen as rather sexist as she takes an authoritarian male's side, the story as such is feminist, as Nell refuses to be a victim of male power. After all, she refuses to succumb to the fates of Ophelia, Tess, or the Duchess.

"My Last Duchess" – an exercise in hermeneutics: The story provocatively juxtaposes the following interpretations of Browning's poem:

- Miss Bessie's academic/conventional approach
- Bill's "scientific" and "factual" interpretation of the poem
- Bill's subjective and emotional approach
- Nell's "accepted" interpretation
- Nell's alternative interpretation of the poem as an act of (female) empowerment

"My Last Duchess" and Atwood's alternative feminism:

- The story denotes Nell's need and longing for role models.
- It subtly plays with the narrator's vulnerability and her acts of female agency.
- Reusing the Victorian poem and subjecting it to different interpretations makes the story a plea for ambiguity but also contextualises Nell's striving for female empowerment.
- At the same time, this technique exposes how, in her efforts, Nell is haunted by texts from the past.
- "My Last Duchess" is thus also one of many stories by Atwood that feature her female characters' refusal to adopt the victim position.

While in "My Last Duchess" the main character feels some solidarity with a murderer only through her endeavour to avoid the pitfalls of female victimhood, Verna in "Stone Mattress" really *becomes* a murderess. In fact, as Shuli Barzilai has demonstrated, Atwood's short fiction shows a "paradigmatic shift away from the 'feminine' tenet of turning the other check to the 'masculine' morality of blow-for-blow" (2017: 326). In the earlier stories, like "Under Glass" or "Betty" (*Dancing Girls*), female victims of male betrayal or abuse tend to respond in a self-effacing and often self-destructive manner. In contrast, Verna's retaliation (like Kat's in "Hairball"), outrageous as it is, introduces an element of "poetic justice" and illustrates Atwood's idea of a "creative non-victimhood".

"Stone Mattress" is a typical revenge story. Having been raped and impregnated by the school's "golden boy" Bob Goreham ("a shining light from a respectable family", *Stone Mattress* 205), then 14-year-old Verna is shipped off to a "church-run Home for Unwed Mothers" (207), where after difficult labour her child is taken away from her. Being denied any support from her family or the law and being told that it was fortunate that someone as morally degenerate could not have any children anymore, Verna resolves to turn the tables and refuses being "Gullible Verna" (205) any longer. Getting the money for an education through "noontime sex" (208), Verna becomes a physiotherapist, "specializing in the rehabilitation of heart and stroke victims" (209). She makes sure she is legally married to her patients before she "helps" them to smoothly pass away in whatever mode offers itself. For Verna, these "innocent" murders are her survival strategy: "all she ever wanted was to be protected by layer upon layer of kind, insulating money, so that nobody and nothing could get close enough to harm her" (201). The chance for her revenge upon Bob Goreham opens later when, on an Arctic cruise, she comes upon her former tormentor and starts to contrive a scheme to get even with the unwitting Bob, who – as it turns out – just went on to get married and have children and grandchildren (211).

It is aboard the *Resolute II* (214) that Verna resolves to act: "She could avoid him throughout the trip and leave the equation where it's been for the past fifty-some years: unresolved. Or she could kill him" (213). Using all her inventiveness and her knowledge from crime novels, she manages to lure her rapist into a well-prepared trap when the ship stops for a landfall on which the passengers may admire "the world's earliest fossilized stromatolites" (216). It is with a stromatolite – also called stone mattress – that she finally kills Bob, not, however, without giving him a last chance: had he apologised upon being told who she was she would have abandoned her plans. However, when he is smirking – just like 50 years earlier – his fate is sealed. Bob, slain by Verna with a sharp stromatolite, is now "sprawled on the rock" (220); just like Verna when she was brutally ravaged on the cold and hard forest ground, he is now "bedded" on his own stony mattress. The stromatolites, with their visible layers of gray and black that record ancient life on earth, assume yet another symbolic meaning in the story. Especially when linked with Verna's earlier reflection, "[h]ow Paleolithic to still feel wounded by any of it" (212), it is suggested Verna herself is the human equivalent of such a multilayered fossil archive, having recorded everything throughout her long and stony life. Verna gets away with her murderous revenge and, like Kat in "Hairball", feels at peace – even though "tired and somewhat empty" (222). The way "poetic justice" is achieved in this story is rather unsettling, as readers will empathise with the murderess and will be torn between understanding and their moral judgment. However, the comic effects and satirical elements that pervade the story counteract a realistic reading, rendering the text a parable about the refusal to accept victimhood.

In Alice Munro's (1931–) work, too, gender issues play a major role, and like Atwood, Munro, too, is wary regarding the tag of "feminist" for her work. For example, she claimed in an interview (Treisman 2012) that "I never think about being a feminist writer". While Atwood is an explicitly political author and activist, Munro confessed after her Nobel Prize win in 2013, "I guess I am not a political person" (Allardice 2013). Her critical impact, in fact, is mostly manifest in her "use of the interrogative short story form" (Hunter 2004), which is most of all characterised by ambiguity. Consequently, Munro's feminism is undogmatic and sceptical of ideological binarism, making her both a feminine *and* feminist author through her refusal to play off one against the other.

The absurdities of "gender scripts" (Kruk 2016: 43) – that is, the putting down of culturally acquired characteristics of femininity or masculinity as biologically determined – are most memorably exposed in Munro's coming-of-age narratives, including *Lives of Girls and Women* (1971) (see also Chapter 4) and the growing-up stories in *Who Do You Think You Are?* (1978). That different rules apply to girls and boys is also critically addressed in "Boys and Girls" (*Dance of the Happy Shades*, 1968) and "Lying under the Apple Tree" (*The View from Castle Rock*, 2006). In the latter story, for example, the narrator sarcastically remarks about bicycles: "All girls who wanted to establish their femininity had to quit riding them" (198). In "The Turkey Season" (*The Moons of Jupiter*, 1982), Munro also problematises such gender stereotypes with regard to homosexuality (Brandt 2016).

Another issue that is repeatedly thematised and questioned in Munro's work is female submission to male authority. In "Nettles" (*Hateship, Friendship, Courtship, Loveship, Marriage*, 2001), codes of femininity are almost comically undermined when the narrator recalls her childhood self's "fanatic feeling of devotion" (163) for nine-year-old Mike. Emblematic of such codes of submission is the fairy-tale motif of the damsel in distress. In the title story of *Hateship, Friendship, Courtship, Loveship, Marriage*, Munro offers an almost carnivalesque feminist revision of this motif. Johanna, the main character, works as a housekeeper for an elderly gentleman and takes care of his granddaughter Sabitha. She is tricked into believing that Sabitha's father, Ken, is in love with her when Sabitha and her friend Edith intercept and forge letters. In Johanna, the letters trigger romantic fantasies, and so she travels out to Saskatchewan with the resolution to get married to the unwitting Ken. What she finds upon arriving in Gdynia is disastrous: nobody picks her up at the train station, and when she finally finds Ken's run-down home, she is confronted with an ill and delirious man who does not even seem to recognise her. It is at this point that Munro sets in motion a comic switch by assigning the role of the brave knight who comes to rescue the fragile princess to Johanna herself. She comes, she stays, and she manages to transform Ken's chaos into a happy family life. As Coral Ann Howells puts it, Munro "has deftly turned romance on its head . . . , subverting the traditional gendered power relationship into celebration of a woman's managerial capacities and a man's gratitude for being rescued" (2009: 177).

Not all challenges of the "damsel in distress" motif end so happily, as is evident, for example, in "The Beggar Maid" (*Who do You Think You Are?*; U.S. edition entitled *The Beggar Maid*). In this story, socially privileged Patrick tries to fit Rose into his fantasy of being the chivalrous hero who saves a helpless lower-class girl, a fantasy that is inspired by the myth of the beggar maid as rendered concrete in Alfred Tennyson's poem and Edward Burne-Jones's painting *King Cophetua and the Beggar Maid*. Though Rose feels, from the beginning, that this analogy does not work for her, and despite her realisation that "[a]ll the time, moving and speaking, she was destroying herself for him" (85), she nonetheless marries Patrick. Eventually, she manages to break free from this marriage and from Patrick's stifling appropriation of her self, but there is one role she cannot escape from, at least emotionally – namely, that of the mother. In fact, "The Beggar Maid" is one of several stories that adapt the plot of *Anna Karenina*, featuring women who break out of suffocating relationships at the price of being cut off from their children. "This is acute pain. It will become chronic" (213), Pauline, the focal character of "The Children Stay" (*The Love of a Good Woman*, 2000 [1998]), is forced to realise after having walked out of her marriage.

In some stories, the toxically patriarchal is exposed in unflinching ways. It crushes the lives of Alfrida in "Family Furnishings" (*Hateship*) and of Mona in "Haven" (*Dear Life*, 2012), who are both shunned from the bosom of the family so that the men of the family can move on – Alfrida for having become pregnant by her cousin and Mona for having become an artist. Male chauvinism is also at the core of "Powers" (*Runaway*, 2004) and "Dimensions" (*Too Much Happiness*, 2009): in the former story, Tessa, who has the gift of second sight, is exploited by her husband, Neil, for medical experiments, while in the latter a husband punishes his young wife, who turned to a neighbour woman for consolation, by murdering their children.

Of particular interest regarding issues of gender are also those stories that deal with the objectification of the female body. In fact, many of Munro's female characters have internalised the male gaze and struggle to protect the vulnerability of their (ageing) bodies. Thus, in "Lichen" (*The Progress of Love*, 2000 [1986]), women are disposable commodities, as David's reflections about Dina suggest: "sooner or later, if Dina allows her disguise to crack, as Catherine did, he will have to move on. He will have to do that anyway – move on" (49f). In several stories in *The Moons of Jupiter* (1982), middle-aged women "inhabit not just the position of object, but of reject" (Mayberry 1994: 64). "Dulse", "Labour Day Dinner", and "Bardon Bus" all foreground the problematic dependence on male approval that prevents the main characters' pursuit of happiness. "Bardon Bus" was inspired by the author's observations in women's dress shops, "the masquerades and attempts to attract love" (Hancock 1987: 222). Having been abandoned by X, the narrator is devastated and afflicted by feelings of listlessness: "I can't continue to move my body along the streets unless I exist in his mind and in his eyes" (*The Moons of Jupiter* 126). The humiliation she feels reaches a climax when she meets up with Dennis, a friend of X's. She not only hopes to be able to find out about X's whereabouts but also strives to make a lasting physical impression on Dennis so that he can tell his friend how attractive and charming she is. However, the meeting has the opposite effect when Dennis makes comments about the life of ageing women: "It's all in the novels and it's in life too. Men fall in love with younger women. . . . You can't compete with younger women". For him, this is a fact to be accepted since "[i]t's probably biologically correct for men to go after younger women" (121). For X, the next one in line, as it turns out, is ten-years-younger Kay. The story ends with a (sad) irony: Kay, with her "new outfit, a dark green schoolgirl's tunic worn with a blouse or brassiere", is just the next one to put on a masquerade for a man.

Even though many of Munro's female characters remain caught in the intricacies of male-female power imbalances, the stories provide profound insights into the mechanisms that apply in each case. Some stories, however, *do* feature reversals of power relations, however implicit or twisted they may be. Apart from the already mentioned Johanna in "Hateship, Friendship, Courtship, Loveship, Marriage", this holds, for example, for Fiona in "The Bear Came Over the Mountain". While this is first a powerful story about ageing, mental decline, and love and affection in a long-term relationship, it also bears out implications of revenge. Fiona's husband, a retired university professor, used to have numerous affairs with his students. Somehow, Fiona and Grant have managed to save their marriage and seem to be happy together until Fiona is diagnosed with Alzheimer's and must be transferred to a nursing home, Meadowlake. Grant, however, from whose perspective the story is told, still senses the hurt to which he has exposed his wife. When Fiona makes friends with another resident at the home, Aubrey, and hardly seems to recognise her husband anymore, there are moments when Grant thinks that she may do this on purpose to take her revenge for his infidelities. Though this possibility is never confirmed, it is obvious that Fiona's attachment to Aubrey is a trying experience for Grant, which also makes him reflect critically on his past behaviour.

Female empowerment also rests in the act of "writing back". In the epistolary story "Before the Change", for example, the main character "writes back" to her former fiancé in the form of a succession of unsent letters. The letters fulfil a therapeutic function for the unnamed protagonist, who struggles to come to terms with the pain inflicted by Robin. However, they are also an act of writing him out of her mind, of erasing him so that she can move on. The most striking form of "writing back", however, can be found in "Material", where the narrator takes her revenge not in the form of a private letter – as she first contemplates – but in the form of a short story. Doing this, she unflinchingly uses her chauvinistic ex-husband Hugo as material, just as he had (mis)used their former neighbour Dotty in his own short story earlier. Unsparingly debunking his inflated personality "[w]ith a letter disguised as a short story, she is able to achieve a degree of exposure that would not otherwise have been attainable" (Schuh 2021: 157).

7.2. Queering the Canadian Short Story

While in the 1980s and '90s, gender issues largely – though not exclusively – focused on inequalities between men and women and on feminist aspects in general, the new millennium has directed attention more strongly on queer identities. This is evident not only from the growing emergence of stories that address LGBTQ issues but also from websites such as "The Arquives – Canada's LGBTQ2+ Archives" or "Casey the Canadian Lesbrarian". In criticism, Terry Goldie's *Pink Snow: Homotextual Possibilities in Canadian Fiction* (2003) and Peter Dickinson and Richard Cavell's *Sexing the Maple: A Canadian Sourcebook* (2006) can be seen as pioneering works in this field, followed, among others, by *Queer CanLit: Canadian Lesbian, Gay, Bisexual, and Transgendered (LGBT) Literature in English: An Exhibition* (2008) and the 2010 focus issue of *Canadian Literature*, titled "Queerly Canadian".

Gender fluidity and queerness are also represented through trickster figures in many Indigenous stories (see Chapter 8). Transcending binaries of male/female, human/animal, material/spiritual, and good/bad on various levels, the trickster is the quintessential negation of heteronormativity. Among the writers who have used the trickster for queering their stories are, for example, Richard Van Camp and Leanne Betasamosake Simpson. *Love Beyond Body, Space and Time: An Indigenous LGBT Sci-Fi Anthology* (2019) provides a pool of stories which interweave LGBTQ themes and two-spirit characters with Indigenous science fiction and fantasy. "[G]ay and lesbian writers of the First Nations", as Terry Goldie and Lee Frew argue, "often call themselves 'two-spirited', which historically referred to someone who was in some way transgendered but today is applied to gays and lesbians and ultimately anyone who is a part of the sexual diversities" (2016: 872).

"Queering", in fact, has now also become a concept that is used in a rather general sense to refer to inclusivity and to the questioning of normative binarism – not only regarding the subject matter but also modes of representation; in other words, the term "queer" is also used to denote "anything outside of the norm" (Goldie and Frew 2016: 873). In this section, however, the focus will be on stories that explicitly address LGBTQ issues and open imaginative spaces for marginalised identities regarding sex and gender.

Probably the most interesting author in this context is Timothy Findley (1930–2002). As Laurie Kruk has observed, Findley "enacted doubleness in his sexual orientation as a gay man, at odds with his middle-class, WASP origins from central Ontario and his privileged childhood in Rosedale, one of the wealthiest suburbs of Toronto. . . . His 'double-voicing' addresses class, gender, and sexuality, with a special interest in questioning dominant depictions of masculinity" (2016: 10). The issue of homosexuality is addressed explicitly only in a handful of (later) stories, with "Bragg and Minna" and "A Gift of Mercy" (*Stones*, 1988) being the "first published examination of marriage between a heterosexual woman and a bisexual man who prefers same-sex partners" (Grace 2020: 310). Two further Bragg-and-Minna stories, which focus on different stations in the couple's life, are "A Bag of Bones" and "Come as You Are" (*Dust to Dust*, 1997). As Sherrill Grace writes, Bragg is "definitely modelled on Findley himself", whereas Minna has been inspired by Canadian writer Marian Engel (2020: 310f). Like most of Findley's characters (including Minna), Bragg is wounded, most of all because "[a]ll his life he'd been taught he was an outcast – part of the scourge upon mankind" ("Bragg and Minna", 25). A recurring trope in Findley's stories that reflects characters' being at odds with their identity is the mirror (Kruk 2016: 30). Thus, in "A Gift of Mercy", Bragg is "looking into the mirror the way most people do who don't really want to see themselves – eyes askance, afraid of meeting other eyes" (*Stones* 36).

In both "Bragg and Minna" (*Stones*) and "A Bag of Bones" (*Dust to Dust*), Bragg is haunted by the fear that he is a "genetic homosexual" (96) and uses this fear as an argument against having children in the many fierce debates with Minna about this issue. In "Bragg and Minna", chronologically the last episode in the story of the couple, Minna, however, *does* finally manage to get pregnant and gives birth to Stella, a baby with six fingers per hand and six toes per foot and a brain defect. Her unconditional love for the child reflects her general attitude to life; she not only refuses to make affection depend on conventional notions of "lovability" but feels particularly drawn to marginalised lives, no matter whether due to social circumstances, sexual orientation, or bodily "defects". While Bragg keeps struggling with his identity as a gay man, it is, in fact, Minna who embodies an all-encompassing openness to the unconventional through her embrace of life and rejection of stifling norms. In "Bragg and Minna", she is diagnosed with cancer of the lungs shortly after Stella's birth and leaves Bragg (and his lover, Col, who was also part of the household), moving to Australia in search of people who will love her baby when she is no longer there. When she is dead, Bragg and Col travel to Australia to scatter her ashes at Ku-Ring-Gai. The exact spot where

Minna had wanted this to be done shows petroglyphs, a man, a woman, and a child who "had long albino hair and one six-fingered hand stretched out for all the world to see forever – and one short leg, for which her parents had made a loving box. Forever. And forever visible" (26). It is only on the two men's flight back to America that Bragg, in a moment of epiphany, deciphers the small figure as a "disfigured" child and recognises his own love for Stella. This might even suggest – if ever so faintly – that he has also come to accept his own being "different".

Since Bragg and Minna are both writers, these stories also abound with meta-narrative references. In Bragg's case, it is interesting to see how he implicitly writes his homosexuality into his stories. Thus, the humour that characterises his writing (but not his life as lived) is produced by rage – rage about how he was treated by others, above all his family, who regarded homosexuality as something that demanded forgiveness or needed to be cured or, in his mother's case, an incarnation of a sin in her (*Stones* 49). The fact that "[a]ll his life he had known he was set aside from the comfortable mass by the fact of his homosexuality" is the source of "the rage that produces his written humour – and the rage, by most accounts, that saved his writing from the spoils of too much darkness" (*Stones* 50), as is disclosed in "A Gift of Mercy". Bragg's tendency to circumvent his homosexuality is captured by his lover Colin in "Come as You Are", who calls him "the queerest queer" (*Dust to Dust* 126) he has ever met: "Minna is still the centre of your life. You still talk *straight*. You never tell gay jokes" (126). Again, the truly inclusive character is straight Minna: it is she who is not bothered at all to be in love with a gay man and whose novels abound with gay characters while, as we learn in "A Bag of Bones", "Bragg had eschewed the subject entirely" in his stories (*Dust to Dust* 99). However, this only goes as far as explicit references are concerned. At a party, he is approached by a queer man who interprets one of Bragg's fictive characters as gay, even though Bragg had thought he had only thematised impotence and how it ruined relationships. Bragg then realises that he "didn't recognize all the possibilities" (135) of his character – a statement that can somehow also be applied to Findley's own work. Those stories which do not explicitly address queerness and homophobia implicitly shed light on LGBTQ issues through Findley's subtle questioning of hegemonic masculinity and of gender politics, in general, as well as his critical unmasking of forms of exclusion and stigmatisation on all levels. In the same manner, those stories that explicitly address homosexuality, like the four Bragg-and-Minna stories, reach far beyond it through their general critique of normative codes which control who is "in" and who is "out".

A completely different approach to homosexuality can be found in Patrick Roscoe's (1967–) stories, especially in the daring collection *Birthmarks* (1990). The book maps the trajectories of people whose lives are characterised by homelessness, drug abuse, and male prostitution – including that of children, as in "My Lover's Touch". In this haunting story, the six-year-old first-person narrator finds himself locked up in a dark room and is beaten and sexually abused by a man who never says a word to his victim. The boy develops a strange and passionate attachment to his tormentor and longs for him in the periods of waiting: "Does he miss me when he goes away? Ache for me as I ache for him?" (34) When he is finally saved and efforts are made to resocialise him into the "normal" life of a schoolboy, this fails. He becomes a prostitute and, all the time, remains full of longing for his "lover's touch" (37). Like so many of Roscoe's well-crafted stories, "My Lover's Touch" is a disturbing read, dealing with self-destructive desires and the dark realms of love *in extremis*. Gay sexuality and desire are also at the core of several stories in *The Truth About Love* (2001), where the author again links the terrifying with the tender, using language that is at the same time brutal and lyrical. This can be observed especially in "From the Laboratory of Love", another story that is haunted by childhood experiences of darkness and images of being caged, and in "The Truth About Love" and "Touching Darkness", where Roscoe experiments with the you-form to render harrowing glimpses into gay relationships and the destructive effects of past abuse (see also Section 5.2.).

Gay sexuality and identity also play a major role in *Calendar Boy* (2001) by Andy Quan (1969–). In the 16 stories, sexual identity is evocatively interwoven with questions of cultural/ethnic identity, featuring Chinese characters who, as gay men, do not fit into their communities while, likewise, experiencing themselves as outsiders in gay communities, where "the white muscle boys" (93) seem to be all the hype. "Immigration" is the most interesting story in this respect. The first-person narrator Albert's recognition of his homosexuality and gradual migration from his former straight circles to gay circles is framed by the history of his Cantonese ancestors and their voyage to Gold Mountain. Albert's drawing of analogies between his homosexuality and the experience of migration is triggered by his parents' fierce reaction when he tells them he is gay and by his endeavours to explain to his mother: "It's not exactly a lifestyle, ma. I can't help the way I am" (171f). Searching for explanations, Albert muses: "Maybe it was planted in my genes somewhere in my family history that I would be a traveller, that I would leave my home" (172). In "How to Cook Chinese Rice", Quan again employs evocative structural devices to depict his first-person narrator's burgeoning sexuality. A meticulous 11-step instruction on how to cook rice provides the organising principle and chapter titles of the story (for example, "7. Heat it up", 11, and "8. Steam it up", 12), and these instructions are – comically – suggested to function as guidelines for the main character's search of a perfect sexual encounter. The title story, in turn, is divided into 12 sections that each represent one month of the year, mirroring the pages of a calendar with perfect white male bodies that Gary clandestinely buys and of one he intends to produce himself. His own calendar is supposed to feature Asian models (including himself), countering the beauty standard of white bodies in gay communities. Even though the calendar project dissolves into nothing, December still brings success for Gary: he is nominated as a model for the cover of *Q Pink News* after a gay Asian group protested against the magazine for almost exclusively showing white guys.

A noteworthy author who has addressed LGBTQ issues in several of her stories is Kathy Page (1958–). "Dear Son" (*The Two of Us*, 2016), for example, recounts a young gay man's conflicted relationship with his widowed, lonely, obese, and impoverished mother. The son, Greg, is the focaliser, and his unfavourable and repulsive thoughts about his mother when she visits him in "the big city" (59) clash uncomfortably with the mother's kindness and gratefulness as rendered through her direct speeches and her letter (which is cited verbatim in the story). However, the story subtly encourages the reader to look beyond the surface pattern of "loving mother" and "ungrateful son" and rather ponder on the reasons for Greg's feelings and behaviour. It transpires that for Greg, growing up with his mother in a small-town environment and filling the void the death of his father had left was stifling. Even though he escaped the "dark terraced house" that was his childhood home "at the first opportunity, to college, the big city, men, freedom, life itself" (59), it is obvious that his act of liberation has not been entirely successful. One such indicator is his vehement reaction to the "Dear Son" salutation of his mother's letter: "This use of the word 'Son', capitalized, this insistence on the indelible connection between them, was another thing that drove him mad" (58). Writing "Son" instead of "Greg" not only foregrounds their familial relationship but also infantilises him. It infringes on his attempts to live the life of a mature and autonomous person, drawing him back, again and again, to a period in his life he does not want to be reminded of, a period when he felt forced to hide his queerness. Instead of confronting his problem, however, Greg just pushes it away by hiding his homosexuality from his mother, hiring a fake girlfriend, making his boyfriend Luke leave the apartment during his mother's visit, and making his new home in the city as different from the family home as possible. It is only in a complete state of drunkenness and when he can no longer bear his discomfort during their dinner in a French restaurant that he blurts out: "I like men . . . I'm gay. Bent. Queer: I've got a boyfriend" (67). The ending is ambiguous: his mother does not seem to have a problem with this revelation and just asks for his boyfriend's name; also, for the first time, his feelings for his mother are not just driven by disgust. On the contrary, when they get home from the restaurant, he takes her arm – not to help her but "to steady himself" (69). However, the last sentence, indicating that, in his drunkenness, the stairs up to his flat were "twice as steep-looking as they really were" (69), leaves it open whether Greg has solved his problem and rid himself of a burden that had weighed on him and that even the therapist could not untangle.

Another intriguing story by Page is "The Kissing Disease" (*Paradise & Elsewhere*, 2014). The story, which displays dystopian elements, is told from the point of view of 14-year-old Gary, who listens to the national radio warning people of the kissing disease that is "transmitted mouth to mouth" (145). As it is, the "virus" is really just expressive of happiness and tenderness, and the propaganda and measures by the authorities set up barriers between people, antagonising them and reducing relationships to mechanical sex. Gary is alienated from his body, his parents, and society. The spell is eventually broken by Tim, a soldier whose unit is stationed nearby to control the "*cordon sanitaire*" (147), a barbed-wire fence that had been erected around the town. Tim is Gary's "best and only friend" (148), but having been brainwashed by the authorities into believing that tenderness and kissing in particular "rot your brain" (149), Gary just meets Tim to wander about town and to have a few pints in the bar "for the clean" (148). Unlike Gary, who has never kissed, Tim remembers how it feels and becomes increasingly fed up with the situation. He tells Gary that none of the "kissers" locked out of town ever tries to get back in – rather, it is the "clean" who try to escape (151). In the end, Tim's longing for tenderness and Gary's recognition of his sexual desire for him gain the upper hand, and they triumph over the imposed moral rigour when they finally commit the "crime" of kissing.

In *The Dark and Other Love Stories* (2017), Deborah Willis (1982–) includes two stories which offer moving portraits of tenderness and erotic longing between teenage girls. In both "The Dark" and "Welcome to Paradise", it is, above all, the narrator who sees the relationship as more than just a close bonding between girls. "It was the closest thing to love at first sight" (13), 13-year-old Jessie says about Andrea, whom she meets at a summer camp; when they sneak out one night to be on their own, it is "with the single-mindedness of lovers" (17). Later in life, Jessie tells her husband about their secret outings and how they took off their clothes at the lakeshore, "but [she] stopped at this point" (22). Similarly, in "Welcome to Paradise", the first-person narrator Hannah recalls her infatuation with Lielle when they both were 14, frequently turning to we-narration to further highlight their strong homoerotic bond. Their habit of breaking into houses in Calgary is described by Hannah as "an adventure, a tragedy – to wed us together" (160), and when she remembers how Lielle "was holding [her] hand" and their "clammy skin stuck [them] together", she adds, "we were married in fear" (163). It is this memory of her first love that keeps coming up and resonates into her later life with her partner and daughter.

Two writers who have repeatedly addressed lesbian love and queer identity are Emma Donoghue (1969–), who is also the editor of the anthology *Love Alters: Stories of Lesbian Love and Erotica* (2013), and Shani Mootoo (1957–), both born in Dublin, the latter to Trinidadian parents. Mootoo's collection *Out on Main Street* (1993) explores how being a woman, being lesbian and being Indo-Trinidadian intersect. Queerness, though in the much broader sense of being "strange" or unconventional, also plays a major role in Barbara Gowdy's (1950–) daringly bizarre collection *We So Seldom Look on Love* (1992). The eight stories all focus on the human body and celebrate its uniqueness, no matter the deviation from norms, no matter if they happen to be corpses, no matter if they have two heads or extra genital organs and legs. In these both beautiful and unsettling stories, it seems, being lovable is disentangled from preconceived notions of beauty, decorum, and norms. The final story, "Flesh of My Flesh", explicitly addresses transgender issues when Marian discovers upon her wedding night that her husband Sam is a trans man. First, Marian is shocked and disgusted and feels that the "'him' she used to love isn't there any more" (175). In the afflicted weeks that follow, Marian comes to understand that "whoever he is he's who she loves" (182) and that this love is a miracle. On the day before Sam is to have the operation that will match his genitalia to his male gender identity, Marian, for the first time, lets Sam become intimate with her. The extraordinary moment of tenderness and sexual pleasure they share implies that their happiness will no longer depend on the masculinity or femininity of their bodies.

Regarding transgender, Casey Plett (1987–), who has herself undergone gender transition, has dedicated much of her work to this issue. Plett is also co-editor of the anthology *Meanwhile, Elsewhere: Science Fiction and Fantasy from Transgender Writers* (2017). In the 11 stories assembled in *A Safe Girl to Love* (2014), Plett provides glimpses into the minds of trans women. In two of the stories, "Twenty Hot Tips" and "How to Stay Friends", she uses you-narration for this purpose, rendering the effect that a part of the narrator-character's self (possibly her future self) encourages and supports the other – still insecure – part of herself. This is evident, for example, when she goes shopping for women's clothes for the first time in the former story or when she is confronted with her cis ex-girlfriend for the first time after her transition in the latter. "Other Women" is a homecoming story, just like "Enough Trouble" from Plett's second collection *A Dream of a Woman* (2021). In "Enough Trouble", the main character, Gemma, moves back to her Manitoban hometown (which shows many similarities to the author's own hometown of Morden, Manitoba) and contemplates whether it was possible for her as an openly trans woman to live there again. About Gemma, the author says that her "upbringing was homophobic and transphobic and this was traumatic, yes, but part of her upbringing was also moving and gentle and filled with grace. Gemma and I have different life histories. But I do feel the same way about my own experiences" (Porter 2021: online).

7.3. Intersections of Sexual and Cultural Identity

I want to conclude with two short story cycles which both interweave cultural or ethnic liminality and marginalisation with issues of sex and gender – namely, Shyam Selvadurai's *Funny Boy* (1994) and Téa Mutonji's *Shut Up You're Pretty* (2019). Even though the former is a narrative of departure, ending shortly before the young narrator's journey to Canada as a refugee, and the latter a narrative of arrival, featuring the main character's first years as an immigrant in Canada, both coming-of-age-narratives establish meaningful connections between cultural and sexual awareness and identity.

In *Funny Boy*, Sri Lankan-Canadian writer Shyam Selvadurai (1965–) traces Arjie's growing awareness of ethnic and sexual otherness in six stories, each of which marks a transitional step in the boy's life. In the course of about eight years, Arjie becomes painfully aware of his twofold "otherness" – that is, his homosexuality in a heteronormative society and his being a Tamil within a Sinhalese majority. While the first and the last story of the cycle focus on Arjie himself, the other four stories illustrate the "normative gaze", which controls and corrects any in-between positions, be they sexual, racial, or political, with regard to other characters who are closely related to Arjie.

In the initial story, "Pigs Can't Fly", transition is brought about by seven-year-old Arjie's brutal expulsion from the "magic" world of the girls he feels drawn to. While being immersed in their favourite game, "bride bride", at their grandparents' house, one of his cousins, who is jealous of Arjie for always playing the part of the bride, exposes the boy's violation of a clear separation of male and female space. When Arjie, dressed up as an Indian bride, is dragged in front of the assembled family, the laughter and quizzical looks of the adults immediately tell the boy that he must have committed a great wrong. Under the spell of this "normative gaze" (Banerjee 2005: 153), Arjie can never again follow his interests and inclinations with ease and self-confidence. Although he is neither able to grasp what exactly the problem of his otherness is nor to understand the meaning of the word "funny", Arjie nevertheless knows that a door has closed.

In the second story, the normative gaze is on Radha Auntie, who, having lived in America for four years, has not only adopted Western ways and styles but also falls in love with a Sinhalese man, which is simply not the done thing for a Tamil. After all, "most people marry their own kind" (54), as Arjie is told by his mother, who is ironically not aware of how her statement – if applied to sexual codes – would have undermined heterosexual norms. That it may be necessary to hide your real identity in order to be accepted is also illustrated in the example of Jegan, a young Tamil who is advised by Arjie's father as follows: "As a Tamil you have to learn how to play the game. . . . The trick is not to make yourself conspicuous" (173). In fact, all the characters in *Funny Boy* whom Arjie feels drawn to (including his first boyfriend Shehan in the penultimate story "The Best School of All") are themselves in some in-between situation as they transgress normative borders, and they all fail in some way. However, by attentively watching, listening, and recording what happens around him, Arjie expands his own perception and finds ways to circumvent some of the absurd moral, social, political, and racial codes which govern society. After all, he does, in the end, not only live his queer identity but does so with a boyfriend who belongs to the "forbidden" Sinhalese. Not even the outbreak of violence between Tamils and Sinhalese in Colombo in July 1983, as chronicled in the concluding story "Riot Journal: An Epilogue", leads to an alienation between the two teenage lovers, even though Sinhalese radicals tear down Arjie's home and burn his grandparents alive in their car. When Arjie weeps "for the loss of [his] home, for the loss of everything that [he] held to be precious" (311), he also weeps for Shehan, whom he must give up when his family prepares to emigrate to Canada. Liminality, as is indicated, will remain a central dimension of Arjie's life, whose family, as his father declares, does not belong to Sri Lanka anymore (204), nor does it yet belong to Canada, where they will arrive as "penniless refugees" (309).

Experiences of being in-between also define *Shut Up You're Pretty* by Congolese-Canadian author Téa Mutonji. The short story cycle maps Loli's jumbled trajectory from childhood to adulthood in 18 short and short short stories which interweave her cultural liminality – belonging to Canada but also somehow to her native Congo – and sexual in-betweenness. The latter is evident in the protagonist's queerness, which is never explicitly stated but "comes through in her thoughts and interaction with her best friends" (Raj Kaur 2019: online).

Loli's relationships with men all come to nothing and, moreover, foreground the men's lack of commitment or their racial prejudice, as is the case with her friend from youth, Dylan, who ends their relationship with the words: "I just never pictured myself with a black girl, you know?" (*Shut Up* 74). The most striking story in this context is the title story. It maps Loli's infatuation with Jonas, a stuck-up Ph.D. candidate who refuses to talk about their relationship; for him, it seems to be an easy sexual one – nothing more. And when Loli asks him, "Is there any meaning in us?" (103), he accuses her of making it all complicated. That Jonas "is not it" is already anticipated at the beginning of their relationship when Loli discloses: "what I felt wasn't electricity but the opposite. Like fingers putting out a light" (99). It is also evident in Jonas's rejection of Loli's poetry. The relationship with Jonas is toxic and almost kills Loli, who eventually frees herself but realises that she is pregnant. In "Women Talking", Loli becomes friends with Steph while waiting for her abortion in the clinic. The two women's observations of and reflections on the other female patients not only shed light on the misery women undergo at the hands of men but, more importantly, highlight female bonding as an essential element of support, thus confirming the author's statement that, to her, "the main themes in the book . . . really centre around womanhood" (C.B.C. Books 2020: online).

Even though in "Sober Party" the narrator concludes, "I had no luck with men, or with women" (127), it cannot be overlooked that it is in her relationships with women that Loli finds community, tenderness, and erotic thrill. This is already evident in the first story, "Tits for Cigs", which captures the beginning of the friendship between Jolie and Loli. Their emotional and physical intimacy grows and finds a sudden end in "If Not Happiness", where Jolie moves in with the much older Henry, leaving 15-year-old Loli heartbroken. In "The Common Room", 17-year-old Loli moves in with Olivia and thinks, when looking at her, "*She might be it*" (83), whereas in "Shut Up

You're Pretty", she realises about her Ethiopian roommate Patty: "She was the smell. She was home" (101). Loli's queer sensitivity is also implicitly suggested by her thoughts when, for example, she observes two little boys holding hands, having no idea "that people might judge them for the gesture" (111).

Loli's cultural in-betweenness is evident on many levels of the story cycle. While some stories, like for example "This is Only Temporary" or "Phyllis Green", explicitly thematise racism, the most interesting aspect regarding Loli's liminal state is her own coming to terms with her Canadian and Congolese identities. When asked by Olivia about her best childhood memory, Loli answers "immigrating" (80), making it obvious that she embraces being in Canada. However, she is strongly shaped by her parents' unfathomable grief, which results in her father's suicide and her mother's becoming a "sadistic mourner" (127). There is no real moving on, it seems, without first accepting who you are. It is, therefore, no coincidence that the cycle is somehow framed and punctuated by Loli's relationship with her mother (Semel 2019: online). "Mother stopped singing once we immigrated" (9), as it says in the first paragraph of the book. After her father's suicide, her mother's "sadness was overwhelming" (67), making Loli move out at the age of 17 in order to breathe. Then, step by step, she draws nearer again until, in the final story, "Tilapia Fish", we find mother and daughter united in the former's kitchen. This reunion has already been anticipated earlier when, upon finding out that she is pregnant, Loli calls Patty's Ethiopian mother in Africa and the "phone call lasted two hours" (108) and when she asks this woman whom she had never met whether she should call her own mother (109).

Due to scattered references to Loli's writing and her proleptic statement, "And then one day, I crowned myself a poet" (127), *Shut Up You're Pretty* may also be read as a "portrait of a young woman as an artist". However, as the concluding story suggests, it is her tentative connection to her roots, to the other part of her cultural identity, that implies, ever so faintly, a happy ending. The book's breaking up of smooth storylines mirrors Loli's life as she experiences it; after all, as Mutonji says in an interview, "[t]o me, life's just as messy and unlinear, even if it's following a clear timeline" (Semel 2019: online). However, the concluding "Tilapia Fish" introduces an element of calm and peace through the trope of homecoming which, by implication, also suggests Loli's acceptance of hybridity regarding both her cultural and sexual identities.

The more strongly activist manifestations of second-wave feminism seem to have established solid ground for the emergence of a broad range of (post) feminisms that are also reflected in the contemporary Canadian short story. They are especially visible in Alice Munro's and Margaret Atwood's alternative and undogmatic approaches to gender scripts, which have provided valuable contributions to a more diverse understanding of the concept of feminism. In addition, the focus has strongly moved to the representation of intersections between gender and Indigeneity or ethnic identities in general. While literary engagements with the repercussions of fixed gender codes on women already defined many stories by female writers in the 1960s, 1970s, and early 1980s, LGBTQ themes started to be taken up only in the late 1980s, with Timothy Findley being one of the pioneers. Since then, stories which challenge heteronormativity are on the rise and fan out the perspectives on sex and gender, thus highlighting the diversity of what it means to be human. Shyam Selvadurai's and Téa Mutonji's intriguing short story cycles, as has been demonstrated, are particularly interesting examples of how short fiction displays intersections and draws meaningful analogies between sexual and ethnic identities.

Works Cited

Primary Works

Atwood, Margaret (1995 [1994]). *Bones & Murder*. London: Virago.
Atwood, Margaret (2006). *Moral Disorder and Other Stories*. New York: Random House.
Atwood, Margaret (2014). *Stone Mattress: Nine Tales*. New York: Random House.
Findley, Timothy (1996 [1988]). *Stones*. Toronto: Penguin.
Findley, Timothy (1997). *Dust to Dust: Stories*. Toronto: HarperCollins.
Gowdy, Barbara (1992). *We so Seldom Look on Love*. Toronto: HarperCollins.
Munro, Alice (2000 [1986]). *The Progress of Love*. London: Vintage.
Munro, Alice (2000 [1998]) *The Love of a Good Woman*. London: Vintage.
Munro, Alice (2002 [2001]). *Hateship, Friendship, Courtship, Loveship, Marriage*. London: Vintage.
Munro, Alice (2004 [1978]). *Who Do You Think You Are?* [*The Beggar Maid*]. London: Vintage.
Munro, Alice. (2006). *The View from Castle Rock. Stories*. London: Chatto & Windus.
Munro, Alice (2007 [1982]). *The Moons of Jupiter*. London: Vintage.
Mutonji, Téa (2019). *Shut Up You're Pretty. Stories*. Vancouver: Arsenal Pulp Press.
Page, Kathy (2014). *Paradise & Elsewhere*. Windsor, ON: Biblioasis.
Page, Kathy (2016). *The Two of Us*. Windsor, ON: Biblioasis.
Quan, Andy (2001). *Calendar Boy*. Vancouver: New Star Books.
Rosco, Patrick (1990). *Birthmarks*. London: Penguin.
Selvadurai, Shyam (1994). *Funny Boy*. Toronto: McClelland & Stewart.
Willis, Deborah (2017). *The Dark and Other Love Stories*. New York: W.W. Norton & Company.

Secondary Works

Allardice, Lisa (2013). "Nobel Prize Winner Alice Munro: It's a Wonderful Thing for the Short Story". Online: www.theguardian.com/books/2013/dec/06/alice-munro-interview-nobel-prize-short-story-literature [accessed: 7 December 2014].
Atwood, Margaret (1972). *Survival*. Toronto: Anansi.
Atwood, Margaret (2018). "Am I a Bad Feminist". *The Globe and Mail*, 13 January. Online: www.theglobeandmail.com/opinion/am-i-a-bad-feminist/article37591823/

[accessed: 10 December 2020]. Also included in: Atwood, Margaret (2022). *Burning Questions: Essays and Occasional Pieces 2004–2021*. London: Chatto & Windus. 335–339.

Bailey, Cathryn (1997). "Making Waves and Drawing Lines: The Politics of Defining the Vicissitudes of Feminism". *Hypatia* 12.3: 17–28.

Banerjee, Mita (2005). "Queer Laughter: Shyam Selvadurai's *Funny Boy* and the Normative as Comic". In: Susanne Reichl and Mark Stein, eds. *Cheeky Fictions: Laughter and the Postcolonial*. Amsterdam: Rodopi. 149–160.

Barzilai, Shuli (2017). "How Far Would You Go? Trajectories of Revenge in Margaret Atwood's Short Fiction". *Contemporary Women's Writing* 11.3: 316–335.

Brandt, Stefan (2016). "'Not a Puzzle so Arbitrarily Solved': Queer Aesthetics in Alice Munro's Early Fiction". *Zeitschrift für Kanadastudien* 36: 28–41.

CBC Books (2020). "Téa Mutonji on How She Authentically Writes Diversity as an Author of Colour". Online: www.cbc.ca/books/téa-mutonji-on-how-she-authentically-writes-diversity-as-an-author-of-colour-1.5467408 [accessed: 19 January 2022].

Devereux, Cecily (2016). "Canadian Feminist Literary Criticism and Theory in the 'Second Wave'". In: Sugars. 845–862.

Gadpaille, Michelle (1988). *The Canadian Short Story*. Oxford: Oxford University Press.

Godard, Barbara (1990). "The Politics of Representation: Some Native Canadian Women Writers". *Canadian Literature* 124–125 (Spring–Summer): 183–225.

Goldie, Terry and Lee Frew (2016). "Gay and Lesbian Literature in Canada". In: Sugars. 862–876.

Grace, Sherrill (2020). *Tiff: A Life of Timothy Findley*. Waterloo: Wilfrid Laurier University Press.

Hancock, Geoffrey (1987). "Alice Munro". In: *Canadian Writers at Work: Interviews with G.H.* Toronto: Oxford University Press. 222.

Howells, Coral Ann (2009). "Intimate Dislocations: Alice Munro, *Hateship, Friendship, Courtship, Loveship, Marriage*". In: Harold Bloom, ed. *Alice Munro*. New York: Bloom's Literary Criticism. 167–192.

Hunter, Adrian (2004). "Story into History: Alice Munro's Minor Literature". *English* 53: 219–238.

Kruk, Laurie (1992). "A Humiliation a Day: Elisabeth Harvor in Conversation with Laurie Kruk". *Antigonish Review* 90: 143–163.

Kruk, Laurie (2016). *Double-Voicing the Canadian Short Story*. Ottawa: University of Ottawa Press.

Mayberry, Katherine J. (1994). "Narrative Strategies of Liberation in Alice Munro". *Studies in Canadian Literature/Études en littérature Canadienne* 19.2: 57–66.

Parkin-Gounelas, Ruth (2008). "Margaret Atwood: Feminism and Fiction". *Modern Fiction Studies* 54.4: 935–938.

Porter, Ryan (2021). "Casey Plett on Truth, Fiction, and the Illusion of Community". *Quill and Quire*, September. Online: https://quillandquire.com/authors/casey-plett-on-truth-fiction-and-the-illusion-of-community/ [accessed: 4 February 2022].

Raj Kaur, Rachna (2019). "Tea Mutonji Adds an Incisive Coming-of-Age Tale to Scarborough's Literary Canon". Online: https://nowtoronto.com/culture/books-culture/tea-mutonji-shut-up-youre-pretty [accessed: 19 January 2022].

Rao, Eleonora (2009). "Margaret Atwood: *Moral Disorder*". *Tolomeo* 12.2: 58–61.

Redekop, Magdalene (1992). *Mothers and Other Clowns: The Stories of Alice Munro*. London and New York: Routledge.

Schuh, Rebekka (2021). *Stories in Letters – Letters in Stories: Epistolary Liminalities in the Anglophone Canadian Short Story*. Berlin and Boston: De Gruyter.

Semel, Paul (2019). "Exclusive Interview: Shut Up You're Pretty Author Téa Mutonji". Online: https://paulsemel.com/exclusive-interview-shut-up-youre-pretty-author-tea-mutonji/ [accessed: 19 January 2022].

Snyder, Claire (2008). "What Is Third-Wave Feminism? A New Directions Essay". *Signs* 34.1: 175–196.

Sugars, Cynthia, ed. (2016). *The Oxford Handbook of Canadian Literature*. New York: Oxford University Press.

Treisman, Deborah (2012). "On *Dear Life*: An Interview with Alice Munro". *The New Yorker*, 20 November. Online: www.newyorker.com/books/page-turner/on-dear-life-an-interview-with-alice-munro [accessed: 13 December 2014].

Suggestions for Further Reading

Bakshi, Sandeep (2019). "The Crisis of Postcolonial Modernity: Queer Adolescence in Shyam Selvadurai's *Funny Boy* and P. Parivaraj's *Shiva and Arun*". *Commonwealth Essays and Studies* 42.1 (Revolution(s)): 1–14.

Goldie, Terry (2003). *Pink Snow: Homotextual Possibilities in Canadian Fiction*. Peterborough: Broadview Press.

Kruk, Laurie (2007). "Mothering Sons: Stories by Findley, Hodgins and MacLeod Uncover the Mother's Double Voice". *Atlantis* 32.1: 35–45.

Löschnigg, Maria (2016). "'Oranges *and* Apples': Alice Munro's Undogmatic Feminism". In: David Staines, ed. *The Cambridge Companion to Alice Munro*. Cambridge: Cambridge University Press. 60–78.

Rasporich, Beverly J. (1990). *Dance of the Sexes: Art and Gender in the Fiction of Alice Munro*. Edmonton: University of Alberta Press.

Rayter, Scott, Donald W. McLeod and Maureen FitzGerald, eds. (2008). *Queer CanLit: Canadian Lesbian, Gay, Bisexual, and Transgendered (LGBT) Literature in English: An Exhibition*. Toronto: Thomas Fisher Rare Book Library.

Tolan, Fiona (2021). "Margaret Atwood's Revisions of Classic Texts". In: Coral Ann Howells, ed. *The Cambridge Companion to Margaret Atwood*. Cambridge: Cambridge University Press. 109–123.

York, Lorraine (1991). *Front Lines: The Fiction of Timothy Findley*. Toronto: ECW Press.

8 Indigenous Short Fiction in English

Stories have always been an intrinsic element of Indigenous cultures and have functioned as specific knowledge systems in Aboriginal communities. As Pueblo storyteller Simon J. Ortez explains in his introduction to *Speaking for the Generations*, "traditional oral stories depict, assert, and confirm the natural evolvement – or the origin and emergence – of Native people from the boundless energy of the universe" (1998: xiii). What is a relatively new phenomenon, however, is the production of written stories in English or French by Indigenous storytellers. While the term "Native American Renaissance", coined by Kenneth Lincoln (1985) to capture the decisive increase of literary works by Indigenous authors, refers to the United States, a similar development can be discerned north of the border. Starting in the 1970s and flourishing from the 1980s onwards, the growing body of Indigenous short fiction in Canada is documented, for example, in Thomas King's seminal anthology *All My Relations* (1990).

In the face of the transformation from oral to written forms of expression, several Indigenous authors have voiced concern about a process which carries with it a certain petrification of hitherto immediate and dynamic modes of storytelling. At the same time, as Okanagan writer and educator Jeanette Armstrong has pointed out, attempts at rendering orality on the written page can be an "extremely exciting aspect" of Indigenous writing (2006: 25). As it is, written stories in English or French that are accessible to a wider reading public now exist side by side with traditional oral storytelling in Indigenous communities.

In this context, it is apposite to introduce Thomas King's description of the vibrant versatility of Indigenous writing. In "Godzilla vs Post-Colonial" (2012: 198), King distinguishes between four major types of stories: tribal, interfusional, polemical, and associational. While the latter three types address wider audiences, tribal stories are in the language of a First Nations community and intended for its members only. Interfusional stories – or "voice pieces" (Gibert 2006: 105) – are characterised by the blending of oral and written modes and often involve the shape-shifting figure of the trickster. Besides King's own trickster stories, examples are Lee Maracle's "Cedar Sings" (*First Wives Club*, 2010), Jeanette Armstrong's "This is a Story" (in *All My Relations*, 1990), and Leanne Betasamosake Simpson's "she told him

DOI: 10.4324/9781003142683-11

10 000 years of everything", "gezhizhwazh", and "gwekaanimad" (*Islands of Decolonial Love*, 2015 [2013]).

Polemical fiction, according to King, "chronicles the imposition of non-Native expectations and insistences (political, social, scientific) on Native communities and the methods of resistance employed by Native people" (2012: 199). Often, Indigenous stories feature elements of the polemical, like many of King's narratives and, in particular, those of Lee Maracle and Leanne Betasamosake Simpson (see Section 8.2.). Finally, associational stories mostly centre on life within Indigenous communities without a specific focus on culture conflict (King 2012: 200). A prime example is Drew Hayden Taylor's collection *Fearless Warriors* (1998), which almost exclusively focuses on the life of a small Ojibway community in central Ontario. A type that is missing in King's four-part taxonomy are stories that eschew ethnic issues altogether. We find such stories in King's own works or, for example, among Haisla author Eden Robinson's stories. These "ethnically neutral" stories, too, are important contributions to the debate since they challenge the common fallacy on the part of readers that automatically equates the ethnic identities of the author and characters. It should also be added that King's classifications are only rough guidelines regarding Indigenous short fiction in English over the past four decades. Looking at the works of authors from different Indigenous backgrounds in the following sections, it will become clear that Aboriginal writing is, above all, characterised by a stunningly wide spectrum of forms and themes.

Despite the diversity of issues addressed in Aboriginal short fiction, there are also themes that are shared by many authors and that reflect the history as well as the present situation of Indigenous peoples throughout Canada and their special relationship with their lands. An issue that resonates particularly strongly in Indigenous writing is the still-to-be-felt effects of the contact between Natives and European settlers. As James (Sákej) Youngblood Henderson observes,

> Colonized Indigenous peoples are still not flourishing. . . . Thus Indigenous peoples are living in a world according to imposed Eurocentric scripts. We are not living our own worldviews or visions. We exist in the contrived institutional and conscious realm of a failed colonization, often wrongly confused with the idea of civilization or modernity.
> (2000: 163–164)

In particular, the consequences of Canada's assimilation policies, including the notorious residential school system, feature prominently in Indigenous writing. These state-funded and church-run institutions included, as Jonathan Dewar (2016: 151) explains,

> industrial schools, boarding schools, student residences, hostels, billets, and even Inuit tent camps in the North. First Nations, Inuit and Métis

children were all subject to the assimilatory goals of the government and proselytizing effort of the various church entities through schooling.

The residential schools have received international attention due to the recent discovery of mass graves at the former Kamloops Indian Residential School and others. Its traumatic and far-reaching effects have been addressed not only in autobiographical writing, such as Chief Dominique Rankin's testimony *They Called Us Savages: A Hereditary Chief's Quest for Truth and Harmony* (2020) and in numerous novels and plays, but also in short fiction. Examples are Lee Maracle's "Too Much to Explain", "Maggie", and "Charlie" (*Sojourner's Truth and Other Stories*); Basil H. Johnston's "Summer Holidays in Spanish" (in *All My Relations*); Drew Hayden Taylor's "The Man Who Didn't Exist" (*Fearless Warriors*); and Leanne Betasamosake Simpson's "jiimaanag" (*Islands of Decolonial Love*).

Another important (and related) theme is the appropriation and stereotyping of Indigenous cultures. Among the numerous examples are King's "One Good Story, That One" (*One Good Story, That One*) and "Tidings of Comfort and Joy" (*A Short History of Indians in Canada*), Simpson's "pipty" (*Islands of Decolonial Love*), and Eden Robinson's "Queen of the North" (*Traplines*, 1996). In "Queen of the North", the author problematises stereotypical non-Native perceptions of Native authenticity. In the middle section of the story, titled "Bloody Vancouver", the narrator and protagonist Adelaine stays with her aunt in Vancouver. Her aunt is an active member of the Helping Hands Society, and when the Society organises a powwow, Adelaine helps her aunt by working the bannock booth. Her last customer is a "middle-aged red-headed man in a business suit" (*Traplines* 206), who, upon finding out that Adelaine is "Indian", becomes obsessed with "authenticity". The young woman first tries to counter him by returning his questions in the same manner: when he asks her "'Are you Indian then?'" (207), she answers "Haisla", but adds, "And you?" (207), thus indicating that his heritage is as "odd" as hers. When she finally hands the tourist his plate of bannocks, he asks, "How should I eat these?" (208) Adelaine considers a rude reply ("With your mouth, asshole") yet answers rather placidly, "'Put some syrup on them, or jam, or honey. Anything you want'" (208). Both her imagined and her actual answer, however, cast some light on the dubious quest for authenticity, which is often only a fascination with the exotic other. Placed at the end of the story collection *Traplines*, this scene may well be read as an implied instruction on how to read Eden Robinson's stories, or, for that matter, stories by Aboriginal writers in general.

Indigenous epistemologies are strongly defined by the "vibrant relationships between people, their ecosystems, and the other living beings and spirits that share their lands" (Coleman 2012: 14). It is, therefore, not surprising that this interrelational dimension is another recurring thematic element in

Indigenous stories. Kateri Akiwenzie-Damm describes this commonality between Indigenous peoples in Canada as follows:

> The Native peoples of this land . . . are fundamentally different from anyone else in this land, fundamentally different from Canadians. The basis of the difference is the land, our passion for it and our understanding of our relationship with it. . . . It is our connection to this land that makes us who we are, that shapes our thinking, our cultural practices, our spiritual, emotional, physical, and social lives.
>
> (1998: 84)

Especially at a time when ecological crises have become one of the most pressing issues of human life on earth, it is essential that we also listen to literary responses to these crises. Indigenous stories, as will be shown in this chapter as well as in Chapter 10, have a great potential to inspire critical discourses on the relationship between humans and their environment.

The fact that from the mid-1980s onwards, a rich body of Native stories in English has been available and continues to grow "has opened up new worlds of imagination for a non-Native audience" (King 1990: ix). In addition, these stories are essential in communicating issues that have for a long time been muted and distorted, providing Indigenous writers with a venue that allows them to write back to the coloniser. What is more, the emergence of Indigenous writers and critics has fostered a dialogue between cultures that may assist processes of decolonisation. These processes, according to Linda Tuhiwai Smith, involve the forging of "a language of possibility, a way out of colonialism", allowing Aboriginal peoples "to make plans, to make strategic choices, to theorize solutions" (2012: 203f). In *Decolonizing Methodologies*, Smith, in fact, brings forth 25 projects, including storytelling, which are proposed as potent strategies to achieve "cultural survival, self-determination, healing, restoration" and "social justice" (2012: 143). At the same time, and especially in the wake of the efforts of the *Truth and Reconciliation Commission* (*TCR*), which commenced work in 2008, we should keep in mind Emma LaRocque's "cautionary note about an 'aesthetics of healing'" (Dewar 2016: 162). Thus, the Cree/Métis scholar warns of making healing "the new cultural marker by which we define or judge Aboriginal literature" (2010: 168) – a development that might again essentialise Indigenous writing and obstruct the view on other facets and qualities of storytelling.

While the power of storytelling is of vital importance within Indigenous communities, the dissemination of stories in written form has now also enabled non-Native readers to partake of that power. It is now up to us to cherish this gift and respond to it with appreciation instead of appropriation. In this vein, Anishinaabe scholar Niigaanwewidam James Sinclair claims that "[r]esponsible and ethical criticisms of Indigenous literatures promote exchanges that include all interested parties, Indigenous or otherwise" and suggests that "we should invite everyone to the literary feast" (2016: 307). It is still important to make clear, however, that "non-Native critics can never and should never claim 'big A' Authority in their discussion of Native texts" (McKegney 2016: 84).

8.1. Humour and Ambushing the Reader: Thomas King

Thomas King's (1943–) hybrid Cherokee/Greek/German cultural background may have contributed to his rejection of monocultural exclusivity. Thus, he acknowledges the definition of Indigenous literature as "literature produced by Native people" yet adds – trickster-like – "as long as you don't ask 'who is Native'" (Lutz 1991: 108). In two essays and a large body of fiction, King dismantles "the destructive hubris of Western civilization" (Riddington 2015: 163). He does so through his playful juxtaposition and amalgamation of Indigenous and Christian mythologies and extensive deployment of humour. Humour, in fact, is King's most "subversive weapon" with which he "ambush[es] the reader" (Atwood 1990: 244).

King is best known for the C.B.C. radio show *The Dead Dog Café Comedy Hour* (1997–2000), his history *The Inconvenient Indian* (2012), which was adapted into a documentary film that premiered at the Toronto International Film Festival in 2020, and his many novels. However, King can also be considered one of the most interesting Indigenous storytellers and one of the most intriguing representatives of contemporary Canadian short fiction. His stories, collected in *One Good Story, That One* (1993) and *A Short History of Indians in Canada* (2005), appeal to the reader not only aesthetically but also because of their extraordinary diversity and originality. The stories assembled in these collections display an overwhelming polyphony of voices and a wide range of different narrative modes. The most significant of these is the author's blending of the oral and the written in his interfusional stories. Indeed, these "voice pieces" bear a particularly strong innovative potential, contrasting most conspicuously with conventional paradigms of the short story in English.

Humour, as mentioned earlier, is a hallmark of King's writing. The comical surface of many of King's stories allows him to take an oppositional stance without becoming too polemical or appearing to lecture his readers. In both *One Good Story, That One* and *A Short History of Indians in Canada*, the comic plays a major role. In the latter book, however, the humour has become significantly darker – a shift that is evident when the relatively light-hearted four trickster stories from the first collection are compared to "Coyote and the Enemy Aliens", the only interfusional story from the second collection.

Regarding King's homodiegetic stories, too, this tendency towards a graver tone in the later book can be observed. While in "Traplines",

"Borders", and "Joe the Painter and the Deer Lake Massacre" (*One Good Story, That One*), a humorous tone dominates despite the criticism, there is nothing funny in the absent-father narratives "Noah's Arch" and "Domestic Furies" (*A Short History of Indians in Canada*), which are both first-person narratives rendered retrospectively from the perspective of a child. The voice of a child also dominates the story "The Dog I Wish I Had, I Would Call It Helen" (*A Short History*), where the dog a boy longs for is a substitute for the father he knows he cannot have, while his mother fails to comfort him.

In several stories written in the third person, King works with fantastic, surrealist, and supernatural elements to highlight the unsettling legacy of colonisation. This is the case, for instance, in "Totem", "How Corporal Sterling Saved Blossom, Alberta, and Most of the Rest of the World", and "A Seat in the Garden" (*One Good Story, That One*), which "emphasize White incomprehension of Aboriginal reality as well as stubborn adherence to stereotype" (Truchan-Tartaryn and Gingell 2006: 17). Although these stories create bafflement and unease in the reader, their general tone mostly remains playful. Ludic humour also characterises several third-person pieces in *A Short History of Indians in Canada*, as in "Bad Men Who Love Jesus", a parody of the New Testament, or "Where the Borg Are", an uptake on the *Star Trek* series. However, King's tendency, in his second collection, to strike a graver note is still there and can also be observed in its surrealist and speculative third-person stories, like "The Closer You Get to Canada, the More Things Will Eat Your Horses", "The Baby in the Airmail Box", or "Tidings of Comfort and Joy". While in these stories King *does* include comic elements, these are hardly fit to elicit laughter. Rather, the disparity between comic representation and outrageous subject matters enhances the monstrosity of what is depicted.

In the following, a closer look at "Tidings of Comfort and Joy" will provide a deeper understanding of King's radical and dark thematisation of colonial trauma and its repercussions in *A Short History of Indians in Canada*. The section on King will close with a case study of "One Good Story, That One", aiming to provide insight into the aesthetic and thematic potential of interfusional stories.

Ironically entitled "Tidings of Comfort and Joy", this story is speculative and dystopian in the sense that it takes to an extreme the commodification of Native life in Western culture: Indigenous people have become consumer articles that can be bought, sold, collected, or thrown out when out of fashion.

Deceptively, the text begins like a nostalgic Christmas story and at first seems to reinforce the expectations raised by the title. Only slowly does the reader realise that what Hudson, the protagonist, looks at through his large bay window is a neatly arranged collection of Indigenous people from various First Nations, whom he has either received as gifts from his wife, Eleanor, or purchased himself from dealers, together with the necessary accessories to make them look more authentic. Hudson's thoughts, to which the reader has access, reveal the attitude of a little boy talking about his toy figures:

> It had been fun playing with the Indians, placing them around the property, figuring out where each grouping should go. Lakota in the open. Cherokee in the hills above the house. Mohawk down by the pond. Chickasaw and Choctaw in the trees.
>
> (9)

On this particular day, however, which happens to be the day before Christmas, Hudson feels strangely uneasy, and when he looks at his collection more closely, he notices that one of the women – "[h]e couldn't tell if it was one of the two Blackfoot that he had picked up at auction on the internet or if it was the Cree maiden that his brother Bert had sent them for their thirtieth anniversary" (10) – was pregnant. Annoyed at the dealer who obviously had sold him "an Indian who hadn't been fixed" (11), he turns to his friends Vince and Franklin for advice and practical solutions. The three men are in a festive mood, merrily humming Christmas songs, when they approach Hudson's Indian camp with the intention of shooting the woman. When they look into the tipi, however, they see that she has already given birth to twins and, luckily, "those are collectible" (15), as Vince tells his friend. To Hudson, the scene seems like the Christian "nativity scene" (14) at Bethlehem: while he may not be aware of the pun (Native/nativity), however, his interpretation clearly indicates Western practices of appropriation.

Hudson cannot wait to tell his wife about the miraculous new addition to the collection, but when she finally calls and Hudson looks out of the window, he sees that all the "Indians" have vanished together with their tipis. This might signify a happy ending, yet Hudson, his wife, and their friends have not learned anything. On the contrary, since all the "pieces" happened to be insured, Hudson merrily resolves to put the loss aside and begin again.

The nightmarish effect of the story mainly results from the seemingly naïve and sober manner in which its outrageous subject matter is presented. While such an incongruity may have a comic potential with less serious topics, it is an additional source of horror in this case. This also applies to the temporal setting: the bizarre disparity between the Christmas context, with its associations of peace, love, and joy on the one hand, and the men's "innocent" preparation for the murder of the pregnant woman on the other highlight the monstrosity of the planned deed and, by extension, of this grotesquely embodied appropriation and commodification of Indigeneity. Emphasising the characters' utter ignorance of their wrongdoing, the story suggests that its ghastly scenarios have become the norm. Using disparity and black humour, it strikingly unmasks White Canadian tendencies to belittle and commodify Indigenous peoples. In *The Imaginary Indian*, Daniel Francis (1992: 103) brings the commodification of Canada's First Nations to the point when he argues that just as "the government was trying to stamp out vestiges of traditional aboriginal culture in everyday life, it was creating a new institution devoted to the preservation of that culture in a contained and manageable form".

Case Study: Thomas King, "One Good Story, That One" – The Interfusional Story

Thomas King's two collections of short fiction contain five interfusional stories: "One Good Story, That One", "Magpies", "The One About Coyote Going West", "A Coyote Columbus Story" (*One Good Story, That One*), and "Coyote and the Enemy Aliens" (*A Short History of Indians in Canada*). Most of these voice pieces are also trickster stories. The trickster is a cultural hero in almost all Native Canadian cultures, a transforming figure who can be human or animal, male or female, good or bad. The trickster is known to the different tribes by various names: Raven on the Pacific Coast, Weesageechak for the Cree, Nanabush for the Anishinaabe, and Coyote for Plains peoples. In stories, tricksters often assume a rather subversive role – they can be destroyers but also preservers. Whereas in King's other voice pieces (with the exception of "Magpies"), the trickster is a major character and agent, Coyote's appearance is only implied in "One Good Story, That One".

In this story, a Native elder (the narrator) is visited by three non-Indigenous anthropologists in search of authentic Aboriginal stories, especially creation myths. What he serves them is their own creation myth, the story of Adam and Eve as recounted in Genesis, in Indigenous disguise. The beginning of King's story already reveals a great number of features which are typical of interfusional stories in general and of King's trickster stories in particular:

> Alright.
> You know, I hear this story up north. Maybe Yellowknife, that one, somewhere. I hear it maybe a long time. Old story this one. One hundred years, maybe more. Maybe not so long either, this story.
> So.
> You know, they come up to my place. Summer place, pretty good place, that one. Those ones, they come with Napiao, my friend. Cool. . . .

172   *The Canadian Short Story from the Mid-1980s to the Present*

> Napiao comes with those three. Whiteman, those.
> No Indianman.
> No Chineseman.
> No Frenchman.
> Too bad, those.
> Sometimes the wind come along say hello. Pretty fast, that one. . . .
> Three men come to my summer place, also my friend Napiao. Pretty loud talkers, those ones. One is big. I tell him maybe looks like Big Joe. Maybe not.
> Anyway.
> They come and Napiao, too. Bring greetings, how are you, many nice things they bring to say. Three.
> All white.
> Too bad, those. (3f)

On the extradiegetic level, the narrator simulates a storytelling situation, inviting the (implied) reader to listen to his story, yet "eliciting not only our attention but also our participation and responsibility . . . as participants in a communal activity" (Truchan-Tartaryn and Gingell 2006: 9). The extradiegetic implication of oral storytelling mirrors the storytelling on the diegetic level, when the narrator pretends to tell his audience, a group of three white anthropologists, an "authentic Native creation story". In fact, however, he feeds them with a parody of their own creation myth as contained in the Book of Genesis – a comic inversion which King also uses in his novels *Green Grass, Running Water* or *The Back of the Turtle*. The simulation of orality is further achieved by the rhetoric of repetition, which is used for emphasis, as a mnemonic device and for creating suspense by delaying the narrative's progression. In the passage earlier, this is visible, for example, when the narrator repeatedly mentions (although each time in a slightly different way) that three "whitemen" came to visit him at his summer place together with his friend Napiao.

An equally prominent feature of the interfusional story is the doubling of the grammatical subject, as seen not only in the title but also, for instance, in "Old story this one" and "Pretty fast, that one". According to Truchan-Tartaryn and Gingell (2006: 9), this technique "serves to clarify and focus the subject in a number of Aboriginal languages"; it also creates an idiosyncratic rhythm. On the syntactical level, the most important repetitive device is the listing of fragmentary sentences. Such enumerations occur especially in the intradiegetic story, when King's trickster-like narrator lists all the things which "that one god" (5) creates:

> Me-a-loo, call her deer.
> Pa-pe-o, call her elk.
> Tsling-ta, call her blue-flower-berry.
> Ga-ling, call her moon.
> So-see-ka, call her flint.
> A-ma-po, call her dog.
> Ba-ko-zao, call her grocery store.
> Pe-to-pa-zasling, call her television. (6)

The slipping in of pseudo-Native words tricks both the extratextual and the fictional audience into believing that they are listening to a traditional "Indian" story. However, the narrator is fair enough to insert clues for the reader as well as for the anthropologists, who are to "watch the floor" and "be careful" (5). The concluding sentence, "I clean up all the coyote tracks on the floor" (10), however, is only meant for the reader's eyes (or ears), providing them with a tongue-in-cheek instruction on how to read the story.

Enumerations like the one quoted earlier produce a ritual effect, recalling an incantation or spell. A comic effect results from the disparity of the items listed. The fact that all of them – the deer as well as the moon and television – are referred to as feminine further suggests a unity that is contradicted by their semantic diversity. At the same time, the use of the feminine as a generic form also foregrounds the importance of the feminine in Native cultures, which King also emphasises by making Eve/Evening a Native woman and depicting her in more positive terms than the white Ah-damn.

Another typical feature of King's interfusional stories is the ample use of adverbs that denote inexactness and uncertainty ("maybe/maybe not") or provide only vague indications of time and place ("somewhere"). Through these, the stories "admit to the limitations of one perspective, and one person's memory, acknowledging that there are always other possibilities"; moreover, they thereby defy "the fixity of written words and the Western proclivity to measure time" (Truchan-Tartaryn and Gingell 2006: 11). Indeterminacy is also in the nature of the trickster figure who, in "One Good Story, That One", makes an appearance through the indeterminate and deceptive story structure itself as well as through the narrator's repeated reminders to watch out for Coyote tracks. Other rhetorical strategies King uses to textualise speech, as summarised by Teresa Gibert, are

> intentional digressions . . . expressions of laughter . . . , elision of verbs, extremely brief sentences, punctuation and line breaks that echo storytelling cadences, together with parataxis, illustrated by a striking proliferation of juxtaposed declarative statements in contrast with an almost complete absence of subordination. (2006: 102f)

The story which the narrator finally offers the anthropologists achieves its comic effects mainly through defamiliarising analogies (the biblical story as Indigenous creation myth). The Christian "master narrative" is subverted by the narrator's irreverent approach, as in the following passage referring to Ah-damn and Evening's nakedness: "Ah-damn and Evening real happy, those ones. No clothes, those, you know. Ha, Ha, Ha, Ha. But they pretty dumb, then. New you know" (6). King also includes scatological jokes and compares both Ah-damn and God to "Harley James", who always shouts and "get drunk, come home, that one, beat his wife" (7). When "that fellow, god, whiteman I think" (9) finally expels Ah-damn and Evening from "that good place, garden" (9), the narrator laconically inserts "Just like Indian today" (9). The most powerful tool for rendering social criticism, however, is the narrative act itself. By reversing cultural appropriation, King and his narrator make "readers understand why Native communities feel offended whenever a story they hold as sacred is treated with the same kind of carelessness, lack of respect or ineptitude by curious strangers (Gibert 2006: 104). The very efficacy of such parodic inversions depends upon the audience's recognition of the pretext to which it responds, and it is only then that the potential of the story as an act of "writing back" (to the coloniser) can be fully realised. Choosing the story of Adam and Eve for his subversive experiment testifies to King's awareness of this.

Elements of oral storytelling:

- Simulation of storytelling situation
- Expressions of laughter
- Elision of verbs
- Rhetoric of repetition and digression

- Doubling the subject
- Enumeration of brief fragmentary sentences
- Storytelling cadences through parataxis, specific punctuation, and line breaks

Further recurring features of King's interfusional stories:

- Ample use of inexactness and uncertainty – defies the fixity of written words in Western written discourses
- Humour and comic effects – disarm and engage readers; potent tool for subversive criticism
- Rejection of fixity and inclusion of comic elements also reflect the indeterminacy and playful nature of the trickster: "Coyote come by maybe four, maybe eight times. Gets dressed up, fool around. Ha, ha, ha, ha. Tricky one, that coyote. Walks in circles. Sneaky" (8).

Ways "One Good Story, That One" can be an act of "writing back":

- Parody of Christian creation myth, which is cunningly disguised as a Native creation story
- Satirical criticism of an authoritarian Christian god
- Radical countering of conventional paradigms of the short story in English through the creative blending of oral storytelling elements with those of print cultures

8.2. "She Had a Big Basket Full of Songs, Stories, Ceremonies": Lee Maracle and Leanne Betasamosake Simpson

Even though Lee Maracle and Leanne Simpson are 21 years apart and originate from different First Nations, their stories show a number of commonalities. Maracle "extensively analyses the situation of the Native within the context of a politics of decolonisation and demonstrates how marginality has been constructed by the hegemonic forces of imperialism and capitalism" (Godard 1990: 194). Barbara Godard's comment on Maracle's writing also applies to Simpson: both are explicitly political authors and can thus be seen in the context of "resistance literature", a mode of writing which, according to Godard, "takes as its starting point the radical fact of its present situation as the culture of a colony" (1990: 199). Another characteristic these two authors share is their combination of the polemical with a highly poetic style – a feature that is particularly striking in Simpson's work. Moreover, in the works of both writers, dialogic structures and an "oral syntax" play a major role. Thematically, colonial injustice and disempowerment are major issues. At the same time, many stories also celebrate practices of healing and the cultural and spiritual values of Indigenous epistemes. Often the reclaiming of what has been lost is linked, in Maracle's and Simpson's stories, with feminist and ecological issues. Even though their output of stories published in English is relatively slim, their diversity is astounding; it can therefore be said of both authors that they have "a big basket full of songs, stories, ceremonies, a language we'd almost had forgotten" (*Islands of Decolonial Love* 128).

Bobbi Lee Maracle (1950–2021) published two collections of short fiction, *Sojourner's Truth and Other Stories* (1990) and *First Wives Club: Coast Salish Style* (2010). She was a member of the Stó:lō nation (part of the Coast Salish) inhabiting the Fraser Valley and lower Fraser Canyon of British Columbia, a region which is also the backdrop of most of her stories.

Maracle preferred internalised modes of narration, especially the first-person voice, for her emotionally gripping stories, yet there is an impressive variety of techniques even within the first-person mode, as becomes clear from the stories in *Sojourner's Truth*. In "Who's Political Here", for instance, a striking narrative about female political agency, "the use of free discourse signals the inseparability of description and process, interpretation and being" (O'Brien 1995: 92). "Free discourse" here denotes the fusion of interior monologue and a knowingly analytic voice, leading to the meaning being "explicitly embodied in action" (92). Through this technique, which also conveys a strong impression of orality, the narrator's domestic multitasking becomes recognisable as a central political act, which is contrasted with her husband's and his friends' "real" political activities such as discussing, postering and organising demonstrations.

In "Maggie", in turn, the author uses a diary mode, whereas "Dear Daddy" is an epistolary story. In "Eunice" and "Lee on Spiritual Experience", various signals make it clear that one is dealing with autobiographical narratives. An oscillation between retrospective and simultaneous first-person narration characterises "Polka Partners" and "Yin Chin", while the most unusual point of view has been reserved for the title story, "Sojourner's Truth", which features the confessional voice of someone lying dead in his coffin. In "World War I", Maracle experiments with the pattern of the trickster narrative, using the first person in the frame to establish contact with the reader and introduce the actual story. Projecting an apocalyptic scenario onto an animal world, this story differs strongly from King's trickster narratives. The reason is mainly that Maracle completely refrains from using comic elements. In contrast, *First Wives Club*, which was published 20 years after *Sojourner's Truth*, gives ample space to the comic, a development that runs counter to that in King's short fiction.

A recurring motif in Maracle's stories is the aforementioned trauma caused by the residential school system. Two stories in particular, "Maggie" and "Charlie", accuse a system which not only alienated children from their families and culture but also literally killed them: Charlie and Maggie both freeze to death as a consequence of the unbearable conditions and cruelties exerted by the school authorities. A closer look at "Charlie" shows how Maracle plays with shifts from external to internal modes of representation in order to stress the monstrosity of these church-run institutions. As the following passage illustrates, the provocatively neutral and generalising description of the children assumes a sarcastic tone, thus highlighting, for shock effect, the Catholic teachers' misconceptions about their pupils:

> Charlie was a quiet boy. This was not unusual. His silence was interpreted by the priests and Catholic lay teachers as stoic reserve – a quality inherited from his pagan ancestors. It was regarded in the same way the religious viewed the children's tearless response to punishment: a quaint combination of primitive courage and lack of emotion. All the children were like this and so Charlie could not be otherwise.
>
> (99)

Whenever possible, Charlie escapes into daydreaming, which is also marked by a shift from authorial to figural narration:

> Charlie's dreams followed the familiar lines of his home. In the centre stood his mama quietly stirring the stew. Above her head, hanging from the rafters, were strips of dried meat. Hundreds of them . . . A little ways from the stove hung mama's cooking tools.
>
> (104)

Maracle uses internal focalisation exclusively for her Native characters (in this case Charlie and his father), reserving sarcastic omniscience for portraying the teachers. The readers' sympathy for the small child freezing to death is thus intensified, as is their condemnation of the crimes committed by the government and the church.

In *First Wives Club*, in contrast, there are several refreshingly humorous narratives, such as, for example, the title story. In general, Maracle developed several novel strategies in her 2010 collection, one of them being a markedly poetic style which conveys the impression of marvellous paintings in words. In "Erotica", "The Café", and "Tiny Green Waves", for example, intense feelings of frustration, anger, or sexual arousal are translated into powerfully graphic images which render the emotions they denote palpable and communicable. While there is still a thematic focus on political issues, these are now more strongly linked to ecological concerns, as in "Cedar Sings" (see also Chapter 10). In general, however, Maracle's 2010 stories strike a more conciliatory note than those published two decades earlier. Even though we still find a clear dissociation from Canada (as a framework of cultural identification), the impression is conveyed that bridges are being built.

In Leanne Betasamosake Simpson's (1971–) *Islands of Decolonial Love* (2013), too, we find both an unflinching critique of colonial interference but also a strong a note of resurgence and healing. The Mississauga Nishnaabeg artist is not only a writer but also a highly acclaimed musician and spoken word performer. This is immediately evident in *Islands of Decolonial Love*, which assembles stories and creative political manifestos as well as songs that can be streamed for multimedia reception.

Simpson's stories and songs are interspersed with words in nishnaabemowin. This not only signifies a reclaiming of Indigenous languages but also – for those not familiar with this language or any Indigenous language – it forces them to slow down, to pay attention, to reread, to get attuned to the rhythm, and to look up words in the footnotes provided. Another noteworthy feature is the consistent use of lower-case letters, a device that is meant to acknowledge the equality and interrelatedness of all things. The connection between people and their environment is at the core of Simpson's entire collection. Thus, for example, in "indinawemaaganidog/all of my relatives", the narrator recognises kinship with the young mi'kmaq man who takes her out in his boat to see a colony of seals through his acknowledgement of kinship with other living creatures when he tells her: "the bird is my family, all of this, the fish, the seals, the water – this is my family" (13).

Interrelational aspects are also foregrounded through the dialogic structure of several of the texts, as in "she hid him in her bones", "leaks", and "smallpox, anyone". The trickster story "gezhizhwazh" embeds the actual story of how gezhizhwazh, an Indigenous transformer figure, defeated wiindigo in a dialogue between an old Anishinaabeg story-teller and a young listener. Wiindigos are powerful cannibalistic monsters who, in this story, "found a way to convince people to buy disconnection, insatiable hunger and emptiness" (109). Wiindigos here stand for the white coloniser, and just when it was believed that they had been defeated "the wiindigo has insidiously reincarnated and come back stronger" (109), having seeped into every aspect of life. This includes "the drugging of women so they couldn't be present at their ceremony. planned c-sections. putting a plastic nipple in the baby instead of her own flesh" (111). The plan of gezhizhwazh was to protect women giving birth since, as she knew, this was how Wiindigo implanted the emptiness in her people that, in the end, turned them into cannibals themselves. The necessity of liberation and decolonising is strongly emphasised in this story, which also illustrates how storytelling is a central factor in reclaiming cultural wholeness and interrelatedness.

In "it takes an ocean not to break", a poignant story about the (im)possibility of healing, dialogic elements are employed, too. The narrative alternates between passages in italics, where the narrator addresses, in her mind, an 18-year-old teenager who tried to commit suicide, and sections in the first-person form in which the narrator processes her sessions with a white "therapy lady", "me the poor depressed Indian. Her the white fucking pathologizing saviour" (83). While the story critically exposes patronising attitudes and the stereotyping of Indigenous people, it also – if only faintly – suggests the possibility of healing through communal responsibility and love. All else having failed, the narrator resolves to act herself: "*i'm getting in the car right now, and i'm driving north to you. . . . i want to pick you up, and i'm going to stitch every one of your broken bones back together with kisses*" (83).

The staging of orality on the printed page plays a major role in Simpson's entire collection; it is a particularly prominent element in her trickster stories like, for example, "gwekaanimad", a story that echoes the style of King's interfusional stories, including the setting up of an oral storytelling situation with reminders to watch out for the interference of the trickster. The story is powerfully decolonising, encouraging the nishnaabag (and Indigenous people in general) to stop mimicking white culture and, instead, to become doers rather than watchers. When white people have their parades, as the narrator discloses, they "put up them metal fences so the watchers can't dance down the streets too. they in the parade. we the watchers" (136). The parade which nishnaabekwe, a special Ojibway woman, in the end not only envisions but actually organises is radically different from the exclusive events of white people and is fittingly named after the strawberries, which "got them roots and runners all entwined. hard to pick its roots that one. all connected underground" (136). To this alternative party, everyone is invited, and there are no watchers; all belong to the one community, including the earth itself, "that turtle", who "likes all those gentle brown feet massaging her back" (138), and all are interweaving, including the animals and "that tricky one" (138).

While many of the texts in *Islands of Decolonial Love* are polemical, some are outright activist, like "nogojiwanong", a composite of four texts. Through its unflinching recording of the wrecking of the land and of Indigenous cultures and its successful reclaiming of the power of nature and of sustainable cultural practices, this story cycle also has a strong ecological impact (see also Chapter 10).

8.3. Drew Hayden Taylor and Richard Van Camp

Both Drew Hayden Taylor and Richard Van Camp set their stories within their respective Native communities – in Taylor's case, a fictive Ojibway community in Ontario, in that of Van Camp, a fictive Dogrib (Dené) community in the North-West Territories. Their stories are mostly associational stories, typically following a "flat narrative line", "lean[ing] toward the group rather than the single isolated character", and ignoring "the ubiquitous climaxes and resolutions that are so valued in non-Native literature" (King 2012 [1990]: 200). At the same time, many of their stories also include stylistic features of orality and are characterised by cultural syncretism – that is, a blend of Indigenous content with elements of Western genres which, in Van Camp's words, reflects the fact that "Aboriginal peoples walk in two worlds" (Vranckx 2012: 74). While both authors make frequent references to *Star Wars* and *Star Trek*, it is, above all, Taylor who has experimented with conventions of science fiction. With Van Camp, it is especially his adaptation of the horror genre, notably in his Wheetago stories, which can be identified as a novel and powerful syncretic strategy.

Drew Hayden Taylor's (1962–) short stories, collected in *Fearless Warriors* (1998) and *Take Us to Your Chief* (2016), mirror the author's own open and intercultural approach to Canadian society, which may have been prompted, as in the case of Thomas King, by his multicultural heritage: "I am an old hand at hybridizing. Perhaps it goes all the way back to my DNA – I'm half Ojibway and half . . . not" (*Take Us to Your Chief* viii). The setting of most of his stories is the Anishinaabe (Ojibway) community of Otter Lake, which may be a fictional version of the place of his birth, the Curve Lake First Nation, Ontario, where he also lives.

Reading *Fearless Warriors*, one immediately senses that the ambivalent first-person narrator, Andrew, whose perspective filters all 12 stories, deserves particular attention. Andrew is a young Ojibway who is an attentive observer of life on the Otter Lake Reserve but generally manages to stay out of the conflicts he tells us about. To a great extent, it is this consistent perspective of the I-as-witness-narrator which makes Drew Hayden Taylor's stories so intriguing because it allows for a double inside/outside perspective.

As a collection of stories linked by narrative voice, place, and community, *Fearless Warriors* represents a short story cycle with its typical significance of the initial and concluding stories. Thus, the initial story, "The Circle of Death", and the final story, "Crisis Management", constitute a kind of frame which further shapes the reader's perception of the narratives in between. In both stories, the actual protagonist is the narrator's sister, Angela, and in both stories encounters between Ojibway characters, and the "white other" are foregrounded in a way which sheds light on Andrew's ambivalent internal/external stance. This may be illustrated by a scene from "Crisis Management", which presents the brother and sister in downtown Peterborough on their way to meet their mother:

> During the cab ride, we had started some small talk with the driver, who finally got around to noticing we were Native.
> "God I envy you guys. Got land, no taxes, hunt and fish when you want, government takes care of all your problems. You people got it made".
>
> I immediately felt Angela's body stiffen and her eyes focus in on the back of this poor guy's head. I grabbed her forearm and quickly whispered into her ear. "No, Angela". She shrugged my arm off saying "Yes, Andrew".
> (*Fearless Warriors* 177)

While the reader never really finds out what Andrew thinks about the driver's remark, there can be no doubt about his sympathies for him. Andrew's general aversion to conflict becomes even more tangible in the central episode of the story. Shortly after the unhappy taxi ride, Angela and Andrew enter a bar, "The Saddle", where they are asked for their IDs:

> My sister and I looked at each other in surprise, wondering whether to be flattered or confused. I'm twenty-six and my sister's two years older than me and it had been a long time since we'd been I.D.'d.
>
> . . . As by habit, I brought out my driver's license to show the man, and my sister offered her Indian status card. He glanced at mine first and quickly handed it back to me. Angela's bore a little more scrutiny. I don't think he'd ever seen one before. Smiling, he passed it back to my sister. "A wagonburner, huh? Welcome to 'The Saddle'".
>
> For the second time that day, I saw my sister's body tense. As a result mine did too.
>
> (180)

Again, the episode reveals Andrew's in-between position: on the one hand, he understands Tom, the bouncer ("The way the man had said those crucial words held no malice or obvious racial hatred that I could detect", 180), while on the other hand, he understands the insult his sister feels as a result of the perpetuation of such distorting clichés. The situation rendered in the quotation almost escalates when Angela grabs the bouncer's vest and will not let go until the perplexed man has apologised for his racist remark. When not even the bar manager can resolve the situation, Andrew secretly bribes Tom with money. This finally does the trick, but Andrew's feelings of relief are mixed with a bad conscience about having deceived his sister instead of fighting for her – for their? – cause. Angela is really the "fearless warrior" referred to in the title, while Andrew prefers to adopt the position of a detached observer whenever he can.

Making the narrator Andrew a non-committed observer rather than an involved character also allows the author to provide his stories with a humorous note, despite their critical seriousness. Thus, for example, the comic absurdity of the bar scene would be lost if the event were told from Angela's point of view. Through Andrew, Taylor offers first-hand insights into the life of the community, viewing it critically and with a touch of benevolent (self-)irony at the same time. This is the case, for instance, in the title story. It starts out with Andrew, his friend William, and their two girlfriends driving home from a night in a bar where William had started a fight with "a couple of farmer boys" (72). While the two girls are furious, William brags about his deed:

> "Oh, don't whine. We're Ojibway men, fearless warriors from a long line of fearless warriors".
>
> "William, your father pours cement".

"Details. It's the spirit of the idea. We got a long history behind us. We weren't gonna let a couple of farmer boys tell us anything, now were we". (72)

This introductory scene is important for the ironic effect of the story: a little later, the car hits a deer which is seriously injured but still alive. As it turns out, William, the "fearless warrior", is unable to free the animal of its pain so that, in the end, it is Andrew who kills the deer with the tire iron. As the passage quoted shows, the "Native mimicry of white pronouncements on authentic Indianness" that Robert Nunn (1998: 110) has identified in Taylor's plays is also a prominent theme in his short stories.

Taylor's stories deal with human life in general, the Native context entering only indirectly and unobtrusively, yet no less effectively than in texts which make Nativeness an explicit issue. This characteristic and his "gently subversive humour" (Nunn 2008: 59) also define the stories in *Take Us to Your Chief*. Again, however, there is unmistakable criticism of "those who showed up one day for dinner and never left" (Taylor 2016: vii), and again, these critical sentiments are clad in irony and – at times – dark humour, as is already evident in the author's "Foreword": "Darn clever those white people. Native people constantly wonder at the clever innovations and devices the dominant culture feels the need to create – everything from vibrators to nuclear bombs" (vii). In the nine stories that make up *Take Us to Your Chief*, Taylor challenges the boundaries of what counts as Indigenous literature by experimenting with sci-fi elements and "filter[ing] them through an Aboriginal consciousness" (viii).

The initial "A Culturally Inappropriate Armageddon", a story in two parts, starts out with a seemingly unspectacular scenario, featuring Emily, Tracy, and Aaron, who found C-RES, "the first community radio station on [their] reserve" (1); it ends in an apocalyptic nightmare. The three C-RES people are among the few survivors in a postapocalyptic world created by aliens who landed in a huge spaceship. Most of the others are either dead or slaves "working in the limestone mines" (16) for the new alien masters: "Who would have guessed limestone was such a valuable commodity on the galactic market? So far, the trio had managed to escape, scurrying from hole to hole, but at the moment they were not revelling in their freedom" (17). Ironically, the aliens had been attracted by the airwaves of a Native "Calling Song", which Tracy had been adamant to broadcast, and had then wiped out most of the human race. It is, above all, through the second part of the story that the space invasion can be read as a punishment for humanity's reckless treatment of each other and of the planet. This part, fittingly titled "Old Men and Old Sayings", features old Willie, situated on a small Anishinaabe reserve a few days before the spaceship is supposed to land. While in Toronto and Ottawa, "[p]eople are holding these welcoming parties! For the aliens! All around the world too" (22), Willie knows that the landing will mean the destruction and enslavement of the planet. He knows because he has read his philosophers, among them George Santayana, who famously said, "Those who cannot remember the past are condemned to repeat it" (23).

Not all the stories in *Take Us to Your Chief* strike such drastic notes. In the title story, the aliens that land near Old Man's Point seem to be more benevolent. The three Ojibway men to whom the Kaaw Wiyaa appear, Tarzan, Cheemo, and Teddy, are mostly characterised by their laziness, sitting at Old Man's Point, drinking beer silently because having "spent so much time together over the years, they practically knew each other's thoughts; thus nothing needed to be said" (139). Ironically it is their "ability to communicate without interacting verbally. Almost a form of telepathy" (144), which the Kaaw Wiyaa have interpreted as the "planet's sophistication" and which had aroused their interest. The name "Kaaw Wiyaa" not only sounds like something fishy (caviar), but the slimy aliens also seem to have tentacles, reminding Cheemo that "I haven't had calamari in a long time" (140), and the chief of his dinner: "Seeing the gills on the Kaaw Wiyaa quiver as it spoke reminded the chief that he had a large and tasty muskie fish back home in his freezer" (141). Having watched *Star Trek* a lot, the chief seems to be up to the task of negotiating with the aliens, even though their methanic smell makes the "diplomatic talk" a bit unpleasant and "would probably fail the environmental assessment" (143). Even though the story is hilariously funny, it does nonetheless create uneasy feelings. The chief, seeing a great opportunity to get rid of his lazy relations, appoints Tarzan, Cheemo, and Teddy as ambassadors to follow the aliens back to Kaaw Wiyaa. Being sceptical at first, the three Ojibway men are soon lulled into their new situation on the spaceship when the drinks they are offered trick them into feeling content and as if at home: "We have tried to replicate the environment we originally approached you in. We hope it is satisfactory, ambassadors from Earth" (146). Through the men's acceptance of the replica of their culture as "real", Taylor evokes analogies, directing criticism against all parties at the same time – the chief for "selling" his own people, the three "ambassadors" for their hopeless indifference and lack of initiative, and the aliens for their "fishiness" and manipulative power that echoes the practices of the white coloniser.

In "Petropaths", the sci-fi dimension consists of the main character Duane Crow's time travel. The story renders his grandfather's eulogy delivered at the 26-year-old Duane's funeral. Being sent to a remote island for his past misdeeds, Duane intensively studies the ancient petroglyphs on the island and feels they speak to him: "Like it was the Earth telling us a story, he said. Or more accurately, he added, like it was some song waiting to be sung" (98). Cracking the code of the sacred site, he manages to travel back in time and decides to make amends for his past crimes by ameliorating the dark history of his people. However, his endeavours to make his grandfather and his community proud of him end in the young man's death. When his grandfather finds him, he "was running a high fever and was barely conscious. A rash of some sort had spread across his face and neck" (109). Since, as the doctors find out, he died of smallpox, a disease that "was stamped out worldwide in the 1970s" (109), Duane must have made contact with the past. There is no happy ending here, only the narrator's realisation that the knowledge of how to use the petroglyphs properly had been lost and the implicitly dawning question of whether it can be reclaimed.

Like most of the other Native authors discussed in this chapter, Richard Van Camp (1971–), too, is not primarily known for his short stories. Nonetheless, the prolific Dogrib writer and storyteller has published no less than five collections of short fiction (besides his remarkable novels, graphic novels, and young adult fiction), the most recent being *Moccasin Square Gardens* (2019). As Sylvie Vranckx explains, "Van Camp also writes to work through his pain concerning the psychosocial problems among the communities with which he has formed connections", including the "intergenerational legacy of the residential schools" (2012: 71). Such collective traumata are, for example, addressed in the title story of *The Moon of Letting Go and Other Stories* (2010). They are also manifest in a loss of cultural affiliations, which, as Van Camp says in an interview with Sylvie Vranckx, is a particularly severe problem with the male young: "I think many young men in our community don't know how to be warriors now and that families have lost how to honour young men and women and welcome them into the inheritance of power and grace" (2012: 82). A story that addresses this problem quite explicitly is "Man Babies" (*Moccasin Square Gardens*). Baby is a 28-year-old man who still lives with and off his mother and whose only interests are his Xbox, TV, eating, booze, and marijuana. The narrator, a good friend of Steve, the man who is dating Baby's mother, comments on this as follows: "that is what our government is counting on: that our warriors remain couch potatoes. That our languages and customs will die. That we will fade out" (86). When Steve finally throws Baby out of his house, however, this leads to an almost miraculous transformation of the young man, who eventually *does* become a warrior.

Healing and empowerment feature even more strongly in "Super Indians" (*Moccasin Square Gardens*), a story about corrupt Chief Danny, who, as the narrator tells us, "is one big stinky loser face. He's always been here, and nothing ever changes. He's made a fortune off of us and our future. Our town looks like a war zone" (35). However, the fate of the Native community of Fort Simmer changes when the narrator, "Dene Cho: a Tłı̨chǫ daydreamer" (27), has an ingenious idea and transforms his dreams of a better future for his people into action. So when, as part of the Canada Day celebrations, the employees of the Fort Simmer's Band office play tug-of-war against the RCMP, Dene's plan is as follows: "How 'bout when they go 'One, two, three', we all let go? And when the RCMP and the fore-fighters fall back we can have a good laugh and we'll buy 'em a coffee, and everything will be good, right?'" (35). What the others do not know, however, is that Chief Danny was not informed about the plan. So he "wrap[s] himself up pretty tight in that rope" (36), and when the RCMP team pulls with all their might, the unworthy chief is flung into a heap of mud – a public disgrace "documented by a hundred cellphones and later posted online in slow motion" (37). This scene, while being exceedingly funny, is especially significant as an act of liberation. It endows Dene with "superhero power" (39), a power that enables him to embark on his larger mission – namely, that of "uncolonizing Chief Danny" and all the other unworthy leaders that prevent the North and its people from thriving.

While in the two stories discussed, the serious topics addressed are wrapped up in humour and the endings leave room for hope, this is not the case in Van Camp's numerous Wheetago stories, where the mythological monster figure and zombies feature as the incarnation of evil. Abounding in graphic descriptions of the cannibalistic monstrosities of the Wheetagoes, these stories draw gruesome pictures of what Lee Maracle (2002: 132) termed "implosion", that is, "when a community blows *inward* instead of up" (Vranckx 2012: 78). Examples are the eco-story "On the Wings of This Prayer", and "The Fleshing", where the bully Dean transforms into a Wheetago (both in *Godless but Loyal to Heaven*, 2013). A particularly "brutal read" (Vranckx 2012: 74) is the diptych of horror stories in *Moccasin Square Gardens*, "Wheetago War I: Lying in Bed Together" and "Wheetago War II: Summoners", which feature an Earth invaded by incessantly multiplying Wheetagoes, devouring humans and/or turning them into monsters and zombies themselves. The strong environmental impact of these stories will be addressed in Chapter 10.

Considering how decisively stories by Indigenous writers contribute to a decolonising of the mind, one may well agree with Richard Van Camp when he talks about "storytelling's medicine power" (Vranckx 2012: 79). Aboriginal short fiction has greatly enriched the Canadian short story thematically and aesthetically. It has contributed to a rethinking of history, to a countering of appropriative Eurocentric practices, to a reinstalment of healing and resilience as powerful cornerstones of Indigenous cultures, and to the resurgence of Indigenous epistemes. Aesthetically, these stories have significantly diversified the landscape of Canadian short fiction. Thus, Eurocentric traditions of short fiction are challenged by focusing on community rather than the lone hero, by fusing conventions of written narratives with orality, and by not recoiling from using humour for rendering serious and dark content.

In different degrees, humour plays a role in the works of all the authors discussed here, being intrinsic to trickster-like storytellers, textual and real. At the same time, it is a potent strategy for subverting Eurocentric discourses on Indigenous peoples, culture, and history. As Eva Gruber puts it,

> Native writers' use of humour in many of its various forms pulls the presumably stable epistemological ground from underneath the readers'

feet and opens their minds to a re-evaluation of their underlying cultural assumptions. Shared laughter at Eurocentric versions of history thus exorcizes the pain inflicted by centuries of misrepresentation and helps to envision a more self-determined future for Canada's Native people.
(241)

Taking note of the upsurge of short fiction by Indigenous authors in the past three decades (only some of which could be considered here in more detail), it can be concluded that Thomas King's prophecy, as voiced in the introduction to his 1990 anthology *All My Relations* (xvi), has really come true: "the potential for Native literature in the next century seems unlimited (we'll be there, you know)". Indigenous short fiction is here and must definitely not be overlooked!

Works Cited

Primary Works

King, Thomas (1993). *One Good Story, That One*. Toronto: HarperCollins.
King, Tomas (2005). *A Short History of Indians in Canada*. Toronto: HarperCollins.
Maracle, Lee (1990). *Sojourner's Truth and Other Stories*. Vancouver: Press Gang.
Robinson, Eden (1996). *Traplines*. New York: Metropolitan Books.
Simpson, Leanne Betasamosake (2015 [2013]). *Islands of Decolonial Love: Stories & Songs*. Winnipeg: Arp Books.
Taylor, Drew Hayden (1998). *Fearless Warriors: Stories*. Burnaby: Talon Books.
Taylor, Drew Hayden (2016). *Take Us to Your Chief and Other Stories*. Vancouver: Douglas and McIntyre.
Van Camp, Richard (2019). *Moccasin Square Gardens: Short Stories*. Vancouver: Douglas and McIntyre.

Secondary Works

Akiwenzie-Damm, Kateri (1998). "We Belong to This Land: A View of 'Cultural Difference'". In: Christl Verduyn, ed. *Literary Pluralities*. Peterborough: Broadview. 84–91.
Armstrong, Jeanette (2006). "Keynote Address: The Aesthetic Quality of Aboriginal Writing". *Studies in Canadian Literature/Études en littérature canadienne* 31: 20–30.
Atwood, Margaret (1990). "A Double-Bladed Knife: Subversive Laughter in Two Stories by Thomas King". *Canadian Literature* 124–125: 243–250.
Coleman, Daniel (2012). "Toward an Indigenist Ecology of Knowledge for Canadian Literary Studies". *Studies in Canadian Literature/Études en littérature canadienne* 37.2: 5–31.
Dewar, Jonathan (2016). "From Profound Silences to Ethical Practices: Aboriginal Writing and Reconciliation". In: Cynthia Sugars, ed. *The Oxford Handbook to Canadian Literature*. New York: Oxford University Press. 150–169.
Francis, Daniel (1992). *The Imaginary Indian: The Image of the Indian in Canadian Culture*. Vancouver: Arsenal Pulp.
Gibert, Teresa (2006). "Written Orality in Thomas King's Fiction". *Journal of the Short Story in English* 47 (Autumn): 97–109.

Godard, Barbara (1990). "The Politics of Representation: Some Native Canadian Women Writers". *Canadian Literature* 124–125: 183–225.
Gruber, Eva (2008). "Humorous Restorifications: Rewriting History with Healing Laughter". In: Kerstin Knopf, ed. *Aboriginal Canada Revisited*. Ottawa: University of Ottawa Press. 220–245.
Henderson, James (Sákej) Youngblood (2000). "Postcolonial Ledger Drawing: Legal Reform". In: Marie Battiste, ed. *Reclaiming Indigenous Voice and Vision*. Vancouver and Toronto: University of British Columbia Press. 161–171.
King, Thomas (1990). "Introduction". In: Thomas King, ed. *All My Relations: An Anthology of Contemporary Canadian Native Fiction*. Toronto McClelland & Stewart. ix–xvi.
King, Thomas (2012 [1990]). "Godzilla vs. Post-Colonial (1990)". In: Konrad Gross and Jutta Zimmermann, eds. *Canadian Literatures*. Trier: WVT. 196–202.
LaRocque, Emma (2010). *When the Other Is Me: Native Resistance Discourse, 1850–1990*. Winnipeg: University of Manitoba Press.
Lincoln, Kenneth (1985). *Native American Renaissance*. Berkeley: University of California Press.
Lutz, Hartmut (1991). *Contemporary Challenges: Conversations with Canadian Native Authors*. Saskatoon: Fifth House Publishers.
Maracle, Lee (2002). *Daughters Are Forever*. Vancouver: Polestar.
McKegney, Sam (2016). "Strategies for Ethical Engagement: An Open Letter Concerning Non-Native Scholars of Native Literatures". In: Reder and Morra. 79–87.
Nunn, Robert (1998). "Hybridity and Mimicry in the Plays of Drew Hayden Taylor". *Essays on Canadian Writing* 65 (Fall): 110.
Nunn, Robert, ed. (2008). *Drew Hayden Taylor: Essays on His Works*. Toronto: Guernica.
O'Brien, Susie (1995). "'Please Eunice, Don't Be Ignorant': The White Reader as Trickster in Lee Maracle's Fiction". *Canadian Literature* 144: 82–96.
Ortez, Simon J., ed. (1998). *Speaking for the Generations: Native Writers on Writing*. Tucson: University of Arizona Press.
Reder, Deanna and Linda Morra, eds. (2016). *Learn – Teach – Challenge: Approaching Indigenous Literatures*. Waterloo: Wilfrid Laurier University Press.
Riddington, Robin (2015). "Got any Grapes? Reading Thomas King's *The Back of the Turtle*". *Canadian Literature* 224: 163–168.
Sinclair, Niigaanwewidam James (2016). "Responsible and Ethical Criticism of Indigenous Literature". In: Reder and Morra. 301–308.
Smith, Linda Tuhiwai (2012). *Decolonizing Methodologies: Research and Indigenous Peoples*. Dunedin: Otago University Press.
Truchan-Tartaryn, Maria and Susan Gingell (2006). "Dances with Coyote: Narrative Voice in Thomas King's *One Good Story, That One*". *Postcolonial Text* 2.3: 1–23.
Vranckx, Sylvie (2012). "'I Carve My Stories Every Day': An Interview with Richard Van Camp". *Canadian Literature* 215: 70–84.

Further Reading

Gibert, Teresa (2001). "Narrative Strategies in Thomas King's Short Stories". In: Jacqueline Bardolph, ed. *Telling Stories: Postcolonial Short Fiction in English*. Amsterdam: Rodopi. 75.
Knopf, Kerstin, ed. (2008). *Aboriginal Canada Revisited*. Ottawa: University of Ottawa Press.
Lacombe, Michele (2016). "Leanne Betasamosake Simpson's Decolonial Aesthetics: 'Leaks'/Leaks, Storytelling, Community, and Collaboration". *Canadian Literature* 230–231: 45–63.

Lee, Robert A. (2016). "Native Short Story. Authorships, Styles". In: Deborah L. Madsen, ed. *The Routledge Companion to Native American Literature*. Abington and New York: Routledge. 412–422.

McCall, Sophie (2016). "Land, Memory, and the Struggle for Indigenous Rights: Lee Maracle's 'Goodbye Snauq'". *Canadian Literature* 230–231: 178–195.

Scott, Conrad (2016). "(Indigenous) Place and Time as Formal Strategy: Healing Immanent Crisis in the Dystopias of Eden Robinson and Richard Van Camp". *Extrapolation* 57.1–2: 73–93.

Van Toorn, Penny (2004). "Aboriginal Writing". In: Eva-Marie Kröller, ed. *The Cambridge Companion to Canadian Literature*. Cambridge: Cambridge University Press. 22–48.

9 Migration and Diaspora

Migration is a central factor in the construction of Canada and of a "Canadian identity". Unsurprisingly, it is, therefore, a prominent theme in Canadian literature, especially in the short story. "After all, it is in the form of cultural practices such as literature that the human factor in migration expresses itself" (Löschnigg and Löschnigg 2009: 9) and that its affective dimension is rendered. In Canada, migration is inextricably linked to multiculturalist policies, which took shape in the 1970s and became institutionalised in 1988. The Multiculturalism Act of 1988 recognises "the cultural and racial diversity of Canadian society and acknowledges the freedom of all members of Canadian society to preserve, enhance and share their cultural heritage" ("Canadian Multiculturalism Act", online). As David Staines elaborates, the

> ongoing and mutually re-assuring nature of the naturalized as well as the native-born voices of Canadians gives the country its unique place as a small-populated but infinitely rich home to the crossroads of the world which has come to this multicultural land.
>
> (2014: 17)

The plurality of voices that has defined the Canadian literary landscape since the mid-1980s is strongly represented in short fiction, which has proved a potent genre for rendering the wide spectrum of issues relating to migration within different cultural and ethnic contexts. Given that migrant identities and exile involve a discontinuous state of being, it is not surprising that authors have turned to short fiction in their search for adequate forms of expression. Through their "foregrounding of the uncomfortable intensity of threshold experiences" (Orr 2015: 251) and their tendency towards fragmentation, short stories seem particularly well suited for capturing experiences of disruption, of "living on the hyphen" (Seyhan 2001: 15), and of being in a state of flux. The recognition of the short story's significance in the context of diasporic writing also finds expression in several anthologies with a focus on multiculturality or on specific ethnic groups in Canada. Examples are

DOI: 10.4324/9781003142683-12

Smaro Kamboureli's landmark anthology *Making a Difference: Canadian Multicultural Literature* (2006/1996), or *Strike the Wok* (2003), a collection focusing on Chinese immigration edited by Lien Chao and Jim Wong-Chu.

Canada's multiculturalism has frequently been likened to a mosaic, whose individual pieces remain identifiable as such while together creating a harmonious whole. In her novel *What We All Long For* (2005), Dionne Brand describes Toronto's multi-ethnic makeup like this: "There are Italian neighbourhoods and Vietnamese neighbourhoods in this city; there are Chinese ones and Ukrainian ones and Pakistani ones and Korean ones and African ones. Name a region on the planet and there's someone from there, here" (4). However, idealist views on multiculturalism and the mosaic have also met with much criticism. As early as 1965, the sociologist John Porter's *The Vertical Mosaic: An Analysis of Social Class and Power in Canada* questioned the myth of a society that offered equal chances of success to everyone, no matter their ethnocultural backgrounds. Porter's critique of persisting hierarchies is also expressed in numerous short stories, such as Dionne Brand's *Sans Souci and Other Stories*, or many of Austin Clarke's stories. In Anosh Irani's "Translated from the Gibberish, Part One" (*Translated from the Gibberish*), the narrator recalls the oath he took in order "to become a Canadian citizen": "I still remember parts of what he [a judge] said. How Canada was this great mosaic, this tapestry of cloth made up of different peoples, and now I was being asked to contribute to it, become part of it" (27). What he finds strange is that in this welcoming ritual, the actual host, that is, the Indigenous population, is missing: "Why aren't they here, as representatives of this great land, to welcome, to educate, to allow us passage into our new home, which was once entirely theirs, and theirs alone?" (27f).

Another critique on the multicultural mosaic, besides that of the glossing over of established hierarchies, concerns issues of ghettoisation and stereotyping. Thus, the mosaic metaphor not only tends to suggest a static division between ethnicities but also bears the danger of essentialising cultural, ethnic, or racial performance. This issue has been memorably addressed by Neil Bissoondath in *Selling Illusions: The Cult of Multiculturalism in Canada* (1994). An example of a short story tackling this problem is Iris Li's "Snaps – a Satire". The story features a writer-protagonist upset about her publisher's wanting her novel to be more Chinese:

> All Chinese writing must be filtered through this filthy sieve of exoticism. Sex becomes magic, dragon-lady sex. Dogs become food. A Grandmother becomes a sagacious fortune cookie. You don't understand the notion that some people can balance their so-called conflicting cultural identities and it becomes boring, becomes normal, becomes something like . . . yourself. Sometimes, we're just not as different as you would like us to be.
>
> (*Strike the Wok* 68f)

While multiculturalism is still the official term for Canada's approach to the coexistence of different ethnic groups within the national frame, interpretations suggesting that ethnocultural communities have clearly definable boundaries are increasingly seen as obsolete. This shift is also evident in a stronger focus on *trans*culturalism, memorably captured by Janice Kulyk Keefer (1991: 16) through the dynamic metaphor of the kaleidoscope. As opposed to the static mosaic, the kaleidoscope foregrounds "the possibility of continuous transformations rather than fixity" (Löschnigg 2013: 254) and the possibility of creating hybrid and transcultural spaces and identities.

While it would be naïve to argue that official multiculturalism has automatically led to a more just society in Canada, it cannot be denied that its propagation has been an important factor in the emergence of writers from various cultural backgrounds, whose stories often feature settings outside Canada. As David Staines observes, these writers

> represent multiculturalism as it is now being manifested in Canadian fiction where the number of native-born writers is increasingly augmented by naturalized Canadian voices, voices that are unafraid to tackle their own chosen landscapes from the safe world that is Canada.
> (2014: 26)

To give some notable examples: most of the stories in Rohinton Mistry's *Tales from Firozsha Baag* (1987) are set in Bombay, while Shyam Selvadurai's collection *Funny Boy* (1994) takes the reader to conflict-ridden Sri Lanka. The 11 stories and vignettes of Makeda Silvera's *Remembering G* (1990) are set in Jamaica. The geographical setting, however, as is the case with many other stories of origin, is not only a physical space but also, as Lucas observes, a psychological one, that is, "a set of social and cultural rules" (1998: 97). Such cultural codes also define the – mostly – India-set stories of Shauna Singh Baldwin's *English Lessons and Other Stories* (1996) or Nalini Warriar's stories in *Blues from the Malabar Coast* (2002). In fact, as Martin Löschnigg has shown, "Canada in recent works by immigrant writers frequently provides a point of departure from which these writers transcend places and chronological strictures, looking back on their old worlds and showing how these intersect with Canada" (2013: 253). The fact that an engagement with the culture of origin is not necessarily bound to geographical or national boundaries is evident, for example, in Zalika Reid-Benta's coming-of-age cycle *Frying Plantain* (2019). Set in Eglington West or "Island Town" (33), as the narrator Kara refers to it, a Caribbean neighbourhood in Toronto, the major cultural backdrop of the stories is Jamaican, including the use of *patois*, an English-based creole language with West African elements (see also Section 9.2.). In fact, urban space, in general, is the spatial context against which most migration stories evolve – an aspect which will be further discussed in Section 9.4.

9.1. Major Thematic Concerns

The themes dealt with in stories about migration and diaspora are manifold, reflecting the often very different circumstances of migrants. In spite of individual differences, however, some recurring themes can be identified. These are the transitory nature of migrant identities and the experience of cultural displacement and alienation. The latter is often connected to being exposed to racism and hostility towards "others". Another prominent theme is living with or in between languages and the straddling of two or more cultures. Feeling that they do not (yet) belong to Canada while at the same time being disconnected from their place of origin, many characters find themselves suspended between here and there. Their search for identity thus becomes another major concern, which is often explored against the backdrop of generation conflicts. Humiliating ordeals the newly arrived must undergo to be "employable", and inhumane working conditions are also recurring themes in migration stories. Focusing on ambivalent experiences of making a new living in Canada, the stories provide critical assessments of the multicultural ideal. Unflinchingly charting immigrant experiences, contemporary Canadian short fiction thus draws attention to the multifarious challenges of trying to settle in a novel and often alien environment.

Cultural displacement is a theme that appears particularly often in diasporic short fiction. Thus, in Caterina Edwards's "Prima Vera" (*Island of the Nightingales*, 2000), Maria finds herself caught in Canada's "never-ending winter", a "prisoner of this cold country", where even her "very thoughts were freezing" and "the ice was pushing in at the windows, at the corners. Reaching for her" (8). Longing for the Italian spring (*primavera*), she finds herself exposed to the bright light of the hospital room where she is to give birth. Her traumatic experiences in the hospital are a trope for an overall crisis, aggravated by prejudicial insults she suffers from the nurse, whose "freckled face scrunched in disgust. 'Italians!'", and the doctor, who attributes her plumpness to too much spaghetti (19). Images of coldness also inform the first-person narrator Lulu's impressions of Canada in Makeda Silvera's *Remembering G* (1991). Speaking from a point "[w]hen the cold tears away at [her] soul" (102) and being confronted with blatant racism, she looks back at her childhood in Jamaica. However, Lulu's vision of her native island is not entirely nostalgic. In fact, as Maria Belén Lucas points out, Silvera's cycle also "depicts the interaction between the black and the white communities on the island, and articulates, from a feminist perspective, the estrangement which the colonizer's racist and sexist culture has wrought among the Afro-Caribbean population" (2000: 256). Through its disrupted chronology, which suggests an interweaving of past, present, and future, and its undermining of coherence in general, *Remembering G* is also a striking example of how the short story cycle lends itself to the rendering of lives characterised by fragmentation and discontinuity.

Many immigration stories depict forms of explicit or implicit racism and provide insights into the humiliating ordeals immigrants often undergo. Examples are Rabindranath Maharaj's "The Diary of a Down-Courage Domestic" (*The Books of Ifs and Buts*, 2002) and Austin Clarke's "Waiting for the Postman to Knock" (*They Never Told Me and Other Stories*), two epistolary stories about Caribbean domestics in Canada. Maharaj satirises the materialistic and patronising attitudes of Canadians through Irma's letters to her husband, Paul. What mostly provokes Irma, a "fifty-five-year-old woman with grandchildren as big as he self" (169), is the arrogance of people at the employment agency, "skinny little children with they mother milk still on they face" (173). The humiliation of being bossed around by teenagers also appears in Lao-Canadian Souvankham Thammavongsa's "Picking Worms" and in the title story of *How to Pronounce Knife* (2020). In the latter, the focaliser Joy's father complains that whatever great jobs they had in Laos did not count in Canada, where they were "being managed by pimple-faced teenagers" (4).

In addition to inhumane working conditions and dire abodes, another recurring theme is the hardships and traumatic experiences of refugees, which often leave them scarred not only physically but also mentally. Memorable examples are the title story of Neil Bissoondath's *On the Eve of Uncertain Tomorrows*, David Waltner-Toews's "Wild Geese" (*One Foot in Heaven*), or selected stories from Téa Mutonji's *Shut Up You're Pretty* and Thammavongsa's *How to Pronounce Knife*. In Thammavongsa's "Picking Worms", the girl narrator is haunted by the memory of her father, who drowned during their flight from Laos:

> He was there, his head above the water, pushing me and my mother across the river, and then I looked back and saw his head go under. He came back once more, and his mouth opened, but he made no sound as he went under again.
>
> (172f)

In Anosh Irani's "Behind the Moon" (*Translated from the Gibberish*), we encounter an illegal Muslim immigrant in Vancouver, "a passport-less creature", who "had used a tourist visa to enter Canada, and was now one of the invisibles" (51). Abdul is exploited by and bound to Qadir Bhai, an immigrant who has made it and in whose restaurant, Mughlai Moon, Abdul works as a cook. His boss keeps the young man's passport in order to prevent him from leaving and has, for five years, been tricking him into believing that he would take care of his obtaining citizenship. Just one step before a friend, another immigrant from India, manages to rescue Abdul from Qadir Bhai's clutches and provide him with the necessary papers, Abdul becomes the victim of white racism and, in consequence, is found out by the police and arrested. Sitting in the back of the police car, Abdul feels that he is morphing into a rat – "a strange feeling, but altogether familiar as well" (72).

The metamorphosis, however, endows him with a feeling of power, making him imagine how he would nibble at Qadir Bhai's passport:

> And he could feel the passport turning into a different shape, the edges tearing, as though a new country was being formed, a country for traitors like Qadir Bhai, where rats like Abdul were in charge, ensuring that promises made were kept, and that when dreams were offered to people, a thousand rats would start singing, nibbling, gnawing in warning, and shame would drip down the jowls of men like Qadir Bhai, just as Abdul's shame had seeped into a country that could have been his.
> (72f)

While in stories such as "Behind the Moon" or "On the Eve of Uncertain Tomorrows", the focus is on the difficulties of being accepted as an immigrant or refugee, the balancing act it takes for immigrants to adapt and move on while at the same time trying to stay connected to their cultural roots is an issue that is even more frequently addressed in Canadian short fiction. Often, the straddling of two (or more) identities, that of the place of origin and that of the place of residency, is shown to be entangled with generational conflicts between immigrant parents and their children, an issue that will receive more attention in Section 9.3.

Living in, with, or between two cultural paradigms may destabilise notions of identity and create rifts between parents and children. However, in migration stories, such liminal experiences are also frequently shown to bear transcultural possibilities, as will be elaborated in Section 9.4.

9.2. Major Voices

The list of Canadian short fiction writers who address migration, cultural displacement, and multi- and transculturalism is long and includes authors with backgrounds from all parts of the world. In the following, I shall name a selection of writers which seem to me particularly representative.

Regarding diasporic short fiction in Canada, writers with a Caribbean background make an exceptionally strong appearance. David Chariandy (2004: 79) mentions the social and historical factors that have led "to the centrality of migrant experiences and 'ex-centric' settings in so much contemporary Caribbean writing". Especially after the Second World War, emigration from the Caribbean to Canada promised better prospects. The best-known authors here are Barbadian-born Austin Clarke (1934–2016), Trinidadian-born Dionne Brand (1953–), and Indo-Caribbean Neil Bissoondath (1955–), born in Trinidad and Tobago. Among these three authors, it is Austin Clarke who often turned to short fiction, while Brand has so far published only one collection of stories, *Sans Souci and Other Stories* (1988). She is rather known for her poems, novels, and essayistic work, in addition to her significance as one of Canada's foremost black lesbian feminist voices. Bissoondath, too, is not primarily known for his short fiction, collected in *Digging Up Mountains* (1987) and *On the Eve of Uncertain Tomorrows* (1991), but rather for his novels and the previously mentioned *Selling Illusions*. Clarke's short fiction appeared in seven collections, from 1971 (*When He Was Free and Young and He Used to Wear Silks*) to 2013 (*They Never Told Me and Other Stories*), plus *The Austin Clarke Reader*, edited by Barry Callaghan (1996), and *Choosing His Coffin: The Best Stories of Austin Clarke* (2003). His stories are mostly set in Toronto, charting the manifold trajectories of immigrant life (see also Section 9.4.).

Other Caribbean writers of note are Jamaicans Olive Senior (1941–) and Nalo Hopkinson (1960–), and André Alexis (1957–), who was born in Trinidad and Tobago and grew up in Ottawa. Senior has made a strong impact with her four collections of short fiction so far, ranging from *Summer Lightning and Other Stories* (1986) to *The Pain Tree* (2015). While the title story of the latter collection delves into Jamaica's colonial past, Senior's penchant for child perspectives (Gadpaille 2009: 162) is, for example, evident in "Lollipop" (*The Pain Tree*). After her mother left for Canada, Katie and her two younger brothers stay with their Gran in Jamaica. When her mother finally succumbs to Gran's repeated complaints that she could no longer take care of her daughter's children, Katie is allowed to join her mother in Toronto. The nightmare that follows appears even bleaker due to the point of view of a child who finds herself on her own most of the time in a Toronto apartment, with her mother going about her own business:

> She works in a hotel in the day but Katie isn't sure what kind of work she does at night. It is work she has to dress up for though, in high heels and everything, or dress down, for she doesn't put much on though she always throws on a jacket before she goes out.
>
> (89)

On the surface, the story may read as an account of child neglect; the subtext, however, suggests that Katie's mother is really the tragic figure, struggling to make ends meet, seemingly living but dead inside. Her confession to Katie, "I was just a pikni meself, never know a thing about life. . . . Make sure you get education first" (89), is the only time in the story when she makes it explicit to her daughter that she was trapped and that she wants her daughter to escape this fate. In Nalo Hopkinson's *Falling in Love with Hominids* (2015), Caribbean myth and creative literary recycling are major elements. Thus, the tale of Bluebeard has not only inspired authors like Angela Carter or Margaret Atwood but also figures in Hopkinson's "Blushing". Antoine de Saint-Exupéry's classic *The Little Prince* plays a role in "Flying Lessons", and "Shift" places Shakespeare's *The Tempest* in an Afro-Caribbean context, rendering the plot from Caliban's perspective.

André Alexis is unique among Caribbean-Canadian short fiction writers, both with regard to his experimental style and penchant for supernatural and absurdist scenarios, which he employs to "create a philosophical investigation of the human psyche" (Staines 2021: 262), as well as his approach to his Caribbean heritage. Referring to Alexis's stories "Horse" and "Kuala Lumpur" (*Despair, and Other Stories of Ottawa*, 1994), Chariandy points out how "Alexis depicts the ethnicity associated with his Afro-Canadian heritage in negative and ultimately threatening terms" (2004: 80) (see also Chapter 6 of this volume).

Cyril Dabydeen (1945–), born in Guyana and of Indian descent, has been a prolific writer of short fiction. From his first collection of short stories (*Still Close to the Island*, 1980), he has expressed his understanding of identity as diasporic *and* global in an ample body of short fiction. As Mariam Pirbhai (2014: online) has phrased it, "Dabydeen has played an integral role in forging a multicultural literary community that looks to differences in ethnicity, race and perspective as the basis for cultural and national enrichment". Dabydeen's transcultural approach is memorably expressed, for example, in the title story of *North of the Equator* (2001) (see also 9.4). Some of Dabydeen's stories seem overly didactic, as in the "debate-structured" title story of *My Multi-Ethnic Friends* (2013), which provides insight into the main characters' committee work that strives to "recommend action that will eliminate racial discrimination in the new Canada now before us" (*My Multi-Ethnic Friends* 52). However, what also defines this story and is, in fact, a characteristic feature of Dabydeen's fiction, is his interrogative style and his persistent and thought-provoking refusal to provide fixity. This can be observed in "Believers", which explores ambivalences in religious affiliations, or in the homecoming narrative "Starapple Canadian" (both in *My Multi-Ethnic Friends*), to name but two of many.

Further noteworthy Caribbean short fiction voices are Antiguan Althea Prince (1945–), Rabindranath Maharaj (1955–), who was born and raised in Trindad and Tobago; Shani Mootoo (1957–), who was born in Dublin to Trinidadian parents and moved to Vancouver at the age of 19; and Jamaican-born Makeda Silvera (1955–). A Jamaican background also defines emerging author Zalika Reid-Benta's award-winning debut collection *Frying Plantain* (2019), which traces Kara Davis's growing up in Toronto's Eglington West neighbourhood, where "[b]ungalow windows boasted the colourful banners of the island flags: red, yellow and green for Guyana; black, and green for Jamaica" (34).

Frying Plantain is also a prime example of the evocation of orality that is so typical of much of Caribbean writing. In the story "Snow Day", Kara and her friends, it seems, engage in a spiteful competition about whose *patois* is more authentic:

> "Ay, look at this, Kara ah take charge! She think she a bad gyal for she break the rules dey", said Jordan, laughing with Rochelle.
> "She'll probably cave halfway to your house and run back to school, Chelle".

"Quiet, Anita. Yuh run yuh mouth too much", I said.

"What's this? Miss Canada gwine fi bust out the patois? Yuh need to stop Ja-fakin' it, Kara".

(32)

Regarding Caribbean stories in general and Jamaican literature in particular, the use of *patois* or other modes that implement the rhetoric of orality into the written text is not only a device meant to render the impression of authenticity but also has a strong political function. It is a "writing back" to the assumed primacy of literacy over orality, which had led to the cultural exclusion of large parts of Caribbean society. As Michael A. Bucknor writes, "Caribbean creole expression is more than pleasing language to the discerning ear; it is political expression to the discerning eye" (2002: 179). Michelle Gadpaille adds that "the history of writing in those islands can be seen as a long, slow resurfacing of the repressed energies of orality, the reclamation of permission to make a spectacle of yourself in public" (2009: 164). Referring especially to stories by female Jamaican authors such as Olive Senior, Hyacinth M. Simpson points out how they "have added to the seemingly endless ways in which oral elements – strategies of composition, transmission and performance – can thus be used to shape narratives that explore the psychological and social aspects of Jamaican life". A memorable example of Olive Senior's use of performative orality is "You Think I Mad, Miss" (*Discerner of Hearts*, 1995), a story that depicts a homeless woman, "Isabella Francina Myrtella Jones" (76, 82), who finds it necessary to inform the people in cars stopping at the traffic light or passers-by about her name. Even though, in the end, she begs for money, her "primary concern is with getting her version of the story out, while refusing to take over the silenced 'fallen woman' role" (Kruk 72). Through simultaneous first-person narration and the excessive use of "you", Isabella's ranting monologues addressed to ten unnamed townspeople have an unsettling effect on the reader, turning her character into one that "haunts like a Caribbean Cassandra" (Kruk 2016: 70).

While much of Caribbean-Canadian writing can also be seen as belonging to African diasporic literature, there have also been authors who have recently immigrated from African countries themselves. M.G. Vassanji (1950–) was born in Kenya to Indian immigrants and moved to Canada from Tanganyika (now Tanzania), where he was raised. The 16 stories (some being only short vignettes) that make up *Uhuru Street* (1990) focus on the Indian community of Dar es Salam. While the ethnic and religious patchwork of Uhuru Street forms the backdrop of the first stories, this setting then loses its importance but remains significant as a point of reference. This holds even for those stories which are set in Germany ("Refugee") or shift between London, Toronto, and Dar ("The London-Returned"). In his second collection, *When She Was Queen* (2005), Vassanji again moves between Toronto, Africa, and beyond.

An interesting new voice in the context of African Canadian writing is Téa Mutonji, who immigrated with her family from the Democratic Republic of Congo and grew up in Toronto. In her debut collection, *Shut Up You're Pretty* (2919), Mutonji gives voice to many of her own experiences in Canada through Loli's struggling with her Congolese heritage, her parents' traumatised selves, and her own chaotic growing up in and integrating into Canadian society (see also Chapter 7).

Among Asian Canadians, writers of Chinese descent have made a particularly strong impact on Canadian short fiction. Even though the Chinese are one of the oldest immigrant groups in Canada (Hatch 1995: 169), their history has long been one of discrimination and silence. In 1885, Canada introduced the Chinese Immigration Act, which imposed a head tax on Chinese immigrants, a discriminatory policy that was aggravated in 1923, with the Chinese Exclusion Act, prohibiting Chinese immigration until its repeal in 1943, when China had become an ally in the Second World War. In the 1970s, Chinese-descended writers first appeared on the Canadian literary scene. Lien Chao (1997: 28) refers to this time as a phase of re-territorialisation when collective identities and the history of institutionalised racial discrimination were placed in the foreground. While the first anthology of Chinese-Canadian writing (*Inalienable Rice*) appeared in 1979, followed by *Many-Mouthed Birds* in 1991, it was only in 2003, with Lien Chao's and Jim Wong-Chu's *Strike the Wok*, that the first anthology of Chinese-Canadian short fiction was published.

Paul Yee's (1956–) and Judy Fong Bates's (1949–) stories are in many ways typical of the phase of re-territorialisation. Thus, Yee has addressed the history of Chinese immigrants in Canada in the collections *Tales from Gold Mountain* (1990) and *Dead Man's Gold and Other Stories* (2002). In Judy Fong Bates's *China Dog and Other Tales from a Chinese Laundry* (1997), the laundry of the title functions as a (stereo)typical setting of stories about the Chinese diaspora in Canada. Although not a short story cycle in a narrower sense, *China Dog* contains a unifying element as the characters of these stories are all members of a community who share the same (traumatic) experiences.

Further noteworthy Chinese-Canadian authors are Evelyn Lau (1971–), Andy Quan (1969–), and Lien Chao (1950–). Largely excluding explicit ethnic markers from the 17 stories collected in *Fresh Girls* (1993) and *Choose Me* (1999), Lau sets herself off from the stories that define the re-territorialisation phase. At the same time, however, many of the stories contain implicit critiques of social hierarchies. Mostly, Lau's protagonists are mistresses, escorts, or lovers in a triangle which usually involves an older wealthy man in a prestigious position and his wife. Interestingly, however, it is always the socially privileged wife who is "othered" and who mostly remains a "ghost wife", while the socially marginalised woman is the one who is behind the narrative voice. Quan's *Calendar Boy* (2001) is striking in its innovative depiction of ethnic and queer identities (see also Chapter 7). Chao is best known as a poet and anthologist, yet with *The Chinese Knot and Other Stories* (2008), she has also brought out an important book of short fiction, one that offers "inner-city snapshots" of Chinese immigrants in Toronto, as the author explains in her introduction to the volume.

Celebrated author Madeleine Thien (1974–) was born in Vancouver to Malaysian Chinese parents who had moved to Canada in the 1960s. Even though Thien has shifted her interest to novels, some stories, like for example "Simple Recipes" and "Map of the City" (*Simple Recipes*, 2001), have received a wide critical echo and have assumed an almost canonical status (see also 9.3). *Simple Recipes* combines stories like "Bullet Train" or "Dispatch", which exclude questions of ethnic identity, with stories that explore migrant experiences – often with regard to how differently these affect first- and second-generation immigrants. Among Southeast Asian voices, an emerging author that needs to be mentioned is Souvankham Thammavongsa (1978–), who was born in a Laos refugee camp in Thailand and raised and educated in Toronto. Her powerful debut collection, *How to Pronounce Knife* (2020), addresses different facets of starting a new existence in an alien and often hostile environment.

Like the Chinese, immigrants from Japan, too, can look back at a long and often troubled history of settlement in Canada. From the late 19th century onwards, Japanese immigrants have settled on the Canadian West Coast. When Japan became an enemy in the Second World War, Canadians of Japanese origin suddenly found themselves enemy aliens; they were stripped of their possessions and interned in the interior of British Columbia and Alberta, with families often being torn apart. A writer who has dedicated a whole collection of short stories to those Japanese Canadians whose lives were shattered by the war measures is Terry Watada (1951–). While some of the stories in *Daruma Days* (1997) capture the haunting atmosphere in the internment camps during the 1940s, others switch back and forth in time, thus also depicting the aftermath of events that were motivated by racism much more than by an actual threat to national security. This is the case, for example, in "The Brown Bomber", "Only the Lonely", and "The Moment of Truth". Another interesting Japanese Canadian writer of short fiction is Hiromi Goto (1966–), a self-proclaimed queer writer, editor, and feminist. Her first collection of short stories, *Hopeful Monsters* (2004), works with elements of magical realism and the uncanny and critically – and to unsettling effect – challenges notions of "normalcy".

Important contributions to Canadian short fiction have also come from Sri Lankan-Canadian Shyam Selvadurai (1965–) (see also Chapter 7) and from the emerging Bangladeshi Canadian writer Silmi Abdullah, whose experiences as a lawyer and an immigrant inform her debut collection *Home of the Floating Lily* (2021). Regarding writers with an Indian background, the most well-known representative is Rohinton Mistry (1952–). Mistry, whose *Tales from Firozsha Baag* (1987) and accoladed novels have earned him a place as one of the most eminent contemporary Canadian writers, was born in Bombay into a Parsi community, itself a diasporic group within India, and emigrated to Canada in 1975 (see also Section 9.4). Further noteworthy short fiction collections which address migrant identities against an Indian background are Shauna Singh Baldwin's (1962–) *English Lessons and Other Stories* (1996) and especially Anosh Irani's (1974–) *Translated from the Gibberish* (2019) (see also Section 9.4). New Delhi–born Rachna Mara (1953–2021) first emigrated to London before settling in Canada in the mid-1970s. Mara's polyvocal short story cycle *Of Customs and Excise* (1991) spans different locations (India, Canada, Great Britain) and generations and offers insight into how the experience of migration has shaped the lives of the four women who represent the main characters in the book.

Literary approaches to migration and transition can also be found in the short fiction of writers from different European backgrounds. In the six stories in Caterina Edwards's (1948–) *Island of the Nightingale* (2000), there is a strong focus on cultural dislocation against the backdrop of the Italian diaspora. At the same time, however, the stories can be seen as depicting different forms of being Italian Canadian, defying stereotypical notions of "Italianness" and doing justice to the multiple (and at times strikingly varied) effects of migration on the characters. In most of Italian-Canadian writer Licia Canton's (1963–) stories (collected in *Almond, Wine and Fertility*, 2008, and *The Pink House*, 2018), migration and the negotiation of different linguistic and cultural systems are a subtly interwoven backdrop rather than the central topic. The 15 stories assembled in *The Pink House* are mostly set in Montreal and feature experiences of the Italian diaspora in a Québécois context. What is mostly foregrounded, however, are the complexities and the depth of familial relationships and the female characters' (mostly successful) juggling of professional life and traditional values.

Of Tamas Dobozy's (1969–) four collections, the two more recent ones, *Siege 13: Stories* (2012) and *Ghost Geographies* (2021), are the most interesting regarding themes of exile and the impact of political turmoil and oppression on lives – on a personal and collective level, as an immediate threat and as traumatic memory. Shortlisted for both the Rogers Writers Trust Fiction Prize and the Governor General's Award, the linked stories of *Siege 13* all revolve around the occupation of Budapest by the Red Army at the end of the Second World War and Hungary's becoming a satellite of the Soviet Union. While some stories, as for example "The Restoration of the Villa Where Tibor Kalman Once Lived", are directly set in Budapest, others, like "The Beautician", lay the scene in Canada decades later, where the Soviet siege of the Nazi-controlled city remains a haunting memory. This and the oppressive communist regime that followed also reverberate in Dobozy's *Ghost Geography*. Thus, in "Ray Electric", we find a successful wrestler who is forced to flee Hungary and does so with a "homemade" balloon, which takes him, his girlfriend, and his best buddy to Austria, from where they move on to Canada. In his review for "The Art's Fuse", Vincent Czyz

(2022: online) finds apt words for Dobozy's style and intent in his "melancholy" and at times darkly humorous investigations into "the inevitable failure of . . . utopias (communism being the most notorious)":

> Borders are arbitrary. Identity is amorphous or hopelessly polyhedral. Boundaries are blurry. . . . The stories also display a penchant for constructing or reconstructing – however imperfectly – wholes from fragments. . . . Dobozy is an anarchist in the best sense of the word: it's not chaos he's enamored of but a way of life untrammeled by political oppression, bureaucratic horrors, legal absurdities. He's drawn to nowhere, blanks, interstices, and in-between states. He's patron saint of forgotten histories and the margin note that's more interesting than the text.

Two other important authors of Eastern European descent are Janice Kulyk Keefer (1952–) and David Bezmozgis (1973–). Keefer's Ukrainian heritage and the question of cultural in-betweenness define several stories in *Transfigurations* (1987) and *Travelling Ladies* (1992). Similarly, Bezmozgis has provided compelling portraits of diasporic subjects. The author's Jewish-Latvian background informs especially his cycle *Natasha and Other Stories* (2004), which can be described as a storified narrative of arrival, rendering the act of migration as a decoding of new cultural contexts. All seven stories are presented by the same first-person narrator, Mark Berman; roughly chronologically, they deal with his Latvian family's attempt at settling in the Russian-Jewish enclaves of Toronto and his development – from age six until adulthood – and the negotiation of two cultures. In Bezmozgis's most recent collection, *Immigrant City* (2019), the actual protagonist is Toronto (see also 9.4). While, again, all main characters of the seven stories are immigrants with a Latvian/Russian/Soviet Union background, the stories also feature numerous encounters with other cultures. "How It Used to Be", in turn, shows elements of dystopian fiction, while "A New Gravestone for an Old Grave" takes the main character, Victor Shulman, "home" to Riga, where he realises the impossibility of returns: "He had returned to the city of his birth, but no place had ever seemed less familiar" (123).

While Bezmozgis – and also Sidura Ludwig (1976–) in *You Are Not What We Expected* (2020) – explore Jewish identities and experiences in Canada, Sandra Birdsell (1942–) and David Waltner-Toews (1948–) speak from a Mennonite perspective. As a Mennonite writer, Waltner-Toews, in fact, represents a "double hyphenation" (Keefer 1995: 190). His *One Foot in Heaven* (2005) is a memorable account of Mennonite communities and multicultural patchworks in general in the Canadian prairies. In addition, the 14 stories that make up this cycle are linked by the themes of migration and loss, stretching from Prom Koslowski's flight from Ukraine as a little boy to his own son Thomas's search for a lost sense of wholeness which he eventually finds neither there nor in Canada but in his relationships with the people he cares for.

In Steven Heighton's (1961–2022) short fiction (three collections between 1992 and 2012), too, the transcultural is probed and analysed. Even though the author's Greek heritage (through his mother) only surfaces occasionally in his stories – as in "The Son is Always Like the Father" (*Flight Paths of the Emperor*, 1992) – the themes of culture clash, cultural idiosyncrasies, linguistic confusions, and the impact of history on present cultural contacts feature prominently in *Flight Paths* and also make an appearance in "Those Who Would be More", the initial story in *The Dead Are More Visible* (2012). Like Mavis Gallant and Norman Levine before him, Heighton looks at Canadians abroad, especially in Japan, where the author himself worked as an English teacher for some time. Many of Heighton's Japan stories illustrate how atrocities committed during the Second World War cast a shadow on relationships in the present.

9.3. Cultural Identity and Generational Conflict

The experience of migration and the challenge of living in between or within different cultures are frequently thematised against the backdrop of generational rifts. In many stories, the cultural drifting apart of parents and children is depicted as a dilemma that confronts first-generation parents in particular. On the one hand, they project all the dreams they themselves could not (or can no longer) fulfil into their offspring, encouraging them to quickly adapt and perform well in their new environment; on the other, it is exactly their children's increasing Canadianness and losing touch with their culture of origin that can prove a painful experience, suggesting an incompatibility between the parents' emigrant and their children's immigrant perspectives.

More often than not, these hardships are filtered through the perspectives of children, as is the case in a number of stories from Lao-Canadian author Souvankham Thammavongsa's challenging collection *How to Pronounce Knife* (2020), in Congolese writer Téa Mutonji's acclaimed *Shut Up, You're Pretty*, or in Zalinka Reid-Benta's *Frying Plantain*. As the title of Thammavongsa's "You Are So Embarrassing" already indicates, for children and especially for adolescents it is often mortifying to witness their parents' inability to fully fit in. In David Bezmozgis's *Natasha and Other Stories* (2004), too, it is the child, Jewish-Latvian Mark Berman, who narrates the story of his family's attempts at settling in Toronto. A key element in these immigrant stories is the inversion of accustomed roles, as the further acculturated children guide their parents, especially in linguistic matters. Thus, Mark Berman, from the beginning, feels the pressure of having to function as "the family's translator, the necessary mediator between a baffled family and alien linguistic territory" (Weber 2004: online).

Often, food or the preparing and sharing of a meal hold a central position as tropes of transgenerational communication (see also Fellner 2013). In the final story of Téa Mutonji's *Shut Up, You're Pretty*, food and the sharing of a meal become emblematic of cultural reconciliation. In "Randy Travis" and in the title story of Thammavongsa's *How to Pronounce Knife* food, too, plays a significant role. In David Waltner-Toews's *One Foot in Heaven*, the Mennonite heritage of Aunt Elsie is rendered through the instructions for baking, truly transcultural since heavily permeated by German expressions which she gives to her "Canadian" nephew. In contrast, food in Caterina Edwards's "On a Platter" functions as an (unwelcome) trigger for the main character's unsuccessfully suppressed memories of her Sicilian past and heritage.

A memorable story that features both generational conflict and the trope of food is Madeleine Thien's "Simple Recipes".

Case Study: Madeleine Thien's "Simple Recipes" – Migration and Generational Conflict

"Simple Recipes", the title story of Madeleine Thien's only collection of short fiction to date (2001), is an unsettling narrative about migrant identities and intergenerational conflict. It features a family who has immigrated to Vancouver from Malaysia and explores the agonising relationship between a home-bound father, his working wife, their teenage son, and their little daughter, from whose perspective the story is told.

Most of the story is set in the hermetically closed space of the family's kitchen, where the narrator's father tries to uphold their traditional culture through the carefully prepared Asian dishes he cooks for them. As the mother works as a sales clerk in a department store and the 12-year-old son plays outside as much as possible, it is father and daughter who occupy the space at home and develop a close bond, the daughter unconditionally admiring her father, "the magician, who can make something beautiful out of nothing" (18). For the father, the food he prepares becomes a symbolically charged substitute for his native language, which his Canadian-born daughter never picked up and which has "left" his Malaysian-born son, or "he forgot it, or he refused it, which is also common, and this made my father angry" (7), as the narrator records. Against this backdrop, the father's preparing rice by sifting it in his hands and dexterously removing any impurities becomes an act that symbolises his attempt at preserving an unadulterated cultural identity. Stripped of the patriarchal authority he would have enjoyed at home, his daily kitchen rituals may also function as compensation.

The story's climax has the family assembled in the kitchen for supper. The mother, in her shop assistant's uniform, and the son, mud-bespeckled from the football field, appear as intruders from outside. While the mother takes off her uniform before sitting down, the boy dirties the tablecloth, thus visualising his rejection of his father's "offering" of communicating through food and the ritual of eating. Tension increases when he refuses to eat the fish his father cooked; it finally escalates when he chokes on a mouthful of cauliflower and spits it onto his plate. While his sister realises that her brother is "drowning" (14), like the fish did in the sink, his father sees this as another insult, "slams his chopsticks down" (14), and slaps his son in the face. Still gulping for air, the son strikes back with a fork and gives vent to his anger, verbally abusing his father and wishing him dead. Shaking with anger, the father sends him to his room and later thrashes him with a bamboo rod, "a more than obvious symbol of the father's Asiancy and patriarchal tyranny" (Löschnigg 2013: 254), as are the chopsticks that significantly contrast with the fork which the son uses to strike out in the immediately preceding scene.

One of the most powerful effects of the story results from the analogy between the boy and the fish. In retrospect, the fish's desperate struggle to breathe as the water drains from the sink transpires as an image for the son's suffocating from the constrictions of the family situation, rendered concrete as he gulps for air. Having earlier observed the fish dying slowly in the sink (8), the daughter's impressions now merge with the picture of her brother choking on the food, "drowning, his hair waving like grass" (14). Her description of her brother, whose "face is red and his mouth open" (14), his "small chest heaving" (15), echoes earlier descriptions of the fish that "is barely breathing" (5), "mouth open, its body heaving" (8). Serving the fish, the father's "spoon breaks skin" (13) in the same way as his bamboo rod "rips the skin on my brother's back" (15). Sizzling in the pan, the frying fish makes "a sound so loud it drowns out all other noises" (10), as will the beaten boy's screams (16). The image of the dying fish also concludes the story, emphasising its symbolic significance and the mature narrator's feelings of complicity and guilt: "Somewhere in my memory, a fish in the sink is dying slowly. My father and I watch as the water runs down" (19).

Before the eruption of violence against her brother, her father's "simple recipes", his daily ritual of cooking rice, his careful removal of impurities, "every motion so clean and sure", gave the narrator the feeling "that all was well in the world" (4). Later, however, when she dreams of him in the shiny kitchen, "he looks out of place" (4). Apparently, she has come to realise that the father's obsession with imperfection was expressive of his failure to open up to Canada, obsessively trying to cling to his Asian identity. Against this backdrop, the "slowly dying fish", as Janice Fiamengo suggests, could also be linked to the father via the "associations of the phrase 'a fish out of water', an expression indicating displacement, maladjustment, the kind of expression used about someone who does not belong – like the father" (2014: 213).

While the main parts of the story take place in the kitchen, there is a frame provided by the narrative's going back and forth, from flashbacks to the parents' past and immigration to Canada to foreshadowing reflections on how this "violence [would] turn all [the daughter's] love to shame and grief" (18) and strongly affect her later life. Even if there has been a break beyond repair, the daughter will continue her relationship with her father yet, as she says, "The unconditional quality of my love for him will not last forever, just as my brother's did not" (17).

Filtered through the perspective of the child, his greatest admirer, the father's brutal punishment of his son comes even more shocking to the reader. However, Thien also conveys very subtly the father's own pain and despair, as well as the mother's and daughter narrator's silent complicity and feelings of guilt.

Thematic concerns:

- Generational conflict
- Cultural displacement and alienation
- Trying to cling to one's roots

Narrative voice and structure:

- The first-person narration alternates between the experiencing child's perspective and reflections of the adult narrating self.
- The climactic escalation of the conflict between father and son is framed by flashbacks and passages that capture the time after the father's outburst of violence.

The "language" of food:

- The kitchen is a hermetically closed, culturally freighted space:
  - The kitchen is the father's domain, where he prepares Asian food for his family.

> - For the narrator, the kitchen represents both a paradise and the setting of her brutal expulsion from it.
> - Rice-cooking is emblematic of Asian culture.
> - The father's ritual of sifting the rice and removing all impurities is a symbolic act reflecting his rejection of cultural openness and hybridity.
> - Cooking becomes a substitute language for the father, whose children refuse to learn or speak his language.
> - Suggested analogies between the slowly dying fish the father prepares for supper and his son add intensity to the already shocking scene of violence.

9.4. Multicultural "Ethni-cities" and Transcultural Possibilities

Edward Soja's term "ethni-cities" (1995: 24) pointedly denotes the significance of urban space as a vibrant "site for the inscription of cultural contact and struggles over empowerment" (Löschnigg 2013: 246). Canada's urban centres represent the idea of multiculturalism in the form of concentrated microcosms, as it were. Characterised by dynamic rather than static parameters and by the blurring of cultural boundaries, the "ethni-city" at the same time provides an ideal tableau against which literature may explore cultural encounters and new configurations can be mapped. The semanticised space of the city fulfils various and often opposed functions in stories that thematise the fluidity of migrant identities. On the one hand, there are stories in which the city appears as a hierarchically segregated space defined by exclusionary principles. Often, these stories render urban space – or the streets, residential areas, houses, and apartments that metonymically represent the city – as a trap. On the other hand, there are stories in which the city engenders imaginary or practised movements which suggest a productive crossing of cultural borders – a crossing "not in order to arrive at some totalized monolithic ideal of Canadianness, but rather to establish a dialogic rather than oppositional field of discourse, to conflate margin and mainstream, dominant and emergent group into an everchanging choreography of differences" (Keefer 1995: 197).

As Judith Misrahi-Barak claims in her exploration of cityscapes in Caribbean-Canadian short fiction (1998: 20), "[t]he city offers the paradox of a territory already composed by and for the other but where an identity of one's own can still be worked out". In several stories from Téa Mutonji's *Shut Up You're Pretty*, Toronto appears hierarchically organised. From the point of view of young Loli, however, Galloway, the Scarborough residential area of the underprivileged, is home and an intact community. This positively connoted internal perspective clashes with the external perspective of the news reports following the death of Darnell, a young black man from the community who was beaten to death, probably because of homophobia. Since this has happened in the Galloway "ghetto of the poor" (45), however, involving a young black man, the murder is dismissed as a fight between black thugs. The victim is described as a "high-school dropout who sold dope and fucked sex workers" (45) while, in fact – and quite ironically – he was studying "law and politics" (47). In general, Toronto's city space figures prominently in Mutonji's story cycle and is strongly semanticised. Already in the first story, "Tits for Cigs", Jolie introduces her new friend Loli to the "boundaries and the places to avoid" and highlights the significance of the "intersection of Lawrence and Galloway", where you "got the best of Scarborough . . .: the low income houses attached to the getting-by houses, attached to the getting there houses" (11). Repeatedly the stories display the social and racial semantics of the city, highlighting the liminality which seems to be inscribed in the places where people live, as in the following description of the view from Ben's balcony in "Old-Fashioneds": "This was the part of Scarborough that turned into Toronto. And the people who lived in this specific building seemed equally in between two identities" (119).

While Loli in Mutonji's story cycle *does* manage to claim her own terrain on Toronto's map and while for the family in Souvankham Thammavongsa's "Chick-A-Chee!" (*How to Pronounce Knife*, 2020), the Saturday trips "to a neighbourhood we wished we could live in" (77) remain an invigorating, imaginative game, Jefferson in Austin Clarke's "Four Stations in His Circle" (*When He Was Free and Young and He Used to Wear Silks*, 1971) utterly fails in his fierce endeavour to belong. Jefferson is one of Clarke's many protagonists who have come to hate themselves and their black (Barbadian) identity due to a long history and personal experience of the hegemonic gaze (Chariandy 2005: 151) that, in Jefferson's case, has become internalised. Having worked at various jobs, denied himself any amenities and withdrawn from his black friends, Jefferson has finally saved enough money to buy a house in Rosedale, one of the wealthiest areas in Toronto. However, already during his frequent excursions to Rosedale to take a look at "his" house, his black skin arouses suspicion, and he is taken for a burglar; when he finally lives in the Rosedale house, the neighbours mistake him for the gardener. Thus, not only Jefferson's dream to belong to white society is shattered, but more importantly, during his obsessive mimicry of privileged white society, he has also erased his black identity or any identity for that matter. He has become a hollow man in a "hollow house . . . , muttering greetings in whispers to his guests, and answering himself" (*Choosing His Coffin* 243) in the bout of madness that closes the story.

Many of Austin Clarke's stories are also memorable examples of how the confined space of houses or apartments – which function as concentrated metonymic representations of urban space – becomes the canvas on which "the isolation and alienation of black immigrants in Canada, and the question of immigrant space allocated to the West Indian in Toronto" (Schuh 2021: 165) is delineated. Thus, as Misrahi-Barak argues, "the house is often depicted . . . as a trap or even a grave, a sort of outgrowth of a city in which it has been impossible to make room for oneself" (1998: 13). This is the case, for example, in "A Slow Death" (*When Women Rule*, 1985), in "Trying to Kill Herself" (*In This City*, 1992), in "Waiting for the Postman to Knock" (*They Never Told Me and Other Stories*, 2013), and in "Canadian Experience" (*Nine Men who Laughed*, 1986). In the latter story, which features an unnamed (and unsuccessful) immigrant in Toronto, constricting and intimidating spaces create a claustrophobic atmosphere, anticipating the protagonist's suicide.

Neil Bissoondath, too, correlates immigrant anxieties with a semantically charged depiction of urban space. In "On the Eve of Uncertain Tomorrows" (*On the Eve of Uncertain Tomorrows*, 1990), Joaquin, a refugee whose precarious position is aggravated by his mutilated body, anxiously awaits the interview that will decide on his status. The setting, a Montreal rooming house, seems to him like a cage that bars him from the real life of the city:

> In the distance, past the complex geometry of withered buildings – garage store-rooms, walls of tin and brick – pressing in on the rear rooming house, the colourless towers of a few tall buildings of the city sit one-dimensional against the sky. They suggest an unknown life, a world of blood and flesh and everyday ambition, a life within his sight but not, yet, within his grasp.
>
> (1f)

Later, he traverses the city on his way to a café, fittingly named *La Barricada*, a meeting place for the hopeless, another prison. It is there that he is involved in saving the life of a woman, an act, it seems, which transforms his feelings towards the city. While, on his way to the café, he did not actively recognise the city but furtively hurried through the streets, his walk back is a leisurely stroll governed by Joaquin's new interest in exploring the city, an interest that has been prompted by his knowledge that "in this city, he has helped save a life" (22). This claiming of urban space, if only for a few moments, may be seen as symbolically prefiguring Joaquin's "placement" in Canada. However, expectations of a happy ending are thwarted when he is back in the rooming house. There, he not only feels imprisoned again but is also disillusioned when he is informed of the refusal of his friend Amin's application for refugee status.

Dionne Brand, too, makes closed segments of urban space functional for her imaginative analysis of ethnic othering. While the city (Toronto) as such appears "claustrophobic" (*Sans Souci* 87) to the focaliser in "No Rinsed Blue Sky, No Red Flower Fences", her apartment is even more menacing: "The apartment had tried to kill her again. She painted the walls as fast as she felt threatened" (85). In "Train to Montreal", too, both urban space in general and the confined space of a train compartment assume a menacing quality. Even though the jazz club featured at the beginning is connoted as "home space", it still depresses the protagonist because it makes her realise that she cannot translate the anger she detects in the music into constructive criticism of the racism she finds herself exposed to. The source of this anger becomes tangible when the safe space of the club is juxtaposed with the – to her – suffocating space of the Toronto-Montreal train she boards: "really shocked at all the white faces on the train" (*Sans Souci* 18), the protagonist falls into a state of immobility, which is further enhanced by a group of white children who "stared blankly and rudely at her" (24). This paralysing feeling of radical exposure receives another twist when she gets off the train, and her walk to the escalator is experienced by her as an ordeal, a transgression through white space. She remains mute when a man explicitly attacks her with crude racist remarks, but inside she is screaming, and the concluding statement that "anger now was close, at her mouth" (29) can be read as an indicator that she will no longer endure such insults silently.

In "Train to Montreal", the trope of hyper-visibility against the backdrop of the cityscape is used to communicate what threatens the diasporic subject. In contrast, however, it is also their *in*visibility which, in some stories, becomes expressive of the marginalisation of ethnic minorities and migrants. This invisibility is often rendered through graphic descriptions of dire living conditions, with basement flats reflecting a low social position. Thus, in Thammavongsa's "A Far Distant Thing" (*How to Pronounce Knife*), the mouldy "one-bedroom basement apartment" (151), separated by a "chain-link fence" and a "dense green forest . . . from all those nice houses farther down the street" (157), makes the child narrator ashamed to invite friends over to her home. In Shauna Singh Baldwin's "Montreal 1962" (*English Lessons*), too, the "grey two rooms" (16) "with their small windows, unnaturally high" (17) designate the couple's obscure position in Canadian society. The "cramped four walls" (17) in this story, however, are miraculously transformed and "filled with sheer lightness" (17) when the wife drapes her husband's brightly coloured turbans over the chairs to dry; the chairs that "stood stiff and wooden as ignorant Canadians" (17). The splendour of this "decoration" becomes a strong statement of the couple's cultural identity as Indian Sikhs, "refusing the drabness, refusing obscurity" (17).

In a considerable number of stories, enclosed segments of urban space materialise as sites of transcultural encounters. In Cyril Dabydeen's Ottawa-based "North of the Equator", for example, the sauna becomes a vast transcultural imaginary for Ravi, the focal character. Sharing the sauna with Pierette, a French-Canadian woman, the two characters' inversely proportional fantasies prepare the ground upon which a third space is created: while Ravi desires to become more familiar with Canada, Pierette longs to visit Jamaica. Transcultural space is created not only through their cross-cultural communication but, more importantly, through Ravi's imagining of teaching a curriculum "that embraces places of origins and cultures from around the world and ties them with the vast Canadian landscape" (9) and his general vision of places melding. In Lien Chao's "Under the Monkey Bars" (*The Chinese Knot and Other Stories*), too, the ideal of a transcultural community is suggested – in this case, in the microcosm of a Toronto playground. In Janice Kulyk Keefer's "Prodigal" (*Travelling Ladies*), in turn, it is the protagonist's return to her dead grandmother's house which makes her claim the Ukrainian heritage she had for a long time rejected and develop a truly hybrid identity. In David Bezmozgis's stories, Toronto becomes not only the eponymous immigrant city of his 2019 collection but also the "site for border crossings, a liminal space, providing opportunities of connection, exchange, trans-action and trans-formation" (Keefer 1995: 181), which for Keefer constitutes an ideal form of multiculturalism. In the title story of *Immigrant City*, the first-person narrator, a Jewish-Canadian writer originally from Soviet Latvia, finds himself "warped" into the magically different world of a Somali community when he picks up a car door he had bought via the Internet. Eventually, however, it turns out that this community does not at all feel that different – rather, the narrator is reminded of his own immigrant past. His daughter Nora, too, feels more and more comfortable with Mohamed's wife and daughter while she waits for her father. When she starts crying, they make a hijab for her to comfort her – a token she does not want to take off when they are on their way back home. The story meaningfully closes with Nora's unwitting comment on the liminal state of the immigrant when father and daughter are on the train back home:

> "Nora, it's our stop", I said. "Do you want to go home or keep going?"
> "Go home and keep going", she said.
>
> (*Immigrant City* 16)

Let me conclude with two compelling representations of transcultural possibilities, Rohinton Mistry's *Tales from Firozsha Baag* and Anosh Irani's *Translated from the Gibberish*. The two authors are not only comparable as to their similar backgrounds; in his short story collection, Irani also alludes to Mistry when his narrator comments on the latter's novel *A Fine Balance* (4) or when reflections on the different blocks of the apartment complex in "Translated from the Gibberish" resonates with the Firozsha Baag-complex in Mistry's *Tales*.

Mistry's 11 *Tales* first introduce the reader to the Firozsha Baag apartment complex in Bombay and its residents, most of them Parsis. While the stories provide glimpses of India's religious plurality ("The Ghost of Firozsha Baag") and the Westernisation of some of the residents ("Squatter"), the theme of migration only emerges gradually. It first appears explicitly in "Squatter" and "Lend Me Your Light" and moves centre stage in the concluding story "Swimming Lessons". The latter reveals that Kersi is not only the narrator and protagonist of *this* story and one out of many characters in some of the others but that *Tales from Firozsha Baag* is actually "his" book, his looking back on and reconstruction of his old world while he has already started his new life as an immigrant in Toronto. Sending the manuscript home to his parents in India and receiving their comments, the volume is also a manifesto of intercultural exchange while, in addition, establishing connections between intra- and extra-textual realities through this *mise-en-abyme* of the writer-reader relationship. The story's transcultural dimension is also underscored by analogies between Firozsha Baag and the apartment complex in Toronto, where Kersi now lives. The strongest connection is the motif of water, linking Bombay's Chowpatty Beach with, first, a sterile indoor pool in Toronto and then the bathtub. It is here that Kersi finally experiences something like a rebirth. Having feared being in and under water, he now, for the first time, dares to submerge, a highly symbolic or even epiphanic act. He resurfaces with a deepened insight into his situation, realising that "[t]he world outside the water I have seen a lot of, it is now time to see what is inside" (249). Through this ending, the story strongly suggests that Kersi will transcend his partly self-imposed status as an outsider and will immerse himself in Canadian society. At the same time, he will uphold the connection with his roots by communicating with his parents but also by creating "imaginary homelands" (Rushdie 1991: 17) in his writing.

Like Mistry's "Swimming Lessons", the two parts of the title story that frame Anosh Irani's *Translated from the Gibberish* connect India with Canada, and like Mistry's story, Irani's abounds with metafictional elements. In addition, the six stories encased by the frame all zigzag between India and Canada, connecting both through the web of storytelling and intercultural exchange while suggesting fragmentation through multimodal elements. The first part of "Translated from the Gibberish" is set in Bombay, where the narrator visits after years of absence; the second takes him back to Vancouver. In both parts, the uppermost concern is the narrator's realisation of his cultural liminality, which he regards ambivalently: "I have two homes, and I have neither" (22). Also, a clear sense of belonging is no longer possible: "I'm going home, and leaving home, at the same time" (198). When asked, in India, about whether he was happy in Canada, he answers no and adds, "but then I'm not happy here [in Bombay] either, because there is no here, here *was*, it no longer *is*" (23). In fact, he questions the existence of "happiness" as such and realises that he does not really want it. What he craves instead is "to combust in such a powerful way that the effects are felt deep in the oceans" (23). What these two stories strongly suggest is that in-betweenness, no matter how challenging, is a powerful catalyst for the creativity of the writer-protagonist, a thinly disguised persona of the author himself. This becomes explicit when the protagonist's boarding pass is fully printed on the page, giving the name "ANOSH IRANI". Seeing the destinations on the boarding pass, "FROM: BOM-PEK; TO: PEK-YVR" (206), the narrator falls into a state of crisis and, in his imagination, gets a new boarding pass (again reproduced on the page) with the destination "OUTER SPACE" (27). The protagonist now seems to have transcended place altogether – looking at the planet Earth and all its diversity and fragility from above, seeing the ongoing terrorism and war, seeing the icecaps melt, knowing that the Earth, "this body is breaking too; it's decaying just like any human" (208). Despite this gloomy outlook, the final story ends with a note of healing, to which the writer can contribute through "some kindness and humour" (210) and through a creative power that results from accepting the in-between, embracing this *and* that rather than this *or* that only.

Multiculturalism is a contested concept. On the one hand, it has clearly fostered the emergence of a plurality of voices and massively contributed to an aesthetic and thematic enrichment of the contemporary Canadian short story. On the other hand, authors have criticised the multicultural ideal as deceptive, as glossing over hierarchical structures and suggesting a static patchwork of clearly separated communities. In general, short fiction writers have thrown light on both the challenges and the possibilities of Canadian multiculturalism and have expanded the understanding of migrant and diasporic experiences through a wide spectrum of perspectives, thematic concerns, and cultural contexts. Moreover, while some stories display "living on the hyphen" (Seyhan 2001: 15) as an experience that leads to disrupted and fragmented selves, others foreground its potential for producing transcultural and creative space.

It takes multiple narratives in different genres employing a rich arsenal of literary expression to tell the "true" story of migration, diaspora, and exile, of exclusion and inclusion in the multicultural fabric of Canada, of the pitfalls and potentials of living with or in the interstices between two cultures. In Canadian short fiction, this multiplicity is realised to the utmost extent even within a specific genre, both thematically and textually, with authors from different cultural backgrounds experimenting with language and narrative expression in remarkably variegated ways. In these stories, the fictionalising of experience becomes a strategy for dealing with the affective dimension of migration and a potent tool for battling ignorance and for generating a cultural climate of mutuality.

Works Cited

Primary Works

Baldwin, Shauna Singh (1996). *English Lessons and Other Stories*. Fredericton: Goose Lane Editions.
Bezmozgis, David (2004). *Natasha and Other Stories*. Toronto: HarperCollins.
Bezmozgis, David (2019). *Immigrant City. Stories*. Toronto: HarperCollins.
Bissoondath, Neil (1990). *On the Eve of Uncertain Tomorrows*. London: Bloomsbury.
Brand, Dionne (1988). *Sans Souci and Other Stories*. Stratford, ON: William-Wallace Publishers.
Clarke, Austin (2003). *Choosing His Coffin: The Best Stories of Austin Clarke*. Toronto: Thomas Allen.

Dabydeen, Cyril (2013). *My Multi-Ethnic Friends & Other Stories*. Toronto: Guernica.
Edwards, Caterina (2000). *Island of the Nightingales: Short Stories*. Toronto: Guernica.
Irani, Anosh (2019). *Translated from the Gibberish: Seven Stories & One Half Truth*. Toronto: Alfred A Knopf.
Li, Iris (2003). "Snaps – A Satire". In: Lien Chao and Jim Wong-Chu, eds. *Strike the Wok: An Anthology of Contemporary Canadian Fiction*. Toronto: TSAR. 66–69.
Maharaj, Rabindranath (2002). *The Book of Ifs and Buts*. Toronto: Vintage.
Mistry, Rohinton (1992 [1987]). *Tales from Firozsha Baag*. London: Faber and Faber.
Mutonji, Téa (2019). *Shut Up You're Pretty. Stories*. Vancouver: Arsenal Pulp Press.
Reid-Benta, Zalika (2019). *Frying Plantain: Stories*. Toronto: House of Anansi Press.
Senior, Olive (1995). *Discerner of Hearts*. Toronto: McClelland & Stewart.
Senior, Olive (2015). *The Pain Tree*. Toronto: Cormorant Books.
Thammavongsa, Souvankham (2020). *How to Pronounce Knife: Stories*. London: Bloomsbury.
Thien, Madeleine (2001). *Simple Recipes*. Toronto: McClelland & Stewart.
Waltner-Toews, David (2006). *One Foot in Heaven*. Regina: Coteau Books.

Secondary Works

Bucknor, Michael A. (2002). "Caribbean and Canadian Literature". In: William H. New, ed. *Encyclopedia of Literature in Canada*. Toronto: University of Toronto Press. 178–180.
"Canadian Multiculturalism Act". Online: https://laws-lois.justice.gc.ca/eng/acts/c-18.7/page-1.html [accessed: 12 December 2021].
Chao, Lien (1997). *Beyond Silence: Chinese Canadian Literature in English*. Toronto: TSAR.
Chariandy, David (2004). "Haunted Diasporas: The Second Generation Stories of André Alexis". *Journal of West Indian Literature* 12.1–2: 79–89.
Chariandy, David (2005). "'That's What You Want, isn't it?': Austin Clarke and the New Politics of Recognition". *Journal of West Indian Literature* 14.1–2: 141–165.
Czyz, Vincent (2022). "Book Review: 'Ghost Geographies' – Dark but Magical Stories of the Dispossessed and the Stateless". *The Art's Fuse*. Online: https://artsfuse.org/247338/book-review-ghost-geographies-dark-but-magical-stories-of-the-dispossessed-and-the-stateless/ [accessed: 8 April 2022].
Fiamengo, Janice (2014). "Understanding a Father's Pain in Madeleine Thien's 'Simple Recipes'". In: Carol L. Beran, ed. *Contemporary Canadian Fiction*. Amenia, NY: Grey House Publishing, Salem Press. 207–219.
Fellner, Astrid M. (2013). "The Flavours of Multi-Ethnic North American Literatures: Language, Ethnicity and Culinary Nostalgia". In: Cornelia Gerhardt, Maximiliane Frobenius and Susanne Ley, eds. *Culinary Linguistics: The Chef's Special*. Amsterdam and Philadelphia: John Benjamins Publishing Company. 241–260.
Gadpaille, Michelle (2009). "'In Exchange for a String of Islands': A Meditation on Diasporic Caribbean Writing in Canada". In: Maria Löschnigg and Martin Löschnigg, eds. *Migration and Fiction: Narratives of Migration in Contemporary Canadian Literature*. Heidelberg: Winter. 160–170.
Hatch, Ron (1995). "Chinese-Canadian Writing: The Silence of Gum San". In: Hans Braun and Wolfgang Klooss, eds. *Multiculturalism in North America and Europe: Social Practices and Literary Visions*. Trier: WVT. 167–179.
Keefer, Janice Kulyk (1991). "From Mosaic to Kaleidoscope". *Books in Canada* 20.6: 13–16.
Keefer, Janice Kulyk (1995). "Writing, Reading, Teaching Transcultural in Canada". In: Hans Braun and Wolfgang Klooß, eds. *Multiculturalism in North America and Europe: Social Practices, Literary Visions*. Trier: WVT. 180–197.

Kruk, Laurie (2016). *Double-Voicing the Canadian Short Story*. Ottawa: University of Ottawa Press.

Löschnigg, Martin (2013). "Spaces of Immigration and Their Models in Contemporary Canadian Literature". In: Klaus-Dieter Ertler and Patrick Imbert, eds. *Cultural Challenges of Migration in Canada/Les défis culturels de la migration au Canada*. Frankfurt am Main: Peter Lang. 245–262.

Lucas, María Belén Martin (1998). "Psychic Spaces of Childhood: Jamaican-Canadian Short Story Cycles". *International Journal of Canadian Studies/Revue internationale d'études canadiennes* 18 (Fall): 93–111.

Lucas, María Belén Martin (2000). "Interweaving Stories: Genre, Race, and Gender at a Cross-Stitch". In: Rocío G. Davis and Rosalía Baena, eds. *Tricks with a Glass: Writing Ethnicity in Canada*. Amsterdam: Rodopi. 251–267.

Misrahi-Barak, Judith (1998). "The Cityscape in a Few Caribbean-Canadian Short Stories". *Journal of the Short Story in English* 31 (Autumn): 9–22.

Orr, Katherine (2015). "Liminality, Metamorphic Experience, and the Short-Story Form: Alice Munro's 'Wenlock Edge'". In: Jochen Achilles and Ina Bergmann, eds. *Liminality and the Short Story: Boundary Crossings in American, Canadian, and British Writing*. London: Routledge. 251–262.

Pirbhai, Mariam (2014). "Introduction to *The Stories of Cyril Dabydeen*". *Guyana Chronicle*. Online: https://guyanachronicle.com/2014/11/15/the-short-stories-of-cyril-dabydeen/ [accessed: 11 November 2021].

Rushdie, Salman (1991). *Imaginary Homelands: Essays and Criticism, 1981–1991*. London: Granta.

Schuh, Rebekka (2021). *Stories in Letters – Letters in Stories: Epistolary Liminalities in the Anglophone Canadian Short Story*. Berlin and Boston: De Gruyter.

Seyhan, A. (2001). *Writing Outside the Nation*. Princeton: Princeton University Press.

Simpson, Hyacinth M. (2005). "The Jamaican Short Story: Oral and Related Influences". *Journal of Caribbean Literatures* 4.1: 11–30.

Soja, Edward W. (1995). "Heterotopologies: A Remembrance of Other Spaces in the Citadel-LA". In: Sophie Watson and Katherine Gibson, eds. *Postmodern Cities and Spaces*. Oxford: Blackwell. 13–34.

Staines, David (2014). "Canada in the World: Literature at the Crossroads". In: Waldemar Zacharasiewicz and Fritz Peter Kirsch, eds. *Immigration and Integration in North America: Canadian and Austrian Perspectives*. Göttingen: V & R Unipress. 15–29.

Staines, David (2021). *A History of Canadian Fiction*. Cambridge: Cambridge University Press.

Weber, Donald (2004). "Permutations of New-World Experiences Rejuvenate Jewish-American Literature". *Chronicle of Higher Education* 51.4 (online).

Suggestions for Further Reading

Chariandy, David (2016). "Black Canadian Literature: Fieldwork and 'Post-Race'". In: Sugars. 539–563.

Dobson, Kit (2009). *Transnational Canadas: Anglo-Canadian Literature and Globalization*. Waterloo, ON: Wilfrid Laurier University Press.

Ertler, Klaus-Dieter and Patrick Imbert, eds. (2013). *Cultural Challenges of Migration in Canada/Les défis culturels de la migration au Canada*. Frankfurt am Main: Peter Lang.

Isaacs, Camille A., ed. (2013). *Austin Clarke: Essays on His Works*. Oakville, ON: Guernica Editions.

Löschnigg, Maria and Martin Löschnigg, eds. (2009). *Migration and Fiction: Narratives of Migration in Contemporary Canadian Literature*. Heidelberg: Winter.
Pirbhai, Mariam (2016). "South Asian Canadian 'Geographies of Voice': Flagging New Critical Mappings". In: Sugars. 583–601.
Sugars, Cynthia (2016). *The Oxford Handbook of Canadian Literature*. New York: Oxford University Press.
Ty, Eleanor (2016). "(East and Southeast) Asian Canadian Literature: The Strange and the Familiar". In: Sugars. 564–582.

10 Narratives of Loss – Domestic and Environmental Contexts

Though radically different in scale, both environmental loss and personal loss are universal concerns. The former has moved into the centre of attention during the last decades; the latter has been a theme of literature from the beginning. In his introduction to *Best Canadian Short Stories 2018*, Russell Smith observes that "Canadian fiction still tends to focus on the domestic and the relational"; however, as he goes on, "it is just as hard as it ever was to make this field of activity exciting" (2018: 14). Pretending that the contemporary Canadian short story mostly engages with red-hot issues that figure prominently in the media (ethnic identities, gender, and – more recently – the environment) would draw a rather distorted picture indeed. Still, Canadian authors have approached the quintessentially human from new angles and have incited readers to reflect on the seemingly familiar in thought-provoking and unconventional terms. Personal loss, in particular, is a recurring motif in contemporary Canadian short fiction, as authors have probed the surfaces of the domestic and relational to provide exciting psychological insights.

To different degrees and in different shapes, the increasing environmental degradation of our planet affects us all and is thus a topic of universal urgency. Since the environmental crisis is not only physical but also a crisis of the imagination (what will life in drastically damaged environments be like for individuals?), it is important to look at what literature can offer to spark interest in ecological issues and assist growing environmental consciousness. Nature and the wilderness have, for a long time, held a prominent position in Canadian short fiction, beginning with Seton's and Roberts's animal stories in the late 19th and early 20th centuries (see Chapter 2). Also, in analogy to Pamela Banting's argument that, "in the Canadian context, regionalism prepared the ground for the subsequent reception of ecocriticism" (2016: 731), works of short fiction that focus on the specificities of distinct regions such as the prairies, the Maritimes or the Pacific Coast, could be regarded as precursors of the eco-story. Despite these earlier developments, however, the focus on the environmental crisis that has been recognised as a global threat in the past decades is a relatively new thematic concern. While it goes beyond the scope of this chapter to compare the significance of eco-stories

DOI: 10.4324/9781003142683-13

in different literatures, it *can* be stated that, especially since the onset of the new millennium, environmental loss has emerged as an important topic in the Canadian short story, as is also reflected, for example, in anthologies such as *Canadian Tales of Climate Change* (2017), edited by Bruce Meyer.

10.1. Domestic Contexts and Personal Loss

An omnipresent theme in the Canadian short story, aspects of personal loss have already been addressed in other chapters of this volume – for instance, with regard to migrant identities in Chapter 9 or the loss of ancestral knowledge, traditions, and habitat among the Indigenous population in Chapter 8. Considering the prominence and universal relevance of this theme, however, it is justified to give it a separate chapter section, even if this can only be selective and exemplary.

Personal loss is centre stage in Frances Itani's moving short story cycle *Leaning, Leaning Over Water* (1998), which deals with a mother's depression and suicide and her family's coming to terms with it. The Ottawa River in which Maura drowns herself is a central presence for all the characters, assuming multiple connotations. In the river's noises, Maura recognises "the sound of sorrow" (24), while her husband, Jock, dreams that it is flowing through him, driving him almost mad after the loss of his wife. After all, it was he who made her live close to the river against her will. For Trude, the daughter and narrator, the river's current becomes a symbol of the elusiveness of meaning:

> I walked to the cliff and stood looking down over rapids. I thought about how sometimes I chose one spot on a single wave and how I tried to hold that spot. No matter how hard I tried or how many times, my eyes shifted in the direction of the current. Against my will, beyond my will, I could not focus on that single spot.
>
> (95)

In her role as chronicler, however, Trude succeeds in holding on to such "single spots", as it were, as she captures episodes from the family's life and tragedies from the fleetingness of existence.

In Debbie-Howlett's Montreal-based collection of linked stories, *We Could Stay Here All Night* (1999), the disintegration of the Wilkinson family is prefigured by the rifts in Montreal's population between Francophones and Anglophones, Catholics and Protestants, and separatists and federalists, culminating in the October crisis of 1970. Again, it is the daughter who narrates the story. She is also the one most strongly affected by the father's disappearance and impoverished life as an alcoholic in a Vancouver trailer park. The fact that his instability, absence, and illness have haunted Diane since childhood is revealed when, as a grown-up, she receives the phone call that she has expected "my whole life" (159), informing her of his death.

Poignant approaches to personal loss can also be found in Elyse Gasco's *Can You Wave Bye Bye, Baby?* (1999). In the second-person narrative "Elements", for example, the nine-month period of pregnancy is set in analogy to the period it takes to come to terms with the loss of a beloved person, which is, in this case, the expecting mother's adoptive mother. In this story, it is in particular through the you-mode that Gasco's profound exploration of the mental strain of mourning suggests universal validity (see also Chapter 5).

An author known for his exceptionally daring dissections of the human condition is Douglas Glover (1948–), whose work is "at once technically experimental and viscerally experiential" (Stone 2004: 7). Glover's unflinching approaches to loss, human destructiveness, resilience, and survival are visible in all his collections of short fiction, including *The Mad River* (1981), *Dog Attempts to Drown Man in Saskatoon* (1985), *A Guide to Animal Behaviour* (1991), *16 Categories of Desire* (2000), and *Savage Love* (2013). "Tristiana" (*Savage Love*), one of Glover's numerous pieces of historical short fiction, is a striking example of how the author sometimes combines the outrageous and the laconic in order to analyse the depths of human savagery. Thus, in the first of the nine sections that make up the story, a man trapped in an isolated hut by a surprisingly early and severe onset of winter survives by killing and eating not only his livestock and dog but also his wife. In the end, however, he laments that "Yet it was imperative to die because of his losses and the embarrassment of curious bones lying about, of which the spring thaws would require an explanation" (15f).

According to Bruce Stone (2004: 7), "suffering is the primary ontological condition" for Glover's characters, who are mostly fierce survivors responding to loss in bizarre ways. A striking example of human suffering *in extremis* is rendered in "A Piece of the True Cross" (*16 Categories of Desire*). The story unfolds against the backdrop of a family home that had, for some time, "served as a tuberculosis sanatorium" (157). Throughout the story, this home emanates an atmosphere of decay and morbidity that envelops and determines the lives of the broken characters. In the centre are a brother and a sister who are bound together by the horrors they have experienced. The story is relentless in its refusal to grant the reader any glimmer of hope other than the grim endurance of loss and suffering, leading the brother – and narrator – to conclude, "It seems impossible that a human being could suffer this much and live. And just when you think you can't stand any more, it gets worse and you discover new possibilities of living" (174). While "the past receded until it was nothing but a presence and a dull ache, like a tumour" (175), it is the future which is identified as most terrible in the narrator's final sentence.

Some stories, however, take a lighter note, fusing loss and sorrow with irony. This is the case in "The Left Ladies Club" (*16 Categories of Desire*), where the narrator, a young woman, is abandoned by her husband Duffy weeks before she is to give birth to their twins. The irony lies in Duffy's attempts to become a novelist, fashioning himself as the main character in each case, thinly disguised as Scuffy, Cuffy, Ruffy or Muffy. In a self-referential twist, his last work, whose protagonist is named Buffy and which, for the first time, includes the abandoned narrator, is titled *The Left Ladies Club*. Duffy's novel, which ends with Buffy's death and features a persona of the narrator with "two teenagers", beautiful, "looking strong and alone" (94), leads to a blend of two ontological levels and of the "real" and the fictive father's and mother's fates. Due to the author's refusal to shy away from taboo, whether sexual or pertaining to violence and cruelty, Glover's aesthetically conscious stories are testimony of literature's licence to *"say everything, in every way"* (Derrida 1992: 36).

Lisa Moore's (1964–) three short story collections are *Degrees of Nakedness* (1995), *Open* (2002) and *Something for Everyone* (2018), in addition to *The Selected Stories of Lisa Moore* (2012). As with Michael Winter (1965–) and Michael Crummey (1965–), Moore's native Newfoundland has intricately inscribed itself upon her narratives. Personal relationships and experiences of loss play a considerable role, as they do in Winter's two collections (*Creaking in Their Skins*, 1994, and *One Last Good Look*, 1999) and in Crummey's *Flesh and Blood* (2003), yet it is Moore in particular who has experimented with new stylistic possibilities to render the complexities of human feelings.

Moore's stories are characterised by fractured chronologies, and meaning often lies hidden in the interstices between fragmented episodes. One of the hallmarks of Moore's work (the author holds a degree in arts and design) is its strongly visual quality. In "The Way the Light Is" and "Melody" (*Open*), for example, Moore elicits novel ways of seeing through verbal "snapshots" of the transformative effects of light and water.

Many of Moore's stories also have a strong sensual element (see, for example, "Granular", *Degrees of Nakedness*) and achieve baffling effects when the erotic melds with the elegiac, as is the case in "Sea Urchin" (*Degrees of Nakedness*). Mapping the narrator's grief over the loss of her father, the story seems to be addressed to her lover, whom she met shortly after her father had died. After 11 years, the bereaved daughter is still "discovering lost pieces of him" (18), retrieving his memory in fractured images that combine to create meaning and eventually allow the daughter to move on. The most suggestive of these is that of a sea urchin on which her father stepped. The only remedy, her father is told, is to "pour heated wax over the foot" (17). This image reverberates later in the story when the grieving daughter describes to her lover the effect of their first kiss:

> It was as though you were pulling my whole self, all the pain from my father's death . . . , siphoning it up through my body into my tongue, and taking it into your mouth, until my tongue felt swollen. . . . Just the sucking seemed to be drawing out the sadness. Heat, like the needles being drawn from my father's foot with melted wax.
>
> (25f)

In "Visitation", included in *Best Canadian Stories 2018*, the accumulation of seemingly randomly organised and temporally disjointed scenes and images mirror the narrator's frenzy after the collapse of her marriage. This personal loss is reflected in the narrator's repeatedly disturbed vision, and it corresponds with a fire at the local fish plant through which a whole community lose their homes and employment. That, for the protagonist, the world is out of joint is further underscored by the strange and sudden stranding of "hundreds of thousands" of cod in the Bay which "were dying all over the sand" (217). Both images, that of the fire and the mass of dying fish, pervade the story, as does the narrator's vision of a menacing male figure. These male "visitations" are accompanied by a strong "stink of rot or sewage" (217), implying notions of toxic masculinity. In the climactic dream vision, the man tries to rape the narrator, yet her cellphone has miraculously transformed into a syringe: "With more effort than I have ever exerted in my life . . . I forced my arm off the bed and drove the needle into his side" (238). It is this surreal act that marks a turning point in the life of the protagonist, as it seems to transform her from a passive victim to an active decision-maker.

"Visitation" is also interesting as it blends personal and ecological loss. Primarily, the strange behaviour of the fish is to reflect the narrator's loss of her mental balance, yet it also points to far-reaching environmental disruptions. Reading "Visitations" as an eco-story, the visitations of the menacing male figment, and his olfactory representation of decay appear as an allegory of anthropogenic aggression. Evoking Newfoundland regional contexts (for instance, through the fish that are an important part of the island's economic history), Moore's use of visual effects and contradictory images, her inclusion of magic and her emphasis on the elusiveness of truth create powerful refractions of seemingly familiar territory.

Personal loss and grief are also central to the work of Guy Vanderhaeghe (1951–), whose domestic dramas, mostly unfolding against the backdrop of the Saskatchewan prairies, are "unflinching depictions of weakness and strength in men and women caught in moments of crisis" (Kruk 2016: 17). All four of Vanderhaeghe's collections, including *Man Descending* (1982), *The Trouble with Heroes* (1983), *Things As They Are* (1992), and *Daddy Lenin* (2015), are peopled with male anti-heroes who are compromised by conventional codes of masculinity and their own weaknesses. This is memorably illustrated by the title story of *Man Descending*: here, the 30-year-old first-person narrator seems to have accepted the downward spiral in which he has been caught: "I know now that I have begun the inevitable descent, the leisurely glissade which will finally topple me at the bottom of my own graph" (193). In contrast, as he observes, his wife "is a hopeful woman" (193). The way the protagonist reflects on his marriage tends to obfuscate identifications of cause and effect. It thus remains open whether it is the couple's implied incompatibility that triggers the narrator's descent or whether it is his self-image as "a man descending" (192) that widens the breach in their marriage.

In "Tick Tock" (*Daddy Lenin*), we find in Charlie Brewster another manifestation of Vanderhaeghe's male "losers", and again his decline is set off against a cutting-edge partner. While Eva is an acknowledged university professor and feminist, Charlie feels that he "belonged in some professional Jurassic Park" (31). Moreover, the masculinity he embodies in Eva's view seems to be a provocation for her: "It hadn't taken her long to conclude that he was the poster boy for the bad hegemonic variety since he was white, heterosexual, and a member of a privileged profession" (32). What Eva does not – or does not want to – know is how Charlie still struggles with traumatic experiences from the past. His parents' ill-advised choice to have their gifted boy skip classes first sets his downward spiral in motion. Much younger than his schoolfellows, he is the victim of their bullying; in turn, this led to his later development into a merciless avenger who, in his frenzy, did not know when to stop. His time in prison is a secret, as are his fractured hands, which have healed on the outside but now start to trouble him again, giving him unbearable pain when an abusive neighbour moves in who regularly beats up his wife. In the story's final confrontation between Charlie and this neighbour, Melvyn Janacek, in an underground garage, the reader expects that Charlie will lose control and thereby also seal his own demise. However, his hands suddenly feel relaxed, "every drop of hurt squeezed out of them" (45), and he refuses to defend himself when Melvyn knocks him down, and he sees the concrete floor "that now rushed up to meet him as he dropped gratefully to it on his knees" (45). The ending is highly ambiguous, leaving it open whether Charlie's refusal to use force is really a victory, laying to rest his own history as a thug and increasing his chances with Eva, or whether it signifies complete resignation, propelling him back to an earlier past when he was "everybody's favourite punching bag" (34). The way this last scene is depicted may suggest the former; however, when we call to mind how, shortly before the physical encounter, Charlie tells Melnyk, "I'm a rusty time bomb. Either that or an old clock running down. Tick tock, tick tock, tick tock" (44), it is suggested that there are no happy endings possible for the protagonist.

Physical ailments or invalidity as reflections of mental crisis or professional and social failure are a recurring element in Vanderhaeghe's short fiction, including, for example, "A Taste for Perfection" (*Man Descending*) and "Live Large" (*Daddy Lenin*). In "A Taste for Perfection", 28-year-old Tom Ogle finds himself in hospital after having collapsed at work. Step by step, and using Tom's internal perspective, the narrative, one of the most gripping Canadian stories on illness and physical decline, traces his loss of control over his body and his "turning into a vegetable" (146). Refusing, first, to understand and accept the seriousness of his condition, he desperately tries to detach himself from the pandemonium of disease and decay "that crept and wheeled past his doorway" (131) during the day, and which does not end by night when "the ward came alive with the sounds of night terrors" (132). In particular, there is his roommate, Morissey, who suffers from a "rare metabolic disorder that was slowly making him waste away, imperceptibly killing him inch by inch, or rather, pound by pound" (137). Being finally diagnosed with an inoperable brain tumour and increasingly losing control over his limbs, Tom is eventually forced to realise that "everyone on this ward was dying", that there was "no escaping", and that there "*was no outside*" (148). On a second level, the story also invites a symbolic reading. Exclusion – of which he becomes painfully aware when he "stood by the window and observed life go on outside the hospital as if he were watching a movie screen" (141) – had already determined Tom's life before he was hospitalised. In fact, Tom seems to be another of Vanderhaeghe's male losers and loners – left by his girlfriend, without any friends or family and with colleagues at work who would not even pay him a visit, he seemed to have lost control over his life long before his brain and limbs gave out. His tumour can thus also be understood as a symbolic rendering concrete of his social failures.

In Billy Constable, the troubled (anti)hero of "Live Large", we encounter a 53-year-old man whose most detrimental weakness is his desire to appear strong and powerful. Entrapped in stereotypical gender scripts, he makes the decisions that eventually lead to his downfall. This begins with his megalomaniac attempt to turn the moderate but sound family business into something grand and impressive. Playing golf with his old mates – as a guest, since he can no longer afford club membership – the story of Billy's rise and fall materialises through snippets of his thoughts and recollections. One of these relates to Malcolm Forsythe, a ruthless businessman and, to Billy's dismay, one of the foursome of their game. Some time ago, he tricked Billy into buying a luxury car he could not really afford. Physical and social decline are made to correlate. Thus, Billy's heart, too, seems to be giving out as he realises the inevitable crash of his business. The ambivalent ending ("It was only June, but Billy Constable figured he had less than twenty minutes of summer left to him. He intended to make the most of it", 130) may suggest that he intends to forestall the coronary by taking his death in his own hands.

As in Alice Munro's work (discussed in the final part of this section), loss frequently combines with guilt in Vanderhaeghe's stories, "1957 Chevy Bel Air" and "Where the Boys Were" (*Daddy Lenin and Other Stories*) being memorable examples. In "1957 Chevy Bel Air", a teenage boy's attempt to break free from the suffocating corset of strict family rules succeeds in the end, yet only at great cost. "Where the Boys Were", in turn, tells the story of two brothers, Bob and Donny, and the younger one's grief when he gets a phone call informing him that Bob was "found frozen to death in an alley in Edmonton" (133). The homodiegetic narrator, Joey Fenton, is the confidant of Donny's wife, Anne, and reconstructs and interprets the events from his point of view. Joey repeatedly inserts references to his fragmented knowledge, admitting that he will fill up the gaps with conjectures as to how it could have been: "There's license taken here, embellishments perpetrated. There will be more. But it's clear that something like that must have happened" (141). Interestingly, this emphasis on the narrator's act of reconstruction makes the story seem more authentic and the narrator more trustworthy. It is also the narrator who, as opposed to Donny's wife, realises that the bereaved brother's untypically emotional outburst of grief mostly results from his guilt, his feeling that he had failed the person to whom he owed his survival in the first place. Their parents being "two mean stupid drunks" (132), it was Bob who brought up and protected his younger brother. When they were 15 and 18, however, their lives took a radical turn with the appearance of Carol DiPietro, the daughter of one of the American managers of the local mine. Much to the dismay of the father, who hated his daughter "hanging out with low-life trailer trash" (142), Carol and Bob fall in love. Their romance comes to an abrupt end when, at the end of summer and against her will, Carol is sent off again to a private boarding school in the U.S.A. When all of Bob's attempts to contact her fail, he suspects that Carol may have been with child and that her father had kidnapped her and their baby and made sure his daughter had no chance to contact Bob ever again. From then on, the mission to find his "ghostly family" (153) becomes an obsession, slowly grinding him down mentally, physically, and economically. Donny, in the meantime, had started his own family with Anne, and the contact between the brothers had become more and more sparse before ceasing altogether. While Donny's failure is nowhere precisely explicated – after all, the narrator is only an external witness – it is mentioned that Bob had asked his brother for help, especially for financial support in order to hire a professional investigator, while Donny had tried to persuade his brother to give up and come home. His guilt is, therefore, that he failed to understand how much Carol and a possible child had meant to Bob. Thus alienating his brother, he has never been able to make up for the gift of life that Bob had made to him when he was a child.

Alice Munro, whose fiction "reveals the recurring problems of everyday life" (Staines 2016b: 2), may well be regarded as *the* most profound chronicler of the mundane, domestic, and relational. In her stories, which Staines – with a nod to Del Jordan's description in *Lives of Girls and Women* – aptly describes as "kitchen linoleum with the deep caves of people's aspirations and failings just beneath the surface" (2016b: 2), the author shows how rewarding it can be to return to the same matters again and again, revealing ever new facets and ambiguities of what it means to be human.

One such matter is that of mothers, especially invalid and/or dying mothers, as seen from the ambivalent perspectives of daughter figures (Hay 2016). This motif appears, for example, in "The Peace of Utrecht" (*Dance of the Happy Shades*, 1968); "The Ottawa Valley", "Winter Wind", and "Memorial" (*Something I've Been Meaning to Tell You*, 1974); "Friend of My Youth" (*Friend of My Youth*, 1990); "Family Furnishings" (*Hateship, Friendship, Courtship, Loveship, Marriage*, 2001); and "Soon" (*Runaway*, 2004). In these stories, the daughter's failure to offer support and reassurance, as well as how this keeps haunting her in later life, is approached from a different angle each time. As Elizabeth Hay argues, going back to the (ailing) figure of the mother is Munro's attempt at dealing with feelings of loss and guilt concerning her own mother, adding,

> There is a special irony here. The kind of material a writer wants to get rid of is the material that recurs, and it is always rich and troubling. The subject of her mother is what Munro called in a *Paris Review* interview in 1994 "my central material in life".
>
> (2016: 180)

Considering this, it is not surprising that Munro revisits this "material" in *Dear Life* (2012). The title story that concludes this collection is one of four where the author – just like in *The View from Castle Rock* – blurs the line between autobiography and fiction. Though not the main motif in this story, it can hardly be overlooked that the mother's illness and death preoccupy the narrator in her later life:

> Something had come upon us that was even more unexpected and would become more devastating than the loss of income, though we did not know it yet. It was the early onset of Parkinson disease, which showed up when my mother was in her forties.
>
> (308)

Again, it is the notion of filial failure, of not having tended her in the final stages of her illness and not having been at her funeral, which the daughter finds herself grappling with. However, at the end of this final story in Munro's final volume, there is a note of conciliatory acceptance of human failure: "We say of some things that they can't be forgiven, or that we will never forgive ourselves. But we do – we do it all the time" (319).

In contrast to stories featuring the perspective of the daughter, stories like "Silence" (*Runaway*), "Deep Holes" and "Dimensions" (both in *Too Much Happiness*, 2009) offer haunting portraits of bereaved mothers. Thus, Doree in "Dimensions" struggles to come to terms with the trauma caused by the violent death of her three children – murdered by her husband, Lloyd, as a punishment for her "disobedience". Seven years later, Lloyd, who is locked up in an institution for the criminally insane, almost manages to reclaim Doree through manipulative letters he sends to her, claiming that he has seen their children – happily existing in another "dimension".

Particularly poignant variants of the mother-daughter configuration can be found in Munro's trilogy of linked stories, "Chance", "Soon", and "Silence" (*Runaway*), where especially in the latter two, loss is a central motif. In "Soon", Juliet comes home to rural Ontario in order to present her baby-daughter Penelope to her parents. However, her home, as she had imagined it, no longer exists. With her illegitimate child and her modern ways, she seems to be an embarrassment to her father (whom she had remembered as open-minded), especially in the presence of Irene, the young and practically oriented woman who helps out about the house since her mother Sara's health has been deteriorating: "Everything here distracted her. The heat, Irene, the things that were familiar and the things that were unfamiliar" (98). The title, however, refers to a significant scene towards the end of the story, when her mother tells her: "When it gets really bad for me – when it gets so bad I – you know what I think then? I think, all right. I think – Soon. *Soon I'll see Juliet*" (124). Again, we find, in Sara, a variant of the invalid mother, and in Juliet the guilt-ridden daughter who only later realises the whole dimension of her filial failures. The story ends with an epiphanic glimpse into the future: after Sara's death only a few months after Juliet's visit, and triggered by a letter she finds years later (which she had written to her partner Eric during this memorable homecoming), "the pain of her memory" (125) starts to surface. She not only realises that home was not "at Whale Bay with Eric but back where it had been before, all her life before" (125) but also becomes acutely aware of the gravity of having denied her mother any sign of love or confirmation when the latter reached out to her in her desperate declaration:

> When Sara said, *soon I'll see Juliet*, Juliet had found no reply. Could it not have been managed? Why should it have been so difficult? Just to say *Yes*. To Sara it would have meant so much – to herself, surely, so little. But she had turned away, she had carried the tray to the kitchen, and there she washed and dried the cups and also the glass that held grape soda. She had put everything away.
>
> (15)

This scene seems to echo an earlier incident as recounted in "Chance". On the train from Ontario to Vancouver, where Juliet is supposed to start a temporary position as a teacher, she rebuffs a fellow traveller who takes the seat opposite her and suggests that they "could just chum around together" (56). This same man, as it turns out later, then committed suicide by throwing himself onto the tracks after a stop: "He wanted somebody worse than I didn't want somebody. I realize that now. And I don't look cruel. But I was" (67), she later tells Eric, a man she gets in contact with because of the fatal incident and who will later become her partner and the father of her child. Unwittingly, Eric foreshadows other, graver failings when he says, "things will probably happen in your life – that will make this seem minor. Other things you'll be able to feel guilty about" (68). In "Soon", this is her rejection of her mother's needs, and in "Silence", it is her unwillingness to grant reconciliation to Eric for an infidelity long ago before he sets out in his boat – and drowns. As Deborah Heller puts it, the three Juliet stories "are unified by the motif of denial or rejection by one person of another's desire for a sign of human fellowship or love" (Heller 2009: 35).

In "Silence", however, the bereaved one is Juliet herself. Here, Juliet's daughter is as old as Juliet was at the beginning of the first story, "Chance", and seven years have passed since Eric's death by drowning. Mother and daughter have moved to Vancouver, where Juliet now works for a provincial TV channel and has become a local celebrity. In the first scene of the story, however, we find her on Denman Island, where she is supposed to meet her daughter, who, out of the blue, as it seems to Juliet, has retreated to the Spiritual Balance Centre and not kept any contact with her mother for six months. When another woman waiting for the ferry says "that Juliet must be looking forward to seeing her daughter again, and Juliet says yes, very much" (127), we are painfully reminded of Sara's futile longing for her daughter, for Juliet. As it is, Juliet will never see her daughter again, and the grief, especially during the first years, grinds her down. Most of all, however, she is tortured by the lack of an explanation. According to her, the relationship between mother and daughter was perfect, and so the diagnosis of Mother Shipton, as Juliet disparagingly calls the sect's leader, that Penelope "has come to us here in great hunger" (132), keeps haunting Juliet until old age.

Does the story, or the triptych as a whole, suggest the workings of poetic justice? After all, on the train ride to Vancouver ("Chance"), Juliet, who holds an M.A. in the classics, is reading E.R. Dodds's *The Greeks and the Irrational* about "cosmic justice" (65). It is true that the story refrains from providing clear explanations for Penelope's rejection of her mother, but does this mean, as Heller argues, that "the trilogy deliberately refuses to provide a context for understanding Penelope's silence as an act of cosmic justice" (2009: 42)? Being explicitly broached in the story itself, this will provide *one* possible interpretation. Moreover, even though the story does not pass moral judgement on Juliet or foreground any maternal failures on her part, the reader will – just like Juliet herself – keep going back, looking for clues. As the title "Chance" already suggests, the trilogy can also be read as a testimony of the caprices of life; those that bring happiness – as the accidental meeting with Eric – and those that bring grief – as the disappearance of Penelope. In all three stories, it is Juliet with whom we are made to identify and who acts as a guide in pursuit of meaning that keeps being deferred. The human need for causal links and predictability clashes, as Munro's stories seem to teach us, with the enigmatic complexities of life and of human relationships. Munro provides disturbing glimpses into the treacherous voids that lurk underneath the seemingly solid and thereby forces us to reassess what we have held as safe and certain.

The Canadian short story abounds with narratives that deal with personal loss in eye-opening ways, challenging our attitudes towards bereavement, grief, and guilt through unusual perspectives and novel means of expression. Having focused on only a handful of representative authors here, readers may also be interested in looking into Elisabeth Harvor's, Elizabeth Hay's, or Alistair MacLeod's stories in this context. Insights into the depths of the domestic and relational are also offered in Margaret Gibson's stories. Another author who could be named here, among many others, is John Gould, whose more than 50 pieces of flash fiction in *the end of me* (2020) offer stunning views on sorrow and our mortality. Through stories such as "Anthropocene" or "Customer Review", Gould's collection is also a prime example of how the environmental and the personal and domestic are often connected, a feature that is also evident in several of Sharon Butala's short stories (see also the case study in Chapter 3). In *Season of Fury and Wonder* (2019), her latest book of short fiction to date, in turn, Butala offers intriguing portraits of loss and ageing.

10.2. Environmental Loss

In critical responses to eco-literature, the focus, in general, has mostly been on poetry, non-fiction, the novel, and – more recently – drama, while the specific potential of short fiction has so far been largely ignored. Notwithstanding the centrality of the short story in Canada, this neglect can also be observed in Canadian ecocriticism and is reflected, for example, in Pamela Banting's substantial chapter "Ecocriticism in Canada" in *The Oxford Handbook of Canadian Literature* (2016), which references a multitude of Canadian eco-texts but largely eclipses short fiction. However, as Richard Kerridge claims, "we may allocate different tasks to different literary forms and genres", and "we need all the different literary forms to do different tasks" (2014: 369). It is, therefore, essential to also pay attention to how short fiction can contribute to environmental consciousness. While the novel lends itself ideally to the depiction of large-scale developments over time and space, the eco-story's strength results, to a large extent, from innovative experiments with narrative voice and a focus on significant moments of crisis. These snapshots typically feature strongly metaphoric language, apt to create lasting images in the reader that make the overwhelming "hyperobject" of climate change and environmental loss tangible. Timothy Morton, who coined and conceptualised the term "hyperobject", describes it as referring "to things that are massively distributed in time and space relative to humans" (2013: 1). This (for human beings) unfathomable scale of anthropogenic change and of the prognosticated "Climapocalypse" (Bloom 2017: 256) is after all one decisive factor that explains the still widespread indifference and inertia (among politicians as well as common people) regarding the urgency of these concerns.

Whereas biodiversity is key to healthy ecosystems, diversity in cultural discourses and literary forms of expression is key to creating a pool of possibilities for dealing with an ecological crisis (Zapf 2020). This pertains to the necessity not only of different genres and media but also of utmost representational diversity within respective text types. The Canadian short story has increasingly taken up the topic of the environmental crisis and brought forth a considerable and growing body of eco-stories, a term I prefer to "eco-fiction", which encompasses eco-stories but has, in criticism, rather been used to denote the novel. Another term, coined by Dan Bloom in 2007 (Goodbody 2020: 133), that is often used synonymously with eco-fiction is cli-fi (short for "the fiction of climate change"), which Goodbody – with a nod to Adam Trexler – defines as "a medium to explain, predict, implore and lament climate change" (2020: 150). That changing environmental circumstances call for new literary responses, however, is evident not only thematically. Rather, Canadian writers have strikingly experimented with different modes of expression to address the challenges of the Anthropocene.

Such innovative approaches can be observed, especially in Indigenous eco-stories. Drawing from ancestral ecological knowledge, making use of the transformative and destructive as embodied by tricksters and the Windigo, and employing elements of oral storytelling, Native Canadian writers like Lee Maracle, Leanne Betasamosake Simpson, Richard Van Camp and Warren Cariou have written thought-provoking narratives that challenge exploitative human behaviour. Many stories by Indigenous authors, in general, are informed by cosmologies that are based on the premise of "the animate nature of the land" (Watts 2013: 23). As Anishnaabe and Haudenosaunee scholar Vanessa Watts further elaborates, "habitats and ecosystems are better understood as societies from an Indigenous point of view" (23). That non-human beings and entities are attested agency, as will be illustrated, is thus an essential element in Aboriginal writing, with the effect that most Indigenous stories are also, in a wider sense, eco-stories. In this chapter, however, the focus will be on stories that explicitly deal with the destructive human impact on the environment. Focusing, first, on Lee Maracle, I will start with a case study on "Cedar Sings".

Case Study: Lee Maracle, "Cedar Sings" – The Canadian Eco-Story

In Lee Maracle's "Cedar Sings" (*First Wives Club: Coast Salish Style*, 2010), the two main characters are a tree and a bird – or rather an individualised and anthropomorphised plant, Cedar, which metonymically stands for the vulnerable West Coast environment, and Raven, the West Coast trickster figure. Cedar and Raven are described not only from an external point of view but also function as centres of orientation and are given a voice, thus inviting empathy with the non-human. Above all, however, the story reverses conventional hierarchies of setting and agents by placing flora and fauna centre stage, while human characters constitute the (threatening) backdrop.

Like most interfusional stories (see Chapter 8), "Cedar Sings" simulates an actual storytelling scenario by addressing an extratextual audience:

> Cedar sings. She stands at the edge of Squamish territory, near Whistler Mountain before it was a ski resort, overlooking Howe Sound. This is the place where you can hear Raven sing, too. Today, the ancestors who inhabit the mountains between North Vancouver and Whistler are dancing – potlatch dancing. If you look close you can see them. They look like sun spots dappling the tips of the wrinkles on the water of the sound. Can you see? No matter. They are there. (69)

Cedar is one of the last trees in (former) Squamish territory, but also in other Salish West Coast territories cedars are in danger due to exploitative logging. Not even the Salish people hear the screams of the trees anymore because they are now glued to their TV sets instead of telling and listening to their own stories. In fact, Raven herself is tempted by this new magic machine: "Once in a while, when she thinks no one is looking, she watches a little TV. Who can resist, it is shiny, lovely, awake and dramatic? Raven cannot resist anything shiny" (72).

However, Raven's weakness has a miraculous effect: she hears on TV about a "machine that can amplify sound thousands of time" (73). In fact, it is "so powerful", the man on TV says, "that you could [even] hear plants talk" (73). Raven and Cedar are both utterly shocked that these white people did not know that plants could talk and feel. What is important, however, is that this information produces an idea in Raven. She does some shape-shifting and steals such an amplifier, hauling it into the forest to make the screaming of the trees audible – at least to the Natives who stop logging and start singing and protesting against the killing of the trees. Even though it is too late for Cedar, who dies at the end of the story, it is implied that her grandchildren may profit from it.

Western consumer goods, as the story suggests, have alienated Indigenous communities from their connection to nature. The use of the trickster figure is ideal for rendering the manipulative power of shiny devices – Raven cannot resist. Raven is not perfect: like all trickster figures, she has good and bad qualities, and often she is a mischief-maker; her most striking feature, however, is her transformative creativity. It allows her to appropriate and instrumentalise the colonisers' electronic toys, use them to redress the damage, and thus subvert the destructive practices of the dominant. Her act is an act of resistance *and* of creative adaptation.

"Cedar Sings" foregrounds destructive cultural practices; it gives voice to those who are normally muted in civilisational discourses and thereby counters notions of anthropocentric dominance. The story, moreover, makes permeable boundaries visible through the ample use of metaphor, thus reintegrating notions of connectivity and fluidity into the binary systems of Western thinking. By using the form of the interfusional story, the text also renders the impression of directly speaking (and thus appealing) to the audience. Finally, "Cedar Sings" can also be read as being representative of the possible environmental impact of literature. Cedar's singing *is* Lee Maracle's writing; the chorus of the West Coast trees, as amplified by Raven's act of cultural appropriation, suggests the regenerative power of combined literary voices and the importance of creating avenues for these voices to be heard.

Narrative style:

- Simulation of oral storytelling
- Frequent dialogues between and focalisation on Raven and Cedar that allow for defamiliarising and thought-provoking perspectives on nature

Main characters:

- Cedar: using a plant as a protagonist and portraying it as a sentient being
    - suggests transspecies kinship and
    - engenders empathy for the non-human.
- Raven:
    - Is a West Coast trickster figure
    - Stands for transformative principles
    - Counters binary concepts
- Moving plants, animals, and spirit figures in the foreground and humans in the background suggests an inversion of centre and periphery and leads to a questioning of human supremacy.

> **Creativity and healing:**
>
> - Countering ecocidal Western practices through a clever appropriation of emblems of Western culture:
>   - TV: a trigger for Raven's act of environmental activism
>   - Amplifier: a technical tool used to make the trees' agony audible
> - Self-referentiality: the chorus of West Coast trees through Raven's intervention can be read as a comment on the power of stories.

Two further noteworthy eco-narratives from Maracle's *First Wives Club* are "Blessing Song" and "Tiny Green Waves". In both stories, all parts of nature are celebrated as animate (animals and plants as well as the sun, the ocean, stones, or the sky) and metaphorically linked to the human sphere in a way that foregrounds their mutual kinship. However, while "Blessing Song" is a story of healing and of intergenerational and interspecies kinship, "Tiny Green Waves" strikes a more elegiac note. Here, the once audible "poetry of this land is buried" (62), as the narrator observes. This loss, as the story suggests, is the consequence of the practices of the European coloniser that are defined by the "desire for more things than he needs" (64), a defective way of life that is referred to as "barracuda culture" (62). Its utmost danger, however, lies in the treacherous appeal it has for Indigenous people themselves, who are trapped into "false desires" that result in distorted visions where the "grey concrete becomes attractive. Vehicle exhaust smells alright, and the maddened place of the self-destructive death-culture of the European world looks so good" (64). There is hope, though: juxtaposing "barracuda culture" and its "genocide of trees, people, stone or anything else" (65f) with the collective force of minnows, "Tiny Green Waves" is also a powerful resistance narrative. The minnow may seem tender in comparison with the barracuda, but since the minnows' mission to swim upstream and against the tide is a joint venture, "including even the relatives we don't like" (63), it is an effective one, a battle not *against* anyone, as in the case of the barracudas, "but rather a fight for creation . . . [which] itself is the only winner" (63).

While an inclusive relationship with the land, including all elements of the environment, non-human life-forms, and spirit figures, informs many Indigenous stories in general, it is of particular importance in Leanne Betasamosake Simpson's *Islands of Decolonial Love* (2013) (see also Chapter 8). The "decolonial aesthetic" deployed in these stories and songs, as Michelle Lacombe notes, "realigns Anishinaabe relationships to land, history, self, and community" (2016: 49). In "nogojiwanong" (the Mississauga name for Peterborough), a polyptych of four texts, past, present, and future are linked, as are records of environmental devastation and stories of active collective resistance to this wrecking and strategies of healing. The first text, "she is the only doorway into this world", is, in fact, a decree in seven paragraphs put together and signed in June 1830 by seven spirit women and knowledge keepers, in which they forbid the new settlers to erect huge hydro dams. Each paragraph starts with the same introductory phrase and then details one of the many damages that such dams would bring to the ecology of the Great Lakes Territory. Paragraph iii, for example, reads as follows:

> iii. it is with great regret that we are writing on behalf of the michi saagiig anishinaabeg that you will not be permitted to build your lift locks, canals and hydro dams because we cannot permit concrete shackles on our mother, she needs to be free to move around in order to cleanse and give birth.
>
> (114)

The second story, "she asked why", is a confession without regrets. Since the European newcomers obviously ignored the decree, the speaker addresses them directly and reveals that it was she who "blew the fucking lift lock up in downtown peterborough" (116). In "she asked for help", in turn, we are offered a trickster narrative, typically deploying humour and oral storytelling elements. Following the futile attempts of the Ashininaabeg to convince their new neighbours, "those ones that moved in beside them" (117), of the toxic effects of their lifestyle and interference with the environment, the young female protagonist decides to take action herself. However, this time, she is not alone but turns to the powerful transformer aanjibines (117) and her two young ones, echo-maker and overseer. With the help of the latter, she summons mishibizhiw, the huge underwater lynx, who then sucks out all the locks that had blocked the water in the Great Lakes water system. With the locks, the neighbours miraculously disappear as well, together with their large houses, lawns, and fences, and the phase of healing can begin. In the concluding "she sang them home", the speaker is a salmon who is sung home and caressed by the now freely floating river. The story is a poetic celebration of life and renewal, with the river vibrating with energy, its heartbeat audible through poetic sound and rhythm, as in the following repeated set of lines: "bubbling/beating/birthing/breathing" (124).

Featuring different text types and foregrounding a "we" and "you" that include the voices and forces of the non-human, "nogojiwanong" is an intrinsically dialogic text that illustrates the idea of cultural ecology and evokes feelings of kinship on all levels. The non-hierarchical approach of the four linked texts that emphasise resistance, mourning, healing, and resurgence is further underscored by Simpson's insistent use of lower-case letters.

Besides excessive logging and the large hydro dams interfering with natural waterways, the bituminous sands in north-eastern Alberta have moved centre stage in eco-critical Canadian arts and literature. As the "world's largest industrial project", being "roundly condemned as producing the dirtiest oil on the planet", the sands have become "the epicentre of the rising global clash" between economic and ecological interests (Takach 2016: 21–22, xvi). The heated controversies over large-scale fracking in this area are reflected in the site's names: oil sands for those who support its economic value and importance for Alberta's identity and tar sands for those critical of its devastating impact on the ecology of the region and far beyond.

Dogrib Tłı̨chǫ writer Richard Van Camp, for example, deploys the Alberta Sands as an emblem of ecocidal and auto-destructive practices in his deeply disturbing Wheetago stories. As Sarah Henzi has shown, "Windigo, Wendigo, Whitiko, Feaster, Boiled Face, Hair Eater or Skin Walker, vampire or Zombie, the mysterious world of shape-shifters and evil creatures has peopled Indigenous mythology since its beginnings, and these creatures are finding their way into contemporary texts" (2016: 469). "The Fleshing", "On the Wings of This Prayer" (*Godless but Loyal to Heaven* 2013), and the two "Wheetago War" stories from *Moccasin Square Gardens* (2019) all display elements of dystopian fiction and "markers of the Indigenous horror genre" (Scott 2016: 80) to drive home the urgency of agency vis-à-vis an increasingly accelerating degradation of the environment. As it transpires in these stories, the return of the cannibalistic monsters was brought about by humankind itself, by their greed and exploitation of the environment. The narrator of "Wheetago War II: Summoners" has his own theory about the deadly invasion:

> They say that Earth had seven billion humans before the Wēetago returned, right? I think that was the Wheetago's magic number. Men warmed the world and the Wheetago unthawed themselves from whatever Hell they were in. I think seven billion was the magic number for the amount of meat they'd need to make the world maggoty with them and their kind.
>
> (64)

In his Wheetago stories, the Athabasca Tar Sands are a recurring locale, connecting, in an unsettling manner, the fictional dystopian world with nightmarish aspects of the "real" world (Scott 2016: 79). "The cannibalistic practices of both the 'tar sands' and the Wheetago are unsustainable" (Scott 82) because, in the end, they consume themselves. In "On the Wings of This Prayer", dreams are thrown from the past into the future, which uncannily foreshadow how the massive excavation activities in the Tar Sands reawaken the Wheetago: "We think those machines must have moved the heavy rocks that covered his limbs. We think his fingers were able to crawl back to the torso and legs and head" (6). The "thrown" dreams, as Scott explains, are "a catalyst with the potential to start a chain reaction that allows for a better future" (83). In all four connected Wheetago stories, these dreams play a significant role, as do Dogrib characters and spirit figures who act as culture-keepers and figures of hope and healing in a world that is infested with incessantly multiplying evil forces.

Setting a possible "future of cannibalistic horror" (Scott 82) in analogy to the "ecocide" (*Godless but Loyal* 7) of the Tar Sands, Van Camp has found a powerful new format to shatter our complacency vis-a-vis environmental degradation in the name of progress. Especially the chronologically last story, "Summoners", with its graphic images of carnage, makes dimensions of environmental and cultural loss shockingly felt. However, even in the face of the seemingly hopeless post-apocalyptic tableau that is evoked at the end of the story, Van Camp forbids a retreat into "doomsday fatigue": after all, the narrator, who survived the carnage, as did Dove, a "Watcher" and "Shifter" figure (57), resolves to reclaim the world from the clutches of the Wheetago, and he invites the addressee (and us as readers) to accompany him in this mission.

The Alberta Sands are also the backdrop of Métis writer Warren Cariou's "An Athabasca Story", where the author makes use of Elder Brother, who, as Robert Alexander Innes notes, "is more than just a trickster" and can be seen as "a synonym for 'our grandfathers'" (2013: 34). Elder Brother stories hold the function of a legal institution (Innes 2013: 38), insofar as this cultural hero's behaviour and the ensuing – positive or negative – results help to explain and reinforce cultural knowledge that ensures harmony within the community and between the community and the land.

Walking over the apocalyptic landscape of the Athabasca Sands, Elder Brother seems like the last survivor of an extinct species and from a time when the "traditional kinship practices of the pre-reserve and early reserve periods" (Innes 2013: 42) were still valid. Using a figure who represents the spirits of the grandfathers allows Cariou to provide a shockingly defamiliarised image of the fracking sites of Northern Alberta, thus rendering as strange and monstrous what has become normal in industrialised societies.

Longing for warmth and unable to accept the new rules that govern this infernal site, Elder Brother approaches an oilman who leans out of one of the "enormous contraptions that clawed and bored and bit the dark earth" (72). Threatened by the oilman, who "talked as if he had not relations at all" (72), Elder Brother has just one more question – namely, what will happen "with all that earth" (72). The impatient oilman answers,

> We're gonna burn it, and burn it, and burn it, until we make so much heat that the winter never comes back! And then even you and the rest of your sorry kind won't be cold anymore. So how would you like that? (72)

The reader may be struck by the irony of this "magical dirt" (73) creating perennial heat and the implications of global warming and also of hell in

Christian mythology. Elder Brother, in contrast, driven by his craving for warmth and eventually also by his greed, digs into the naked soil himself to get his share. The earth, however, whose screams of pain he had ignored, takes its revenge. Locked in the soil's tarry grip, Elder Brother is dug up by the huge machines and processed into petroleum. Detrimental practices, as this story drastically suggests, cannot be countered by imitating them. While Raven in Maracle's "Cedar Sings" appropriates and transforms a device of Western technology and thus uses it for a reintegrative purpose, Elder Brother's act only *seems* revolutionary while actually being affirmative. Cariou's outcry against humankind's detrimental dependence on non-renewable resources echoes forth in Elder Brother's unremitting attempts to "get your attention" (75) when, for example, you hear a "knocking and rattling sound deep down in the bowels of the machine" of your car (75).

On the whole, the story, like the others discussed earlier, narrativises Native knowledge systems, transgressing boundaries between human and non-human spheres and between spiritual approaches to the environment and those driven by rational anthropocentrism. Moreover, by adopting a radically defamiliarising point of view and by attributing agency to human-made facilities, "An Athabasca Story" critically emphasises the threatening dimensions of technological progress in general and of fracking in particular. Fracking, in fact, was already addressed by Rudy Wiebe in the 1980s in "The Angel of the Tar Sands" (*The Angel of the Tar Sands and Other Stories*, 1982). In this surreal story, set around Fort McMurry, Alberta, business as usual is disturbed when the workers accidentally dig up an angel. Of the three witnesses, only Bertha is able to understand parts of the live celestial figure's Hutterite German. While she immediately quits her job, the superintendent and Tak, the other worker, quickly recover from their initial shock, ignore the warning, and resume their work at the plant.

Ecological issues make a particularly strong appearance in Indigenous short fiction. However, non-Native writers, too, have increasingly started to address the precarious state of the environment and have done so through a wide array of different narrative approaches to make the urgency of these concerns visible, comprehensible, and tangible.

Thus, post-apocalyptic and dystopian modes can be found in Matt Cohen's "The Bone Fields" (*Living on Water*, 1989; quoted from *And Other Stories*, 2001) and Keath Fraser's "Taking Cover" (*13 Ways of Listening to a Stranger*, 2005). Cohen, as Cheryl Lousley notes, has produced "some of the most environmentally engaged fiction in contemporary Canadian literature" (2013: 247). While she exclusively focuses on his novels, "The Bone Fields" demonstrates that his short fiction, too, merits closer ecocritical study. It is a powerful story about ecological damage, resilience, and survival. At the centre is the authoritarian freak Stigson, who founded a cult to which the first-person narrator (and later murderer of Stigson) belongs, too. According to Stigson, the world is deliberately poisoned by radiation from alleged accidents in nuclear power stations. These poisonings, so his conviction, are necessary to get rid of the weak and to prompt a new beginning. The people of the cult are the last survivors: while Stigson believes in their transformation and survival, the narrator accepts the demise of humankind, which will enable the planet to "commence the multi-million-year process of healing" (115). For now, though, like Jimmy/Snowman in Margaret Atwood's *Oryx & Crake*, it is the narrator who survives when he kills Stigson. However, whether his survival indicates a new beginning remains doubtful.

In Fraser's "Taking Cover", too, the world has become uninhabitable due to radiation: "The World is contaminated. It's a fate worse than death" (90), as the voice addressing the survivors in a hermetically sealed emergency dome informs them. The effect of the story, which renders concrete the limits of life in a collapsed ecosystem, is significantly enhanced by the format of a public announcement explicitly addressed to an audience. This group of survivors, as the narrative seems to suggest, could be ourselves in the not-so-distant future – considering ongoing dictates of a global market and warfare against both fellow human beings and the environment.

Another interesting author in this context is Kathy Page, whose *Paradise & Elsewhere* (2014) stuns the reader with innovative and thought-provoking approaches to environmental loss. Her pieces of mythopoeic fiction, in particular, offer unsettling perspectives on modern societies and their disconnection from the environment. Mythopoeia, a term that came into use, in particular, through J.R.R. Tolkien in the 1930s, means the making of myths. In several of Page's stories, mythopoeia is used to reclaim sustainable ancient knowledge and to create mythic communities that function as foils to our present societies. Examples are "G'Ming", "Lak-ha", the Gothic mythopoeic piece "Saving Grace", or the we-narrative "Of Paradise". The latter features a community of females living in a paradisiac state until they are visited by a stranger whom they recognise as human but yet different. The stranger, referred to as "she" but recognisable as a man to the reader, unbalances the women's harmonious coexistence with and appreciation of their surroundings. Demanding more and more and never being content, the traveller, who stands for man's subduing of the earth, spoils the "infinity of time" which the women's sustainable life had enabled so that, in the end, their paradise has become "an invisible landscape, which we carry buried inside of us and now can reach only rarely, by intricate acts of memory and forgetfulness" (36).

"We" is also frequently (though not consistently) used in "The Ancient Siddanese", the most interesting of Page's mythopoeic eco-stories. While in "Of Paradise", the first-person plural highlights the communal aspects of the female society, their acting and living as an intact collective, the "we" in "The Ancient Siddanese" designates a group of tourists visiting the relics of the ancient city of Sidda; however, they may also stand metonymically for modern society in general. Like "Of Paradise", the Sidda story, too, uses utopian and elegiac elements to mourn the demise of an ecologically healthy society that "refrained from eating meat or using animals as beasts of burden . . . avoided trade and eschewed science" (58) and where lives were based on the belief that "individuals should leave nothing behind them" (52). Making the

Siddanese an autonomous community of *blind* people, the author, moreover, draws on the myth of Tiresias, suggesting that their blindness gave the Siddanese the ability to foresee what would come. Thus, instead of bending nature to their will, they, as is indicated, left the place when it dried up and moved on. The story, however, does not only allow glimpses into the past but also offers an uncanny cosmic view into the future. Reflecting on how different tour guides at different times offer different interpretations of the sites of the past, Page imagines a future guide who may not even be human, offering the tourists a bird's-eye view of the planet Earth:

> We're nearing the end of our tour. Just one more thing – below is the planet earth. Mostly desert now, though once it was uniquely fertile and inhabited by many forms of life, one of which came to dominance, and, we guess, was responsible for the change. . . . These beings left their mark, but had no culture to speak of, and have often been compared, in their compulsion to build and multiply without thought, to the blue beetles which caused such havoc on our planet some years ago.
>
> (59)

Another striking eco-story in Page's *Paradise & Elsewhere* is "We, the Trees", where a young man, fittingly named Joshua, tries to draw attention to the ecocidal (and suicidal) practice of large-scale deforestation. The story's focaliser is Paula Jacobs, a professor of journalism for whose class Joshua signed up because of her reputation for open-mindedness. Even though Joshua largely fails to do the assigned work, Paula is taken by him, "his powerful connective smile" but also his devotion to a larger cause which she cannot fully comprehend until she is guided – by a hand-drawn map she received from his e-mail account – to an old forest where she finds him dead, propped against a tree, his legs "buried thigh-deep, as if he too has roots" (99). Months earlier, Joshua had informed Paula about research that showed how trees could communicate via "a fungal web that connected their roots" and that "every tree was interconnected by this mycorrhizal network and it was as if the forest had a vast, communal brain" (93). Joshua has sacrificed himself not only to achieve cross-species communication but also to find an effective way to draw attention to the dying woods. "*We, the Trees*" (100), reads the first line of the note he has left for Paula, knowing she would

> unearth the rest of the story and then tell it, not just once but repeatedly . . . , she must continue to speak out in person, on screen, in print, online – she must and would use every possible medium to spread the story of their sacrifice.
>
> (101)

It is *their* sacrifice because Joshua could do this only due to the human network he is/was part of, a network that not only stands in analogy to the organic system of the forest but that, according to the young activists, needed to be actually connected to that of non-human nature. This story not only resonates with Margaret Atwood's *Surfacing* or with Donna Haraway's daring ecocritical concepts as articulated in *Staying with the Trouble: Making Kin in the Chthulucene* (2016), but also, on a meta level, thematises the necessity of telling the stories of the impending death of the planet in ever new ways, and through ever new media, so that new forms of life may evolve before it is too late.

While the perspective of trees is suggested in both Lee Maracle's "Cedar Sings" and Kathy Page's "We the Trees", Zsuszi Gartner goes yet another step further in her dazzling piece of we-narration "The Second Coming of the Plants" (*Best Canadian Short Stories 2019*). In this story, the "we" designates the plants telling their story from their own point of view. Having been the ones who "gave this benighted planet lungs" (61), thus making the development of other life forms possible in the first place, the plants, after millennia of suppression, are now planning on their second coming. Knowing their Shakespeare – "Does a milkweed not bleed?" (60) – and revolting against "the routine massacre of walking palm and Brazil nut tree; the agonies of the Japanese willow and jasmine at the hands of their bonsai torturers" (61), the plants resolve to strike back; they will become active and "explode taxonomies" such as "the yoke of Linnaean binominal nomenclature" in favour of "criss-cross borders" 61). "The Second Coming" is unique among eco-stories not only for its unusual narrative voice but also because of its satirical tone, which conveys the malady of humankind's fatal alienation from and interference with the flora in a vibrantly comical and yet thought-provoking manner.

What Gartner's and other eco-stories discussed here show is a strong penchant for variants of we- and you-narration (see also Chapter 5) and a tendency towards dialogic modes or devices which create the illusion of directly reaching out to an addressee. That new situations and challenges also call for novel responses is particularly visible in this narrative trend, as is confirmed by a look at Margaret Atwood's environmental short fiction. Atwood's fame as a spokesperson against environmental loss rests mostly on her dystopian novels (above all, her *MaddAddam* trilogy of 2003, 2009, and 2013) and her public speeches. However, her short fiction, too, presents inspiring perspectives on the ecological crisis we are facing. Thus, for example, "The Age of Lead" (*Wilderness Tips*, 1992) "ends with a final vision of global pollution where 'wilderness' has become an outmoded concept in a postmodern world" (Sturgess 2000: 95), while in the dystopian tale "Torching the Dusties" (*Stone Mattress*, 2014), environmental issues are unflinchingly juxtaposed with generational conflicts. It is, however, in *The Tent* (2006), where Atwood uses the format of flash fiction and experiments with both we- and you-narration that the author's search for effective and affective literary modes to address human abuse of the environment is most strikingly visible.

In "Faster", "Eating the Birds", and "Something Has Happened", the first-person plural suggests (Western) civilisation as a whole, including the readership, whose complicity in the destruction of a once-intact eco-system is thus exposed. Among the second-person eco-narratives in *The Tent*, "Time Folds", "Tree Baby", and "The Tent", the title story is of particular interest because of its self-conscious references to the writer's responsibility for "talking back" to destructive trends. In "The Tent", the apocalyptic scenario created by an accumulation of words denoting chaos and decay is not only the world the narrator/central character inhabits but also – through the multiple references of the "you" – the environment the addressees find themselves thrown into. The narrator/protagonist has taken refuge in a tent made of paper on whose walls she frantically tries to record everything before it is lost, being compelled to "cover every available space on the paper with writing" (144). The paper and writing metonymically testify to the importance of literature in the face of crisis. However, the writer is painfully aware of the challenge of providing an accurate account: "it must tell the truth about the howling, but this is difficult to do because you can't see through the paper walls and so you can't be exact about the truth, and you don't want to go out there, out into the wilderness, to see exactly for yourself" (144). The urgency of the crisis (the "howling" outside) is conveyed by the "clomping of leather-covered feet", the "scratching", "scrabbling" and "sound of rasping breath" (146) the narrator hears; eventually, the crisis culminates in an autodafé:

> Wind comes in, your candle tips over and flares up, and a loose tent-flap catches fire, and through the widening black-edged gap you can see the eyes of the howlers, red and shining in the light from your burning paper shelter, but you keep on writing anyway because what else can you do?
>
> (146)

This ending is highly ambiguous: on the one hand, the writer in the burning tent seems to be doomed, as is her writing; on the other hand, however, it is due to the gaps torn by the fire that she can now not only hear but also see – even if her life is in acute danger. Finally, her unabated resolution to keep on writing suggests ongoingness and the writer's responsibility to defy resignation no matter how hopeless the situation may be. Through the strong appellative effect that results from the consistent use of you-narration, the narrator's final heroic act is carried over to the reader, appealing to them to carry on reading and writing as long as it is possible. This highly self-referential text can, of course, also be read as Atwood's coded comment on the political impact of her own work in the wake of the increasingly threatening environmental and political concerns at the beginning of the new millennium.

In the "Introduction" to *Canadian Tales of Climate Change*, editor Bruce Meyer recalls an incident from April 2015, when Margaret Atwood spoke at a high school literary festival and her question, "Where are all the Canadian writers who should be addressing the greatest crisis of our age"? (2017: xv) was met with silence. This episode was the trigger for Meyer to bring forth his anthology. However, what is more interesting is that both Atwood and Meyer, when he says that "the idea of Cli-fi, the fiction of climate change, had not entered the Canadian imagination as a convenient topic. It remained an inconvenient truth" (xvi), seem to have overlooked the growing body of Canadian stories that *do* broach these red-hot issues. It shows, in other words, that the Canadian eco-stories that appeared in the past two decades have not yet been fully recognised. It is, thus, up to critics and teachers to pay closer attention to the steadily growing output of Canadian stories that *do* address the greatest crisis of our age and thereby contribute to the circulation of texts that offer novel and thought-provoking perspectives on our engagement with the environment. After all, in the words of Bruce Meyer, "imagination is our human barometer" (2017: xvii); however, it is only if we keep paying attention to it that "the power of art and literature to transform lives and transform society [can] . . . change hearts and minds in Canada" (Bloom 2017: 257) and beyond.

Works Cited

Primary Works

Atwood, Margaret (2006). *The Tent*. London: Bloomsbury.
Cariou, Warren (2012). "An Athabasca Story". *Lake: Journal of Arts and Environment* 7 (Spring): 70–75. Online: www.lakejournal.ca.
Cohen, Matt (2001 [1989]). "The Bone Fields". In: George Bowering, ed. *And Other Stories*. Vancouver: Talonbooks. 99–122.
Fraser, Keath (2005). "Taking Cover". In: *13 Ways of Listening to a Stranger: The Best Stories of Keath Fraser*. Toronto: Thomas Allen. 89–99.
Gartner, Zsuzsi (2019). "The Second Coming of the Plants". In: Caroline Adderson, ed. *Best Canadian Short Stories 2019*. Windsor: Biblioasis. 59–66.
Glover, Douglas (2000). *16 Categories of Desire*. Fredericton: Goose Lane.
Glover, Douglas (2013). *Savage Love*. Fredericton: Goose Lane.
Maracle, Lee (2010). *First Wives Club: Coast Salish Style*. Penticton: Theytus.
Moore, Lisa (2004 [1995]). *Degrees of Nakedness. Stories*. Toronto: House of Anansi Press.
Moore, Lisa (2018). "Visitation". In: Russell Smith, ed. *Best Canadian Stories 2018*. Windsor: Biblioasis. 209–239.
Munro, Alice (2004). *Runaway*. Toronto: McClelland & Stewart.
Munro, Alice (2012). *Dear Life*. London: Chatto & Windus.
Page, Kathy (2014). *Paradise & Elsewhere: Stories*. Windsor: Biblioasis.
Simpson, Leanne Betasamosake (2015 [2013]). *Islands of Decolonial Love: Stories & Songs*. Winnipeg: Arp Books.

Van Camp, Richard (2013). *Godless but Loyal to Heaven: Stories*. Winnipeg: Enfield & Wizenty (eBook).
Van Camp, Richard (2019). *Moccasin Square Gardens: Short Stories*. Vancouver: Douglas and McIntyre.
Vanderhaeghe, Guy (1992 [1982]). *Man Descending*. Toronto: Stoddart Publishing.
Vanderhaeghe, Guy (2015). *Daddy Lenin: And Other Stories*. Toronto: McClelland & Stewart.
Wiebe, Rudy (1982). *The Angel of the Tar Sands and Other Stories*. Toronto: McClelland & Stewart. 188–191.

Secondary Works

Banting, Pamela (2016). "Ecocriticism in Canada". In: Cynthia Sugars, ed. *The Oxford Handbook of Canadian Literature*. Oxford: Oxford University Press. 727–754.
Bloom, Dan (2017). "Afterword". In: Bruce Meyer, ed. *Canadian Tales of Climate Change*. Holstein, ON: Exile Editions. 256–257.
Coleman, Daniel (2012). "Toward an Indigenist Ecology of Knowledge for Canadian Literary Studies". *Studies in Canadian Literature / Études en littérature canadienne* 37.2 (online).
Derrida, Jacques (1992). "This Strange Institution Called Literature: An Interview with Derrida". In: Derek Attridge, ed. *Acts of Literature*. New York and London: Routledge. 33–75.
Goodbody, Axel (2020). "Cli-Fi – Genre of the Twenty-First Century? Narrative Strategies in Contemporary Climate Fiction and Film". In: Löschnigg and Braunecker. 131–153.
Hay, Elizabeth (2016). "The Mother as Material". In: Staines. 178–192.
Heller, Deborah (2009). *Daughters and Mothers in Alice Munro's Later Stories*. Seattle: Workwomans Press.
Henzi, Sarah (2016). "Indigenous Uncanniness: Windigo Revisited and Popular Culture". In: Deborah L. Madsen, ed. *The Routledge Companion to Native American Literature*. Abington and New York: Routledge.
Innes, Robert Alexander (2013). *Elder Brother and the Law of the People. Contemporary Kinship and Cowessess First Nation*. Winnipeg: University of Manitoba Press.
Kerridge, Richard (2014). "Ecocritical Approaches to Literary Form and Genre: Urgency, Depth, Provisionality, Temporality". In: Greg Garrard, ed. *The Oxford Book of Ecocriticism*. Oxford: Oxford University Press. 361–376.
Kruk, Laurie (2016). *Double Voicing the Canadian Short Story*. Ottawa: University of Ottawa Press.
Lacombe, Michele (2016). "Leanne Betasamosake Simpson's Decolonial Aesthetics: 'Leaks'/Leaks, Storytelling, Community, and Collaboration". *Canadian Literature* 230–231: 45–63.
Löschnigg, Maria and Melanie Braunecker, eds. (2020). *Green Matters: Ecocultural Functions of Literature*. Leiden and Boston: Brill, Rodopi.
Lousley, Cheryl (2013). "Knowledge, Power, and Place: Environmental Politics in the Fiction of Matt Cohen and David Adams Richards (2007)". In: Ella Soper and Nicholas Bradley, eds. *Greening the Maple: Canadian Ecocriticism in Context*. Calgary: University of Calgary Press. 247–272.
Marshall, Susanne (2008). "'As if There Were Just Two Choices': Region and Cosmopolis in Lisa Moore's Short Fiction". *Studies in Canadian Literature / Études en littérature canadienne* 33.2: 80–95.

Meyer, Bruce (2017). "The Climate of the Times: An Introduction to Canadian Cli-Fi". In: Bruce Meyer, ed. *Canadian Tales of Climate Change*. Holstein, ON: Exile Editions. xi–xvii.

Morton, Timothy (2013). *Hyperobjects: Philosophy and Ecology After the End of the World*. Minneapolis and London: The University of Minnesota Press.

Scott, Conrad (2016). "(Indigenous) Place and Time as Formal Strategy: Healing Immanent Crisis in the Dystopias of Eden Robinson and Richard Van Camp". *Extrapolation* 57.1–2: 73–93.

Smith, Russell (2018). "Introduction": In: Russell Smith, ed. *Best Canadian Stories 2018*. Windsor: Biblioasis. 7–16.

Staines, David, ed. (2016a). *The Cambridge Companion to Alice Munro*. Cambridge: Cambridge University Press.

Staines, David (2016b). "Introduction". In: Staines. 1–6.

Stone, Bruce (2004). "Douglas Glover". *The Review of Contemporary Fiction* 24.1: 7–57.

Sturgess, Charlotte (2000). "Margaret Atwood's Short Fiction". In: Reingard M. Nischik, ed. *Margaret Atwood: Works and Impact*. Rochester: Camden House. 87–96.

Takach, Geo (2016). *Scripting the Environment: Oil Democracy and the Sands of Time and Space*. London: Palgrave Macmillan.

Watts, Vanessa (2013). "Indigenous Place-Thought and Agency Amongst Humans and Non-Humans (First Woman and Sky Woman Go on a European World Tour!)". *Decolonization: Indigeneity, Education and Society* 2.1: 20–34.

Zapf, Hubert (2020). "Literature and/as Cultural Ecology". In: Löschnigg and Braunecker. 52–73.

Suggestions for Further Reading

Deen, Leesa (2015). "Rings within Rings: In Conversation with Lisa Moore". *The New Quarterly* 133 (Winter): 58–61.

De Falco, Amelia and Lorraine York (2018). *Ethics and Affects in the Fiction of Alice Munro*. London: Palgrave Macmillan.

Glover, Douglas (2019). "The Literature of Extinction". In: Douglas Glover. *The Erotics of Restraint: Essays on Literary Form*. Windsor, ON: Biblioasis. 179–184.

Lester, Barber (2006). "Alice Munro: The Stories of *Runaway*". *ELOPE: English Language Overseas Perspectives and Enquiries* 3.1–2: 143–156.

Löschnigg, Maria (2020). "The Function of Literature in Environmental Discourses". In: Löschnigg and Braunecker. 17–51.

McCall, Sophie (2016). "Land, Memory, and the Struggle for Indigenous Rights: Lee Maracle's 'Goodbye Snauq'". *Canadian Literature* 230–231: 178–195.

Smythe, Karen E. (1992). *Figuring Grief: Gallant, Munro and the Poetics of Elegy*. Montreal and Kingston: McGill-Queen's University Press.

Trexler, Adam (2015). *Anthropocene Fictions: The Novel in a Time of Climate Change*. Charlottesville and London: University of Virginia Press.

Afterword

"Clearly the short story is alive and thriving in the hands of Canadian writers", Diane Schoemperlen concludes her introduction to *Best Canadian Stories 2021*, adding that "the best short stories are disruptive in all the best ways, diverse in all senses of the word, always looking back and leading us forward" (7). Literature is affected by the cultural, political, and global contexts from which it emerges and which, in turn, it affects through expanding (and often empathically unsettling) the minds of its readers: "The more evident the expanding depth and breadth of our realities", Paige Cooper reminds us, "the more rigorous the duties of our imaginations" (2020: 6). What does that have to do with the short story? Authors who opt for the poetics of brevity make a conscious choice and employ the specific parameters of short fiction for responding creatively to the concerns of their times, for processing anxieties and foregrounding the delusions of our increasingly complex world. Each literary genre is equipped with its own specific representational modes and is thus able to address similar issues in decisively different ways. Acknowledging this is the basis for literature to unfold its full cultural and aesthetic impact. In other words, in order to "do their jobs", short stories have to be recognised as distinct imaginative knowledge systems. It is thus necessary, on the part of critics, scholars, and teachers, to provide more space for the inclusion and consideration of short stories when they discuss the role of fiction in the context of, for example, climate change, diasporic experiences, decolonisation, the digital turn, or issues of sex and gender.

In the telephone interview with Adam Smith following the announcement of the 2013 Nobel Prize, Alice Munro expressed her hope that the Nobel Committee's choice would spark interest not only in Canadian literature but, above all, in the short story:

> Because it's often sort of brushed off, you know, as something that people do before they write their first novel. And I would like it to come to the fore, without any strings attached, so that there doesn't have to be a novel.
>
> (Smith: online)

There can be no doubt about how the prize boosted international interest in Munro's work and drew attention to Canadian literature. However, in the early 2020s, short fiction still seems to be "wandering in the shade" of its more widely received sibling, the novel. This is the case even in Canada, where the cultural infrastructure is perhaps more conducive to the proliferation of short stories than in many other countries. The fact that despite the richness of Canadian short story writing, publishers and readers still seem to prefer novels may have several reasons. One of them, as indicated by Munro, may be that the novel is still seen as the more important genre, an observation that is further confirmed when we think of how short story cycles such as Selvadurai's *Funny Boy*, Itani's *Leaning, Leaning Over Water*, and Munro's own *Lives of Girls and Women* have repeatedly been defined and marketed as novels to render them more attractive. Another reason may be the novel's greater accessibility and potential to immerse readers through their longer engagement with it. However, it is exactly from the short story's tendentially more artistic fabric that its genre-specific power arises. This is also the reason that the short story – much like poetry – needs more avid advocates drawing attention to its unique potential and providing anchor points for readers to connect to its enriching complexity.

As it is, there is still a strong bias in favour of the novel in literary histories, introductions, and handbooks. While the short story is usually granted a separate chapter, it is often strangely excluded from genre-transgressing, thematically oriented sections. Thus, the impression is nourished that the short story may be an interesting aesthetic game of no significant cultural relevance. The neglect of the short story is particularly astonishing in book publications on Canadian fiction. The term "fiction" includes both the novel and the short story, as one would expect. However, the inclusion of the short story is very often limited to those authors who have only or mostly written short stories, such as Mavis Gallant or Alice Munro.

I should, therefore, want to conclude with a plea for including the short story more strongly in critical works on Canadian literature and, in particular, on Canadian fiction. The short story may be a "minor" genre, as Adrian Hunter (2007: 2) suggests, due its specific "elliptic, fragmentary, fleeting, suggestive and ambiguous nature"; however, this quality is exactly what makes it "ideally calibrated to the experience of modern life" (Hunter 2007: 46). The short story, therefore, as well as its unique response to the multifarious concerns of the past, present, and future, is anything but minor – an argument I hope to have illustrated with the present volume.

Works Cited

Cooper, Paige (2020). "Introduction". In: Paige Cooper, ed. *Best Canadian Stories 2020*. Windsor, ON: Biblioasis. 1–7.

Hunter, Adrian (2007). *The Cambridge Introduction to the Short Story in English*. Cambridge: Cambridge University Press.

Schoemperlen, Diane (2021). "Introduction". In: Diane Schoemperlen, ed. *Best Canadian Stories 2021*. Windsor, ON: Biblioasis. 1–7.

Smith, Adam (2013). "Interview: Alice Munro, 2013 Nobel Prize Laureate in Literature". Online: www.youtube.com/watch?v=djHreNp-HvY [accessed: 5 May 2022].

Index

Abdullah, Silmi 199
   Home of the Floating Lily (2021) 199
Adderson, Caroline (1963–) 121, 127, 133, 137, 140, 240
   Best Canadian Stories 2019, ed. 238, 240
   Pleased to Meet You (2006) 121, 133–134, 137
      "The Maternity Suite" 121
      "Shhh: 3 Stories About Silence" 133–134
Alexis, André (1957–) 10, 22, 103, 109, 127, 132–133, 137, 195–196, 213
   Despair and Other Stories (1994) 109, 127, 132, 137, 196
      "Horse" 132–133, 196
      "Kuala Lumpur" 196
      "My Anabasis" 109, 127
Alford, Edna (1947–) 94
   A Sleep Full of Dreams (1981) 94
Armstrong, Jeanette (1948–) 164, 186
   "This is a Story", in: *All My Relations* (1990), ed. Thomas King 164
Arnason, David (1940–) 45, 65, 68, 103, 116
   The Demon Lover (2002) 116
      "A Prelude to America" 116
      "The Succession" 116
Atwood, Margaret (1939–) 3, 10, 11, 13, 20, 23, 26, 30, 36, 44, 57, 65–66, 67, 68, 71–72, 77, 92–93, 95, 96, 101, 103, 105–107, 113, 116, 117, 118, 130, 136, 139, 140, 141, 142, 143–148, 160–163, 168, 186, 195, 236, 238–240, 242
   Alias Grace (1996) –6, 57
   Bluebeard's Egg (1983) 142

   Bones & Murder (1995) 20, 23, 105–107, 116, 117, 142, 145, 161
      "Gertrude Talks Back" 20, 142, 145
      "Happy Endings" 105, 106–107
      "Let Us Now Praise Stupid Women" 107
      "The Little Red Hen Tells All" 107
      "Murder in the Dark" 72, 105, 118
      "The Page" 105
      "She" 13
      "There Was Once" 105–106
      "We Want It All" 116
      "Women's Novels" 105
   Burning Questions: Essays and Occasional Pieces 2004–2021 (2022) 162
   Dancing Girls (1977) 147
      "Betty" 147
      "Under Glass" 147
   Good Bones (1992) 105, 118
   The Handmaid's Tale (1985) 142
   The Journals of Susanna Moodie (1970) 26
   MaddAddam Trilogy (2003, 2009, 2013) 238
   Oryx and Crake (2003) 236
   Moral Disorder (2006) 95, 142, 143, 146, 161–162
      "The Art of Cooking and Serving" 143
      "My Last Duchess" 3, 142–147
   Murder in the Dark (1983) 72, 105, 118
   Stone Mattress (2014) 11, 23, 30, 143, 147, 161, 238
      "Stone Mattress" 143, 147–148
      "Torching the Dusties" 238
   Surfacing (1972) 238
   Survival (1972) 26, 140, 161

The Tent (2006) 105, 113, 116, 117, 142, 238, 239, 240
  "Eating the Birds" 13, 116, 239
  "Faster" 239
  "Heritage House" 116
  "Life Stories" 105
  "Orphan Stories" 105
  "Post-Colonial" 116
  "Resources of the Ikarians" 116
  "Salome Was a Dancer" 142
  "Something Has Happened" 239
  "The Tent" 105, 113, 239
  "Three Novels I Won't Write Soon" 105
  "Time Folds" 239
  "Tree Baby" 113, 239
Wilderness Tips (1991) 143, 238
  "The Age of Lead" 238
  "Hairball" 143, 147, 148

Baldwin, Shauna Singh (1962–) 121, 191, 200, 209, 212
  English Lessons and Other Stories (1996) 121, 191, 200, 209, 212
  "Montreal 1962" 209
  "Simran" 121
  "Toronto 1984" 121
Bates, Judy Fong (1949–) 198
  China Dog and Other Tales from a Chinese Laundry (1997) 198
Bezmozgis, David (1973–) 22, 35, 95, 127, 201, 202, 210, 212
  Immigrant City (2019) 201, 210, 212
  "How It Used to Be" 201
  "Immigrant City" 210
  "A New Gravestone for an Old Grave" 201
  Natasha and Other Stories (2004) 95, 201, 202, 212
Birdsell, Sandra (1942–) 53, 94, 127, 139, 201
  Agassiz Stories (1987) 53, 94
  Ladies of the House (1984) 94
  Night Travellers (1982) 94
Bissoondath, Neil (1955–) 22, 190, 193, 195, 208, 212
  Digging up Mountains (1987) 195
  On the Eve of Uncertain Tomorrows (1991) 195, 208, 212
  "On the Eve of Uncertain Tomorrows" 193, 194, 208
  Selling Illusions. The Cult of Multiculturalism in Canada (1994) 190, 195

Blaise, Clark (1940–) 71, 73, 76–77, 95, 97
  Man and His World (1992) 76
  "Meditations on Starch" 77, 95
  A North American Education: A Book of Short Fiction (1973) 76, 77, 95
  'The Keeler Stories' 76
  'The Montreal Stories' 76
    "A Class of New Canadians" 76
    "Eyes" 76–77
  'The Thibidault Stories' 76
    "Words for the Winter" 76
Bowering, George (1935–) 3, 10, 65, 71, 95, 103, 105, 108–111, 117, 118, 132, 240
  Flycatcher (1974) 71
  "How Delsing Met Frances & Started to Write a Novel" 71
  A Place to Die (1983) 71, 108
  "A Short Story" 71, 108
  The Rain Barrel (1994) 108, 117, 132
  "Being Audited" 108–109
  "Discoloured Metal" 3, 109–111
  "Little Me" 132
  "Staircase Descended" 108
Brand, Dionne (1953–) 141, 190, 194, 208–209, 212
  Sans Souci and Other Stories (1988) 190, 194, 208, 209, 212
  "No Rinsed Blue Sky, No Red Flower Fences" 208
  "Train to Montreal" 209
  What We All Long For (2005) 190
Buchanan, Tom Thor 102
  "A Dozen Stomachs", in: *Best Canadian Stories 2018*, ed. Russell Smith 102
Butala, Sharon (1940–) 3, 53, 54, 57–60, 68, 69, 227
  Coyote's Morning Cry (1995) 58
  Fever. Stories (1990) 53, 58, 68
  "Gabriel" 3, 53, 57–60
  "The Prize" 53, 58
  The Perfection of the Morning (1994) 58
  Queen of the Headaches (1985) 58
  Real Life (2002) 58
  "Saskatchewan" 58
  Season of Fury and Wonder (2019) 58, 227

Callaghan, Morley (1903–1990) 8, 9, 47, 48, 51–53, 68, 69
  "All the Years of Her Life" (1936) 52, 68

"A Cap for Steve" (1952) 52
"Last Spring They Came Over" (1927)
    51, 68
"The Shining Red Apple" (1935) 52
Canton, Licia (1963–) 200
    Almond, Wine and Fertility
        (2008) 200
    The Pink House (2018) 200
Cariou, Warren (1966–) 44, 228,
    234, 240
    "An Athabasca Story" (2012)
        234–235, 240
Chao, Lien (1950–) 21, 23, 190, 198,
    199, 210, 213
    The Chinese Knot and Other Stories
        (2008) 210
    "Under the Monkey Bars" 210
    *Strike the Wok. An Anthology of
        Contemporary Canadian Fiction*
        (2003), ed. Lien Chao and
        Jim Wong-Chu. 21, 23, 190,
        198, 213
Clarke, Austin (1934–2016) 22, 127, 190,
    193, 194, 195, 207–208, 212,
    213, 214
    The Austin Clarke Reader (1996), ed.
        Barry Callaghan 195
    *Choosing His Coffin. The Best Stories
        of Austin Clarke* (2003) 195,
        207, 212
    Nine Men Who Laughed (1986) 208
        "Canadian Experience" 208
    They Never Told Me and Other Stories
        (2013) 127, 193, 195, 208
        "Waiting for the Postman to Knock"
            193, 208
    In This City (1992) 208
        "Trying to Kill Herself" 208
    *When He Was Free and Young and
        He used to Wear Silks* (1971)
        195, 207
        "Four Stations in His Circle" 207
    When Women Rule (1985) 208
        "A Slow Death" 208
Coady, Lynn (1970–) 10, 77, 103, 104,
    113–114, 117, 127, 130,
    137, 140
    "The Drain", in: *Best Canadian Stories
        2020*, ed. Paige Cooper
        104, 117
    Hellgoing (2013) 104, 117, 130
        "Clear Skies" 104
        "Dogs in Clothes" 130

Play the Monster Blind (2000)
    113–114, 117
    "Batter My Heart" 113–114
    "Ice Cream Man" 113–114
"Someone's Recording" – in: *Best
    Canadian Stories 2018*, ed.
    Russell Smith 130, 137
Cohen, Matt (1942–1999) 71, 103, 235,
    240, 241
    Living on Water (1989) 235
    "The Bone Fields" (also in: *And
        Other Stories* (2001), ed. George
        Bowering 235–236, 240
Cooper, Paige 117, 121, 243, 244
    Best Canadian Stories 2020, ed. 104,
        117, 244
    Zolitude (2018) 121
        "Slave Craton" 121
        "Vazova on Love" 121
Crane, Dede 127
    The Cult of Quick Repair (2008) 127
        "What Sort of Mother" 127
Crawford, Isabella Valency
    (1846–1887) 26
Crummey, Michael (1965–) 121, 219
    Flesh and Blood (1998; expanded
        edition 2003) 121, 219
        "Roots" 121
Cushing, Eliza Lanesford
    (1794–1886) 26

Dabydeen, Cyril (1945–) 196, 209,
    213, 214
    My Multi-Ethnic Friends (2013)
        196, 213
        "Believers" 196
        "My Multi-Ethnic Friends" 196
        "Starapple Canadian" 196
    North of the Equator (2001) 196
        "North of the Equator" 209–210
    Still Close to the Island (1980) 196
Dobozy, Tamas (1969–) 200–201
    Ghost Geographies. Fictions
        (2021) 200
        "Ray Electric" 200
    Siege 13: Stories (2012) 200
        "The Beautician" 200
        "The Restoration of the Villa
            Where Tibor Kalman Once
            Lived" 200
Donoghue, Emma (1969–) 127, 156
    *Love Alters: Stories of Lesbian Love and
        Erotica* (2013), ed. 156

Dore, Deirdre Simon 129
  "Your Own Lucky Stars", in: *Best Canadian Stories 2018*, ed. Russell Smith 129

Edwards, Caterina (1948–) 127, 192, 200, 203, 213
  Island of the Nightingales (2000) 127, 192, 200, 213
  "Home and Away" 127
  "On a Platter" 203
  "Prima Vera" 192
Engel, Marian (1933–1985) 44, 72, 152
  Bear (1976) 44
  Inside the Easter Egg (1975) 72
  The Tattooed Woman (1985) 72

Fawcett, Brian (1944–2022) 136
  Cambodia: A Book for People Who Find Television Too Slow (1986) 136
  "The Huxley Satellite Dish" 136
  "A Small Committee" 136
  "Universal Chicken" 136
Findley, Timothy (1930–2002) 26, 141, 152–153, 161, 162, 163
  Dust to Dust (1997) 152–153, 161
  "A Bag of Bones" 152–153
  "Come as You Are" 152–153
  Headhunter (1993) 26
  Stones (1988) 152–153, 161
  "Bragg and Minna" 152–153
  "A Gift of Mercy" 152–153
Fleming, May Agnes (1840–1880) 26
Flood, Cynthia (1940–) 103
Fraser, Keath (1944–) 54, 68, 71, 103, 235–236, 240
  13 Ways of Listening to a Stranger (2005) 235, 240
  "Taking Cover" 235–236, 240
Fraser, Raymond (1941–2018) 65, 71, 73, 77
  The Black Horse Tavern (1972) 77

Gagliese, Lucia 131, 137
  "Through the Covid-Glass" – in: *Best Canadian Stories* 2021, ed. Diane Schoemperlen 131, 137
Gallant, Mavis (1922–2014) 2, 9, 32, 66, 67, 71, 72, 73, 78–82, 95, 96, 97, 202, 242, 244
  The Collected Stories of Mavis Gallant (1996) 79

The Cost of Living (2009) 79
  "Madeline's Birthday" 79
From the Fifteenth District (1979) 79
Home Truths: Selected Canadian Stories (1981) 73, 79, 80–82, 95, 96
  "The Ice Wagon Going Down the Street" 32, 80–81
  "Orphan's Progress" 79, 82
  "Saturday" 79
  "Up North" 79–80
  "Virus X" 80
My Heart is Broken (1964) 71
The Other Paris (1956) 66, 67, 79
  "The Legacy" 67
Garner, Hugh (1913–1979) 9, 47, 48, 66, 68
  The Yellow Sweater (1952) 48, 66
  "The Legs of the Lame" 47
  "One-Two-Three Little Indians" 47–48, 68
  "The Yellow Sweater" 47
Gartner, Zsuzsi (1960–) 10, 102, 116, 238, 240
  "The Second Coming of the Plants", in: *Best Canadian Short Stories 2019*, ed. Caroline Adderson 102, 238, 240
Gasco, Elyse (1967–) 77, 113, 114, 117, 140, 218
  Can You Wave Bye Bye, Baby? (1999) 114, 117, 218
  "Elements" 218
  "You Have the Body" 114
Gibson, Margaret (1948–2006) 139, 227
  Desert Thirst (1998) 139
  The Fear Room (1996) 139
  Sweet Poison (1993) 139
Glover, Douglas (1948–) 10, 13, 21, 24, 25, 101, 103, 121, 218–219, 240, 242
  16 Categories of Desire (2000) 218, 240
  "The Left Ladies Club" 218–219
  "A Piece of the True Cross" 218
  Dog Attempts to Drown Man in Saskatoon (1985) 218
  A Guide to Animal Behaviour (1991) 121, 218
  The Mad River (1981) 218
  Savage Love (2013) 101, 121, 218, 240
  "Tristiana" 218
Godfrey, Dave (1938–2015) 71, 103
  Death Goes Better with Coca-Cola (1967) 71

Index

Goto, Hiromi (1966–) 199
  Hopeful Monsters (2004) 199
Gould, John (1959–) 101, 103–104, 117, 118, 127, 129, 130, 227
  the end of me (2020) 101, 103, 117, 129, 130, 227
    "10 Things" 129
    "Anthropocene" 227
    "Bones" 129
    "Customer Review" 129, 227
    "Ex" 129
    "From the Journal of Dr. Duncan MacDougall of Haverhill, Mass." 130–131
    "Pulse" 103
    "Squirrel" 103–104
    "Via Negativa" 129
    "Welcome" 129
  Kilter (2003) 101, 118
  The Kingdom of Heaven: 88 Palm-of-the-Hand Stories (1996) 101
Govier, Katherine (1948–) 139
Gowdy, Barbara (1950–) 10, 44, 156, 161
  We So Seldom Look on Love (1992) 156–157, 161
    "Flesh of My Flesh" 157
  The White Bone (1998) 44
Grove, Frederick Philip (1879–1948) 9, 48, 50, 53, 68

Haliburton, Thomas Chandler (1796–1865) 26, 27–29, 30, 45, 46, 89
  The Clockmaker; or the Sayings and Doings of Samuel Slick of Slickville (1837) 28–29, 45, 46
Harrison, Susan Francis (1859–1935) 26, 27
  Crowded Out and Other Sketches (1886) 27
Harvor, Elisabeth (1936–) 139, 162, 227
  Let Me Be the One (1996) 139
Hay, Elizabeth (1951–) 139, 223, 224, 227, 241
Heighton, Steven (1961–2022) 77, 113, 115, 117, 121–122, 128, 129, 202
  The Dead Are More Visible (2012) 115, 117, 128, 202
    "Noughts & Crosses: An Unsent Reply" 128
    "OutTrip" 115
    "Swallow" 115
    "Those Who Would be More" 202
  Flight Paths of the Emperor (1992) 122, 202
    "A Man Away from Home has No Neighbours" 122
    "The Son is Always Like the Father" 202
Hodgins, Jack (1938–) 2, 30, 59, 72, 82–86, 95, 96, 97, 163
  The Barclay Family Theatre (1981) 82, 85, 96
  Damage Done by the Storm (2004) 82, 85–86, 95
    "Astonishing the Blind" 85
    "The Drover's Wife" 85–86
    "Galleries" 85
    "Over Here" 85
  The Invention of the World (1977) 83
  Spit Delaney's Island (1976) 82, 83–85, 95
    "Every Day of His Life" 84
    "At the Foot of the Hill, Birdie's School" 84
    "Separating" 83
    "Spit Delaney's Island" 83–84
Hood, Hugh (1928–2000) 19, 20, 23, 66, 71, 72, 73, 75–76, 95, 97
  After All! (2003) 75
  Around the Mountain (1967) 71, 72, 75
  August Nights (1985) 75
  Flying a Red Kite (1962) 19, 23, 71, 75
    "Flying a Red Kite" 20, 75–76, 95
  The New Age/Le nouveau siècle (1975–2000) 75
  None Genuine Without Its Signature (1980) 75
Hopkinson, Nalo (1960–) 195
  Falling in Love with the Hominids (2015) 195
    "Blushing" 195
    "Flying Lessons" 195
    "Shift" 195
Howlett, Debbie (1964–) 95, 217
  We Could Stay Here All Night (1999) 95, 217
Huggan, Isabel (1943–) 95, 139
  The Elizabeth Stories (1984) 95

Irani, Anosh (1974–) 103, 190, 193, 200, 210, 211, 213
  Translated from the Gibberish. Seven Stories & One Half Truth (2019) 190, 193, 200, 210, 211–212, 213

"Behind the Moon" 193–194
"Translated from the Gibberish"
    (Parts One and Two) 190, 210,
    211–212
Itani, Frances (1942–) 95, 139, 217, 244
    Leaning, Leaning Over Water (1998)
        95, 217

Jameson, Anna Brownell (1794–1860) 26
    Winter Studies and Summer Rambles
        (1838) 26
Jarman, Mark Anthony (1955–) 10,
        112, 121
    19 Knives (2000) 112
    My White Planet (2008) 112, 121
        "Bear on a Chain" 121
        "In Terminal Three (More Fun
            in the New World with
            the Symbionese Liberation
            Army)" 112
    New Orleans is Sinking (1998) 112
Johanson, Reg (1968–) 101
    "A Titan Bearing Many a Legitimate
        Grievance", in: *Best Canadian
        Stories 2018*, ed. Russell
        Smith 101
Johnston, Basil H. (1929–2015) 166
    "Summer Holidays in Spanish", in:
        All My Relations (1990), ed.
        Thomas King 166

Keefer, Janice Kulyk (1952–) 81, 82, 96,
        139, 191, 201, 206, 210, 213
    Transfigurations (1987) 201
    Travelling Ladies (1992) 201, 210
        "Prodigal" 210
Kellough, Kaie (1975–) 134
    Dominoes at the Crossroads (2020) 134
        "Ashes and Juju" 134
King, Thomas (1943–) 4, 10, 20, 22, 23,
        30, 48, 87, 102, 103, 118, 164,
        165, 166, 167, 168–175, 176,
        179, 180, 186, 187
    *All My Relations. An Anthology of
        Contemporary Canadian Native
        Fiction* (1990), ed. 164, 166,
        186, 187
    The Back of the Turtle (2014) 172, 187
    Green Grass, Running Water (1993) 172
    The Inconvenient Indian (2012) 168
    One Good Story, That One (1993)
        20, 23, 166, 168, 169, 171,
        186, 187

"Borders" 169
"A Coyote Columbus Story" 171
"How Corporal Sterling Saved
    Blossom, Alberta, and Most of
    the Rest of the World" 169
"Joe the Painter and the Deer Lake
    Massacre" 169
"Magpies" 171
"The One About Coyote Going
    West" 171
"One Good Story, That One" 4, 48,
    87, 166, 169, 171–175
"A Seat in the Garden" 48, 169
"Totem" 48, 169
"Traplines" 168
A Short History of Indians in Canada
    (2005) 166, 168, 169,
    171, 186
"The Baby in the Airmail Box" 169
"Bad Men Who Love Jesus" 169
"The Closer You Get to Canada,
    the More Things Will Eat Your
    Horses" 169
"Coyote and the Enemy Aliens"
    168, 171
"The Dog I Wish I Had, I Would
    Call It Helen" 169
"Domestic Furies" 169
"Noah's Arch" 169
"Tidings of Comfort and Joy" 48,
    166, 169–170
"Where the Borg Are" 169
Knister, Raymond (1899–1932) 8, 9, 47,
    48–51, 53, 68, 69
The First Day of Spring. Stories and Prose
    (1925/1976) 68, 69
    "The Fate of Mrs. Lucier"
        49–50, 68
    "Horace the Haymow" 50
    "Mist Green Oats" 49
    "Peaches, Peaches" 49
My Star Predominant (1934) 50
Kreisel, Henry (1922–1991) 53

Lau, Doretta 129
    *How Does a Single Blade of Grass Thank
        the Sun?* (2014) 129
        "God Damn, How Real is
            This?" 129
Lau, Evelyn (1971–) 22, 141, 198
    Choose Me (1999) 141, 198
    Fresh Girls & Other Stories (1993)
        141, 198

Laurence, Margaret (1926–1987) 26, 35, 53, 56, 57, 67, 69, 71, 72, 89, 94
  A Bird in the House (1970) 53, 67, 72, 89
  The Diviners (1974) 26
  The Tomorrow Tamer (1963) 71
Leacock, Stephen (1869–1944) 27, 28, 29–32, 33, 35, 45, 46
  Arcadian Adventures of the Idle Rich (1914) 30
  Literary Lapses (1910) 30
  Sunshine Sketches of a Little Town (1912) 27, 29, 30–32, 33, 45
    "The Hostelry of Mr Smith" 31
    "L'Envoi. The Train to Mariposa" 30–31
    "The Marine Excursions of the Knights of Pythias" 31–32, 45
Leprohon, Rosanna (1829–1879) 26
Levine, Norman (1923–2005) 67, 70, 71, 78, 96, 202
  I Don't Want to Know Anyone Too Well and Other Stories (1971) 78
    "A Canadian Upbringing" 78
    "I Like Chekhov" 78
    "In Lower Town" 78
  One Way Ticket (1961) 71
  Thin Ice (1979) 78
    "We All Begin in a Little Magazine" 70, 78, 96
Li, Iris 190, 213
  "Snaps – a Satire", in: *Strike the Wok: An Anthology of Contemporary Canadian Fiction* (2003), ed. Lien Chao and Jim Wong-Chu. 190, 213
Ludwig, Sidura (1976–) 201
  You Are Not What We Expected (2020) 201
Lyon, Annabel (1971–) 10, 122, 137, 140
  Oxygen (2000) 122, 137
    "Song" 122

MacLeod, Alistair (1936–2014) 2, 19, 23, 82, 86–89, 95, 96, 97, 141, 163, 227
  As Birds Bring Forth the Sun (1986) 82, 87
    "The Tuning of Perfection" 87, 88
  Island (2000) 19, 23, 82, 87, 88, 95
    "Clearances" 19, 82, 88
    "Island" 82
  The Lost Salt Gift of Blood (1976) 82, 87
    "The Boat" 87
    "The Return" 87–88
  No Great Mischief (1999) 86
  "Remembrance" (2012) 82, 88
Maharaj, Rabindranath (1955–) 127, 193, 196, 213
  The Book of Ifs and Buts (2002) 127, 193, 213
    "The Diary of a Down-Courage Domestic" 127, 193
Maracle, (Bobbi) Lee (1950–2021) 4, 22, 44, 102, 127, 130, 141, 164, 165, 166, 175–177, 185, 186, 187, 188, 228–231, 235, 238, 240, 242
  First Wives Club. Coast Salish Style (2010) 164, 176, 177, 228, 231, 240
    "Blessing Song" 231
    "The Café" 177
    "Cedar Sings" 4, 164, 177, 228–231, 235, 238
    "Erotica" 177
    "Tiny Green Waves" 177, 231
  Sojourner's Truth and Other Stories (1990) 102, 127, 141, 166, 176, 186
    "Bertha" 141
    "Charlie" 166, 176–177
    "Dear Daddy" 127, 128, 141, 176
    "Eunice" 176
    "Lee on Spiritual Experience" 176
    "Maggie" 130, 166, 176–177
    "Polka Partners" 176
    "Sojourner's Truth" 102, 176
    "Too Much to Explain" 141, 166
    "Who's Political Here" 141, 176
    "World War I" 176
    "Yin Chin" 176
Mara, Rachna (1953–2021) 35, 95, 200
  Of Customs and Excise (1991) 95, 200
Marche, Stephen (1976–) 135
  "Twinkle, Twinkle", in: *Best Canadian Stories 2018*, ed. Russell Smith 135
Marshall, Joyce (1913–2005) 9, 47, 48, 60, 62, 63, 64, 68, 83
  Any Time at All (1993) 62
  Blood and Bone (1995) 64
  A Private Place (1975) 62, 63, 64, 68
    "The Enemy" 63
    "The Little White Girl" 63
    "The Old Woman" 63–64, 83
    "Salvage" 63

McCulloch, Thomas (1776–1843) 26, 27–28, 29, 30, 45, 89
  The Stepsure Letters (1862) 28, 29, 45
Metcalf, John (1938–) 2, 8, 70, 71, 73–75, 78, 95, 97
  Standing Stones: The Best Stories of John Metcalf (2004) 73
    "Gentle as Flowers Make the Stones" 74–75, 95
    "Girl in Gingham" 75
    "Polly Ongle" 75
    "Private Parts" 75
    "The Years in Exile" 75
Mistry, Rohinton (1952–) 22, 35, 95, 127, 128, 191, 199, 210–211, 213
  A Fine Balance (1995) 210
  Tales from Firozsha Baag (1987) 95, 128, 191, 199, 210–211, 213
    "The Ghost of Firozsha Baag" 210
    "Lend Me Your Light" 210
    "Squatter" 210
    "Swimming Lessons" 128, 210–211
Mitchell, W.O. (1914–1998) 53
Moodie, Susanna (1803–1885) 26, 35
  Life in the Clearings Versus the Bush (1953) 26
  Roughing It in the Bush (1952) 26
Moore, Lisa (1964–) 103, 140, 219–220, 240, 241, 242
  Degrees of Nakedness (1995) 219–220, 240
    "Granular" 219
    "Sea Urchin" 219
  Open. Stories (2002) 219
    "Melody" 219
    "The Way the Light Is" 219
  The Selected Stories of Lisa Moore (2012) 219
  Something for Everyone (2018) 219
  "Visitation", in: *Best Canadian Stories 2018*, ed. Russell Smith 220, 240
Mootoo, Shani (1957–) 156, 196
  Out on Main Street (1993) 156
Munro, Alice (1931–) 1, 2, 3, 7, 9, 13, 17, 18, 19, 23, 24, 35, 50, 57, 61, 66, 67, 71, 72, 73, 89–95, 96, 97, 103, 119, 123, 127, 128, 138, 139, 140, 141, 142, 148–151, 160, 161, 162, 163, 214, 222, 223–226, 240, 241, 242, 243, 244, 245

Dance of the Happy Shades (1968) 67, 71, 73, 148, 223
  "The Piece of Utrecht" 223
  "The Time of Death" 67
Dear Life (2012) 93, 149, 163, 224, 240
  "Dear Life" 224
  "Haven" 149
Friend of My Youth (1990) 223
  "Friend of My Youth" 223
Hateship, Friendship, Courtship, Loveship, Marriage (2001) 13, 148, 149, 161, 162, 223
  "The Bear Came Over the Mountain" 150
  "Family Furnishings" 149, 223
  "Hateship, Friendship, Courtship, Loveship, Marriage" 128, 148–149, 150
  "Nettles" 148
  "Queenie" 13
Lives of Girls and Women (1971) 3, 13, 67, 72, 89–94, 95, 96, 119, 148, 223, 244
  "Age of Faith" 91
  "Baptizing" 91
  "Changes and Ceremonies" 92
  "Epilogue: The Photographer" 92–93
  "Flats Road" 91
  "Heirs of the Living Body" 92
  "Princess Ida" 91
The Love of a Good Woman (1998) 128, 149, 161
  "Before the Change" 128, 151
  "The Children Stay" 149
  "The Love of a Good Woman" 13
The Moons of Jupiter (1982) 148, 150, 161
  "Bardon Bus" 150
  "Dulse" 150
  "Labour Day Dinner" 150
  "The Turkey Season" 148
Open Secrets (1994) 127
  "Carried Away" 128
  "A Wilderness Station" 57, 127
The Progress of Love (1986) 73, 149, 161
  "Lichen" 149–150
Runaway (2004) 149, 223, 224, 240, 242
  "Chance" 224–226
  "Powers" 149
  "Silence" 224–226
  "Soon" 223, 224–225

Something I've Been Meaning to Tell You (1974) 223
   "Material" 151
   "The Ottawa Valley" 223
   "Winter Wind" 223
"The Strangers" (1951) 67
Too Much Happiness (2009) 17, 23, 149, 224
   "Child's Play" 17, 18, 19, 20
   "Deep Holes" 224
   "Dimensions" 149, 224
   "Too Much Happiness" 13
The View from Castle Rock (2006) 90, 96, 148, 161, 224
   "Lying Under the Apple Tree" 148
Who Do You Think You Are? (U.S. title: *The Beggar Maid*; 1978) 73, 90, 91, 95, 148, 149, 161
   "The Beggar Maid" 90, 149, 161
Mutonji, Téa 95, 141, 142, 157, 159–160, 161, 162, 163, 193, 198, 202, 206, 207, 213
   Shut Up You're Pretty (2019) 95, 141, 142, 157, 159–160, 161, 193, 198, 202, 206, 213
      "The Common Room" 159
      "If Not Happiness" 159
      "Old-Fashioneds" 207
      "Phyllis Green" 160
      "Shut Up You're Pretty" 159–160
      "Sober Party" 159
      "This is Only Temporary" 160
      "Tilapia Fish" 160
      "Tits for Cigs" 159, 207
      "Women Talking" 159

Page, Kathy (1958–) 16, 17, 20, 23, 44, 101, 116, 127, 140, 155, 161, 236–238, 240
   Paradise & Elsewhere. Stories (2014) 101, 140, 155, 161, 236–238, 240
      "The Ancient Siddanese" 236–237
      "G'Ming" 236
      "The Kissing Disease" 155–156
      "Lak-ha" 101, 236
      "Low Tide" 140
      "Of Paradise" 140, 236
      "Saving Grace" 236
      "We, the Trees" 237–238
   The Two of Us (2016) 14, 23, 155, 161
      "Dear Son" 155
      "Red Dog" 14, 16, 20

Plett, Casey (198–-) 129, 157, 162
   A Dream of a Woman (2021) 157
      "Enough Trouble" 157
      "Other Women" 157
   "Hazel & Christopher" – in: *Best Canadian Stories 2020*, ed. Paige Cooper 129
   Meanwhile, Elsewhere: Science Fiction and Fantasy from Transgender Writers (2017), ed. 157
   A Safe Girl to Love (2014) 157
      "How to Stay Friends" 157
      "Twenty Hot Tips" 157
Prince, Althea (1945–) 196

Quan, Andy (1969–) 154–155, 161, 198
   Calendar Boy (2001) 154, 161, 198
      "Calendar Boy" 154–155
      "How to Cook Chinese Rice" 154
      "Immigration" 154

Reid-Benta, Zalika 141, 191, 196–197, 202, 213
   Frying Plantain (2019) 141, 191, 196–197, 202, 213
      "Snow Day" 196
Richler, Mordecai (1931–2001) 30, 66, 67, 72
   The Street (1969) 72
Roberts, Charles G.D. (1860–1943) 3, 27, 36–37, 40–45, 46, 216
   Earth's Enigmas: A Book of Animal and Nature Life (1896) 37
      "Do Seek Their Meat from God" 3, 37, 40–45, 46
   Kindred of the Wild (1902) 37
   Wisdom of the Wilderness (1922) 37
Robinson, Eden (1968–) 22, 165, 166, 186, 188, 242
   Traplines (1996) 166, 186
      "Queen of the North" 166
Rooke, Leon (1934–) 71, 103, 117, 132
   Painting the Dog (2001) 103, 117, 132
      "Art" 103
      "The Heart Must from Its Breaking" 103
      "Sing Me No Love Songs I'll Say You No Prayers" 132
      "Want to Play House" 103
Roscoe, Patrick (1967–) 101, 112–113, 117, 153, 154, 161
   Birthmarks (1990) 153–154, 161
      "My Lover's Touch" 153–154

Index   255

The Truth About Love (2001) 101,
        112–113, 117, 154
    "The Cage" 101
    "From the Laboratory of Love" 154
    "Touching Darkness" 112–113, 154
    "The Truth About Love" 154
Rose, Connie Barnes 95
    Getting Out of Town (1997) 95
Ross, Sinclair (1908–1996) 3, 9, 47, 48,
        53–57, 58, 59, 60, 68, 69, 71
    As For Me and My House (1941) 54
    The Lamp at Noon and Other Stories
        (1968) 54
    "A Field of Wheat" 54
    "The Lamp at Noon" 3, 54–57, 58,
        60, 68, 69
    "Not by Rain Alone" 54
    "The Painted Door" 54

Sawai, Gloria (1932–2011) 53
    A Song for Nettie Johnson (2001) 53
Schoemperlen, Diane (1954–) 10, 65,
        103, 105, 107–108, 117, 118,
        135, 137, 139, 243, 245
    Best Canadian Stories 2021, ed. 137
    Double Exposures (1984) 107, 118
    Forms of Devotion (1998) 107–108,
        117, 135
    "How to Write a Serious Novel
        About Love" 107–108
    "Innocent Objects" 135
Scott, Duncan Campbell (1862–1947) 8,
        27, 30, 32–35, 45, 46
    In the Village of Viger (1986) 8, 27, 30,
        32–35, 45
    "Josephine Labrosse" 34
    "The Little Milliner" 33
    "No. 68 Rue Alfred de Musset" 34
    "Paul Farlotte" 34–35
    "Sedan" 33–34
    "The Wooing of Monsieur
        Cuerrier" 34
    The Witching of Elspie (1923) 32
    "Labrie's Wife" 32
Selvadurai, Shyam (1965–) 22, 95, 142,
        157, 158–159, 161, 162, 163,
        191, 199, 244
    Funny Boy (1994) 95, 142, 157, 158–159,
        161, 162, 163, 191, 244
    "The Best School of All" 158
    "Pigs Can't Fly" 158
    "Riot Journal: An Epilogue"
        158–159

Senior, Olive (1941–) 127, 141, 195,
        197, 213
    Discerner of Hearts (1995) 197, 213
    "You Think I Mad, Miss" 197
    The Pain Tree (2015) 195, 213
    "Lollipop" 195
    Summer Lightning and Other Stories
        (1986) 195
Seton, Ernest Thompson (1860–1946) 3,
        27, 36–40, 43–44, 45, 46, 216
    The Birds of Manitoba (1891) 36
    Wild Animals I Have Known (1898) 36,
        37, 38, 45, 46
    "Lobo – the King of
        Currumpaw" 36
    "Silverspot. The Story of a Crow" 3,
        36, 37–40, 43–44
Shields, Carol (1935–2003) 3, 16, 26,
        103, 120, 123–126, 137,
        138, 139
    Dressing Up for the Carnival (2000) 123
    "Dressing Up for the Carnival" 123
    "Dying for Love" 3, 16, 120,
        123–126
    "Edith-Esther" 123
    "Ilk" 123
    "Keys" 16, 123
    "A Scarf" 123
    The Orange Fish (1989) 123
    "Block Out" 123
    Small Ceremonies (1976) 26
    Various Miracles (1985) 123
    "Flitting Behaviour" 123
    "Home" 123
    "Various Miracles" 123
Silvera, Makeda (1955–) 95, 191,
        192, 196
    Remembering G (1991) 95, 191, 192
Simpson, Leanne Betasamosake (1971–)
        151, 164, 165, 166, 175, 176,
        178–179, 186, 187, 228,
        231–232, 240, 241
    Islands of Decolonial Love (2013) 165,
        166, 176, 178, 179, 186, 187,
        231–232, 240, 241
    "gezhizhwazh" 165, 178
    "gwekaanimad" 165, 179
    "indinawemaaganidog/all of my
        relatives" 178
    "it takes an ocean not to break"
        178–179
    "jiimaanag" 166
    "leaks" 178, 187, 241

"nogojiwanong" 179, 232
"pipty" 166
"she hid him in her bones" 178
"she told him 10 000 years of everything" 165
"smallpox, anyone" 178
Smith, Ray (1941–2019) 10, 65, 71, 72, 73, 77–78, 95, 97
  Cape Breton is the Thought-Control Centre of Canada (1969) 71, 72, 77–78, 95, 97
    "Cape Breton is the Thought-Control Centre of Canada" 77–78
    "Smoke" 78
  Lord Nelson's Tavern (1974) 78
Smith, Russell (1963–) 101, 118, 130, 135, 137, 216, 240, 242
  Best Canadian Stories 2018, ed. 101, 102, 118, 129, 130, 135, 137, 216, 220, 240, 242
  Confidence. Stories (2015) 130
    "Raccoon" 130
    "TXTS" 130
  Diana: A Diary in the Second Person (2003) 130
Svendsen, Linda (1954–) 95
  Marine Life (1992) 95

Taylor, Drew Hayden (1962–) 22, 165, 166, 179–184, 186, 187
  Fearless Warriors (1998) 165, 166, 180, 186
    "The Circle of Death" 180
    "Crisis Management" 180–181
    "Fearless Warriors" 181–182
    "The Man Who Didn't Exist" 166
  Take Us to Your Chief (2016) 180, 182, 183, 186
    "A Culturally Inappropriate Armageddon" 182–183
    "Petropaths" 183–184
    "Take Us to Your Chief" 183
Thammavongsa, Souvankham (1978–) 193, 199, 202, 203, 207, 209, 213
  How to Pronounce Knife (2020) 193, 199, 202, 203, 207, 209, 213
    "Chick-A-Chee!" 207
    "A Far Distant Thing" 209
    "How to Pronounce Knife" 193
    "Picking Worms" 193
    "Randy Travis" 203
    "You Are So Embarrassing" 202

Thien, Madeleine (1974–) 4, 22, 199, 203–206, 213
  Simple Recipes (2001) 199, 213
    "Bullet Train" 199
    "Dispatch" 199
    "Map of the City" 199
    "Simple Recipes" 4, 199, 203–206, 213
Thomas, Audrey (1935–) 71, 103, 117, 118, 123, 137
  Ten Green Bottles (1967) 71, 123, 137
    "If One Green Bottle" 123
  Two in the Bush (1981) 103, 117
    "Initram" 103
Traill, Catherine Parr (1802–1899) 26, 35
  The Backwoods of Canada (1836) 26

Valgardson, William Dempsey (1939–) 15–17, 20, 23, 24, 67, 72
  Bloodflowers. Ten Stories (1973) 72
    "Bloodflowers" 72
  God is Not a Fish Inspector (1975) 72
  Red Dust (1978) 72
  What Can't be Changed Shouldn't be Mourned (1990) 15, 23, 72
    "A Matter of Balance" 15–17, 23, 24
Van Camp, Richard (1971–) 151, 179, 180, 184–185, 186, 187, 188, 228, 233–234, 241, 242
  Godless but Loyal to Heaven (2013) 185, 233–234, 241
    "The Fleshing" 185, 233
    "On the Wings of This Prayer" 185, 233
  Moccasin Square Gardens (2019) 184, 185, 186, 233–234, 241
    "Man Babies" 184
    "Super Indians" 184–185
    "Wheetago War I: Lying in Bed Together" 185, 233
    "Wheetago War II: Summoners" 185, 233–234
  The Moon of Letting Go and Other Stories (2010) 184
Vanderhaeghe, Guy (1951–) 9, 53, 73, 141, 220–222, 241
  Daddy Lenin and Other Stories (2015) 73, 220, 221, 222, 241
    "1957 Chevy Bel Air" 222
    "Live Large" 221, 222
    "Tick Tock" 221
    "Where the Boys Were" 222–223

Man Descending (1982) 53, 73, 220, 221, 241
  "Man Descending" 220–221
  "A Taste for Perfection" 221–222
Things As They Are (1992) 220
The Trouble with Heroes (1983) 220
Vassanji, M.G. (1950–) 95, 197, 198
  Uhuru Street (1990) 95, 197
    "The London-Returned" 197
    "Refugee" 197
  When She Was Queen (2005) 198

Waltner-Toews, David (1948–) 193, 201, 203, 213
  One Foot in Heaven (2005) 193, 201, 203, 213
    "Wilde Geese" 193
Warriar, Nalini (1954–) 191
  Blues from the Malabar Coast (2002) 191
Watada, Terry (1951–) 199
  Daruma Days (1997) 199
    "The Brown Bomber" 199
    "The Moment of Truth" 199
    "Only the Lonely" 199
Watson, Sheila (1909–1998) 9, 48, 60, 64–66, 68, 69
  "Antigone" 64–66, 68, 69
  "The Black Farm" 64
  "Brother Oedipus" 64
  "The Rumble Seat" 64
Wiebe, Rudy (1934–) 53, 72, 235, 241
  The Angel of the Tar Sands and Other Stories (1982) 235, 241
    "The Angel of the Tar Sands" 72, 235
  "Where is the Voice Coming From" 72
Willis, Deborah (1982–) 121, 137, 140, 156, 161
  The Dark and Other Love Stories (2017) 121, 137, 156, 161
    "The Dark" 156
    "Last One to Leave" 121
    "Welcome to Paradise" 156
Wilson, Ethel (1888–1990) 9, 47, 48, 60–62, 68, 69, 71
  Mrs. Golightly and Other Stories (1961) 60, 68, 69, 71
    "Haply the Soul of My Grandmother" 61–62
    "Hurry, Hurry" 61
    "I Just Love Dogs" 60
    "Mrs. Golightly" 61
    "Mr. Sleepwalker" 62
    "On Nimpish Lake" 61
    "Till Death Us Do Part" 61
    "We Have to Sit Opposite" 61, 62, 69
    "The Window" 61, 62
Winter, Michael (1965–) 219
  Creaking in Their Skins (1994) 219
  One Last Good Look (1999) 219

Yee, Paul (1956–) 198
  Dead Man's Gold and Other Stories (2002) 198
  Tales from Gold Mountain (1990) 198

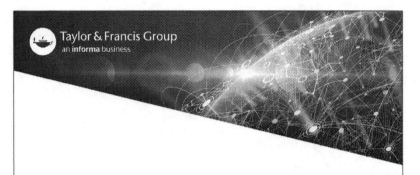

Printed in the United States
by Baker & Taylor Publisher Services